D1606760

GOOD PLACES AND NON-PLACES IN COLONIAL MEXICO

The Figure of Vasco de Quiroga (1470-1565)

Fernando Gómez

University Press of America,® Inc.
Lanham · New York · Oxford

Copyright © 2001 by
University Press of America,® Inc.
4720 Boston Way
Lanham, Maryland 20706

12 Hid's Copse Rd.
Cumnor Hill, Oxford OX2 9JJ

Library of Congress Cataloging-in-Publication Data

Gómez, Fernando (Gómez-Herrero).
Good places and non-places in colonial Mexico : the figure of
Vasco de Quiroga (1470-1565) / Fernando Gómez.
p.   cm
Includes bibliographical references.
l. Indians of Mexico—Government relations. 2. Quiroga,
Vasco de, 1470-1565. 3. Indians, Treatment of—Latin America.
4. Utopias—Latin America. 5. Spain—Colonies—America—
Administration. I. Title: Figure of Vasco de Quiroga (1470-1565).
II. Quiroga, Vasco de, 1470-1565. III. Title.
F1219.3.G6 G66   2001   972'.02—dc21   00-053201 CIP

ISBN 0-7618-1924-X (cloth : alk. ppr.)

⊖™ The paper used in this publication meets the minimum
requirements of American National Standard for Information
Sciences—Permanence of Paper for Printed Library Materials,
ANSI Z39.48—1984

In Memoriam
Silvia Zierer Melià (1969–1997)

April is the cruelest month…

Contents

Abbreviations

American Historical Review: AHR
The Americas: TA
Anales de Literatura Hispanoamericana: ALH
Anuario de Historia del Derecho Español: AHDE
Boletín del Archivo General de la Nación: BAGN
Colonial Latin American Review: CLAR
Cuadernos Americanos: CA
Estudios de Historia Novohispana: EHN
The Hispanic American Historical Review: HAHR
Hispanic Review: HR
Historia Mexicana: HA
History and Memory: HM
Jahrbuch fur Geschichte von Staat, Wirtschaft und Gesellschaft
    Lateinamerikas: JGL
Journal of Medieval and Renaissance Studies: JMRS
Law and Society Review: LSR
Missionalia Hispanica: MH
Modern Language Notes: MLA
Nueva Revista de Filología Hispánica: NRFH
Renaissance Quarterly: RQ
Revista de Crítica Literaria Latinoamericana: RCLL
Revista Iberoamericana: RI
Revista de Literatura Latinoamericana: RLL
Revista de Indias: RDI
The William and Mary Quarterly: WMQ

Preface

This work will defend the historical existence of early modern (Latin) American utopias, and their meaningfulness, for us today, if only in their incomplete, negative or future-oriented formulations. This work historicizes the theme of the city of equals (utopia), in relation to the early Spanish colonization of the Americas. To energize the crisis or dissociation between utopianism and Hispanism, this work will address the legal or repressive American circumstance. Colonial literature in the young, if imperial, romance language (Spanish) in the Americas is here, for us, predominantly the theory and practice of the law. Against the historicity of modernity, our ground will thus be colonial Latin America, i.e. the pre- but also post-USA Americas, which does not conform to conventional readings of utopia. This work introduces the historical figure of Vasco de Quiroga (1470-1565), into the international cultures of scholarship. Quiroga, one of the four judges or *oidores* of the Supreme Court (or *Segunda Audiencia*) in the Americas (1530-1535), and the first bishop of the region of Michoacán, is for us an influential, if neglected, figure historically to be situated inside the decision-making circles of power and privilege in early colonial Mexico. This work will provide the most thorough account of Quiroga's complete textual production, and a comparative evaluation of the complete historiography on Quiroga. Our thesis is that Quiroga represents the historical efforts for the betterment of the American Indian polity under Spanish coloniality. In the heterogeneous historical horizon of early modernity in the Americas, Quiroga's colonial literature will mean, for us, the traumatic belief in the reformation of the Indian crisis, within the historical world of possibilities and limitations available to a *hidalgo letrado indiano*. We will defend that Quiroga's texts constitute the socio-historical vehicle for American proto-egalitarianism always according to the early modern protocols of Spanish legality. The reformation of this early modernity will occur precisely during the strongest winds in the sails of the early modern Spanish-mediated globalization of the American life-world (the first to the second phases of capital accumulation and the transitional years from Charles V to Philip II). To historicize some of these agonies of early colonial legality in New Spain, we will step into the delineated dance floor of this individual name, Quiroga. Against unconvincingly narrow or genre-centered readings of utopia, chapter one will carve out the necessary spaces of differentiation for colonial utopianism; chapter two will concretize the theme and social function of the city of equals; chapter three will address Quiroga's proposals for the reformation of the colonial economy of Indian labor, segregation politics, the repression of slavery, the reparation of the rule of law and the temptations of uneven official messianism; chapter four will synthesize the official discourse of early modern globalization and the American theater of state surveillance and control of peoples and duties apropos the manufacturing of a clean record for Quiroga in his post-*oidor* years. If Hispanism is the blind spot of the international cultures of (utopian) scholarship, Quiroga's colonial utopianism, always within the imaginary location of colonial Latin America, is also the blind spot of international Hispanism, uneasy in a world which often gets called western, repressively.

Acknowledgments

This work, surely a preliminary protocol in the cultures of scholarship, took most of my time in the last three years. I wish first to thank the examining committee for the cooperation in the completion of this process. My debt to Walter D. Mignolo, advisor and Frederic Jameson, is, literally, immense. This work would not be here today had I not met with them inside and outside the classroom. I hope that some of this work will manage to convey, if only tangentially, some shreds and threads of the rare emotion I have felt in their acquaintance. I wish to thank Lúcia H. Costigan and Margaret Greer for their timely support and intelligent criticism of this not yet final product.

Duke University has meant an exceptional platform for the completion of this doctoral program. I wish to thank the Department of Romance Studies at Duke University for the financial assistance, especially the one-year stipend for research and writing at the end of the Ph.D. program. I wish to thank the financial support of the Duke-UNC Center for Latin American Studies for summer research and travels to Latin America in the early years of the Ph.D. program. I also wish to thank the Graduate School at Duke University for its two-time generous financial support so that I could attend some necessary professional meetings.

I would like to mention some other important names. Lee Sorenson and Yunyi Wang at Lilly Library gave me late-night employment, and unrestricted access to photocopy machines and the video collection. Eve Himler, Linda Purnell, Rebecca Gomez and Alice Poffinberger, in the Inter-library Loan Section of Perkins Library were always prompt and efficient in handling the voluminous traffic of foreign-sounding material this work could not have done without. The colorful section of the digital culture and Vasco de Quiroga included in chapter one, surely the most insisted single name in this work, would not have been possible without the acquaintance with Laura Cousineau and Steve Cramer, Reference Librarians at Perkins Library. Their web classes opened a brave new world for me. I wish to thank Mark A. Thomas, State Documents and Maps Librarian and Linda McCurdy, Director of the Rare Book, Manuscript and Special Collections, Dalton-Brand Reference and Research Room at Perkins Library. They allowed me to get to know the Utopian Collection and some essential tools for map-making. They also gave their time to the students in the SP114 course "The Colonization of the Americas" (Fall 1998), so that they could have a hands-on approach to the endlessly changing historical elaboration of geographies which includes all of us. The Medieval and Renaissance Working Group at Duke University, under the guidance of Ronald G. Witt, provided venues for intellectual criticism with abundant collegiality, mango cake and red wine. Pegge Abrams, Director, and Charlynn Burks at the Language Learning Center were always there for me with the audiovisual technology for my teaching and my research. I also wish to thank Sarah Schroth, Associate Curator, Duke University Museum of Art (DUMA), who joined the teaching experience of the aforementioned course with enthusiasm. DUMA granted me a generous exchange fellowship with the *Museo del Prado* for late Spring 1999. Sir John Elliott sent me some rigorous criticisms and many suggestions. Already feeling at home in Mars: I wish to thank Yvonne Yarbro-Bejarano, chair of the Department of Spanish and Portuguese at Stanford University for her guidance. I also wish to thank the Center for Latin American Studies at Stanford University for a research grant that took me to the *Archivo de Indias* (Seville, Spain) in the summer of 2000. New trips to Seville and elsewhere will be needed in consolidating some themes and points developed in this work and also in pursuing some new venues of investigation. Many thanks to Janet Cooper for the meticulous preparation of the final manuscript. This would have been a nightmare without her assistance.

Finally, I want to express my gratitude to my parents, Cándido and Virginia for their trans-Atlantic money wires. I felt I haven't been alone in the *soledad enamorada* of the writing process. Gwendolyn sent me the right music at the right time: Amancio Prada, Lluis Llach, Silvio Rodriguez, Keith Jarrett and many others helped me destroy again and again the serpents of the sea. In the desolation momentarily called Durham, many thanks to Debbera Carson, Jorge Marturano, Mary Visconti, Tom Caldwell, Luis Avilés and Ivette Hernández for their friendship. Finally, to KP, for too many things.

Statue of Quiroga in the city of Quiroga (Michoacán), reproduced in Rubén
Landa's *Don Vasco de Quiroga* (Barcelona: Biografías Gandesa, 1965).

Chapter I

ଞ୍ଜର

The No-Good Place of Early Modern
(Latin) American Utopias in a World
Which Often Gets Called Western

1. Introduction

The initial declaration of authorial intention for this first chapter will say that it will create spaces of originality and differentiation as regards early modern American utopias mostly for following chapters to substantiate, or else this work will fail. We here wish to historicize one concrete example of social experimentation for the betterment of a commonwealth (or utopia), as we find it situated in the early modern trans-Atlantic horizon of the Americas (or pre-USA Americas). Against conventional wisdom on utopias, this work will intervene critically into international scholarship explicitly concerned with the time-honored theme of the city of equals (our second definition of utopia). We will do so with a weary eye towards what we have perceived to be the crude trivialization of sixteenth- and seventeenth-century Hispanic American utopias. With this laborious title, "The No-Good Place of Early Modern (Latin) American Utopias in a World Which Often Gets Called Western," we initially wish to generate some whirlpools of estrangement and unpredictability inside conventional meanings about political happiness (our third definition of utopia). This must be done mostly, we believe, historically. This long title means mostly that we wish to generate, if only negatively, the "good" out of the omission (no-place), of the historical makings of American egalitarianism, and that we have no option but to tinker with all these corsetted concepts involved in the mental operation, "utopia," "Western," "Hispanic" and "America." It is of course easier said than done, yet the historical elucidation of the Hispanic utopia in the *Indias Occidentales* is the road we here want to take.

The critical analysis of the early modern circumstance as pertains to our selected social experimentation will take us to the official or politico-juridical culture in the *Indias Occidentales* (or sixteenth- and seventeenth-century *América con acento*). We do not wish to acquiesce to "proper" taxonomies for the "utopian" genre for reasons which will be explicit soon. Consequently, we must advance the alternative, more encompassing notion of utopianism or the necessarily conflictive horizon of the not-yet. Following Maravall, our favorite history is the history of the future,[1] which for us does not make sense without utopianism, or its failures. We have three main goals in mind: first, we will defend the existence and the meaningfulness of practices under the general nomenclature of early modern Hispanic American utopias; second, we will tease out concrete historical content under early modern American utopias in the most unpredictable place of places, colonial writing inside the repressive or legal circumstance,[2] precisely in the colonial horizon of verticalities, social conflict and struggle (or dystopia); and third, we will place the relatively little-known historical figure of Vasco de Quiroga in the center of our scholarship. Always uneasy in between English or Spanish, we will advocate the sharpening of mechanisms of perception and/or imagination with a keen eye on power/knowledge differentials; and we will ironize the great divide between them around pre- but also post-USA American utopias. The individual name of Vasco de Quiroga is for us here the red thread to follow in trying to put all these pages together. Quiroga, with or without all the textual incoherences by and about him, is for us the historical coherence of this work. Yet, we will have to circumvent him, and play occasionally the game of hare and hounds with our readers, should we wish to catch—if only momentarily—a fleeting glimpse of collectivities and utopianism. This work wishes to think of itself as mostly an exercise in the historical imagination.

So, let us imagine that we are not acquainted existentially with "utopia" (or happy forms of egalitarian commonwealth), and that we fail to understand that misery holds no dominion or that collective need has become a weird, unintelligible theology. Let us imagine that when we try to visualize human landscapes of happiness or collective labor,[3] warmth and intelligence, we fail and we try to hide and color the embarrassment with "busyness." It is not too difficult to imagine that we might have tried some time ago some of these so-called "proper" utopian texts, and we found them rather shoe-flavored and monotonous, a silly exercise and a waste of time. And so we, self-appointed creatures of good taste, decided to make a big break with this confusion, and leave it behind, like noisy pieces of outmoded technology, an old-fashioned hat or the hospitality of our uncouth country cousins. And we say out loud that the utopian tradition is a thing of the past and we feign unacquaintance. That was just the entertainment of a penniless doctoral candidate! And there are perhaps no longer distinct images, landscapes, faces or names associated with utopia except perhaps negatively *The Stalker* (1979) by Andrei A. Tarkovskii. But this would mostly mean our own resistance to look into how deep the cut of devastated landscapes of misery in ourselves by dystopias of hypocritical individuation, monetarized exchange and cardboard language

We do not wish to go gentle into this night and we are willing to admit to the embarrassing failure in the hope that something good will come out of it: one, that we cannot make convincing existential claims to know "utopia," or that utopianism is still the history of the future; and two, that we have not enjoyed the bookish contours of classic utopian figurations, and that we are not supposed to enjoy these fearful symmetries any longer since most scholarship has mostly made them into a rather unwelcoming place for the Hispanic tradition. We have no option but to try to energize these human landscapes of foreignness and historicity in the hope that we engage our fears and desires, if only obliquely, along the way.

So, since we did not understand "utopia," we have turned to some general literature on utopias. After consultation, it dawns on us however that we still do not know what this *thing* (utopia) means historically and socially in relation to the Americas. Rather than sweeping this unknowingness under the carpet, we wish to put it right in the middle of the living room for everybody to see. Let us imagine that life never took us to Mexico, that we are not Mexicans, and that we do not feel any particular need to go to Mexico. It would then be natural to shuffle feet, raise eyebrows and ask, "Who?" a bit nervously upon hearing the name of the historical figure of this work, Vasco de Quiroga (1470-1565), since we haven't seen (let us continue imagining) the locations named after him, the commemorative statues in public parks[4] and some of the portraits in the north-western state of Michoacán, but also in Mexico City. We may mention the illustrations to the monumental *Crónica de Michoacán* (XVIII Century) by the Franciscan Friar Pablo Beaumont,[5] the symbolic mural painting—Vasco de Quiroga side by side Thomas More—designed by Juan O'Gorman for the *Gertrudis Bocanegra Federal Public Library* in the city of Pátzcuaro, Michoacán,[6] or the magnificent murals created by Diego de Rivera for the National Palace in Mexico City.[7] Inside Mexico, it is not possible not to have heard of Quiroga, who is also automatically associated, among colonial scholars, with the name of Silvio Zavala.[8] Outside Mexico, as this is our case, it is quite another story. The non-visual quality of Quiroga's legal treatises will not help us much either.

Chances are most of us will not be making the connection between the abstract and rather unusual noun of "utopia" and the traceable concreteness of Vasco de Quiroga. Again, this ignorance would come to us naturally outside Mexico and the presumption of knowledge on our part would be guilty of the same arrogance we are here set to undermine. If familiar names of other dead white males will surely come up easily for us around "utopia," like Thomas More, Tomasso Campanella or Francis Bacon,[9] we will not be able, not even at gun point, to stutter a good couple of lines on this rather obscure Spanish-sounding name of Quiroga. The standard response in most of us will be the absence of a soundbite.

Most likely, we will be unable to qualify why on earth this foreign-sounding name found a modest niche, a few good lines, in a few good encyclopedias, but not all.[10] This low profile of Vasco de Quiroga, which may or may not include the largely Mexican mantra of *defensor de Indios*, is the norm in relation to standard narratives on Early Modern utopianism. This work wishes to disrupt this sorry state of (scholarly) affairs, if ever so slightly.

We wish to historicize the historical legitimacy of this soundbite ("defender of the Indians"), as pertains to Quiroga. Our analysis will need, however, to ramify and engage standard frames of vision of early modern utopianism as they pertain to the West Indies of Spanish America. We will do so assuming an initial position of suspension of the affirmation or the negation of this aforementioned cliché, for the main reason that we wish to insert Quiroga's individuality into the collective set of lettered repressive practices, horizons and limitations, proper to a high state official in early New Spain. That is, our Quiroga will gain three-dimensionality in the social role of the *hidalgo letrado indiano* and American utopianism will historically make sense in relation to this social role with all its limitations. All individualities will have to assume a rather precarious position in this collective forum of the repressive culture. Early Modern utopianism must here necessarily incorporate a second passenger on equal footing, that of colonization (or dystopia). Always in relation to Quiroga, we will talk about colonial utopianism, or utopianism in the colonial world, to thus differentiate it better from metropolitan or European utopianism (the imaginary place where all these aforementioned "naturalized" male names are to be included). This work on colonial utopianism will grow stronger in the invigoration of this differentiation from metropolitan or conventional utopianism.

Yet we do not wish to radicalize or isolate the colonial specificity. Within the rather limited dance floor, i.e. the individuality of Quiroga, we set out for the critical investigation which will, of necessity, relativize and hopefully overcome the limitations of "proper" genre analysis. If successful, this work will represent a loss of innocence, also ignorance, and so we wish to introduce the most encompassing notion of utopianism. In what is surely a stretch to the historical imagination, we want to untie the tight historical knot of modernity and coloniality.[11] Our initial suggestion is that this trans-Atlantic stretch will elaborate convincingly that utopianism cannot permanently nest in either abstract notion indefinitely, and that it must instead necessarily cut across the coexistence of modernity and coloniality in the foreign horizon of early modern Americas or officially New Spain. This work will hopefully deliver concrete content, the bureaucratic "busyness" of the repressive culture, for this argument in favor of the historical meaningfulness of colonial utopianism.

Yet, most classic utopian accounts do not look too good for us since they leave Hispanic practices out. The scholarly landscape is thus a bit more distressing than the one enunciated thus far. It is not that Quiroga's name is rarely mentioned in relation to the historical makings of the good place which is not yet here (utopia); conventional wisdom, most of the utopian traditions will say, explicitly or not, that there is no such thing as any one convincing American utopia in the early modern "world" which fits the bill. In other words, it is not that Quiroga happens to be the ugly little duckling who fails the English test; we would be quite happy to concede to the relative banality of this individuality, whose single-minded defense would almost always be a futile exercise (like the "treading on the shimmering light" of the single name as we appropriate Luis de Góngora's famous line). It is rather the entire American continentality, suspiciously within a certain chronology, that fails to fit the bill of classic utopias. To challenge this damaging myopia on utopianism, we here wish to make the name of Quiroga a paradigmatic symptom of a larger, more troubling disposition.

Quiroga is mostly for us paradigmatic of the ignorance and silence over human practices and experiences which we could only hastily synthesize under the continental name of America. Thus, we are about to tread on the shimmering light of the single name which will hopefully help us gain imaginary vistas into vaster landscapes of human endeavors. Our work emerges from the always tense juxtaposition of Hispanism and America historically in relation to early modern utopianism. Through this individuality, Quiroga, we will explore most concretely some of these heterogeneous horizons of early modern political reformation as they directly relate to the Spanish-vehicled colonization of the officially-called New Spain (or sixteenth- and seventeenth-century Mexico). By doing so, we hope to challenge some of these easy silences regarding colonial utopianism.

The distressing conventional argument we wish to oppose will implicitly or explicitly articulate that, *they* do not have it (the "good") ever. We stretch this cryptic formula thus, so that "they," this heterogeneous or foreign ghost of the historical imagination, cannot ever deliver the "goods" for "us" here and now.[12] This generic formulation will often win the historical argument precisely by the deliberate simplification of vocabulary which closes down on myopic visions of horizons, as though "they" were under some kind of biblical curse! Poorly formulated arguments often betray the fat capons of prejudice flying quite high upon imaginary fields of unacquaintance and ignorance! The presentation of fresh new evidence, which we will do here, and the increasing sophistication in argumentation, which we will try to do here, will not however necessarily shoot these flying capons down to the historical ground of early modernity. Yet, this is quite explicitly, precisely what we wish to do.

Two things are clear: one, that there is no easy option between debilitation or invigoration of referentiality, which could behave like a two-edged knife, all too easily in multi-directional and unpredictable fashion; and two, that these "goods," like the empty goods promised by the abstract sign of "utopia," will only gain its inter-subjective three-dimensional content historically (we will see some of this prejudicial content in relation to the digital culture). We do not wish to get caught in the trap of nominalism of "utopia." The social mechanism of incipient egalitarianism in early modern Americas is what we are here after. Against the playful lightness of fictional referentiality, we will try to come to terms most concretely with the harsh, repressive explicitness of the referential mechanism in Spanish Indian Law (or *Derecho Indiano*).

We must still go deeper into these troubled waters of international scholarship. The conventional argument will run negatively thus: the Spanish language will fail historically to manufacture utopias during the classic early modern period of gestation of utopias. They do not exist *even* in the land of evasion and inexistence, and should these by any computational mistake exist, they will be of lesser value or negligible detail. Should any Spanish utopias exist, these unicorns will be, first, the exception which will have to conform to the "European" norm, and second, they will be second rate (that's always how the country mouse will get talked about by the city mouse). This distressing argument is mostly made in a language other than Spanish, which is, explicitly or not, put "there" as we will soon see.

To undermine the conventional argument that there is no such thing as one single early modern Hispanic utopia, we need to highlight that it is not that pre-USA human experience is not ever "here"; it is rather that the pre- and post-USA Americas are *never* here with us today making demands for an egalitarian society. An anti-Spanish sentiment, mostly in the contemporary USA setting, is precisely built on the over-simplification of the Spanish colonization of the Americas. More concretely, conventional arguments will mean the erasure of the "Latin" of "Latin America" and also the systematic underrepresentation of the Spanish articulation of knowledge production inside international cultures of scholarship. This standard mechanism of dehistoricization, or idealization, will confer almost ontological privilege to the fourth or post-Second World War moment of capital accumulation with the gradual exclusion of all others (the vernacular use of "modern" in the American idiom means precisely this post-Second World War moment of "glory").[13] This fourth moment, clearly one in a series of interrelational systemic changes, is trumpeted into the singular modellic moment of human culmination *precisely* by deliberately refusing to look closely into others. Against this disconnected seriality or chronology, we need to put historical wheels of crisis and transformation and add historical landscapes to this rather static and poor historical vision. We will also need to chase down this American ostrich, drag its head out the hole of ignorance and stubbornness, and point out the historical horizon of greener fields of pasture in continuity with the Hispanic tradition.

Yet, there is no kidding that we are "here" in the repression of historicity which defines the USA, and this work emerges precisely to try to stretch this rather atrophied popularized historical imagination, which clings stubbornly to this ostrich hole of this fourth stage of capital accumulation as global culmination. But still, and this is the key turn to the screw, as it is almost exclusively narrated in the English language (or vicariously in French, German and Italian) but *not* in Spanish. We did not choose to be in this marginal corner and yet this work will have to find its place precisely by going against the grain of this rather resilient prejudicial belief, which is always already the tick of the superiority complex of power and privilege (Ginés de Sepúlveda and Quiroga will give us ample evidence of this tick in following chapters). We are not fooling anyone in that we are not happy with what we see happening around us. And so we wish to wrap the shiverings of this historical imagination precisely by making use of some of the historical lessons which come to us today in the language, mostly in the USA, of the garbage collectors, migrant farm-workers, the lumpenproletariat in departments of foreign languages in big universities, the sorry-looking English-corsetted *roto* Spanish. We have not failed to notice the alarming juxtaposition in prestigious American universities of general courses such as Spanish for Law Enforcement Personnel, Business Spanish, "Experiential Learning" [*sic*] and Contract Learning side by side courses in Masterpieces of Spanish Literature, Culture and Civilization of Spain and Latin America, Spanish Prose of the Golden Age and Representative Authors of Spanish American Literature. In the emotional vicinity of this broken national idiom, we will turn a deaf ear to the delicacy of big-business monolingualism, and instead try to create solidarities by pressing harder the historical texture of a global, all-inclusive synchronicity. Historicity is the realization of the throbbing pulse in your wrist here and now. Coloniality is the awareness of the historical cut, even by negligence, of the throbbing pulse of entire collectivities.

We will thus here try to open up this historicity to the heterogeneity of the Quiroga findings, which we will figuratively place out there on the scholarly tables for the scavenging of the historical imagination. This cannot be done without some appropriate restlessness as to the neglected utopian figurations in the pre- and also post-Enlightenment moment of early modernity in the colonial Americas.[14] If periodizations are no natural demarcation lines, the conventional American use of "modern," we find an indeed impossibly tight corset which will cut our breathing.[15] If early modernity means for us the teething troubles of capitalism colonizing the Americas, Spanish, an empty signifier and never an entirely innocent sign of the "good," will signify for us eminently an imperial language of rather seclusive, repressive officialdom in these heterogeneous American horizons. It will do so with a historical inferiority complex against the undisputed supremacy of the language of high culture, Latin. This communicational vehicle, Spanish, will help us allegorize some of the early reconfigurations and commotions as they historically relate to the first-phase global process of capital accumulation. Quiroga's legal culture will represent the early attempts for the change of some of these early commotions and reconfigurations for the betterment of "indianized" American populations. This work will historicize power differentials as they pertain historically to the Spanish literature for the law enforcement of early New Spain.

Our historicization of colonial utopia must do its job inevitably inside international platforms of utopian scholarship. Historically, the notion of "literature," as we will see in closest detail in the following chapters, is not the automatic sign which speaks to us candidly and transparently. "Literature" in the colonial world, or "colonial literature"—almost like the voice of the oracle—will not make easy, graceful sense at first glance. That is why we feel the need to insist and denaturalize this apparent meaninglessness which will most likely take us by surprise. The efforts to try to understand the notion of "colonial literature" in either Spanish or Latin, as relates to the *letrado* Quiroga will take us to the most counter-intuitive or unlikely of places: the legal, or repressive, culture. We must highlight the virtual inexistence of this association of colonial utopianism and colonial legality in most historiographies on utopianism and also colonial Latin American literature. This is one of our claims to originality.

We wish to bring Lalinde-Abadía's equation, i.e. legality is repression, to the rather abstract, cardboard notion of "utopia," seemingly a new thing with Indian feathers for the early modern Americas. Better yet, the official record of practices of inclusion and exclusion of social agents from social goods, or the law, is the historical circumstance for early egalitarian tendencies in this heterogeneous historical horizon. Quiroga will represent for us the concreteness of these early egalitarian tendencies. We will place imaginary wheels underneath "utopia," our Trojan horse, and we will approach the early modern horizon of the Americas, officially New Spain, mostly with a critical eye on the law which will be no other than Spanish Indian Law (or *Derecho Indiano*). Early modern American utopia thus becomes for us an Indian utopia, the betterment of the polity for the majority of the early modern American populations, as manufactured by the non-Indian official figure of Quiroga. We will need to fill up the no-good historical place of Vasco de Quiroga inside international utopianism. This work is the most comprehensive critical presentation of this historical figure in the high society of international scholarship on utopianism. This is our second claim to originality.

We will have to provide some generalizations as to the collective legal practice of university-trained petty nobility or *hidalgos* in the early commotions of Spanish colonization. The manufacturing of the reformation of the early establishment of the colonial polity, theoretically for the betterment of the American majority by these non-humanist *letrados*,[16] means primordially that we will focus on the legal profession. Colonial literature means mostly for us here legal or institutional literature, very much like today the American political class comes mostly from law schools and not from departments of literature, let alone foreign literature. Quiroga's colonial literature is hence, we must emphasize, legal literature in the double sense of legal theory and courtroom litigation. Rephrasing the distressing table of contents under "Spanish" in one representative American university, the experiential learning of Quiroga's Spanish, mostly for political business only, is historically never the expression of the self, but rather the official vehicle for a set of proposals for the hasty fix of the fractures of the rule of law. Quiroga's official utopia always promoted the rule of the colonial law in times quite close to a state of siege. Quiroga's repressive literature, historically in a dystopian or colonial world, will not lend itself easily to grand pronouncements about the felicity of the genius or the trans-historical inspirational longevity of the masterpiece. We do not feel the need to talk this talk anymore. In fact, we would rather leave it behind, like an old-fashioned four-wheeled automobile for the ants to be eaten away. It is only the rigorous historicization of this colonial literature which will manage to deliver the meaningfulness of this rather intimidating and shamelessly archaic use of repressive language, Quiroga's. This work will thus try to bring the "there" of the historical heterogeneity, if only imaginatively back to our often unconscious, three-dimensional socio-historical circumstance.[17] It is with this old-fashioned time machine under the arm—Quiroga's endeavors, almost like a jack-in-the-box—that we wish to knock on the readers' doors of perception. It is this official repressive bundle of early modern rationalities for the betterment of a polity that we will be exploring to try to see if we achieve some shreds and threads of political happiness any differently or any better today. If early modern utopianism is the whipped cream, and the name of Thomas More, the cherry on top, Quiroga's repressive textualities are, at least for us, the green vitamin of the spinach historically hiding inside the cream.[18]

So, against the conventional charges of the inexistence and meaninglessness of pre-Enlightenment Spanish American experimentation, our scholarship will join others' efforts and try to rewind the hands of the historical clock to better reconfigurate historical centers of power and privilege across the Spanish Atlantic.[19] We will have to signify without falling into the trap of proposing role models of human perfection. To release the fierce repression of this global historicity, we would instead rather belabor the most salient colonial imperfections negatively and most concretely as pertain to our chosen historical figure. Our goal is to try to achieve occasional glimpses into the social totality, tensions and struggles, which give historical form to early modern and colonial New Spain. The Western world, or the "West" as the brutal reduction customarily granted to us by political scientists has it,[20] is not for us a warm, friendly place. Yet we here feel we must make room for the rather miniscule name of Quiroga. Quiroga will be the wedge with which to hopefully break open some of the rather crude and uninspiring soundbites on early modern utopias. Hopefully amid these ruins, we wish to move towards and beyond Quiroga's orthodox or official vision, with all its limitations, as regards the West Indies of America.

This work will thus logically make the following claims. First, there is at least one American project for political reformation (or utopia) associated with the name of Vasco de Quiroga. Second, this early modern American utopia does not historically "fit" into conventional understandings or the proper rules of decorum of the utopian genre, and we will have to flesh out imaginatively the historical three-dimensionality of this colonial unfittingness. Third, the critical exploration of this colonial specificity will take us waist-deep to the rather esoteric protocols for the official construction of social truth. And fourth, the utopian theme of the city of equals will for us turn into the always bittersweet confrontational process of politico-juridical negotiation. It is our task, mostly in the following chapters, to make fit most concretely at least some of these egalitarian tendencies into this early modern dystopian and colonial repressive circumstance. This is where we must imagine Quiroga's fight for intelligibility, and our critical analysis will look into the complete textual typologies "by" and "about" Quiroga. This colonial fracture is our moment of pain and truth and we will cling to it as that which hurts with meaning still relevant for us today. Humanistic niceties will not historically fare well in this repressive culture. Historical persuasion will here work, and we are almost using Machiavellian language, not entirely by equivocation and deceit, but rationally with a rationality not entirely unacquainted with authoritarianism and force. Colonial law is no Sunday picnic on a sunny day. Quiroga's politico-juridical reformation will have no choice but to signify inside these historical whirlpools of harrowing social signification. Following Lalinde-Abadía, we must necessarily turn a deaf ear to dialogic, conversational models for the making of a more egalitarian polity. This is particularly true in Quiroga's case.

The rather counter-intuitive notion of "colonial writing," at least mostly in the young imperial romance language, is thus to be historically understood inside officialdom. Quiroga's repressive culture in this early *novohispano* setting will remain at the level of conventional politics (or policy), always already in tactful negotiation with the early colonial status quo. Colonial utopianism will not historically rise to the level of revolutionary politics (chapter four will elaborate on how Quiroga's politics will remain at the conventional level of *De Translatio Imperii* formulations). Yet, his colonial utopianism, quiet reformation if you wish, will have to be understood at the more localized, nitty-gritty level of the manufacture of a believable policy for a sustainable Indian polity. Quiroga will represent, with abundant limitations and contradictions to be sure, the traumatic belief in the reformation of the early trans-Atlantic and colonial world. His reformation thus cuts unevenly across his institutional politics, i.e. the solid endorsement of the early modern orthodoxy of the imperial lexicon, and his strong, local reformist policy to change the early dramas of the so-called Indians in trans-Atlantic New Spain.

So, we are here about to lose at least some of the conventional, perhaps unconscious historical innocence. We thus set sail to navigate these unquiet waters of silence and neglect, the no-place of American utopias in the western world, the no-association of early modern utopianism and the repressive culture and the no-good place of Vasco de Quiroga. These waters are not, as in Silvio Rodriguez's song, without long and transparent serpents of the sea and we will highlight some of these as we go along. This historicization will have to make historical sense, diachronically inside international cultures of scholarship on early modern utopianism. With a weary eye for sea serpents, "utopia," like "America" in the "American" idiom, is not impoverished for no reason. Against some of these no-good reasons, this historical work emerges.

2. Tarrying with the Negative: The No-Place of Early Modern (Latin) American Utopias in the Western World

There might still be some doubts as to the need for this work. We might still not see the argument regarding the systematic exclusion of Spanish American utopias. If the next section will say that Spanish scholarship says that America is the country of utopia, this one will say exactly the opposite: Hispanic America, negligible detail, is *never* the country of utopia.

But we might want to make some easy money along the way: you go bet there is not a whole lot of literature on utopianism and hispanism, that there is not a whole lot of literature on utopianism and Latin America, and that there are not many convincing historical accounts, mostly in English, on utopianism and the early modern non-USA (Latin) Americas. We guarantee you that the name of Vasco de Quiroga will almost never be there, and so you will find yourself with some money in your back pocket before your friends get a chance to read this work.

The conventional point of departure will be the English intellectual Thomas More (1477-1535), the manufacturer of the early modern neologism of utopia. Classic utopias will classically crystallize inevitably around More's exquisite Latin dialogue, *Utopia* (1516), which will remain the measuring rod, but also the whipping post as to the appropriateness of the nomenclature of "utopia" for pre- or post-early modern egalitarian dispositions. We have swept Latin under the carpet a number of times now so that English patrimonialization will make More's narrative into the perennial model for future generations. The slipperiness of utopianism, the historical "anything" which attains some shreds and threads of the egalitarian ideal, will have to sit pretty in the pillory of More's *Utopia*, still no doubt a delightful, ironic narrative. The makings of saintliness for More but also for Quiroga, as we will soon see, is not far away from this rather pious vision.

We guarantee you most, if not all conventional accounts, mostly in the English language, will systematically circumvent American manufacturings of Early Modern utopianism. The early modern American "ground" is simply neither "there" nor "here" in the supposedly global horizon of vision for the historical imagination. The early modern Americas is, according to most, if not all utopian literature, the rather distant wasteland which will never produce inspirational lessons for the future. We will challenge some of these unhealthy conventions. Yet, let us tarry with this conventional negative. Let us still initially behave as though we were the proverbial donkey fixated upon the dangling carrot hanging in front of the nose: we have nothing else but the five or six letters of the Latin-sounding "utopia" and the *tabula rasa* of colonial Latin America. The inexistence and the meaninglessness of colonial Latin America, inside which we must surely insert Quiroga, is the beginning for our historical research on American utopias.

To demonstrate the systematic elaboration of the permanent no-place of early modern (Latin) American utopias in the western world, we propose this constellation: *The Dictionary of Imaginary Places*,[21] *The Recent Encyclopedia of Utopian Literature*,[22] *Utopian Thought in the Western World*,[23] *The Principle of Hope*,[24] *Utopics: Spatial Play*[25] and finally *Realistic*

Utopias: The Ideal Imaginary Societies of the Renaissance.[26] We would like to add, almost at the biographical or anecdotal level, two further experiences which will support this negative argument that there is no such thing as early modern American utopias.

These experiences will be: first, we got acquainted with the Utopian Collection, located in the Rare Books and Special Collections Section at Perkins Library, Duke University;[27] and second, we participated in the *The Society for Utopian Studies–1997 Annual Conference* at The University of Memphis,Tennessee (Oct. 16-19, 1997).[28] A cursory examination of the former catalogue and its holdings, as well as the attendance to the latter conference, or the perusal of the conference program, will reinforce the conventional dictum. That is, whatever the slippery and cunning "utopia" means, these sources will say, explicitly or not, that it is almost exclusively the literary male exercise of the imagination as manufactured by the pen, yet almost exclusively in the imperial languages (English, French, German, Italian, Latin) and not Spanish. Better yet, whatever "utopia" may mean, this written thematization of the ideal world will mostly concentrate around the restrictive chronology of the XVIII century onwards (let us say 1776, the *Declaration of [American] Independence*).[29] This general literature will rarely, if ever make any association, except by implicit contrast, between utopian literature and the repressive culture. Classic or metropolitan utopias will thus be any kind of idealization of the polity, be it pedagogic endeavors or didacticism, fictionalized flights of evasion and entertaintment, even political messianism, except those social practices, not necessarily textual, mostly intelligible inside the legal circumstance. Quiroga, our concrete historical example of written and non-written *negotium* of repressive labor, proves this dissociation wrong.

Pre-XVIII-century Americas, should this imaginary site be mentioned at all in these utopian sources, will almost exclusively amount to background decoration or inspiring muse for this scribbling male pen in an imperial language of high culture (but again, *not* Spanish or Portuguese, let alone Amerindian languages). The utopian tradition is also guilty of this Anglo-centered impoverishment of historical vision. If "America" is almost exclusively the USA, "Europe" is contemporary rich Europe, which is the reductive referentiality for the social sciences in the USA setting. This is the simplified version of Europe which will travel imaginatively to post-XVIII-century America, carrying in its backpacks the copyright to the utopian tradition (this will also be Mario Góngora's take as we will soon see). So the manufacturing of the imaginary sites for the English-only trans-Atlantic plateau, third and fourth moments of capital accumulation according to Arrighi's serialization, will have to repress systematically all traces of the first Spanish/Genoese moment. Quiroga's historical ghost is likewise nowhere to be seen inside the no-place and good place of the utopian tradition.[30]

So it is appropriate to get a bit suspicious. *The Dictionary of Imaginary Places*, illustrated by Graham Greenfield, including maps and charts by James Cook, obliterates any trace of the early modern Americas. With some surprise, we noticed that there was no entry for America, and that the entry "Amerika" (thus with "k"), told readers to turn to Franz Kafka. The entry "utopia" began by saying, "[It was] fifteen miles from the coast of Latin America, formerly known as Sansculottia." America is here the inaccessible land of perennial non-referentiality.[31] References to the Hispanic world included the predictable references to the most famous Argentinian Jorge Luis Borges, the myth of *El Dorado*, the episode of Montesino's Cave, the grotto of La Mancha explored by the inevitable knight el Quijote, and the Arcadia Tunnel, "a subterranean passage from Arcadia in Greece to Naples in Italy, only to be used by unhappy lovers," in relation to Lope de Vega's *Arcadia* (1598). It is quite telling that the closest *The Dictionary of Imaginary Places* gets to the coast of Mexico is the *Treasure Island* of Robert L. Stevenson (1883).

The bulkiness of this volume strongly suggests three distressing messages: first, the rather artificial divide of imaginative fictionalization and reality (this utopian literature is, however, appropriately situated spatially and chronologically in relation to an individual author, work, etc.); second, "utopia" appears to be little more than European manufacturing of literary make-believe, which grotesquely circumvents pre-USA America and refuses to consider at least imaginatively the history of the future or post-USA America; and lastly, there is the feeling, at least in this reader, of the banality of the entire enterprise of "utopia" which is implicitly and narrowly defined as the mere thematic fictionalization of ahistorical contentment. This contentment, which is supposed to be the readers' contentment, is brittle and false due to the ocean-like silences.

We must linger a bit longer at the doorstep of this unfriendly house of classic utopias. The luxurious package of *The Recent Encyclopedia of Utopian Literature* makes the sin by omission perhaps all the more disturbing as regards the so-called "global" mapping of utopia which is no doubt profoundly myopic and fiercely monolingual. The gold of this Sierra Madre is however quite scarce. The entry "utopia" states quite flatly,

[T]he creation of perfect worlds is almost exclusively a Western proclivity, although writers like John Milton, John Bunyan, James Hilton, Hermann Hesse and Malcolm X draw heavily of Eastern lore and philosophy and on Hebrew and Arabic scriptures, which are dotted with alluring distant playgrounds with romantic names like Shambhala and Nirvana.

This conventional nutshell is what we will fight against: the almost ontological differentiation of rich nations—the rich are here always wiser—which is accompanied by these anxiety-producing adverbs and floppy clauses which fail quite miserably to fly above the ground of the historical imagination. This is a rather dehistoricized and decontextualized tableau for the predictable ethnicities, languages, nationalities and genders. We need to run away like the plague from these Bloch-like psychological approaches to utopianism and need to relativize or historicize these content-free, so-called "romantic" ruminations: from where are we looking East if not from the blurring of historical positionality, which is always a position of historical power and privilege? And isn't this game of heterogeneities, in which desemanticized "utopia" is always already "there," a rather symptomatic gesture which represses historicity? We would argue it is so.

Snodgrass takes utopia to mean the banality of "stressfree human life," which leaves pre-Enlightment America out of sight. This *Encylopedia of Utopian Literature* has nothing to say about what officially got called *Indias Occidentales*. The identification, even mystification of the abstract noun of utopia with More's prototype will consequently come as no surprise. Yet More is in some ahistorical limbo with no speculation as to the most likely role or function of his literary production. Snodgrass's taxonomical impulse will place the historical slipperiness of "utopia" inside thematic boxes. Hers is a sorry-looking collection of old shoes: nature's delights, good will and altruism, industrial refinements, social engineering, fantasy, theocracy, otherworldliness, peace by default and prophecy. Three-dimensional, socio-historical utopianism is thus sapped out, flattened out and banalized conventionally in the following adjectives: "individual, impractical [and] quimerical." This silliness will surely give inspiration to nobody. Against the distant Orinoco murmurs of the New World, there will also be decontextualized quotes from Shakespeare's *As You Like It* (1599) and *The Tempest* (1611).

The second entry on utopia in *The Recent Encyclopedia of Utopian Literature* speaks mostly thematically about More's *Utopia*. We may read this final evasion of a pronouncement:

[It] has been labeled a utopian fantasy, social satire, pure communism, an impractical scheme of social regeneration, and a humanistic system for bettering the world. One theory proposes that he modeled his regulated society on the Incan civilization that sprang up in the vicinity of the fictional island of Utopia [*sic!*] and was revealed to Europe in 1513 through the expeditionary observations of Vasco de Balboa. More's rational pagans, who resemble Plato's Republicans, are remarkably devoid of Christian principles. More's purpose in presenting a community outside the Judeo-Christian ethic is obvious: In order to lambaste the excesses and animosities of Christian Europeans, he extolled the virtues of a heathen people who lived amicably by reason.

Anything goes here side by side the perceptible repression of early modern Americas. Utopianism is little more than the fictionalization of easy worlds in this kind of consumer-friendly self-service paradise of comfortable interpretations. Snodgrass deliberately shies away from positionality inside a merry-go-round of floating geographies which does not carry much meaning after all. This calculated, yet clumsy tentativeness is surely intended to cover all possibilities and yet it will cover none. More's "obvious" ethic is of course not obvious at all in this unsubstantiated appeal to authorial intention, which is never the end of any discussion.

It will not be easy to sift some grain from Snodgrass's hide-and-seek tactics as regards the historical slipperiness of utopianism. The reader will have to help himself to a bunch of "theories" and historical figures. We will run into the literary epic of the *Aeneid*, Orwell's *Animal Farm* (1945), William Dean Howells and Dulcinea del Toboso, Saint Augustine and the *Autobiography of Malcolm X* (1965), Dante Alighieri and Anthony Burgess, allegory, materialism, baptism and bestiality. We will surely be first tempted to imitate Michel Foucault and laugh at this colossal incoherence. There will no order to these utopian things, Sondgrass will blow no whistle, and there will be some giddiness about this momentary floatingness. Yet, initial laughter will subside fast. This apparent plethora of utopian information hides landscapes of misery. It is possible to simplify this wild array of utopian things at least to one negative: no Spanish utopias. J. L. Borges is missing, yet Cervantes is predictably present. Quiroga is of course not mentioned. Early modern Americas are not ever mentioned. Amid this apparent randomness, the message is loud: this so-called "Western" proclivity proclaims that pre-USA Americas are negligible detail. Reading in between the explicit and the implicit, Snodgrass's understanding of utopia appears to be little more than the principle of tolerance with no concrete background and no good historical reasons.

The one single most comprehensive utopian piece by Manuel and Manuel gives to us the same distressing news. "They" do not have "it," the good:

> [T]he utopian propensity is common to the Western world. The Italian architectural utopias of the Renaissance and the French social utopias of the eighteenth and nineteenth centuries were among the heights of utopian expression, and the Pansophic vision of the...seventeenth century had a deep Germanic and Lutheran coloration.... [U]topia in general has not been geographically exclusive. The relative unity of Western culture has guaranteed the rapid diffusion of utopian ideas irrespective of the countries in which they originated.... [T]he absence of a sustained utopian tradition in Spain is peculiar, though free-floating utopian affect may have somehow attached itself to the figure of Don Quixote. The manuscript of an Enlightenment utopia, *Descripción de la Sinapia, península en la Terra Austral*, has recently been published but it hardly modifies the generalization that Spain was relatively untouched by the utopian main current until the penetration of Marxist and anarchist thought. Danes, Swiss, Poles, Czechs, and members of other European nations have written utopias, though the overwhelming number of Western utopias—whatever their national origin—were first printed in Latin, English, French, Italian or German.[32]

The Manuels, following Zavala, will include a passing remark to Quiroga's projects with no mention of the legal circumstance of his reformation of coloniality.[33] Ricard is also quoted with almost identical information.[34] Quiroga is kind of "there" historically, a perennial second fiddle, always approached tangentially or mostly forgotten in the orchestra of utopia, due to his location in the shadows of early modern Americas. This work will change this sorry state of neglect. With Manuel's predictable stereotype, reminiscent of Franco's tourist-attracting motto, "Spain is different," it is no wonder that we must follow Maravall and consistently downplay the folkloric appeals to the exceptionalism of the Iberian peninsula. We may recall the French abuse to the representative of the Republic of Miranda in Luis Buñuel's *The Discreet Charm of the Bourgeoisie* (1972), because this is precisely what the utopian tradition has done with the Hispanic tradition. The Manuels are far from being the only ones doing this ugly thing.

We still need to register one more abuse. We have in mind Eliav-Feldon's *Realistic Utopias*. This volume, slim and more manageable, apparently unpretentious, but also more mediocre, is, precisely for all these reasons, more damaging in the explicit articulation of the conventional negation of the existence and meaningfulness of early modern Spanish American utopias. Eliav-Feldon illustrates the genre argument with tabulations and taxonomies within the chronology, which is also ours, of 1516-1630. Her narrow definition of "utopia" is conventional: "a literary work describing an ideal society created by a conscious human effort on this earth." "Realist" here means "not dependent on any supernatural...or on any divine intervention," and also "not escapist dreams of fantasy." A list of eight great themes includes: good government, idealization of existing societies, designs of ideal cities, glorification of a primitive Golden Age, world empires and plans for universal eternal peace, theocratic millenial kingdoms (plans or experiments), and "utopias proper" [*sic*]. Vasco de Quiroga and the Jesuits in Paraguay are included in the theocratic millenial kingdom section, and excluded from "proper utopias," which are taken to be "[the] ideal imaginary societies described in their entirety as if functioning in the present." The photograph of this "proper" utopian team, almost like a soccer team, includes thirteen members of predictable language, gender and race backgrounds.[35] Eliav-Feldon's conventional nutshell is again perfect for all its conventional wisdom on early modern utopias. This is the narrow vision of early modern utopias this work wishes to relativize and reframe.

By pushing the genre argument, Eliav-Feldon exemplifies the unequivocal taxonomic impulse side by side these blunt-knife thematic definitions which do not convincingly cut the historical figure of the ideal polity, which is always already in constant historical motion. Eliav-Feldon focuses on the skeleton of a certain understanding of the utopian form as that of the genre-specific fictional narrative devoid of any socio-historical content, let alone social role and function. With little hesitation, her analysis will go to dismiss the historical importance of the emergence of the American "ninth circle" even at the deficient level of mere inspirational background for fictionalization of ideal polities: "One has the impression that they could all have been written even if Columbus had never set sail." Juggling slippery referentialities, utopianists are said to be satisfied to build their imaginary cities on the soil of Europe. Eliav-Feldon has only slight regard for the "pathetic attempts to realize the utopias by using the Indias of the New World as the human material." Her language is quite brutal:

Why were there some countries or nationalities which (to the best of my knowledge) did not produce in that period even a single utopia proper?...

[W]hy none in Spain? Was it the preoccuppation with colonization in the New World which diverted the attention of the Spanish humanists from imaginary societies to real social experiments? Or was it the rule of the Inquisition and the enforced religious uniformity that prevented the appearance of utopias proper which are, as was indicated above, a product of a fundamentally secular impulse: to create a perfect society here and now by human powers alone? These are merely tentative speculations which require further research beyond the scope of this study. (p. 15)

This prejudicial belief, which is perceptibly a second-hand knowledge, arouses the ire which drives this work. This repudiated imaginary site, trans-Atlantic Hispanic world, will be our fighting ground for power and desire. Following chapters will fill up Eliav-Feldon's doubts which do not however hesitate to demonize the absence of the proper utopian genre among non-metropolitan locations. It does not occur to her that "proper" utopian forms are always historical creatures potentially intelligible according to their fittingness to social needs and goods generated by the original socio-historical circumstances. Eliav-Feldon however states that this utopian model (the "good") is for others (the "they" of non-English, Spain, pre-USA Americas, etc.), to imitate docilely irrespective of those circumstances. An inflexible causality for utopian endeavors is thus firmly established: utopianism cannot be anything else in the early modern chronology except an "European" creation ("European," in the narrow, anachronistic and contemporary sense of rich European nation). Conceding to her own ignorance, Eliav-Feldon's message is non-ambiguous: it is doubtful that there will be the case of a convincing incorporation of a Spanish representative, let alone the possibility of the change of this framework (Stelio Cro's findings of *Sinapia* are mentioned as "belated" products).[36] No one single Spanish candidate, insistently like Cinderella's big sisters, will ever fit convincingly Eliav-Feldon's anti-Spanish glass slipper-model for the "proper" utopian genre.

Realistic Utopias mostly constitutes a conventional intervention, with or without convincing arguments, into patrimonialist conceptions of cultural capital. We are dealing with the high visibility of Oxford University Press. These distressing dispositions for the systematic exclusion of things Spanish are tremendously meaningful and vastly exceed Eliav-Feldon's modest scholarship, which may pull it off precisely by treading firmly on the conventional path of early modern utopias. Early modern utopias "proper" are here to be the cultural capital of early modern metropolitan narratives articulated in all imperial languages, English, French, Italian and German, but *not* Spanish, the apparently good-for-nothing vehicle for quasi-western none-too-bright delta caste in this brave new world. But whose genre are we talking about here?[37] We have here no choice but to try to untie the knot of a narrow understanding of the genre analysis of proper utopias, and move this conventional understanding, for us no longer convincing, towards the critical analysis of the social mechanism of historical egalitarianism.

So, we here in contemporary America want to assume the historical legacy of this repressed, second national language, Spanish. We do not wish to kneel in front of this god of the utopian genre. Genre is rather for us quite undistinguishable from the conventional rules of the social game, what legally gets called the "due process" of law, which is always already up for grabs according to the appointed magistrates of high interpretation. This work will expand on Eliav-Feldon's fifth chapter on law and order. If this is just one, if hegemonic, narrativity of the repressivity of social regularity, our work will analyze the literariness or the *modus operandi* as the most likely intelligible condition of political possibility and social meaning in the horizon of early colonial West Indies. Our exegesis, running against received modes and moods as regards the historical creature of "literature," will have here instead to square the circle with the always shifting rules of the legal game. Quiroga's repressive literature, our tight knot of historical reasonableness and unreasonableness, will of necessity challenge conventional knowledge on early modern utopias. Our emphases on the drastic practicalities of utopianism, or political reform in this colonial world, will have to bring about, quite unlike Eliav-Feldon, the production of legal treatises and confrontational argumentation in courtroom litigation (Eliav-Feldon notices that More, Agostini and Bacon were jurists and that Doni and Rabelais had all formally studied law). Law and literature in early modernity go historically hand in hand and so do, distressingly to be sure, the rule of law and the rule of force (or the profession of "armas y letras").

Quiroga will represent for us the stupendous occasion for the rigorous historical semanticization of the notion of the "intellectual." Quiroga is not one. Nor is he a writer, as we tend to understand the notion today. Quiroga never dreamed of becoming either. His is the rather different lettered (or *letrado*) practice of the high state official dealing with the early commotions of the American world. Quiroga's social practice, inside which "writing" is but one and not the most crucial portion, must be imagined instead quite close to the homework of an influential politician and also almost entirely the endless paperwork chagrin of a high-ranking bureaucrat. Colonial utopianism is not understandable separated from state bureaucracies. Quiroga's dry prose which following chapters will analyze in close detail, is thematically the city of equals, particularly the *Rules* and *Regulations*. Yet, the harrowing expressivity of this repressive literature will surely make us grit our teeth more than once. Quiroga's literature is no fun or light entertainment and yet the likely boredom of the contemporary reader is historically, rigorously a non-argument.

In relation to the abstraction of the betterment of the West Indies, or "las Indias mejores" in the expression of Las Casas, we better learn fast to make the imaginary site of colonial Latin American Studies the permanent site of the new and the unpredictable, always inside its marginalization among international cultures of comparative scholarship in either English or Spanish. Still another turn to the screw: if "theory," like the human creation of "utopia" is the "good," then "theories" must surely historically, socially come to us today, against Snodgrass, not exclusively from "American" or "Euro-American" locations. Our proposition will always be for the widening of the historical horizons.[38] Our imaginary site, colonial Latin America, must precisely emerge from the fractures of this American idiom which will insistingly try to dust off early modern Americas, officially the *Indias Occidentales*, under the carpet of "America" or the "Western" world. Colonial Latin America must thus logically be articulated, almost always at least in the United States, from the standpoint of unfittingness or unacquaintance. And we will have to do so always tactfully in between mechanisms of (de)differentiation and referentiality (the "heres" or "theres" of necessarily interdependent belief systems).

In this oppressive world, we feel we need some fresh air. Tinkering with Snodgrass, "theories," like "utopias" must instead, of necessity, be in the plural form everywhere. Utopias, even in the negative or dystopian form in a colonial world which is not behind us, must be always already there where you want to find them. And these collective dispositions are always carrying the utopian potential of change for the better, if only negatively. Betterment is for us no other ideal than the city of equals, and the historical lesson in human plasticity and unpredictability is precisely what we may wish to call utopianism. So, we will find this historical lesson in relation to the figure of Vasco de Quiroga, which is clearly not the end of history and never the last man, but still strongly inspirational moment in the negative form of the not-yet under tremendous circumstances. To historicize human plasticity and unpredictability—this is the promise of this work—we will have to go to the most unpredictable of places, the repressive culture. The global reframing will take us, following Abu-Lughod,[39] to the "trans-Atlantic, American or ninth" commercial circuit of social exchanges which will fit beautifully with Arrighi's first moment of Genoese cooperation with early Spanish colonization of the Americas. This no-place of Quiroga's repressive literature is our place.

Quiroga's colonial literature is, we must emphasize, primordially legal literature. Against the thick silences of the utopian tradition, we will be looking closely into the crises and transformations of this early modern social experimentation inside the official Spanish house. To do this, we know we have to frustate some of the conventional expectations regarding early modern utopianism as pertains mostly the para-legal writing proper to daydreaming activity and libidinal satiety. It is safe to say that Quiroga's literature has little or none of the stress-free, highly privatized eupsychia in the freetime of a short weekend. Instead, Quiroga will signify for us almost entirely the opposite: the holding of public office, the busy world of negotiation of repressive meanings, bureaucratic homework, laborious trans-Atlantic traveling in the pre-airplane era with a weary eye on the sustainability of subalternized populations already colonized by the teething troubles of the proto-capitalist world-system. This drama truly does not fit into conventional dictionary definitions of utopia. How could it? Quiroga's official articulations of the *locus* of the city of equals inside this dystopian world, have indeed little to do with Morean delicacy of diction—there will be no litotes[40]—and also little to do with the time-honored *locus classicus* of the "world upside down."[41] In the global village of early modernity, Quiroga's uneasy early modern legalese for the making of social truth has few of the Latinate understatements for the efforts to change social intelligibility since it is historical creation inside the loud drama of colonization, the law-making negotiations in the Court of Valladolid and the acrimonious litigation in New Spain. It is high time to pick up some Hispanic glasses to see into the early modern makings of an egalitarian society in this dystopian world.

3. The Spanish Divide:
The Americas Is the Country of Utopia

This section has been designed to ironize its relation with the preceding one: if English scholarship says there is no such thing as an early modern American utopia proper, Spanish scholarship will instead say that America is the country of utopias, or in the early modern neologism, the *fontano lugar* of all utopias. This is the commonplace in Spanish historiography which almost sounds like an ontological argument. We will give it scholarly body and finally break it open most concretely in relation to the genealogical tree of Vasco de Quiroga. In the meantime, we do not wish to iron out this mutual, if unbalanced unfittingness between English and Spanish. Quite the contrary, we wish to assume this tension fully. Historically, it is not to be doubted that the prestige of languages comes and goes.[42]

In the multilingual setting of early colonial Americas, the early notion of "colonial fracture" will mean for us the permanent fracture of the rule of law as pertains to the early modern trans-Atlantic state of rights (or *estado de derecho colonial indiano*). Most concretely, the brainchild of the Valladolid Debates, the one-day flower of theoretical egalitarianism in the New Laws (1542-3) will represent this "fracture" of the rule of force (or Quijano's "coloniality of power"). Quiroga's endeavors must be understood precisely in the early ruins of this nominal state of rights. This early colonial ruin must be imagined in the scaffolding of the following adjectives: nominal, unregulated, underregulated, unenforced, unenforceable legal configuration of rights. This double bind, or how to say "no" or "not-yet" to a seemingly non-operative body of rights under coloniality, must of course also highlight the historical position of unfittingness for entire American populations. Like the proverbial fox and the sour grapes, this undecidability must remain unresolved and almost beyond reach so, since neither the full endorsement of the law of a colonial state nor the complete disregard of its legal scaffolding structure appear to be a fully satisfactory position for the early modern Indianized majority of the American population. Quiroga's social experimentation, obviously internal to the early modern state machine, will have to be understood, also quite uneasily, in between these two untenable positions.

The scholarly task of *insistere vestigiis* takes us initially to J. L. Abellán's *Historia Crítica del Pensamiento Español* (1979-1986),[43] and also to the arguably most important historian of the early modern period, at least for us, J. A. Maravall, also with a genuine curiosity for Hispanism and utopianism. We suggest the *Oposición Política bajo los Austrias* (1972),[44] *Utopía y Contrautopía en el Quijote* (1976)[45] and *Utopía y Reformismo en la España de los Austrias* (1982).[46]

Now, the Americanist vocation within this classic Spanish historiography is a strong antidote, if only initially, against conventional English repudiations. Abellán, Chair of the *Historia del Pensamiento Hispanoamericano* (Complutense, Madrid), provides a narrative with the emotional center in continuous slippage between the language called Spanish or *español* and the official nation formation called *España*, under intense scholarly siege, in Abellán's words, at least during the last two centuries. The second volume of this aforementioned project deals with the sixteenth century, the apple of the eye of Hispanic historiography, traditionally called *La Edad de Oro*. Abellán typically semanticizes this century as one of innovation, optimism, liberation from the shackles of atavism, of the sudden explosion of technology and creativity, fresh-air openness, expansionism and growth, the golden age of imperial domination and historical concentration of power and privilege. Colonization is a notion Abellán will not use often. He will instead speak of the "discovery" of America, which will almost tangentially add a continental dimension to the *España/español* oscillation. Yet, Abellán does not give a narrative of imperial celebration. Within the mold of the "history of the ideas," continental America emerges as the hitherto evergreen imaginary site for "renaissance" and permanent "(self-)discovery."[47] If the English tradition semanticizes pre-USA America as the desolate place where utopia could not have possibly flourished, this visible representative of Spanish historiography, a peninsularist if you will, semanticizes pre- and also post-USA America as the perennial imaginary site which cannot possible be anything else but desirable utopia. The demonization of English scholarship, implicit in the charges of inexistence and meaninglessness, meets here with the idealization mechanism at least by some salient examples in the Spanish historiography.

Abellán exemplifies the prodigious longevity of the attribution of the utopian potential to a relatively distant heterogeneity called America. This is done via an axiological inversion: America *is* the other non-European side of human things where the grass is always greener.[48] Abellán will not hesitate to semanticize the early modern Americas as *the* quintessential utopia.[49] Bypassing the evergreen problem of the "unfittingness" of the Spanish Renaissance,[50] continental America will signify rebirth, the nominal and universal dignity of man,[51] and the humanistic "naturalness" of diction in the young romance language.[52] Against Weber and Hegel, (Latin) America is the imaginary place of social possibility, which is always clearly differentiated from the almost always dystopian Anglo-Saxon ogre.[53] The longevity of this non-USA "New World paradise" is certainly prodigious already since the sixteenth-century expansionism,[54] but also later among Baroque writers[55] and contemporary public intellectuals.[56]

In order to keep this myth alive, Abellán will look for shelter mostly in one-dimensional thematic readings. America, truly a big semantic elephant of collective signification, is thus manufactured reductively into a mysterious kind of depopulated ground for the dreams of the European imagination.

Abellán agrees with the English tradition about the inexistence of one convincing Spanish utopia proper (the eighteenth-century narrative *Sinapia* is the belated exception which confirms the norm). Yet, Abellán will still speak confidently about abundant utopian elements in this cherished century. Often without the economic dimension or political benefits, Abellán's thematic naturalization of semiotic practices will come dangerously close to the abyss of idealistic dehistoricization. Abellán's narrative is, or was, the conventional narrative that students at the University of Salamanca, the prestigious house of learning during Quiroga's times, got exposed to a few years ago.

Abellán introduces the following projects: Columbus's mythico-missional enterprise, León-Pinelo's cumbersome erudition of paradisal America, Quiroga's village hospitals, always painted with Zavala's colors, all of which will pale by comparison to the "utopian anthropology" of Las Casas. In almost all scholarship of the period, Quiroga will be always sitting pretty in the shadow of the towering Dominican. Abellán's understanding of American utopianism will place the dance of ecclesiastical robes at the center of the historical imagination. There are three classic examples: Las Casas's failed Vera Paz colonist settlements, early Franciscanism in New Spain and the Jesuits in Paraguay. Abellán's semantic content of early modern American utopias appears to be little more than peaceful Christianization of the Indians by monastic groups. Franciscan millenarianism is mentioned, however tangentially.[57]

Quiroga receives no small attention for a second fiddle. Under the heading of Erasmism, Quiroga is made into one salient representative of this prestigious intellectual tradition in the Americas (Bataillon is to blame for this commonplace). Abellán follows Zavala's generic account of Quiroga's *Ordenanzas* and *Información en Derecho*. These descriptive accounts will credit Quiroga with a progressive anti-slavery stance, which chapter three will have to challenge. There is no word about the most likely legal circumstance for these two textualizations, typologically very different. Quiroga's village-hospitals are said to fulfill historically the Christian imperative "love thy neighbor" (we will include soon Grijalva's descriptions), against the eloquent silence over colonization. So, Abellán's intimation is that Quiroga's utopianism means the early modern Christianization, under Erasmian influence, of American populations. Close to Snodgrass, Erasmism here means little more than a vague idea of peace-making tolerance.

The equation "civilization or barbarism," or backwardness, is here explicit. Ecclesiastical idealization of "primitive" populations is put against normalizing "civilization" (Christianity, Spanish and Latin and Early Modern proto-capitalism). Early modern utopianism appears for Abellán to generate an unmistakable axiological reversion: American plasticity exists in so far as its utopian potential travels through all these prefixes: pre-modern, proto-capitalist and also post-capitalist. Early modern utopianism is thus, also for Abellán, unintelligible without the historical circumstance of the expanding world-system of capitalist civilization. Better yet, early modern and colonial utopianism is not intelligible unless within and against the early commotions of this expanding world-system.

In other words, Abellán's encomium of primitivism, mostly in relation to Las Casas, is radically not evasion or nostalgia. It is rather the inspirational drive for human sustainability weathering these early modern civilizational commotions which will continue well until our own century. Las Casas's pro-Indian stance, prefiguring Rousseau's mythification of the Good Savage, is said to exemplify this mechanism of survival and idealization, seemingly against all odds. The early modern global world will also be waiting, like Kavafy, for the barbarians to come to this civilization and change it for the better. We take Abellán's utopianism, via Las Casas, also to mean the not-yet-fulfilled deflation of all hierarchical axiologies on both sides of the Atlantic, yet within the non-negotiable frame of Christianity. This primitivism, against the early modern timeliness of Spanish-vehicled proto-capitalism in the Americas, finally means the resolution of the early problems of unity or diversity of the *genus homo*. Under universalized Christianity, there is one all-encompassing, yet continually expanding humanity which must be ideally structured horizontally. This horizontal articulation (or the value of justice which is undistinguishable from sameness), of all human life forms is how we understand Abellán's vision of Las Casas's historical importance: the non-negotiable dogma of the unity of the *genus homo*. So, Las Casas's lesson "so modern, because it is so primitive," is unmistakably, also for us, a history for the future. The attractiveness in Las Casas's oppositional practices against the early verticalities of barbarism and civilization in the Americas, remains no doubt inspirational also for us. Quiroga's historical signification, by contrast, will have to be included among these ecclesiastical robes, yet institutionally much more locally and repressively articulated, pushing for the institutionalization of proto-egalitarianism in the state of Michoacán. Against the collective impact of monasticism, we chose to tread on the shimmering lightness of an always fragile individuality, Quiroga.

Yet, we must move from ideation to the institution of the ideation. We want to insufflate three-dimensional life and historical plausibility into the mechanisms of idealization, and we want to do so by highlighting the inter-generational processes of institutionalization and its shortcomings. For this reflection, we will turn to the intellectual production of J. A. Maravall, former professor at the *Universidad Complutense*, Madrid and member of the *Real Academia de la Historia*. Maravall's emphasis is correctly placed on the collectivities manufacturing utopia (we dare generalize early modernity as a proto-individual age). We do not wish to neglect the notion of historical failure, or intermittent paralogism, consubstantial to the socio-historical institution of "utopia" as corresponds to the Early or pre-revolutionary Modernity in the Americas.[58] Hence, we are willing to use "reformation" (originally, *reformismo*) in relation to Quiroga's legal practice.

The notion of "reformation" also means something else. It is intended, against Abellán, to repudiate the "hypocritical concession" of endorsing a big discontinuity between the Middle Ages and the Renaissance (O'Gorman's position will be identical to Maravall in this regard). "Reformation" thus signals the slow motion of thickly-textured social complexities embedded amid inter-generational continuities on both sides of the Atlantic. Final cuts are not so easy to come by, historically. Maravall, a crucial inspiration for us to try to articulate the necessary three-dimensionality to any "history of ideas," also reads early modernity as the quintessential moment of utopian crisis.[59] And by this rich notion, we must include its dense semantic field, which includes problem or malfunction, belief and crisis of belief or long-lasting hesitations, pluralization and relativization of worlds and proto-capitalist expansionism, inventiveness and intellectual challenge, dynamism and intercontinental space flows of commodities and peoples, money scarcity, interruptions, critical juncture, labor reconfigurations, social struggle or *desencuentros*, paralogism or confusion and verticalities of multi-lingual (mis)communication. Early modern *Indias Occidentales* is for us the permanent "Indian" site of utopian crisis, which will get incorporated, not by plebiscite, into the driving force of first-phase global process of capital accumulation in a world system which is still with us today. This permanent site of utopian or Indian crisis will constitute the existencial circumstance for our state official, Quiroga. His horizon, which should not be too entirely foreign to us, is the historico-political satisfaction of the problem of need for a so-called "Indian" majority of the early modern American population.

According to Maravall, modern signs of fatigue and frustration with the everyday world will suffer the electric shock of the *novum* which will energize the collective unconscious and all dream factories.[60] This *novum*, or America, will historically unleash a tremendous utopian potential (or *carga utópica*).[61] For Maravall, pre-USA America emerges historically as the proper utopian ground.[62] Against Hegel's myopia,[63] Quiroga's colonial utopianism will already prefigure most of these abundant vertical contradictions, but also most of the egalitarian potentialities embedded in this civilizational world-system, which as we will soon see is for Quiroga radically not the end of history.[64] This Hispanic utopianism in the sails of first-phase capitalism—manufactured inside officialdom—will be historically in place amid the early social ruins of the colonization of the Americas. This work will grow out of the nitty-gritty, never-pretty analysis of this human potential for transformation and change under these surely tremendous circumstances. We promise no easy, one-day epiphanies and little euphoria. Quiroga's utopianism, which is tangible for us as the official, dry bureaucratic paperwork amid larger piles of official, dry bureucratic paperwork, will prove arduous, intricate, tedious, at times truly exasperating. Yet, we must patiently learn to seek for some utopian warmth historically hidden precisely in the modern library husk of all these surely uninviting adjectives.

Against English conventions, Maravall finds this "utopian potential," an expression dear to him, meaningful in the sixteenth-century Hispanic world and literary tradition. In his secularizing emphasis, America is made coextensive with this utopian energizing of collective energies:

> [P]ero parece cierto que fue ante todo el factor del descubrimiento y colonización del continente americano, lo que abrió las puertas hacia los caminos de Utopía, entre ciertos grupos de la sociedad castellana. En el segundo cuarto del siglo XVI no hay, a mi entender, otros grupos en Europa que se vean más fuertemente arrastrados hacia tales empresas (tal vez por eso, más que escribirse en el papel—aunque no faltan ejemplos de literatura utópica estimables—se pretendió levantarlas en la realidad de Méjico al Paraguay)[65]

Maravall's socio-historical vision will prevent us from getting trapped, like naive country rabbits, in a narrow genre analysis of utopian literature (we must imagine an illiterate society on both sides of the Atlantic). America jumps out of the banal role of mere wall-paper decoration, inspiring muse and naturalized background to the value of a cause: early modern America manufactures utopia fittingly already in these "proto-industrial" times.[66] Early Modern utopianism in the colonial world is historically in the antipodes of entertainment or evasion,[67] and so is its literature. This utopian plasticity, i.e. the slippery anything of dynamism and change, must thus historically fit into this early, quintessentially "new" modernity,[68] inside the chronology of 1529-1605,[69] which is also the chronological knot of this work (Quiroga's Mexican years (1536-1565), and Arrighi's periodization fracture, 1550s, between the first and second phases of capital accumulation). For Maravall, a degradation of this impulse for change will follow hereafter (this is consistent with Ortega y Gasset's vision). With the migration of capital to the Netherlands, the progressive disengagement of the imperial state attributes from the protocols of universal catholicity and the progressive secularization of capitalist logic will cause a generalized crisis of belief (this is also Ortega y Gasset's enigmatic definition of modernity, the bankruptcy of all claims to legitimacy). It is against this debilitated state of the historical imagination, but mostly in the peninsular context, that Cervantes's primitivism, the outmoded chivalric model, will represent, for Maravall, a salutary corrective in the ironic form of dystopian disenchantment.

To bring historical speculation to the most concrete, perhaps most convincing ground of argumentation, we must address social role and function. The historical novelty of modernity will find the social machinery of the permanent armed forces, the incipient predations by monetarized proto-capitalist economy and the (un)makings of state bureaucracies. Early modern utopianism in the colonial world must be imagined, mostly among early generations, as the social practice of the University-trained, male non-primogenitors of the petty nobility overseas (the *hidalgos letrados indianos*). This is the social vehicle for the implementation of early modern utopianism in the colonial world. These social agents, expelled from *mayorazgo* bonds and legally dispossessed, will constitute the wedge through which the estate society will slowly crumble.[70] Quiroga was one of them.

So, should we remain faithful to Maravall, we must also semanticize utopia near these "primitive" impulses towards a greater collectivization of energies, resources and needs, already in the sails of capitalist individuation and free wage labor (chapter three will give us this landscape most concretely). Against the slow productivity of loan policies typically practiced by the *mayorazgo*, state bureaucracies will operate differently, surely adrift in the rather intermittent, intercontinental flows of hard currency. Fraud was never far away from this picture.[71] Quiroga, often underneath the parasols of Christian rhetoric, is to be imagined at this triple juncture: the medium of proto-capitalism, the inspiration of collective monasticism, and the repressive circumstances, with numerous irregularities and hesitations, of state bureaucracies overseas. Capitalist expansion created social fractures inside which we must situate the members of the petty nobility or the *hidalgos*.

The loss of power of religious institutions, or secularization, sees the rise of state structures, historically inside which we must situate a codified verticality of managers. The most proficient among these managers will be the technicians of the alphabetic letter, the *letrados*. In the sails of proto-capitalism, we must situate these early modern money-mediated conditions for egalitarianism. In the commotions of early capitalism, we must come to terms with the darker side of colonization of the Americas, or *Indias Occidentales* as the permanent site of crisis as literal as massive depopulation. In these social ruins produced by the Spanish colonization of the Americas, we must imagine the social protocols of the repressive culture. "Primitive" monasticism, quite intimate with "modern" state structures, will constitute a strong inspirational force for change and transformation. We must imagine Quiroga's colonial utopianism as the project for change and reconstruction of these early ruins in the Michoacán region of New Spain with American-Indian populations called Tarascan-Purepechas. The legal circumstance in early modern New Spain, with or without "primitive" dispositions, will constitute our ideal theater for critical reflection of the "idea" of utopia. Quiroga's measures will try to square the new economic circle repressively and channel subalternized collectivities through the individuation process of incipient wage labor. Holding tight the historical knot of paralogism and authoritarianism, we will look closely into this repressive mechanism which will try to generate some shreds and threads of egalitarian legitimacy inside these proto-capitalist opportunities.

We will end this section with the inclusion of some cautious skepticism regarding early modern utopianism and the Americas. We have in mind Chilean colonial historian Mario Góngora's evaluation of utopianism and the Americas:[72]

> Both types of notion, the eschatological and the Utopian, represented the application to America of traditional Christian hopes or of the products of an intellectualised and sentimental Western mentality. In both cases, they were ideal historical interpretations of great importance, because they incorporated the newly discovered lands into the spiritual history of Europe, even though, paradoxically, the precise manner of this incorporation resulted from the concept of them as countries which were new and different from Europe; in any case, these notions were not generated from within America, but were derived from Christian or modern European processes of thought. The designation of America as a "Mundus novus," which was to achieve such wide currency after the letter of Vespucio naturally ignored, by implication, the old pre-Columbian cultures; and, despite the efforts made

by the numerous chronicles of the colonial period to recapture the memory of the old empires, and sometimes to evaluate them from a humanist standpoint, the eschatological and Utopian term 'New World' proved more powerful, because it came closer to satisfying Renaissance and modern aspirations. America became a sort of compensation design which, it was hoped, was an anticipation of the course to be followed by Europe. In British America, which lacked the counterweight of the old Indian empires, the notion of the 'New World' a even greater force, and it was to develop its great power of attraction after 1776.

With an emphasis on the attraction of the *novum*, egalitarian endeavors appear here to recede to being European endeavors. In Góngora's view, America is no more than the ground for the foreign utopian ideation process which will come to be produced precisely in the emphasis on continental differences. The American difference already appears to be always in subordinated relation to the European value or cause. Utopia is the brainchild of the Western or European first-generation male imagination, mostly among newly-arrived soldiers, travelers and ecclesiastical robes, similar to Klaus Kinski's opera dreams in the Brazilian jungle in Herzog's *Fitzcarraldo* (1982). We find Góngora's reading of endtime figurations unsatisfactory. A convincing analysis must surely not stop docilely at the "being" of things and people. This is not "about" the metaphysical being, but about the seemingly endless socio-historical doing and undoing with things and people. We feel that Góngora, admired maestro, essentializes here somewhat positionality. In the inter-generational continuity which is history, all second generations born in America are already American, whatever this adjective may mean in relation to the slipperiness of utopianism in the Americas. Our history is *not* about "being" or "not being" American, but about doing and the failures of doing American utopias.

There is no question that official visions of the social endgame (or eschatologies) are strongly inflected by time-honored millenarianism, mostly, but not exclusively among monastic groups, which are also inside Christian hermeneutics. There is also no question that we are always dealing with historical processes in motion, proto-capitalism, christianization and hispanicization which will cannot be historically understood without accounting for the incorporation of the periphery of the Americas to the expansionism of the "new" world-system. Early modernity must be imagined as the unprecedented, trans-Atlantic space flows of things and peoples inside which destructurations and verticalities, but also proto-egalitarian or horizontal restructurations are simultaneously taking place. The social reading of colonial utopianism comes to the rescue to try to differentiate convincingly the rich tapestry of repressive experimentation which does not make sense without the historical ground of the American *Indias Occidentales*. In the modern house of American officialdom, the political utopia of our *hidalgo letrado indiano* is not the ritualized recreation of indigenous memories of a different world.[73] Our approach to Quiroga's first-generation political reformation, no doubt a historical vehicle formed by proto-capitalism, Christianity and bureaucratic habits, will shy away from Bloch-inspired psychologized retreats into some kind of poetic plenitude.[74] Not to get caught in the antlers of essentialism, we will be particularly careful to illustrate the seeds of egalitarianism within social structures in motion, which historically have nothing to do with fictionalizations of evasion (in fact this leisurely possibility of a narrative is in the historical antipodes of Quiroga).[75] To historicize Quiroga's utopia of colonial reconstruction, we will have to deal with the insufficiencies of discourse analysis in the exegesis of the institutional or collective paralogism of repressive structures. We may advance that, following Lalinde-Abadía, Quiroga's repressive culture will grow precisely out of these colonial paralogisms or fractures which will also challenge our endeavors. Finally, Quiroga's repressive compensation of an utopian design will not be declared indigenous in the sense that the legal profession would not have been a real historical possibility for the immense majority of the American population ten years after the seize of Tenochtitlán by Hernán Cortés (1521). Indigenous or majoritarian access to the lettered city in early New Spain is an unthinkable during Quiroga's lifetime, and we hope that following chapters will recreate even more persuasively, if negatively, this historical impossibility or dream of a majority of the population *not* having access to the production and distribution of social goods for the prompt satisfaction of their needs. Quiroga's early modern colonial utopianism must be understood within the unthinkable horizon of this Indian utopia. We dare call Quiroga's repressive protocols an *indigenista* practice. After this perhaps lengthy preparation, it is now high time that we step inside Quiroga's colonial neighborhood.[76]

4. Treading on the Shimmering Light of a Single Name: Vasco de Quiroga

Following upon Warren, the basic presentation of Vasco de Quiroga, our *hidalgo letrado indiano*, inside international cultures of scholarship will have to say that he was born in 1470 in Madrigal de las Altas Torres (Avila,

Spain), which is Queen Isabella's birthplace, and also the site of the Cortes of Castile in 1475-1476. Our protagonist was a member of the Quiroga family, which also includes his nephew, Gaspar de Quiroga in the visible position of Cardinal-Archbishop of Toledo. Vasco de Quiroga studied jurisprudence, Medieval Canon Law, in Valladolid, the Washington of the sixteenth century, and it is not too unrealistic to conjecture that he might have been if only somewhat acquainted with the other center of knowledge production of the period, the University of Salamanca. There is a lack of information regarding Vasco de Quiroga's early years. Warren did not however hesitate to state that he gained reputation early in his political career in Granada and the north African city of Oran, Algeria in 1525. If the name of Quiroga finds a niche in most encyclopedias, it is mostly for his Mexican years which extend, always according to Warren, from his arrival in New Spain in December 16, 1530, until in death in Uruapán, México in 1565. Acuña has dated a trip to the Iberian peninsula during 1547-1554, Bernal Díaz del Castillo, Hernán Cortés's faithful soldier, will put Quiroga at the negotiating tables in the Valladolid Debates (1550-1551).

We have said that Quiroga's plans for the reformation of early coloniality are the ones available or fitting to a *hidalgo letrado indiano*. That is, Quiroga's colonial literature is part and parcel of the social practice inside the lettered city historically available to a male, non-first son of noble status (or *segundón*), disenfranchised by the *mayorazgo* institution, yet with formal or university training, and by virtue of this technical knowledge of legal letters, capable of holding office overseas (or *indiano*). Quiroga will become one of the four judges or *oidores* of the Supreme Court of the Americas, the *Segunda Audiencia* (1530-1535), and the first Bishop, from 1536 until his death, of the northwestern diocese of Michoacán, of a size larger than actual France and with a population, according to Enrique Dussel, of 1.3 million people. Most estimates give the round figure of 30,000 people for these alternative communities, the so-called "village-hospitals" (or *pueblos-hospitales*), sponsored largely by Quiroga's *oidor* wages. Most literature names three communities, Santa Fé de los Altos de México, Santa Fé de la Laguna de Pátzcuaro and San Nicolás de Pátzcuaro.

Complete primary sources by Vasco de Quiroga include: the *Carta al Consejo de Indias* (1531), the *Reglas y Ordenanzas para el Buen Gobierno de los Pueblos Hospitales* (1532), the most elaborate *Información en Derecho* (1531), the disputed *De Debellandis Indis* 1552), and his Last Will or *Testamento* (1565). There are several possibilities for the archival enquiry of some other items associated with Quiroga: one, the *Britannica*

Encyclopedia recently responded to us about the impossibility of verifying the attribution of a "volume of sermons" to the "Franciscan" Quiroga; two, Marcel Bataillon encouraged the search for a possible epistolary exchange between Vasco de Quiroga and his intimate friend Juan Bernal Díaz de Luco, Bishop of Calahorra and one of the pillars of the *Consejo de Indias*;[77] three, Nicolás León has mentioned a text called *Doctrina Cristiana* by Gutiérrez-González, which printed in Seville in 1553 and the expenses were paid by Quiroga;[78] four, the *Diccionario de la Historia de España* finally mentions the printing, also paid by Quiroga, of a *Manual de Adultos* (1504). We have been so far unsuccessful in establishing the true nature of these records.

According to Tena Ramírez, the legal extinction of these alternative communities occurred in 1872, 340 years after their foundation.[79] How could we today imagine them? We need to turn to Juan de Grijalva's account.

5. Idyllic Enclosures of Indian Christianity: Juan de Grijalva

The Augustinian Friar Juan de Grijalva (1580-1638), constitutes for us the earliest, best account of Quiroga's village-hospitals. We believe this is the closest we can get today to the eyewitness account of Quiroga's Indian communitarianism tightly bound by intolerant Christian belief:

> Había [a] dos leguas [de] Mexico un pueblo que se llama[ba] Santa Fé, fundado de [*sic*] los Indios que, ya convertidos, querían vivir [una] vida más perfecta al modo apostólico, y como en vida religiosa. Al cual [pueblo] venían los Indios de diversas partes con todas sus familias, y eran ya tantos, que pasaban de doce mil vecinos. Fue autor de este santo instituto el Licenciado Vasco de Quiroga, Oidor de la Real Audiencia de México y persona de gran celo y cristiandad, [el cual] después fue dignísimo Obispo de Michoacán. Este gran varón compró todas aquellas tierras de la redonda de Santa Fé, que son muchas y buenas, y daba estas tierras a los que allí se recogían para que allí sembrasen y [se a]cogiesen. Lo que parecía ser suficiente para el sustento de sus familias. Y que lo restante del tiempo lo gastasen en ejercicios de perfección. De manera que aquellos Indios imitaban en algo a los religiosos viviendo de tierras comunes, y ocupándose en oración y vida perfecta. (pp. 54-5)[80]

Perfection is, unambiguously for Grijalva, a sedulous exercise in word and deed of the Christian belief, which is also unquestionable dogma, also for the so-called Indians. Quiroga's *oidor* wages made the sustainability of this Indian Christianity a real possibility. After the brief mention of the second hospital foundation in the region of Michoacán, it is howerver the Santa Fé settlement which grabs Grijalva's attention. This is said to be the truest motherly nursing house for children, and the house of learning and music. Sixty-eight years after Quiroga's death, Grijalva maps out this utopian topography eloquently thus:

> Edificó un hospital de la cuna [*sic*] en este mismo pueblo de Santa Fé, donde los Indios que quisiesen, así de la ciudad de México como de otra cualquiera parte, pudiesen llevar sus hijos, para que allí se los criasen. Movióse a esta obra [el hecho de] que se hallaban multitud de niños ahogados en las acequias, y muertos por las calles. Discurríase veramente sobre este caso porque no se hallaba cierta la causa. Algunos dijerom que hacían aquello los Indios, desesperados de la bajeza y servidumbre en que se veían después de [ser] conquistados. Y así daban la muerte a sus hijos, viendo que nacían para tan triste vida. Pero sin duda no era esta la causa como después pareció. Lo que les movió era que por no tomar trabajo las madres de criar sus hijos les daban la muerte, tanta era la fiereza y barbaridad de esta gente. Averiguó esta costumbre este gran varón [Quiroga] y para remediar este grande mal, edificó este hospital y dio aviso en toda la tierra, que la madre que no quisiera criar a sus hijos, los llevase a aquel hospital donde se criaban con todo cuidado y regalo, dándoles leche, de comer y de vestir todo el tiempo que era necesario. Junto a este hospital hizo un Colegio donde los muchachos y adultos deprendían [*sic*] a leer y escribir, canto llano y canto de órgano, y todo género de instrumentos músicos [*sic*], para que en aquella iglesia y en otras muchas fuera nuestro Señor servido y alabado. De modo que era como seminario de Indios que habían de servir a las iglesias. Pegado a éste hizo un hospital donde se curasen todos los enfermos con tan buena división y orden como se podía desear. Hasta hoy dura este grande edificio con pinturas antiguas que entretienen y mueven harto a los que las miran. (p. 58)

Total numbers for the Santa Fé commonwealth speak of 12,000 neighbors (or "vecinos"), or 30,000 peoples (or "personas"). After Fintan B. Warren, who also follows upon his fellow Franciscan Pablo Beaumont,[81] this is today the standard estimate, no doubt with fluctuations. This commonwealth includes the role-model assistance of the Augustinian Friar Alonso de Borja, who died before our *oidor* in 1542 (p. 202). Grijalva depicts thus a strict, clockwork quasi-monastic regimentation of social energies:

lo que restaba del tiempo gastaban en oración y contemplación, [y] guardaba [Alonso de Borja] todas las ceremonias de la Religión estando el solo con tanta puntualidad como si estuviera allí un convento de muchos Religiosos. No perdía disciplina ni ayuno, ni cosa virtuosa, ni ceremonia, todo a fin de que los Indios se estampasen en aquella vida. Hacíanlo así los Indios de muy buena gana, y con grandísima perfección, porque además de que aquel fervor nuevo, y aquel espíritu los movía. La gente de suyo es ceremoniática [*sic*], y puntualísima en la ejecución de los órdenes que se les dan acerca del culto exterior. En amaneciendo se juntaba todo el pueblo y rezaba la doctrina cristiana, decíales misa, y predicábales todos los días. En acabando, que no era temprano, se iban a sus casas a comer un bocado, y luego los que tenían que hacer en su labor, se iban a ella. Los demás, se volvían a la iglesia, unos a deprender [*sic*] la doctrina, otros a enseñarla, de modo que todos estuviesen ocupados en obras virtuosas. A la oración se juntaban todos por barrios en todas las esquinas, donde había cruces altas, y siempre adornadas de juncia [*sic*] y flores, donde cantaban la doctrina, y luego pedían a nuestro Señor les tuviese de su mano para que aquella noche no le ofendiesen. Y de aquí tuvo principio la ceremonia que después se estableció en toda la provincia de cantar la doctrina por barrios de noche en las esquinas y por la mañana en la iglesia.... Todos los viernes ayunaba todo el pueblo y había disciplina seca [*sic*] en la iglesia a prima noche después de haber dicho todas las oraciones. Esta de la disciplina se hace sólo en la Cuaresma en toda la provincia, con esto parecía aquel pueblo convento de religiosos más que república de seculares. (pp. 55-56)

Grijalva's writing attests to this exquisite timeliness and observation of religious ceremony among new Christian populations in the Americas. Quiroga's secular commonwealth is almost undistinguishable from the harshest rule of monasticism, a collective ideal which is no doubt, for Grijalva and others, the sole discourse of social legitimacy in early modernity. Most if not all other accounts, scholarly or not, will follow Grijalva's original celebration of this secular monasticism (a kind of sixteenth-century precedent to Ernesto Cardenal's secular communities in the Solentiname archipelago by the lake of Nicaragua). A quiet, utopian landscape of dutiful obedience is thus semanticized by Grijalva. The political meaning of this Christian exceptionality must necessarily take into account the surely belabored privilege or immunity from forced labor and tribute:

El privilegio que su Majestad dio entonces a los hospitaleros, no sé si se extendió a todos, pero sé que se practica en todos, siendo refrenados de tributo y servicio personal todos los que en ellos sirven. Y entran cada semana fuera de estos, seis Indios y seis Indias, que voluntariamente se ofrecen, y en los pueblos mahyores doce Indios, y otras tantas Indias. Y en tiempo de necesidad más. Y esto con tanta devoción, que no es menester apremiarlos como lo experimentamos en todo los demás repartimientos. Y así son los más bien servidos, y de mayor regalo a su modo que hay en la cristiandad. Y la caridad que se debe alabar e imitar es, la que tienen con los enfermos peregrinos, quienes además de la cura, y regalo que les hacen en lo agudo de la enfermedad, luego pueden, lo llevan de hospital en hospital o ya en hombros o ya acompañándole hasta su tierra, pareciéndoles que la mayor piedad para con ellos es volverlos a su patria. (p. 219)

Yet, what is really happening inside these idyllic village-hospitals? Besides Quiroga's succinct normative depictions, which we will analyze closely in the second chapter, Grijalva's constitutes the best description:

Para estas buenas obras les ordenan los ministros que trabajen de [*sic*] comunidad. Y todo el pueblo hace sementeras de trigo y de maíz, y las cogen con gran fidelidad [*sic*]. Crían ovejas, y todo aquello que puede ser de interés para la sustentación de los pobres. Y está tan introducido esto, que los oficiales mecánicos que hay en el pueblo, como son herreros, carpinteros y los demás, todos trabajan para el hospital tales días, y los mercaderejos [*sic*] en sus tratos. Y en fin en todo aquello que hay granjería tiene parte el hospital. (p. 219)

We see the non-conflictive collaboration of efficient agrarianism and the mechanical arts, and the collectivization of social energies. Quiroga's utopianism is a commonwealth of and for Christian workers. It is possible to imagine an incipient money economy penetrating the unconscious interstices of this historically intolerant ritualization of rites of passage according to Christian belief:

[Y] así es el ordinario recibo pasados de mil pesos, y en algunos llegan a tres, y a cuatro mil pesos, que son pocos teniendo el servicio de balde con otras muchas ayudas de costa. Todo entra en poder del [Prior] y mayordomo, de que dan muy buen cuenta. Además del gasto que se tiene con los enfermos, gastan mucho en una Capilla, que siempre tienen allí de la Concepción de nuestra Señora, tan adornada de plata y ornamentos, como la Iglesia principal. Allí recibe[n] los enfermos el viático santo, y la extrema unción, que no es pequeña comodidad. Porque así se administra con gran decencia, y los enfermos no reciben vejación. Allí depositan el cuerpo difunto, hasta que le llevan a la sepultura. Y allí hace[n] sus estaciones los que conivalecen dándole gracias a Dios y ofreciéndole la vida, que de nuevo reciben, y pidiéndole salud, para con ella servirle. Entre las cosas devotas, y más bien fundadas que hay en estos hospitales, es la misa y [la] procesión de los Sábados en memoria [*sic*], y a devoción de la limpia concepción de nuestra Señora. Adornan una imagen que en todos tienen de bulto en sus andas, y aderézanlas con todas las flores que la tierra y el tiempo ofrecen. Y desde la Iglesia la llevan al hospital en hombros de cuatro Indios, que también llevan guirnaldas y cadenas de flores y con cruces y ciriales, y el preste revestido. Y todos los Indios del pueblo con velas encendidas en las manos, y con repiques de campanas y tantas trompetas y ministriles, que no es más alegre ninguna de las Pascuas. Y de esta manera llegan al hospital donde se canta la misa de la limpia Concepción con gran devoción y alegría de todos. (pp. 219-220)

A money economy is already clearly perceptible in this management of costs and expenditures typically with the liberal, yet centralized hand of hospital authority. Quiroga's communities are to provide healing and also the necessary Christian ceremony for the failure of healing in the rite of passage of death. This is Grijalva's description of Quiroga, surely one likely beginning for his saintliness:

Estaba contentísimo el Licenciado Vasco de Quiroga viendo puesto en ejecución su deseo y tan lucida su obra. Exhortaba a los naturales a que prosiguiesen con la vida comenzada, que amasen y respetasen mucho a sus ministros, y que le[s] obedeciesen en todo como si fuera un ángel del cielo. Todo el tiempo que podía, huía de los negocio de la Audiencia y se iba a Santa Fé, dándose a la oración, y a otros ejercicios virtuosos. Edificó allí una casa en un nacimiento de agua, la que va a la ciudad, que por el sitio y disposición de ellas [*sic*], y por la memoria de tan espirituales varones, como allí han estado, levantan el espíritu y cabían [*sic*] particular consuelo a todos los que entran en ellas. Tiene el cielo allí una serenidad tan grande, las sombras tan frescas, los aires tan puros, las aguas tan claras, el silencio tan admirable, que todo está causando barruntos del cielo. Y todo convida a la contemplación. Aquí pasaba muchos días este gran varón a quien por muchas cosas comparo yo al grande Ambrosio, que de los negocios y judicatura secular le llamó Dios para Obispo de su iglesia, porque era así, que siendo secular cuidaba más de los negocios eclesiásticos, que de los propios de su oficio y de su casa. (p. 56)

This is the *fontano lugar* which will get repeated innumerable times inside and outside popular versions of Quiroga.[82] The allegorical language which speaks of the depopulation or naturalization of the ideal polity, i.e. the *locus amoenus* of impressive serenity, refreshing shadows, clean waters and admirable silence, is also here: Quiroga's happiness is meant to be collective happiness after doing the right thing. Writing in what he calls the "fourth age," the Augustinian Prior Grijalva does not bargain praises and admiration for Quiroga's legacy originally in the "first age" of "subjugation of the province to Castille (p. 10)." Quiroga is thus the inspirational paragon of modesty and virtue for centuries to come,

> Lo que ayudó mucho a estas fundaciones, y el principal motor y patrón de tan santa obra fue aquel santo prelado y singular varón Don Vasco de Quiroga, primer Obispo de Michoacán, cuya memoria es respetada por todos, y cuya vida debieran imitar todos. Ya dijimos de la manera que fundó el colegio y hospital de Santa Fé, siendo Odior de México. Consagróse después Obispo de Michoacán año de 1537, y fuélo veintiocho años, sin querer admitir otros obispados que le ofrecieron. Cuando volvió de España para dar asiento a las cosas de su iglesia, hízolo con tan gran santidad y perfección, que en cosa ninguna le halló inferior a aquellos santos Padres antiguos, que gobernaban la iglesia en sus principios. Entre otras cosas pues, que santamente instituyó, fue la fundación de estos hospitales en todo su obispado, así por la noticia que se llevaba [*sic*] de Santa Fé, donde experimentó lo mucho que nuestro Señor se servía en ellos, y de la gran necesidad que dellos tenían estos pobres, como por lo que allá conoció de su pusilanimidad y cortedad, y de lo poco que curaban de su vida, y regalo. Y que habiendo de acudir a ello los ministros (como acudían) era el único remedio el de los hospitales. De su renta fundó el famoso hospital de la Concepción llamada Santa María y San Marta de Pátzcuaro, para el cual alcanzó grandes jubileos e indulgencias, y una cédula de Su Majestad reservando a los Indios e Indias que en el sirven, de tributo y servicio personal, a título de hospitaleros. (p. 218)

Quiroga becomes the almost ahistorical vector for the delivery of the gift of life and the satisfaction of need among the neediest. Grijalva's Christian commonplace—justice is sameness under Christianity—speaks of no distinguishable content for this ethnicity, the Tarasca-Purépechas, which could be, at least theoretically, anybody, like you and me. Unlike the patience of good ethnographies, Grijalva's conception of justice is akin to classic utopianism; there will be no tolerance for differentiating features of any kind. In what is also a commonplace to both early modern utopianists, More and Quiroga, Grijalva's early hagiography speaks of a rather peopleless landscape which of necessity will have to exercise restraint and shy away from social intercourse. There is historically, so it appears, no alternative: it is either Quiroga's rigorous utopian monasticism or the surrounding dystopian landscape of early colonial ruins and death:

Yo oí decir a uno de los mayores ministros de nuestros tiempos que averiguó que los Indios Tarascos, desde el día que los oleaban [*sic*], se daban por despedidos de la vida, y desde aquel punto no hacían ya remedios para la vida, ni comían un solo bocado, persuadidos a que contravenían a la ordenación divina, el día que procuraban la vida después que con la extrema unción estaban preparados para la muerte. Y este santo Religioso [Alonso de Borja] pasaba todo el día en los hospitales, y por su propia mano les daba de comer, conociendo la necesidad grande que había de su asistencia y persuadóme a que debió de haber algún fundamento de éstos [*sic*].... En fin, aquellos hospitales se fundaron en tan buen hora, que han crecido, duran hasta el día de hoy, con tan gran asistencia de los religiosos que desde que cae el indio enfermo, hasta que muere, o se levanta sano, siempre le asisten religiosos para consolarle, curarle y regalarle. (p. 218)

Quiroga's colonial utopianism is, at least according to Grijalva, the institutionalization of the Christian understanding of death as the rite of passage towards something else. This is the standard account of hospital activity until to this day. The following chapters of this book will work out the contrast between these supposedly idyllic social landscapes and the always tense negotiations which inform the repressive culture. The theme of the Christian city of equals will have to come to terms with the rather arid landscape, no color and no respite, of the legal discourse as practiced by the *hidalgo letrado indiano* Quiroga. Colonial utopianism, at least according to Grijalva's idyllic Christian communitarianism, will not historically do without the repressive unpleasantness of Quiroga's legal literature.

6. Genealogies-I: Cultures of Scholarship on Quiroga

We are now concerned with the relatively discreet profile of Quiroga inside the Hispanic historiographic tradition. Quiroga rarely gets much coverage in scholarly circles. Yet, when he does, he has consistently good press, which is no doubt a bit intriguing regarding a political figure in a visible high-ranking position during the early traumatic moments of colonization. Political figures and their legacies, with or without hagiographies, are rarely loved by everybody. Quiroga appears to be the exception. Let us see why and how this is so.

The entries for *Quiroga* and *Michoacán* in the *Encyclopedia Britannica* speak of his "success" and the veneration among Mexican natives for his legacy.[83] The *Enciclopedia de México* mentions examples of institutional recognition as well as indigenous devotion to "Tata Vasco" mostly in the Michoacán region. Regional crafts are said to originate from his teachings.[84] Enrique Krauze's *Mexico: Biography of Power* repeats the enduring theme "of outstanding example of missionary love for the Indians...free of intolerance, strongly constructive but still protectively paternal."[85] Eduardo Galeano, a leading poetic voice from Uruguay, mentions Quiroga as one historical example of the other kind of *hispanidad* of mutual discovery among equals ("de igual a igual"), for the history of the future.[86] Following Zavala, *Memoria del Fuego*, Galeano's truly prodigious choral work of poetic historicization, semanticizes the name of Quiroga thus:

> Cristianismo primitivo, comunismo primitivo: el obispo de Michoacán redacta las ordenanzas para sus comunidades evangélicas. El las ha fundado inspirándose en la *Utopía* de Tomás Moro, en los profetas bíblicos y en las antiguas tradiciones de los indios de América. Los pueblos creados por Vasco de Quiroga, donde nadie es dueño de nadie ni de nada y no se conoce el hambre ni el dinero, no se multiplicarán, como él quisiera por todo México. El Consejo de Indias jamás se tomará en serio los proyectos del insensato obispo ni echará siquiera una ojeada a los libros que él, porfiadamente, recomienda. Pero ya la utopía ha regresado a América, que era su realidad de origen. La quimera de Tomás Moro ha encarnado en el pequeño mundo solidario de Michoacán; y los indios de aquí sentirán suya, en los tiempos por venir, la memoria de Vasco de Quiroga, el alucinado, que clavó los ojos en el delirio para ver más allá del tiempo de la infamia.[87]

González-Dávila throws incense at the Quiroga niche in his "theater" of the primitive Church in the *Indias Occidentales*.[88] Pope John Paul II is said to have hailed Quiroga for this "heroic missionary and civilizing work," in a 1990 visit to Mexico. The Latin American Episcopal Conference (CELAM) called him "intrepid fighter for justice and evangelizers of peace."[89] The contentious philosophy and theology of liberation present no disagreements. The name of Quiroga, all the way from eighteenth-century scholarship (Moreno, León and Aguayo Spencer), Zavala's touchstone scholarship, O'Gorman and Fernández's early idiosyncratic essays, to Kripper-Martínez's latest evaluation has endured an amazing continuity in good standing, if mostly in a modest, second-fiddle location. With little or no acquaintance with Quiroga's uncomfortable literature, Quiroga's good trappings will oftentimes become quite undistinguishable from Christian saintliness.

We wish here to propose a more secular reading. Our main interest is the social translation of the most salient utopian meanings historically associated with Quiroga. If Quiroga, it is clear, does not have the individual intellectual stature of Bartolomé de Las Casas, Francisco de Vitoria, or Ginés de Sepúlveda, his historical profile has nonetheless generated quite a consistent amount of traceable literature of varied quality. This is no small feat.

Quiroga's texts are of no easy access to the general public. The most accessible, most comprehensive material is perhaps the recent anthology arranged by Serrano-Gassent (1992),[90] which, despite being most of our basic textual ground, does not rise to the convincing level of a scholarly edition. This anthology does not wish to challenge conventional reading of Quiroga as the "protector of Indians." There is no critical engagement with previous material and it adds no new material.

Little, if anything, is known about Quiroga outside the Hispanic tradition. There are no translations of Quiroga's work into the contemporary lingua franca of English. The fingers on one's hands will suffice to keep count of the reliable sources not in Spanish. In Spanish, most of the work, of a rather regional and apologetic kind, has been mostly done by Mexican historians. The mention of Quiroga is thus exceedingly rare among colonial scholars outside the Mexican context. Except for Zavala's early efforts, we are not aware of any serious attempts to link Quiroga to a larger utopian tradition. Nor are we aware of any serious attempts to link colonial Latin America to the utopian tradition, despite the abundant literature on monasticism, Franciscans in New Spain and Jesuits mostly in colonial Paraguay. The same is true the other way round: we are not aware of any serious attempts to link critically the Utopian tradition and the Hispanic tradition inside colonial studies. The repressive culture is never mentioned among these efforts. This is the imaginary site of originality and differentiation this work on Quiroga wishes to occupy.

What we are here proposing is a double task: to hispanicize utopianism and to force hispanism to look intently into the historical ugliness of colonization, also the negative definition of utopianism if you will. This work is not the celebration of imperial endeavors, quite the contrary. Yet, we do not wish to beat the Spanish donkey while the English donkey roams unimpeded mostly in the grey fields of the historical imagination. By feeding the former donkey with the hard-swallowing grass of colonial Latin American fields of pasture, this work makes the claim to historicize Quiroga's utopianism precisely by bringing it inside the repressive culture. Particularly after the critical production of *De Debellandis Indis* by René Acuña (1988),[91] we believe it is high time for a comprehensive and revisionist (i.e. profoundly historicist) critique, without apologies, of Vasco de Quiroga's repressive utopianism in the colonial circumstance.

It is however in the historiographic tradition of the critique of the ideation of the "New World," i.e. Edmundo O'Gorman, where we wish to situate our general exegesis of colonial utopianism. We initially share some of O'Gorman's reticence as regards the "incident of Humanism," "the certain air of playground of the period," and some of his critique regarding the "schematic and puerile" *Utopia* of Thomas More (1478-1535).[92] Yet we find O'Gorman and Fernández's early disparaging comments on Zavala's early discovery, idiosyncratic and unhelpful as though mostly designed to piss him off.[93]

Periodization is tricky business. Yet we wish to propose three main periods for scholarship on Quiroga: prehistory, classic and contemporary. Our reading of the Quiroga scholarship will fill up some holes in Warren's biographical research.[94] The pre-history must surely include the textual reconstructions of primary sources by Juan José Moreno (1766), Aguayo Spencer (1970) and Nicolás León (1940). This is largely a descriptive work that will most often shy away from any critical engagement with the primary material. Mostly apologetic literature, it will stylize Quiroga into Christian saintliness while the bats with baby faces of colonization will fly out the window of the historical imagination. Moreno's sources are, according to Warren, now lost. Warren also critiques Aguayo Spencer's romanticized account, *Don Vasco de Quiroga: Taumaturgo de la Organización Social seguido de un apéndice documantal* by Rafael Aguayo Spencer (Mexico: Oaris, 1920). Leon's work on the *Proceso de Residencia* (1536), will turn out to be fragmentary and unstable as chapter four will detail. We must make explicit that textual reconstruction is exceedingly difficult in relation to Quiroga's primary sources which have come to us mutilated, decontextualized and romanticized by ecclesiastical or national incense.[95] Our work will have to explain the whys and wherefores of these textual deficiencies, also how these may be dealt with, but not solved, and finally how some of these complexities may rise to the level of historical significance. Early modern colonial textualizations are almost always profoundly unstable grounds we cannot do without.

The City Council of Michoacán has been publishing since 1940 selections of these two aforementioned scholars, Moreno and León. This old material includes several versions of the *Ordenanzas*, besides good general introductions to the history of the region[96]. We believe our analysis of the technicality of "protestation," will enrich Zavala's commonplace on Quiroga, still very much alive today. The work of the Franciscan Pablo Beaumont, the already mentioned *Crónica de Michoacán* (dating from the second half of the eighteenth century), also sheds some early light on Quiroga. Pre-history closes down, besides the Grijalva source, with the anonymous account by *Relación de Michoacán* (1541),[97] of the prehispanic past and the present disasters of the *First Audiencia* before Quiroga's arrival in New Spain.

The classic period puts Quiroga on the scholarly table. It must begin with the well-known Mexican scholar of the colonial period, Silvio Zavala.[98] We call it classic in the sense that it sets the main tone or the commonplace for Quiroga, in scholarly but also popular versions, until today.[99] With truly impressive scholarship, Zavala was the first one, we believe, to bring into sharper focus the second fiddle of Quiroga. He was the first one to make, already in the 1930s, the formalist or thematic comparisons between Thomas More's *Utopia* (1515) and Vasco de Quiroga's *Rules and Regulations* (1532). Zavala's studies, reprinted numerous times, will include no substantial changes. And yet these constitute with no doubts the most faithful to the Quiroga legacy, closely following recent developments and producing a series of critical responses to these developments (for example, his disagreements with Acuña we will see in chapter four). The extensive four-volume biography on the first Bishop of Mexico City, Fray Juan de Zumárraga by García Izcalbaceta (1947), may be very well included in any in-depth contextualization of the period, since it also includes information about some archival primary references to Quiroga. The main biography of our historical protagonist is with little doubt Fintan Warren's *Vasco de Quiroga and his Pueblo-Hospitales of Santa Fé* (Washington, 1963), which was not improved by Rubén Landa (Barcelona, 1965). Almost all accounts on Quiroga's life draw from Warren's information and we are no exception. Mariano Cuevas has also contributed with some primary material.[100]

Computer databases released at least six monographic studies on Quiroga from the 1960s until the 1990s. These could well function as the transition period from the classic to the contemporary period. These six references are: *The Ecclesiology of Vasco de Quiroga* by Gregory A. Banazak,[101] *Collision of Utopias* by Bernardino Verástique,[102] *La Acción Pastoral de Don Vasco de Quiroga* by Manuel Jesús García-Ceballos,[103] *Don Vasco de Quiroga: Oidor of New Spain* by Paul S. Lietz,[104] *The Politics of an Erasmian Lawyer, Vasco de Quiroga* by Ross Dealy,[105] and finally *Don Vasco de Quiroga (Protector de los Indios)* by Francisco Martín-Hernández.[106]

Dealy's early, brief account, with a rather limited access to Quiroga's sources, wishes to make Quiroga the disciplined disciple of Erasmus of Rotterdam in New Spain. Following Bataillon,[107] Dealy will make Quiroga's main text of the *Información en Derecho* reproduce Christian *topoi* of Erasmian inspiration. Some glimpses of Quiroga's *oidor* political profile and some chroniclers' accounts, with the exclusion of Grijalva's, will be offered, yet Dealy's approach is mostly concerned with influences and communications of Christian sources. This history of religious ideas, within a disposition to treasure Christianity, is probably the most resilient approach to Quiroga. We must include Martín-Hernández, Verástique, Banazak and García-Ceballos.

Martín-Hernández, makes Quiroga into an anti-slavery, peace-loving character who will not hesitate to raise doubts about the Spanish colonization. With no words for the legal culture, Quiroga is, according to Martín-Hernández, someone who understood human nature and human dignity and who logically advocated respect and coexistence. Martín-Hernández's manufacturing of saintliness defends that Quiroga defended human rights, and that he loved the marginal and the poor. Following chapters will engage with this popular belief on Quiroga.

Verástique basically rewrites Warren in a stacatto style, which betrays the art of some unacknowledged translator. There is no new information. The silence over Quiroga's social role opens up the Americas to the utopia of Christianization. Christianity is for Verástique the transcendental or transhistorical moment of truth-belief and, despite the title, *Collision of Utopias: Vasco de Quiroga's Mission to the Purehepecha-Chichimec of Michoacán*, there is little insinuation of a collision of worldviews. The only desirable world is the totalizing Christian world. Quiroga is, for Verástique, the catalyst of this Christian utopia mainly understood to be peaceful persuasion of non-believers by word and deed. Perfection is unambiguously full-fledged, sincere Christianity with some occasional dissonance among monastic groups. The Americas are thus made into a heterogeneity which should be grateful since, "the existence of a time and place of perfect spiritual and material well-being is a fundamental archaeological layer of Western culture." This spiritualization of historico-social energies, but without Bataillon's meticulous textual empiricism, is a common precedent on Quiroga which will die hard.

Also in this ecclesiastical neighborhood, Ceballos-García focuses almost exclusively upon pastoral preoccupations. If the secular position gives itself away in the apellation of "theocracy,"[108] all of these authors will instead speak of utopianism in the timeframe of colonial Latin America mainly as the Christian-inspired welfare system for the neediest. Pastoral work, according to Ceballos-García, plows the virginal American fields and the epic of the Christianization of New Spain goes, with Quiroga, in the right direction. Utopia here means refuge for the nomadic, shelter for the homeless, the right place for Christian instruction, the learning of arts and crafts, the invigoration of commerce and the splendor of liturgical ceremonies. There is little insinuation of any kind of historical dissonance in this idyllic description. Ceballos-García also closes ranks for Quiroga's saintliness. The Spanish high state official and later bishop of Michoacán becomes a paragon of pastoral solicitude. Utopia is here the colonial institution of the bishopric. Next to Las Casas, the first Bishop of Michoacan is, always according to Ceballos-García, also with a well-deserving fame in an expanding Christian world.[109]

Holding hands with these Christian authors, Banazak is however the only one who will present some criticisms to Quiroga. His work is concerned with how the Christian Church tries historically to become an institution for the poor or Indian sectors in the Americas, and mostly fails. Banazak, for whom this failure is nevertheless meaningful, still grants Quiroga compassion for the oppressed. Yet he is quick to point out serious flaws in Quiroga's conception of the Church. Quiroga's explicit acceptance of the historical imposition of Hispanocentrism, as he calls it, and the incompleteness of his preferential option for the poor, makes him a historically flawed religious model. This "locus theologicus for the New World," as Banazak calls it, is thus historically "marred." Banazak's work, an offshoot of Gutiérrez's theology of liberation, will keep Quiroga in this unresolved contradiction, which believes "in the redemptive mystery of the poor," yet not fully.[110] In a rather rigid polarization between Spaniards and Indians, Quiroga becomes, still with some doubts—also for Banazak—a modelic figure, only second to Las Casas.

The socio-historical translation of the Christian virtue of compassion takes us to the colonial institution of American bishropics and the collaboration with state structures in the institution of royal patronage (or *Patronato Real*). Enrique Dussel's *El Episcopado Hispanoamericano* (1969-1970),[111] an inevitable archival reference for the early history of the Christian Church in the Americas, examines the function of this institution. Dussel defends the thesis that the bishopric structures, inside the Christian Church, constitute the social mechanism for the manufacturing of the social good for the majority of the population. The early bishops, Quiroga among them, defended the threatened well-being of the Indians. Pastoral duties to the American populations are, according to Dussel, an unquestionable and desirable political ideal, which is mostly carried out by this politico-ecclesiastical labor of prudence.[112] In the always shifting official geography of New Spain, Michoacán is a middle-size bishopric "of importance" (*sic*, with quotation marks in the original). Several factors are considered by Dussel such as population, "cultural infrastructure" [*sic*], total input of tithes, etc. (v. 2, p. 99).[113] Like other bishoprics, Michoacán is economically affiliated to the Crown allocation of tithes (v. 1, pp. 71ff).[114] Quiroga constitutes a singular case in the sense that his election appears to have been more open than usual (v. 2, p. 134). Quiroga is not initially affiliated with any one monastic group. In the vicinity of the New Laws (1542-3), the bishops will become, for Dussel, the foremost colonial institution to defend the rights of the Indians. Dussel proposes the defeat of the official disposition for the implementation of egalitarianism during Quiroga's final years, 1544-1568.

Inside the vastness of the West Indies, the Bishopric,[115] Quiroga, also for Dussel, stands out as an extraordinary bishop (1538-1565), with a clear pro-Indian or *indigenista* agenda. Capitalizing on his peace-making skills, Quiroga's republic allows for the Indians to live "without the influence of the Spanish," yet always in acquiescence to the evangelical message. With words that he would probably modify today, Dussel equates the protection of Indian well-being with the civilizing mission, and both of these with the desirability of preaching the Gospel (v. 3, p. 57). Inside the Michoacán bishopric, which we must imagine "larger than the actual France" (v. 5, p. 116), Dussel estimates a population of 1.3 million, which is no negligible social detail.[116]

The 1960s saw the publication of three biographies of Quiroga. There is however no evidence of any communication among them. Dussel (1969) does not quote from either Warren (1963), or Landa (1965).[117] Dussel's biographical vignette of Quiroga reproduces nonetheless a striking similarity in content: Quiroga's good press. This means "boundless generosity, exemplary piety, sleepless nights devoted to prayer" (v. 5, p. 115), a "gigantic personality" because he is a "civilizing Christian" force (p. 119). The notion of utopia is explicitly mentioned only once in relation to More's *Utopia*, a reference which is originally taken from Moreno (there is no reference to Zavala). Quiroga's hospital-villages, also a "humanist ideal" (v. 6, p. 367), are praised because they represented indigenous collectivist self-ruling. With no operative notion of "private sin," these multi-ethnic hospital communities gave historical form to the common good.[118] Quiroga is, also for Dussel, the "most intelligent of those Spaniards who set foot on American soil" (p. 122), an exemplary figure who, despite his high ranking, was devoted to a dignified poverty (p. 123).

The contemporary period of scholarship on Quiroga may well start with the Mexican scholar René Acuña, who recently edited a complete edition of the controversial treatise *De Debellandis Indis* (México, 1988), previously considered to be lost. Controversy here means the endorsement, according to the decorum of Early Modern political theory of the *justos títulos*, of the Spanish colonization of the Americas. Despite Zavala's misgivings, Acuña's work essentially substantiates Bataillon's early intuitions (1965) about Quiroga's political personality.[119] Acuña's meticulous reading will help us situate Quiroga's political position in relation to most of his contemporaneous figures (chapters three and four will elaborate on this). The importance of Acuña resides for us in the change from hagiographies to what we would simply like to call a rigorous practice of historicism. There is no need, with Bataillon, to apologize for directing the torchlight inside the saint's flower-decorated historical niche. Acuña's research on medieval sources is certainly impressive. This convoluted, uneasy framework will constitute the basic structure at least in relation to *De Debellandis Indis*. Acuña complements Herrejón-Peredo's early work,[120] yet it goes further, through the detailed engagement with textual dilemmas, into necessary territories of imaginary speculations as to the likeliest conditions of possibility, but also impossibility, for Quiroga. Our debt to Acuña, also his good spirits, will become apparent.

We have already mentioned the most accessible pocketbook edition of Quiroga's texts gathered by Serrano-Gassent's *La Utopía en América* (1992). The *Debellandis Indis* and the *Proceso de Residencia* are not included here. Serrano-Gassent breaks no new ground, and the vindication of humanism dies hard, despite some precisions on the contrary.[121] Among the latest works on Quiroga, there is a recent off-shoot of the Zavala tree, *El Humanismo en el Nuevo Mundo* by Raúl Horta,[122] which is symptomatic of a deeply entrenched "Hispanist" understanding of the colonial period as practiced inside Mexico. There are finally these partial approaches: Gomes-Moreira's reconstruction of further theological-judicial sources,[123] Tena-Ramírez's account of the perpetuation of these hospital-villages until the nineteenth centuries,[124] and Miranda-Godínez's uneven work on the pedagogy of the *Colegio de San Nicolás de Pátcuaro*.[125] The latest piece which has come to us is the chapter "Discourse of Domination, Discourses of Hope: the Contradictory Vision of Don Vasco de Quiroga" by Kripper-Martínez,[126] which tries to generate some gray areas of historical ambiguity about Quiroga.

Against this scholarly background, the perhaps comfortable consumption by the few, happy literate European males of early modern fictionalizations of an ideal world will metaphorically morph into Quiroga's schematism of a similar ideal world, or the city of equals. The colonial difference inside the horizon of early colonial Mexico will, however, cling to the three-dimensional imaginary context of courtroom legalisms and discursive political negotiations. Quiroga's colonial utopianism is to be understood generally as the efforts to restore the badly damaged legality of coloniality. This is our explicit challenge: to be able to flesh out the three-dimensionality, or the social text, of the totality of the repressive textualizations "near" the name of Vasco de Quiroga. Against the celebratory account by Zavala, Quiroga's defense of the most fragile and majoritarian social sectors (or *indigenismo*) will need to be revisited, and historically modulated, in relation to his politico-ecclesiastical profile in New Spain. We will see Quiroga's reformation largely contained within hegemonic parameters of intelligibility and diplomacy. This work, we wish to advance, will make it quite clear that there is no explicit pronouncement by Vasco de Quiroga against the expansive totality of the imperial model or the colonial state, which should not be taken to mean that Quiroga offers no global critique of state malfunction or institutional criminality. Against the commonplace that states that Quiroga defended the indigenous populations, we will show that he did not in principle repudiate the extremity of slavery, one historical form of unfreedom among others, in colonial Mexico. Nor did he advocate plurality of belief systems in his village-hospitals (Quiroga will be no "liberal" as we tend to understand the notion today). Inside the more encompassing colonial arrangement of forced labor, Quiroga will propose proto-capitalist contractualism with its utopian or egalitarian potential for the reformation of coloniality. There is no doubt that there is a tremendous social cost and also dangers in this operation. If it is true that Quiroga's claims to legitimacy will move within a Christian horizon of intelligibility, "near" Antonio de Guevara's official Erasmism, our emphasis on Quiroga's working clothes will need, however, to highlight the high-ranking trans-Atlantic repressive *letrado* practice proper to the official reformation of the Indian polity. The most concrete historical delineation possible of this synthetic formula, the repressive reformation of the West Indies, is what this work is all about.

These are some of the reasons why this work will characterize Quiroga's colonial reformation as a quiet or partial reformation always in the vicinity of historico-political privilege. Colonial utopianism is this official reformation from above. It is clear that membership in the repressive decision-making circles means, then as now, at least a good chance for the fight over historico-social configurations of power and privilege. It is also true that the explicitness or literalness in the discourse of legality means, then as now, a social position of power and privilege (*roto* subalterns cannot "speak" repressively quite yet). Quiroga's American texts are therefore to be imagined as historically meaningful in this vicinity of the global qua Spanish house of power and privilege. Quiroga's intricate legalism is the cultural merchandise early "Indians" could not have understood, let alone manufactured. Inside this horizon of lettered legalism, there will no attempt to make of Vasco de Quiroga a radical figure. There will be no desperate search for Che Guevaras in Quiroga's closet. Quiroga's colonial literature will consistently refuse to question the legitimacy of the established authority. For him, this was historically a non-issue. Outside the status quo, there was for Quiroga nothing imaginable or desirable, despite the early colonial commotions. Yet within official protocols, repressive proposals for change and transformations were articulated with a muscular romance language.

7. (Un)predictable Genealogies-II: Digital Culture for a Popular Quiroga

But surely serious scholarship must not always take the dance floor! We confess a disposition for light literature, and so we wanted to give it a try with "website literature." One solitary afternoon, after coffee and muffins, we decided to search the web for the names of "Michoacan" (thus with no accent) and "Quiroga." What we found in these electronic non-places was predictably commonplace, yet some unpredictable twists which we believe to be not entirely meaningless. Thus we decided to create this section immediately after the scholarly genealogies on Quiroga. We confess we find that there is something a bit insidious about the electronic lightness of this mostly anonymous literature.

We have already mentioned Enrique Krauze's *Mexico: Biography of Power*.[127] The succinct sixteenth-century legacy presents to the contemporary imagination the by now familiar Spanish *tableau vivant* of ecclesiastical figures: the Dominican Bartolomé de las Casas, the humanist Ginés de Sepúlveda, the Dominican Francisco de Vitoria, the Franciscans Zumárraga, first Arch-bishop of Mexico, Pedro de Gante and Bernardino de Sahagún, the manager of the monumental compilation *The General History of the*

Things of New Spain. In Krauze's English-only version, the double foreignness of these Spanish names sticks out. Quiroga, a Spanish name made Mexican, is also included in this *tableau vivant* of the *padrecitos* who were "at the heart of one of the most extraordinary chapters in the religious history of the West: the conversion of millions of Indians to Christianity" (p. 5). Following the electronic rules of the soundbite, Krauze's Quiroga is, at least according to this website, mostly Zavala's Quiroga.

Quiroga's business-card presentation is typical: he is said to have been a secular priest who "adapted the ideas of Thomas More's *Utopia* with considerable success to the Indians of the ancient Tarascan Empire in Michoacan" (all accents are gone). Quiroga said that the indigenous were like "soft wax" (*sic*, with quotation marks in the original) without a sign of "arrogance, ambition or covetousness" (idem). He is spoken of as "the most outstanding example of the missionary love for the Indians, in his case free of intolerance, strongly constructive but still protectively paternal." The Santa Fé hospital-towns are described to be "an installation of a group of Indian families in ten houses that shared a common patio, a Church, and cells for the friars." Growth happened soon: "seventy houses, several orchards, fields of maize, wheat, barley, and flax, pens for animals and poultry." The "utopia" of Santa Fé de la Laguna "put down strong roots and began to multiply across what is now Michoacan." Krauze calls them "[an] economic and social success." Success here appears to be a kind of gentle, orderly early stage of capitalism, i.e. manufacturing, which is credited to Quiroga. Success also means for Krauze the self-disciplined allocation of one trade or craft to each town to thus avoid ethnic conflict and unfair economic competition. A clockwork orange of an exchange network is said to have taken over the whole arena. The life in these hospitals is explained thus:

> Each town would center around a "hospital" in the medieval sense of the word, an institution that would welcome not only the sick but also the poor, the hungry, and even travelers in need of a place to stay. Within the hospital-towns, the main features of life were the practice of religion, work in the fields, and the learning of skills. Children were required to go to mass and catechism, taught to read and write in Spanish, and trained in a specific craft: bricklaying, tanning, carpentry, metalworking, ceramics, or textile production. Three kinds of authority were recognized: natural authority (the Indian patriarchs), the principales [*sic*] elected by vote of the heads of each household, and the rector (community priest). The use of domestic servants was not allowed, and collective cooperation was encouraged in the fields and in public projects. (p. 6)

Krauze reads Quiroga's *Rules of Good Government* according to Zavala's fashion. If these rules are said to have in place from 1563 to 1776, Quiroga's legacy is still, according to Krauze, alive:

> In 1996 the town of Santa Fé de la Laguna still exists as an Indian community, with the same hospital and church built by Quiroga. In the Tarascan area many communities still practice the same crafts assigned to them by the bishop. And in other towns the hospitals still stand, enduring emblems of a man venerated by the descendants of those Indians who called him "Tata Vasco." (p. 7)

This is the contemporary soundbite on Quiroga. The webpage links took us to several other unpredictable places. We have selected three representative sites: the tourist information of the Michoacán region, and the websites associated with two individuals, Gianni Riotta, a former journalist of the Italian newspaper *Corriere della Sera* and Jim Tuck, a freelance writer residing in Guadalajara, Jalisco (Mexico). We have finally abandoned the historical circles of ecclesiastical robes in the hope of some other news. Let us see what these electronic sites give to us.

Web-surfers planning to visit the Michoacán region will have access to abundant official snippets of Quiroga's life. These snippets will be dubious or devious, or both, yet there will always be in the vicinity of the aforementioned commonplace. There is, concretely, one full-page presentation of our historical figure. Quiroga's electronic credentials will summarily read:[128]

> Oidor y obispo de Michoacán nació en Madrigal de las Altas Torres, Avila, España. Fue juez de comisión en Valladolid y fue nombrado oidor de la Nueva España. Existen dudas acerca del lugar donde Quiroga realizó sus estudios, pero la mayoría de los historiadores suponen que fue en Salamanca, donde hizo la carrera de abogado, misma que concluyó en 1515.

This attribution of Salamanca to Quiroga is doubtful, yet there is the alleged foundation of a second Salamanca by our historical figure in the Michoacán region in 1563.[129] This electronic profile will select the following highlights: Quiroga's participation in the *juicio de residencia* against the *First Audiencia* officials with the charge of guilty ("[e]l mal trato que habían dado a los indígenas y sobre todo el asesinato del jefe de los tarascos perpetrado por Nuño de Guzmán, habían provocado la rebelión de los michoacanos"). Hence, Quiroga is the peace-maker among indigenous and

Spaniards. He is also the first one to pay any attention to the social and religious situation of the vanquished. The hospitals, despite the awkward syntax, "eran instituciones de vida comunitaria, ideas que tomó de su formación humanística, que incluía ideas de Tomás Moro, San Ignacio de Loyola, Platón y Luciano." These embellishments of high European culture thus adorn Quiroga's apparent neutralization of colonization.

Información en Derecho, qualified as famous ("célebre"), is synthesized thus, "en la que condena enérgicamente a los encomenderos, hombres perversos quienes no conviene que los nativos 'sean tenidos por hombres sino por bestias' [*sic*, with quotes in the original] y defiende apasionadamente a los indios, que no merecen perder la libertad." Quiroga's achievements are typified thus:

> "formó allí [Morelia] un género de cristianos, a las derechas como iglesia primitiva" [*sic*, with quotes in the original]. Urbanizó muchas poblaciones, principalmente la ciudad de Michoacán, concentrando sus principales barrios en el de Pátzcuaro, los cuales proveyó de hospitales e industrias, para las cuales instruyó a los indígenas. Su recuerdo en Michoacán es imperecedero, donde todavía, al referirse a él, se le llama "Tata Vasco." Murió en Uruapan en 1565 y sus restos fueron enterrados en la catedral.

In relation to these unattributed quotation marks, we may infer the likely candidates of Aguayo Spencer, Juan José Moreno or Nicolás León. The glaring absence of the word "colonization," possibly not the most appealing old-fashioned marquee for web-surfers, potential tourists and customers, is to be noted. Without it, readers will be forced to assume an unbearable lightness of being mere consumers of banalized cultural difference.

The site *Pátzcuaro. Introducción* for the *Red de Desarrollo Sostenible* (*RDS*),[130] introduces the lacustrine area as being "of great importance for the identity of the Michoacan people." The site establishes an amazing pre-Columbian continuity through the also silenced Spanish colonization. Quiroga sticks out: "It was in antiquity the site of the Purpecha empire, its actual generations still live here, and this was the place where Vasco de Quiroga undertook his legendary utopia" (p. 1). Nothing else is made explicit in the advertising of this ideal vacation area. Under the heading of "Tianguis and Mercados,"[131] another site credits Quiroga with the introduction of arts and crafts in the region. Far away from belletrism, this electronic prose gives a still latent vernacular popularization of Quiroga:

> En Michoacán, el obispo Vasco de Quiroga introdujo nuevas técnicas para trabajar el cobre. También enseñó a los indios productos nuevos como el

hierro y la laca. Detrás de los conquistadores llegaron los artesanos que enseñaron sus especialidades a los aprendices indios. Los nativos aprendieron rápidamente y pronto compitieron con sus maestros iniciales. No obstante, durante mucho tiempo los artesanos locales fueron mirados de arriba a abajo, pues se consideraba que todo lo español era superior. Pero con el tiempo llegó la independencia y un espíritu nacionalista invadió México. (p. 1)

The subsection "unknown Mexico-colonial"[132] mentions Quiroga profusely in relation to squares, fountains and institutions, the ancient college of San Nicolás among them. Pátzcuaro is said to be the spiritual cultural capital "del pueblo Purépecha (mal nombrado como Tarasco)."[133] Here, Quiroga's legacy is still an inspiration: "organizó en la región varias aldeas modelo [*sic*], u hospitales-pueblo [*sic*], impulsó también el desarrollo comunitario del comercio, la educación, la salud y las artes y oficios." Are not these the explicit values of civilizing modernity and capitalism? With the silence over colonization, isn't this an official endorsement of these "modern" values to thus better attract the attention and the wallets of potential visitors?

The website *Gaceta Consular: Mexico, Present in the Heart of Texas*,[134] sponsored by the General Consulate of Mexico in Austin, Texas includes the following information under the section entitled "History and Tourism." It is mostly an invitation, not without misinformation, to the enjoyment of seductive natural beauties:

The ancient cradle of the Tarascan Empire is now a state of volcanoes and lakes, the proud possessor of a diverse climate and geography. During the viceroy period, Vasco de Quiroga, a Franciscan monk already advanced in years and known as "Tata Vasco" to the natives, devoted the remainder of his life to teaching the natives how to use the natural resources they had available. Today's famous crafts of Michoacan descend from those taught by "Tata Vasco." Michoacan was the home of Mexico's first institution of higher education, and its conservatory of music is the oldest in all the Americas. Great palaces of the viceroy period can also be found, in a land of scenic views and beautiful lagoons, where a kaleidoscope of water, flowers, and land provide a feast for the eyes. (p. 2)

Quiroga, high state official of the Spanish state, is thus "naturalized" into a venerable, monkish teacher who delivers the goods to the "natives" against this postcard rendition of a foreign Mexico. It is easy to get lost in this virtual geography which must surely stretch referentiality to an almost breaking point. We found a rather amateurish bilingual recreation of the possible genealogies called, *The Quiroga Name*,[135] which includes an all-male list of famous Quirogas. It includes our former *oidor*, "famous for his personal crusade to aid the conquered peoples of Mexico," among the Argentine leader of the Andean provinces and the Uruguayan author of "The Decapitated Chicken."

The site *Casa Maya: House of the Spanish Language and Fine Arts*,[136] aiming at an international English-speaking audience, offers a variety of courses which will "aid in the understanding and exchanging of ideas with the people of Pátzcuaro, whose culture and way of life remain unchanged by the encroachment of the 20th Century." The course topics include: 1. general aspects of Mexican history, 2. history of the development of Michoacan culture in the fourteenth century to the sixteenth century, 3. the Michoacan conquest and early years of the sixteenth century, the work of Augustino religious order, Franciscanos and Jesuits, 4. the work of Vasco de Quiroga and the utopias of the sixteenth-century Michoacan and 5. the life and work of artists and intellectuals contemporary to Michoacan.

The site "Morelia, patrimony of humanity"[137] mentions Quiroga in passing in relation to the change of the bishopric seat from the Tarascan capital of Tzintzuntzan to the city of Pátzcuaro in 1540. In 1979, the center of higher education "Vasco de Quiroga" was founded in Morelia. In 1992, this center acquires the official status of *Universidad Vasco de Quiroga*.[138] Its website literature reads:

> Como guía espiritual, Don Vasco de Quiroga, ha legado una fe profunda, cristiana, que mantenga el humanismo y el deseo de bienester en todos los hombres, fortaleciendo los valores humanos con el fin de construir hogares unidos que conlleven a una estabilidad social; por eso la UVAQ sigue los principios de toda Universidad de inspiración cristiana con orientación católica, constituyéndose en comunidad de inspiración cristiana, siempre a la vanguardia de la educación superior, ofreciendo calidad académica humana. Nuestro Servicio Social. En congruencia con el espíritu de Don Vasco de Quiroga el servicio social busca fortalecer ese sentimiento de solidaridad activa con los que menos tienen, pueden o saben. Es una experiencia agradable que todo alumno vivencia [*sic*] íntegramente en la UVAQ. (p. 1)

This electronic congruence, often with the broken grammar of these anonymous website *letrados*, finds further support in a discourse delivered by the *licenciado* Fernando Juárez-Aranda, President ("rector") of the

Universidad Michoacana de San Nicolás de Hidalgo.[139] To a delegation of local institutions (ANUIES), Juárez-Aranda will claim direct lineage to the following genealogy: Vasco de Quiroga, Miguel Hidalgo, José María Morelos, Melchor Ocampo, Pascual Ortiz Rubio, etc. Our main protagonist is introduced in Zavala's predictable fashion: "se caracterizó por tener una honda raíz humanística, proyectada en una recia utopía americana, que aún late en el corazón de los michoacanos (p. 1)."

Some previous scholarly stylization of Quiroga into saintliness is to be taken quite literally. Electronic wires delivered to us what appears to be a journalistic report signed by Arturo Sierra-Reyes entitled, "First Encounter of the *Nuncio Apostólico* with Mexican indigenes."[140] Sierra-Reyes highlights the deep emotion in Justo Mullor García, Archbishop of Morelia and bishop of Tacámbaro, at the sight of the faces of indigenous childen, women and elderly drenched in rain. The cause of the report: the two-day visit of Mullor-García, short after the Vatican appointment, to the Zirahuen *municipio* (county) of Salvador Escalante in November 1997. Sierra-Reyes's tabloid prose speaks of a mutual discovery: "El nuncio fue conquistado por los indígenas, aunque también es cierto que el corazón de ellos fue conquistado por el nuncio, hombre con carisma."

The meeting is quite 'spectacular, yet not without some problems. According to Sierra-Reyes's eye-witness account, we must imagine a magnificent sight of indigenous welcome to the Vatican representative. Hundreds of flower-containing kegs will be placed as far as one-kilometer away from the main entrance to the *pueblo* of Zirahuen. These flowers are appropriately of yellow and white colors. Houses, main streets and the main-square area are embellished for the occasion. An aromatic pine-variety folliage called *guinumo* is sprinkled over these kegs and roof gardens or *pérgolas* of most private homes. The local priest Rafael Barajas-Sandoval extended invitations to the local population and all visitors began to gather at 5:30 p.m. in front of the hotel Zirahuén to greet the distinguished guest. People gathered, always according to Sierra-Reyes, as the threat of the hurricane Ricki was mounting. They endured a three-hour delay with intermittent though strong rain. By the time *Monseñor* Mullor arrived, it was already dark.

All prayers for a timely rainfall failed miserably. Mullor's arrival and parade (*romería*) were accompanied by abundant, if intermittent rain. Sierra-Reyes notices that many indigenes appeared quite unconcerned about both the delay and the rain and remained motionless in the pouring rain perhaps aware that the meeting was really with and for them. Our visiting journalist

confesses to have been in the dark during most of the ceremony: "La mayor
parte de la ceremonia se desarrolló en la lengua purépecha, de tal manera
que los no indígenas, que éramos la minoría, nos quedamos ayunos [*sic*]
del contenido de los mensajes purépechas" (p. 2). The official delegation
finally arrived. It included besides Justo Mullor, the all-male delegation of
Rogelio Patiño, bishop of Apatzingán, Carlos Suárez Cázares, bishop of
Zamora and Jesús Sahagún, bishop emeritus of Lázaro Cárdenas. The Papal
representative is called "Tata Justo Mullor," which he found delightful ("un
título hermosísimo").

Remembering the peoples who received the evangelical message from
"Tata Vasco," Justo-Mullor calls for a new evangelization. Our journalist
appears not to have had problems this time with the translation system:

> Nueva evangelización quiere decir que cada uno de nosotros, ustedes y
> yo, los obispos, el clero, todos los seglares, de todas las etnias, seamos
> más Jesucristo y menos nosotros mismos. Porque el drama de nuestros
> cristianos es que somos nosotros mismos siempre y dejamos poco espacio
> para Jesucristo. La nueva evangelicación es dejar espacio a Jesucristo en
> nuestras propias vidas para que sea el rey de nuestro corazón. Para que
> sea el rey de nuestras familias. Para que sea el rey de México. Para que sea
> el rey del mundo. Para que sea el rey de todos los grupos humanos. (p. 3)

Sierra-Reyes provides a detailed account of some of the stellar moments
("momentos emotivos"), inserted in the one-hour-long presentation of
offerings (*ofrendas*), to the distinguished visitors. By the hundreds, these
comprise the children's dance of the elderly (*Danza de los Viejitos*), an
enormous painting of Vasco de Quiroga, a wooden horse decorated with
flowers and carrying fruit, bread and maize, and a rich variety of the region's
famous craftmanship, including chirimoya fruit from Tingambato, highlights
from Santa Fé de la Laguna and wood crafts from Pichátaro. The Vatican
representative did not hesitate a bit to try on a traditional hat. Several multi-
colored wool garments were also offered to the ecclesiastical representatives,
all of whom did likewise.

Always according to Sierra-Reyes, the festivities conclude with a free
dinner and dance. The site literature ends with the announcement of the
meetings of Justo-Mullor, who also had a breakfast meeting with the governor
of the region, Víctor Manuel Tinoco-Rubí, in the city of Morelia, and the
Sunday mass celebration in the Basílica of *Nuestra Señora de la Salud*,
Pátzcuaro where the initial beatification proceedings of "Tata Vasco, el
obispo protector de los indios purépechas" (p. 5) were officially announced.

Wired Quiroga inevitably cuts an international figure. Gianni Riotta's website includes the comments of one of his readers, Guido Silvestri, on our historical protagonist. Gianni Riota, originally affilliated with the prestigious newspaper *Corriere della Sera*, created in 1998 a section called "Pensieri & Parole" ("Thoughts & Words")[141] for the letter-exchange of information with his readers. Among these, Silvestri signs the e-mail entry on Quiroga. An all-Italian site, this two-year enterprise is, as of February 7, 1999 (my access date), Gianni Riotta's, but only nominally. He is no longer a journalist in the aforementioned newspaper. The initial message under "Benvenuti" ("Welcome"), not as warm as the previous indigenous welcome to the Vatican representative, opens to a site which is no longer interactive or updated. In a follow-up farewell note, Paolo Virtuani, presumably Riotta's colleague in the *Corriere della Sera*, highlights the site's success, the tremendous letter traffic and the output of some 7,300 letters in twelve months. Virtuani also mentions Gianni's next appointment, co-director of the newspaper *Stampa*. Yet, despite closing down the section, Virtuani continues, the readers' letters sent to Gianni in the *Corriere della Sera* will remain virtually available for the near future.

So, it is not entirely by choice that we became acquainted with Riotta and Silvestri in this site still available, yet no longer updated. The virtual *deus ex machina* of the database search mechanism did it for us. And so we found ourselves all of a sudden in the all-Italian no-place of a wired world also addressing "our" Quiroga for a non-specialist audience. The alleged popularity of the site will put in circulation a rather popular profile of Quiroga. This site, giving yet another spin to the rather unpredictable referentiality of "Quiroga," is however not entirely meaningless. Following the automatic selection of Silvestri's letter out of those several thousands, we now turn to it most concretely.

Silvestri's letter to Riotta's section is entitled "Vasco de Quiroga: Leftist Catholicism avant la lettre" ("cattocomunista ante litteram"). After a brief holiday in Mexico, Silvestri wishes to share his experiences with the readers of the *Corriere della Sera* as they relate to the name of Vasco de Quiroga. Due to relatively little acquaintance of the Italian public with the historical profile of Quiroga, Silvestri thinks his explicit attempt at an introduction is warranted. According to Silvestri, sixteenth-century New Spain offered no exciting prospects for the majority of the population caught in the middle of two equally undesirable factions. There are the Aztecs, not exactly "friendly" ("teneroni") and their thousands of sacrifices, and the the sudden arrival of a handful of bearded "conquistadores" (the Spanish word emerges authentically in the Italian narrative), which imposed their "infamous" ("famigerate") *encomiendas*. Levels of heterogeneity are thus presented, we must remember, to an original Italian audience, which is now no doubt also wired and global.

This colonial institution, the *encomienda*, is said to have rooted out the native culture which, together with epidemics, brought these Indian populations from twenty-five million to the one-million brink of extinction (Silvestri speaks of the "indiani del Centramerica"). In this "saddest" context, Quiroga's pragmatic-romantic profile ("al contempo romantica e pragmatica [figura]"), represents the historical neither-nor option or the third way. Quiroga's career thus takes flight in magnificent fashion: from judge to official priesthood for the benefit of all American indigenes. Yet, Quiroga's militant catholicism transcends details and puts into practice the Christian "principles" ("piuttosto che curarsi dei dettagli teologici cercò di applicare i principi evangelici all vita di tutti i giorni degli indigeni d'America"). Quiroga's missions were, according to Silvestri, relatively unconcerned with Christian doctrine ("si dava agli indiani un'infarinata di cristianesimo"), and their importance dwells in collective instrumentalization of the new techniques which were also introduced by Quiroga ("gli si insegnavano nuove techniche di coltivazione della terra e di produzioni di manufatti sulla base della più evoluta tecnologia europea"). Quiroga is thus the messenger of the good news of European technology which the American Indians took fast advantage of. Silvestri does not mention the Tarascan-Purepechas by name. Village specialization in Quiroga's missions ("comunità-villaggio") is however highlighted. An ideal of friendly complementarity in production and consumption of goods is said to have existed. Silvestri mistakenly adds that adults worked eight hours a day. (Quiroga's *Ordenanzas* mentions six hours.) All decisions were taken collectively inside every single community but also among all of them. Silvestri comments that Quiroga did not personally profit from this enterprise. He died in poverty in 1565. Rumor has it that the veneration of his name still continues and that the indigenes call him "the saint" ("da quanto mi è stato detto, ancora oggi gli abitanti dei villaggi che idealmente discendo no dalle comuni da lui fondate ne venerano il ricordo chiamandolo semplicemente 'il santo'"). So, in similar fashion to Sierra-Reyes's previous journalistic report, Silvestri's eye-witness account will also state for the Italian public that "they," passing through all these imaginary layers of wired heterogeneity, still venerate him. Silvestri concludes that this is a clear sign of Quiroga's exemplarity. His coherent Catholic communism was thus able to create a few happy islands for the poor Amerindias "shocked" by the conquest ("e del suo cattocomunismo da sogno capace di creare le poche isole felici per i poveri amerindi cosí scioccatti dalla 'conquesta' [*sic*, with quotation marks in the original]"). So, Silvestri suggests that it is not such a conquest after all.

There is in Silvestri some secular attraction for the demonstrations of faith among others as relates to Quiroga's historical legacy, no doubt a relative novelty and heterogeneity to the Italian public. If Silvestri's electronic pen depicts a Quiroga who closely resembles Pier P. Pasolini among the poor scoundrels of Rome, and chapters two and three will have to come back to this Franciscan vision, his simplistic reading nonetheless repeats some of the objections raised in their day by Fernández and O'Gorman.[142] Silvestri ends his letter with a rather flat-footed failure of an axiology: Quiroga's lived history is "interesting" and "moving" at the human and Christian levels ("la sua vicenda di uomo e di cristiano mi è sembrata interessante e anche commovente"). Silvestri's experiential claim to the historical legacy of Quiroga during his recent visit to Mexico is exclusively para-textual. There is no explicit textual ground for his assertions. Silvestri does not mention any literature by or on Quiroga, which he claims is almost inexistent ("non si trovano molte tracce nei libri di storia"), except in some fliers ("per certi versi").

To his one early anachronism, communism, others will follow in the conclusion: Quiroga's myth is a kind of "Schindler's list" which puts hospitality right there in the middle of the Indian holocaust ("una specie di 'Schindler's list' [*sic*] nell'olocausto degli indiani del Centramerica. Grazie dell'ospitalità"). Silvestri's introductory mapping of Quiroga for his compatriots is bewildering: communism, Hollywood-produced nazism, via Steven Spielberg's 1993 film, the touristic postcard version of Mexico and *Corriere della Sera* Italy against some dark heterogeneity of Spanish colonization of the American Indians ("indiani del Centramerica"), who are still somehow prodigiously alive and faithful to Quiroga. Far from being exceptional, this hasty rendering of Quiroga, but also of the Colonial Period at large, is not so uncommon as we might perhaps like it to be. Yet, there is one redeeming aspect of this Spanish-created horror, and one exemplary lesson for the ages: Quiroga's exceptionalism is the white sheep against so many black sheep but also wolves. The computer printout of "Schindler's List" will further bewilder the historical imagination: "The true story of the enigmatic Oskar Schindler (played by Liam Neeson), a member of the Nazi party, womanizer and war profiteer, who saved the lives of more than 1,100

Jews during the Holocaust." The film is no better. According to Silvestri's casual pen, Quiroga is like Liam Neeson, the Spaniards like the Nazis, the Indians like the Jews and all so-called "historical" ingredients for the culture of entertainment and tourism not exclusively for Italy and the USA. Inside this perhaps unconscious game of heterogeneities, Silvestri gives another spin, with or without appropriate bibliography, to some "black legend" which is always "there." Silvestri's distressing writing is thus fitting to the always indefinite place of the now global wired world, precisely for all the casualness and unpretentiousness. Silvestri's Italian prose is however painfully predictable of unconscious and collective beliefs about some distant and heterogeneous imaginary site called Colonial Latin America. There is no recorded response from Riotta to Silvestri's letter. We have sent an e-mail message to the latter in the hope that we make his acquaintance. There is still no answer by the time this book is sent to print.

While web-surfers will get to experience the colloquial, almost familial Italian-only feel of Riotta's site, Jim Tuck's personal site, *Mexico Connect*[143] is emphatically less chummy in its business-only character. This distinctly American character is, although explicitly catering to an USA audience, also open to the home-free decenteredness of global consumers. Within this wild wired world, Tuck's American idiom dishes out a no-nonsense direct, politesse-free self-presentation with little of the old world chattiness. If Riotta's small photograph looks like the industrious, clean-looking cousin we never had, i.e. a journalist-looking bespectacled young man in ironed tie-and-shirt *prêt-à-porter* outfit leaning over a desk with lots of papers and pencils, the "Jim Tuck Biography" Section, by contrast, includes the black-and-white, almost in-your-face close-up of a gray-haired middle-aged bespectacled man in a tie-less neck-unbuttoned white-shirt looking at you calmly straight in the eye. There is a modest pen sticking out of Tuck's frontal shirt pocket. There is no smile. Tuck's photo is sending you the message that you don't want to mess around with him.

Mexico Connect includes three subsections: a three-page photo-embellished "Jim Tuck Biography," a three-page Quiroga section, entitled "Vasco de Quiroga: Notes on a Practical Utopian (1470-1565)," and a lengthier eight-page section, "Jim Tuck Home Page," which includes all necessary references to the historical merchandise Tuck is selling to potential customers.

Tuck's biography speaks of a well-travelled man. Following upon his graduation in history from Princeton in 1951, he served in the First Marine Air Wing in Korea as a radio correspondent. "After a brief and unsatisfying exposure to the Madison Avenue rat race" (journalism?), "he made the Big Break in 1958." For the last forty years, he has been a freelance writer still with a special attraction for historical issues. Tuck's writing career began in the late fifties. A look into his first life, mainly under the pseudonym of "Irving O'Malley," will find, in his own words, numerous contributions to men's magazines. These include articles like "Veracruz—Steaming Port of Call (Girls)," "The Day They Smeared Hitler's Massacre Battalion," "How Many Hollywood Playboys are Gay Boys?," and "I Am the Love Slave of a Voodoo Priestess." Tuck says that he now "winces" at this early period of his life, when he also tried "serious, less lucrative writing" for magazines like *Catholic World*, *Negro Digest* (today *Black World*), and several other unnamed political magazines. There are no titles for some of these more serious contributions.

In an early date, Tuck became affiliated with the *Fodor Guides*. He served as the Regional Editor in Mexico between 1970-82 with a parenthesis in Romania between 1978-80. His self-described vitae speaks of chapters for *Fodor's Mexico*, *Fodor's Budget Mexico* and *Fodor's Eastern Europe*. Tuck mentions that for this latter contribution, he was awarded "a Diploma of Honour" by the Romanian government, during "the hated Ceausescu regime." Tuck's travel-guide material has seen the light of magazine publication in numerous locations, from Toronto to San Francisco, Boston to Detroit. Taking into account the column of opinion "Insight Straight," created in 1991, and syndicated by *Continental News Service*, San Diego in 1994, the list of Tuck's non-book publications recently exceeded the 1,000 mark.

The 1980s made Tuck return to "his first love: historical writing." He has published since 1982 five books of "historical nonfiction." These include the Mexican themes of the Cristero Rebellion, Pancho Villa and John Reed as the romantic representatives of the revolutionary ideal, a biography of Karl Radek, leading defendant of the 1937 Stalin Purge Trial, a study of the relationship between McCarthy and the Hearts Press, and an examination of the "split" in America's "liberal community with the Communists" (thus, with capital "C"). Tuck's home page includes complete information of these books, including synopsis and praises. The author highlights that "[p]articularly gratifying to Tuck were favorable comments about the McCarthy book from Arthur M. Schelinger Jr. and Gore Vidal."

Finally, the site highlights Tuck's "active" political profile, and his affiliated association since his college days with the "liberal anti-Communist Americans for Democratic Action (ADA)." The McCarthy book is said to have been dedicated to two Princeton graduates and personal friends who "lost their jobs during the McCarthy madness" (p. 2). The biography ends with the information that Tuck lives with his wife María Ruiz in Guadalajara, Jalisco, Mexico. There is a final reference to a near trip with his wife to Singapore and Malaysia.

So, what's the point of Jim Tuck's colorful website profile here? Tuck is also a self-appointed historian. His electronic literature is designed to catch the eye of people interested in colonial Latin America:

> It occurs to me that the material on Mexico that I'm producing on a continuing basis would be ideally suited to survey courses in Latin American History programs a/o for reference purposes. Educators and textbook publishers please take note.

Tuck confesses to being a gargantuan Renaissance man:

> My first choice is anything of a historical, cultural and political nature— interesting historical anomalies, think pieces on current events and trends, etc. Here I'm [in no] way limited by any time-frame; chronology can range from Marcus Aurelius to Monica Lewinsky.

Among these vast panoramic vistas, "our" Quiroga is the only one individuality which will make it to Tuck'website. What follows is the summarized account of Tuck's electronic version of popular Quiroga.

This subsection under *Mexico Connect* is entitled "Vasco de Quiroga: Notes on a Practical Utopian (1470-1565)." It is mostly a biographical summary account of Quiroga which begins by saying that, against the "hopelessly visionary and impractical" utopias of Plato, Augustine and More, "[which] never existed outside the minds and published works [*sic*] of their creators," Quiroga is to have created a "real-life Utopia." Tuck's emphasis on Quiroga's utopian pragmatism thus appears to lead us into the Hispanic road not taken by Eliav-Feldon's aforementioned *Realistic Utopias*.

Quiroga is introduced to have been "a Spanish churchman greatly influenced by More. Yet, unlike More, he was in a position to give a practical application to his vision of a just society (p. 1)." Tuck's fast prose accounts for Quiroga's "facts" fast: "Trained as a lawyer, he took holy orders somewhat late in life. But the Church recognized his ability and promotion came rapidly." Quiroga's complicated political profile comes up in the colonial world. Tuck differentiates metropolitan and colonial practices: "Where *audiencias* in Spain were simply courts of justice, in the colonies they were more powerful and also performed legislative and executive functions." Nazi imagery will predictably color Tuck's adventure-packed account, almost in an Indiana Jones's style, of the First *Audiencia*,

> Its President in 1529 was that Himmler of the Spanish colonial era, Nuño Beltrán de Guzmán. Guzmán's reign of corruption and terror in Mexico City [*sic*] ended only when the courageous Bishop Juan de Zumárraga managed to smuggle a message to the Crown by entrusting it to a sailor on a ship bound for Spain.... In the course of [Nuño's] rampage, a Tarascan king was dragged behind a horse and then burned alive because Guzmán thought he was withholding information regarding a gold treasure. (p. 2)

So, against this hellish background, the "good guy" comes in:

> Guzmán was eventually apprehended, first being confined to a dungeon in Mexico [*sic*]. Then, in an event that could have been taken from a medieval morality play, Quiroga sat on the tribunal that ordered that Guzmán be returned to Spain in chains, where he spent the rest of his life as a prisoner. But there remained the task of cleaning up the mess [*sic*] Guzmán left behind. That's where Vasco de Quiroga came in. Never in history have two men exercising a strong influence in a given region been more polar opposites than Nuño de Guzmán and Vasco de Quiroga.

So, Tuck's hyperbolic fiction makes our venerable Quiroga into the moral cleaning lady of this historical morality play. Tuck also makes Quiroga attend the "first phase" of the Council of Trent against all evidence on the contrary. There is no mention of the Valladolid Debates. Tuck will not hesitate to assert that Quiroga "took several Indians with him to Europe and presented them at the Spanish court." Upon returning to Mexico, Quiroga is credited with bringing the banana trees to the region of Michoacán. With banana tree importation, "Quiroga was also free to put his dream of an ideal community into practice (p. 3)." He did so by insufflating More's "epic work" into "the local Indian population." Tuck will proclaim the "outstanding success" of these communities. The explicit content of this success amounts to "religious instruction, arts and crafts and self-government." Confusingly, Tuck adds however, "Bit by bit, the Indians came to realize that the kindly Bishop was as much as representative of the European race [*sic*] as the sadistic *conquistador* [*sic*, in italics in the original]." More confusingly, the next paragraph states a Zavala-like reading of Quiroga's experiments: "Like many utopian communities, the settlements created by Quiroga had elements of a primitive socialism. Each person worked six hours a day and contributed on an equal basis to the common welfare" (p. 3). Tuck's conclusion is that "Tata Vasco" left an "indelible mark." Selective non-competitive craftsmanship is still in place in the region: "You go to Paracho for guitars, Tzintzuntzán [*sic*] for pottery, Santa Clara for copper products and Nurío for woven woolen goods." A typological synthesis finally brings history together: "The Spanish colonial era was one of astounding diversity. It could produce a daring conqueror like Cortés, a monster like Nuño de Guzmán and a reformer as enlightened and benevolent as Vasco de Quiroga." We take it that this is Tuck's "more serious, less lucrative" writing.

Not many people appear to disagree with this "Quiroga" who mostly amounts to the concrete sign for some resistence to domination. We still do not know why Tuck included this web page on Quiroga. This is the only one individualized page devoted to any one historical figure and there is no book attached to this information. A bait for potential customers with an appetite for things "historical"? Another historical name on the Mexican side to add to Tuck's travel-packed writing vitae? This rather sloppy presentation of ungrounded historical "facts" on Quiroga is, however, no sign of the weakness of the commonplace, but rather the opposite. The website medium, inside which Jim Tuck, Gianni Rotta and many others are located, sprawls Quiroga's commonplace of colonial law into the global political landscape with new and less than new information. This communicational platform, precisely because of the seductiveness of electronic paralogism, is also no doubt making a non-negligible contribution to the signification of colonial Latin America. It is also inside this imaginary site, with or without wires, that Quiroga is to be located, historically in relation to our contemporary meaning-making practices. There are surely many more Tucks, Silvestris and Rottas out there. That's why we decided, inside the narrow Quiroga-delineated circle of social signification, to make these sites representative of larger, invisible, seemingly free-floating expressivities which are not always, needless to say, convincing and persuasive. These, although constituting a rather long-lasting textual body of popular Quiroga, are clearly not. The digital culture already penetrated by consumerism may have already colorized the sign "Quiroga" and the sign "Colonial Latin America" well beyond the clumsy reach of our imagination. It is with this sudden realization that following chapters will suggest other interpretations in the hope that these surely impoverished soundbites may get altered, if ever so slightly.

8. Some Early Conclusions

To historicize our new thing with feathers, "utopia," in relation to the Hispanic tradition in relation to our imaginary ground of the early modern Americas, we have been quite explicit in that we must challenge the hegemonic socio-historical imagination in relation to both cultures of scholarship in English and Spanish. To display some restlessness at some of the customary, perhaps unconscious ways of talking, but also keeping silent about the city of equals, we have been here willing to follow the literalism of the name: early modern utopia is for us the rather obscure name of Vasco de Quiroga. We believe that the literalism in a work explicitly constructed upon the quicksands of this individual name, is still the winning card, at least initially: the existence and meaningfulness of American utopias is for us Quiroga. And we find this early modern utopianism historically intelligible mostly inside the repressive protocols of the official culture in the early colonial *Indias Occidentales*. We find this colonial utopianism meaningful and still inspiring mostly in relation to this new thing with Indian feathers: proto-egalitarian tendencies as having an impact upon the immense majority of the American population during Quiroga's lifetime. Yet, we have been quick to point out that intelligibility, or reasonableness, is—as it cannot be otherwise—also a historical creature, as is its negative cousin, unreasonableness. Consequently, we must logically defend that rationality and paralogism are tied up together with Quiroga's repressive culture, which is also not entirely unacquainted with authoritarianism and the rule of force. The harrowing expressivity of Quiroga's colonial literature will have to emerge out of these surely uneasy conditions of production.

Chapter one has hopefully carved out some utopian potential in the conventional utopian forest: early modern America is for us the inspirational country of utopian potential. To this exploration, we are willing to tread on the shimmering light of a single name, Vasco de Quiroga. This initial chapter has quantified and qualified the most comprehensive account yet on Quiroga. We have also dwelt on the predictabilities of the digital culture on Quiroga in the hope that these are not entirely meaningless. Now, what will follow is the critical exegesis of the individual trees: Quiroga's primary textual body. So, we will shift gears from the "about" Quiroga to the "by" Quiroga with and without all historically meaningful hesitations. Some dignified scholars will of course come with us along the way. Chapter two will look into the clockwork social orange of Quiroga's *Ordenanzas de Buen Gobierno* (1532), and some of the contradictions in his *Last Will* (1565); chapter three will analyze the various economic proposals for the reformation of coloniality in his most ambitious *Información en Derecho* (1535); and finally chapter four will look closely into the repressive contrasts between two small pieces, *De Debellandis Indis* (1552), and Nicolás León's edition of the *Juicio de Residencia* (1536). A historically complex and vital, also contradictory figuration of this colonial utopianism associated with the concrete name of Vasco de Quiroga should thus emerge fully to the historical imagination by the end of this work.

Quiroga's colonial literature is not cakes and ale. Unlike Frank Capra's easy rendition of victory over corruption in high places, the historical lesson of colonial Latin America as pertains to Quiroga's colonial utopianism is more subdued and quiet in its obvious goals, also harder to digest. When Quiroga, our designated Mr. Smith, goes to the Washingtons of early modernity, i.e. Mexico City, Valladolid and Salamanca, he will not be so naive as to want the political goals to come to his hands as easy and fast as a happy ending to a Hollywood film. What will follow is the complete textual evidence produced by, but also about, our high state official in his efforts to reform corrupt and criminal political structures in early New Spain. There will be no easy confessional moments, no sudden epiphanies and no happy evasions and endings. Quiroga's history is simply not out there, done away with in some dust-gathering collection of difficult texts, mostly forgotten in some foreign-sounding library. Quiroga's utopia of reconstruction, little to do with evasions, is not toast. Quite the contrary, Quiroga is for us the concrete name for the production of historicity which constitutes us. Whether we know it or not, whether we want to know it or not, we are Quiroga in the sense that we are history, inevitably in the making. And it is this sudden realization that we are all in the thick of history, i.e. that history is the pulsating vein underneath the skin, which we wish to call historicity. So, Quiroga's repressive literature is the historical creation which is hardly ever didactic, fun, and not entirely unacquainted with the flying bats with baby faces of authoritarianism and force. This repressive literature will surely make us grit our teeth more than once. Following chapters will have to substantiate as concretely as possible, our initial proposal for a meaningful colonial difference as pertains to early modern utopianism. To the critical analysis of each one of Quiroga's texts, we now turn.

Section of Juan O'Gorman's mural painting for the Gertrudis Bocanegra Federal Public Library in the city of Pátzcuaro. The original is included in Silvio Zavala's *Recuerdo de Vasco de Quiroga* (Grijalbo Mondadori, S.A., 1965).

Chapter II

ഇൗ ൽ

The Utopian Desire for a Regulated Society in a Colonial World: Quiroga's Ordenanzas *and Last Will*

1. Introduction

This chapter proposes the main hypothesis that political reformation (or utopianism)[1] in the foundational period of the colonization of the Americas must of necessity come with most, if not all, of the normative and prescriptive trappings of the law. It is not that colonial reformation cannot afford to neglect the already inevitable politico-juridicial discourse of the early modern state in the midst of perplexing crises and growth. It is rather that colonial reformation, in order to have any chance to make any difference, must of necessity internalize most of the normative or prescriptive protocols, textual and otherwise, proper to the tentacular hegemony of Spanish Indian Law (or *Derecho Indiano*).

Inside this vast, intricate jargon of authenticity, colonial utopianism will endeavor implicitly or explicitly to carve out, and certaintly with partial successes and abundant limitations, a differentiated social place for those social sectors, historically the majority of the American population, who officially had not much of a place, or none at all. Colonial utopianism will have to operate within and against this unreasonable negative of social degradation and try to make something good out of it. Still better, this utopian (un)doing within and against the colonial world will be inevitably conditioned by the social positioning of the main figure in these pages. Vasco de Quiroga's utopian legalism obviously does not come out of nowhere. It is the brainchild of the social circles in the vicinity of the Spanish Indian Law, the University-trained *letrado* in canon law. But it is also largely the product of the petty nobility, the *hidalgo*, and the high-ranking state official, the *oidor*, who felt the time-honored seductions of rigorous monasticism.

For all these interrelated influences, colonial utopianism does not come to us with a smiling countenance. We will see it assuming a rather severe, almost authoritarian formulation in the middle of fierce legal feuds over land and bodies. Quiroga's desire for reformation of the early colonial world does not quite fit into the still common understanding of early modern metropolitan utopianism. This norm of belletrist, humanist, metropolitan playground of the alphabetic letter is instead an almost unlivable forcefield for the majority of the American populations in the colonial context which directly concerns us here. We want to state clearly that this norm is simply no good for descriptive or normative purposes for the colonial Americas and that this work precisely grows out of this unfittingness. Political reformation in early colonial Mexico comes to all readers today with plenty of disagreeableness and severity, in its demands for drastic transformations always in the middle of truly dramatic living situations. In the blurry contours of the licit and the illicit, the historical lesson tells us that the (political) game was, as it is still today, a matter of life or death. There was no time to waste. Trying to hold on to some indigenous generational continuity, the reformation call will mostly be for a more strict regulation of the social body. This utopian legal intervention, perhaps the most lasting legacy of colonial reformation, was always on the verge of genocide.[2] We must accordingly give life support to our historical sensisibility and rearrange our mental furniture against most of the information gathered in the first chapter if we wish to look critically at the historical figure of Vasco de Quiroga.

To illustrate the quality of this colonial utopianism, we are proposing that our main subject Vasco de Quiroga (1470-1565), one of the four judges (*oidor*) of the highest judicial-political apparatus of the *Segunda Audiencia* (1530-1535), and later first Bishop of the diocese of Michoacán in the central-western part of Mexico since 1537,[3] exemplifies this distinct historical modulation of colonial utopianism. According to his two main biographers, Warren and Landa, Quiroga's most likely arrival in Mexico, as a man of the state, is not until the early days of 1531,[4] already a sextagenarian, only ten years after the destruction of the Aztec capital of Tenochtiltlán by Hernán Cortés, and four years before the arrival in New Spain of Viceroy Mendoza in 1535. The time frame for this work will be from 1531 to the death of Quiroga in Uruapan in 1565 at the biblical age of ninety-five.[5] It is the legacy of Quiroga's social practice during these 34 years on both sides of the Atlantic that helped him secure a brief niche in most encyclopedias. Barely known outside the national boundaries of Mexico, and scarcely mentioned by most scholars in the early modern period, we wish to break this silence and historicize critically the individual and collective significance of Vasco de Quiroga in relation to the slippery notion of utopianism. This sixteenth-century utopianism will prove to be almost entirely foreign, certainly unappealing and strongly unsettling (Tena Ramírez extends the longevity of Quiroga's legacy, as pertains to one of the institutions he founded, the Colegio de San Nicolás de Pátzcuaro, until the late date of 1872).[6] The much silenced legacy of Quiroga, inside international cultures of scholarship, reaches us today well after the ruins of Quiroga's institutions. This chapter will address two legal documents written by Quiroga. *The Rules and Regulations for the Government of the Hospitals of Santa Fé of Mexico and Michoacán* (1532), and, since endings often make good beginnings, the *Testament* (1565).

We are proposing that Quiroga signifies the quiet reformation of political structures in the colonial world. We understand quiet, or partial, in the historical sense of a political effort which tries to improve, but never dismantle or repudiate, the larger colonial status quo, which is to be largely considered chaotic and criminal especially in the foundational years (from the second half of the sixteenth until the second half of the seventeen century). We must advance that, perhaps to the surprise of most contemporary readers, utopianism (or political reformation) and the expansion of the West (or colonization) are not, in relation to our main subject, mutually exclusive. Quite the contrary the former is part and parcel of the latter. The political possession of the strongest, the Spanish Empire, is never, for our high state official, in dispute. The dispute instead refers exclusively to the regulatory conditions of such possession. The crisis of the Spanish Empire will be semanticized as an impassable historical opportunity for growth, but also an obligation, for the creation of a more egalitarian global commonwealth. We wish to qualify this reformation inside modernizing structures with a civilizational or ethnocentric prejudice, and we ascribe the value of a cause to the double crisis of the absolutist state and the severe decline of the indigenous population in the Americas to which Quiroga's legal reformation will be responding at its best. Quiroga's historical variety of colonial utopianism corresponds to the legal bureaucratization of this civilizational or transformative prejudice, not yet defunct.

We must undoubtedly take into account the social extraction of Quiroga, a sexagenarian peninsular and high state official by the time of his arrival in 1531 in New Spain, but also a lettered *hidalgo* and fundamentally a man well-versed in the intricacies of Spanish law.[7] Sixteenth century reformation will take place inside the high walls of the state, the social practice of the lettered privilege and the legal profession. And in Quiroga's case, we have the courageous, yet ultimately self-limiting scope and latitude of an individual intervention. Unlike the most enduring collective ventures of the mendicant orders of the Franciscans, Dominicans and Augustinians, of ample diffusion in New Spain, and of particular incidence in the Michoacán region, Quiroga's individual intervention will also manage to mobilize a considerable collective dimension. Quiroga, however, will have to enter into negotiations with these collective alternatives with quite considerable economic might and intellectual pedigree for the continuation of his visionary project after his death.

The contrast with the contemporaneous figure of Thomas More (1477-1535), explictly acknowledged as inspiration ("dechado") in Quiroga's most elaborate *Información en Derecho* (1531), will perhaps give us a better view of the social positioning of our main subject. It is already a classic account, in J. A. Maravall and others, to envisage the sixteenth and seventeenth centuries as a transitional period of highly praised creativity situated in the great divide of feudalism and capitalism.[8] Utopianism—Utopia is after all More's neologism—is historically confined to, and also defined by, the tensions and contradictions of this period in between two distinct modes of production. Maravall has traditionally characterized this historical transition with a pervasive feeling of exhaustion of old European forms and with an acute curiosity towards social experimentation mostly in the new horizon of the Americas recently encountered. This largely Europe-centered reformation will be the prodcut of the incipient figure of the bourgeoisie. More, a bourgeois despite himself in Maravall's account, will manufacture in *Utopia* (1515) the social contradictions of his class belonging.[9] The dream of a much improved society is produced in the early modern shadow of European expansionism. New Spain will historically give us the discreet charm of a parallel to this incipient bourgeoisie, the almost empty-handed and frequently illiterate *hidalgo* version of the soldier, and the University-trained and largely disinherited second sons of the petty nobility, engaged in the state or Church bureaucracies and generally wishing in the Americas for a way up the social ladder.

We are thus suggesting the most plausible historical condition of possibility for the manufacturing of colonial utopianism in early New Spain is one that is embodied in the social figure of the lettered *hidalgo*.[10] Quiroga was one of them.[11] Far from More's fictionalized account of an ideal polity, colonial utopianism will materialize repressively, explicitly in its repudiation of ambiguity of meaning. Our likely contemporary enjoyment as regards More's humanistic belletrism, the text of irony and double-entendre, will get a bit rarefied if we are reminded of the historical comforts and privileges of an incipient bourgeoisie, a social sector on the rise in the centuries to follow, which surely provided most of the few, happy members who had access to such a high culture—the lettered Latin artifact of *Utopia*—with the subject theme of the ideal polity. Quiroga's *ordenanzas* could not historically afford this kind of luxury.

More's Latin representation of an ideal polity will translate into a rather undisguised harshness of unlikely possibility in the Americas. Quiroga proposes to the highest authorities a critical reformation of the colonial world built upon a lapidarian, even authoritarian construction of social signification. With this goal, Quiroga's writings resist pleasantness and tastefulness. Nothing is more foreign to them than the quality of wit and playfulness. They are not the product of *otium*. Early modern literature rarely is, and early modern literature in the colonial world almost never is. Quiroga's *ordenanzas* instead constitute an arduous *negotium* in courtroom litigation.

There is another strong seductive inspiration to Quiroga's model of alternative life. Like More, our *hidalgo* and high state official will also approach social institutions parallel to, and oftentimes undistinguishable from, the centralizing state, namely ecclesiastical institutions. In the last twenty-five years of his life, the former judge Vasco de Quiroga will become the first bishop of the newly-created diocese of Michoacán established upon former Tarasca-Purépecha territory.[12] We must certainly incorporate the strict social codification of mendicant orders in our dealings with Quiroga's colonial utopianism.

Unlike the more secular notion of More, time-honored aesthetics of social asceticism, or monasticism, is a fundamental source of inspiration for colonial utopianism. The non-negotiable renunciation of individual ownership, the strict communitarian synchronism of social energies, and the centralization of monetarized wealth will be central ingredients to Quiroga's imagination of an alternative polity. Josefina Muriel has told us that in the village hospital of Nuestra Señora de la Concepción y Santa Marta in Pátzcuaro, "The regime of life was exceedingly severe."[13] Muriel also notes, "Whenever free from *Audiencia* obligations, Quiroga often retreated to his cell in the Hospital of Santa Fé under the guidance of the Augustinian friar Alonso de Borja." The severity of this Franciscan ethos permeates Quiroga's *ordenanzas*.

A monastic rigor is clearly perceptible in Quiroga's *ordenanzas* which here demand our close attention. These will constitute an unresolved combination of contradictory impulses, the rise of individualism and its firm negation, the rise of money and its prohibition, the tentacular growth of state legislation and the creation of para-state enclaves in an early century of the irrepressible advance of a capitalist global market economy.[14] Quiroga will be combining the conflictive trepidations of a prominent state official, truly a maker of social reality, with the seductions of iron-like obedience and monastic seclusion. Quiroga's call for reformation of selected sectors of the American society, inside the larger frame of a still largely incipient colonial world, will somehow manage to keep alive this truly heterogeneous amalgam of life options and tensions. Because of this tight knot of contradictory impulses, the Quiroga solution appears to be a distinctly early modern repressive instance. Let us take a close look into this.

2. The Inflexible Dictum of the Cenobitic Life

It appears quite plausible that a meagre, stale and foreboding quality of early modern utopian neutralization may be strongly related to the time-honored social institution of monasticism.[15] These regulated social forms, para-state forms if you will, considerably older than early modern statism, may be said to provide strong seductive models for utopian figurations of an Early Modern polity.[16] Such is the contention for Quiroga's *ordenanzas* (or rules). Quiroga is the individual condition of possibility for such monastic-inspired communitarianism to take place.

Social experimentation in colonial Mexico takes the form of rigid and disciplined regimentation. We may be allowed to speak of monasticism as a time-honored form of the institutionalization of social energies according to a strict dictum. The term "rule" thus acquires a meaning broader than our customary one. We dare equate monastic rule to worldview. The rule represents a worldview for communitarian purposefulness. The rule is the only habitat and it is non-negotiable. Obedience is instead the sole commendable social practice. Monastic life is indeed profound communitarianism constructed upon an inflexible or ritualistic, also cherished ideal of renunciation (or *canonica vita*). One is tempted to say that the rule may well operate like a broad horizon of expectations and conditions of (im)possibilities, which provides a desirable social fittingness and closure to the complete subordination of the individual member to the social sphere of a same-sex cloistered existence.

The rule forces a series of straight edges upon this secluded social realm, the rule "keeps it straight" in the etymological sense, and arranges with no exceptions regular patterns of global predictability of roles and duties. The strength of the rule-as-the-ideal comes precisely from the fearful symmetry of this being-one-with-the-community which may be exemplified, for instance, in the homophonic quality of Gregorian chant until today (the Benedictine Monks of Santo Domingo de Silos of Spain for instance, recently popularized in the US). We may understand this fearful symmetry in the radical and faceless sense of almost ahistorical egalitarianism. The rule is after the clockwork intensification of an achieved synchronism of the social polity. "Rectus," "straight" and "true" in the carpenter's sense, communal and homophonic in unvarnished repudiation of liberal tolerance or individual expressivity, a meaningless phrase and truly an anachronism here.[17] Expressivity is, for example in the rule of St. Benedictine, the prescription of silence, the prohibition of laughter, a structured cell life in fundamental solitariness.

The monastic ideal exemplifies a strong desire for the total triumph of the rule. That is, the subject-work-in-project (the monk) must inhabit in complete obedience the explicit dictum of the rule without leaving any feature of his life outside an inflexible communitarian life rhythm (we wish to recall Andrei A. Tarkovskij's magnificent opening in *Sacrifice* (1986)—the glass of water, the bicycle and the dead tree—for a delicate recreation of some of this monastic ethos). In claiming to approach a sacred quality of human existence, the rule must be "totalitarian" and ubiquitous, or nothing. The rule is not to be negotiated. Sacredness is (re)produced and heightened by the collective mechanism of ritualization inflexibly prescribed by the rule. It is mainly by virtue of self-discipline and devotion that the individual makes it his. There can be no relaxation of the normative rigors, except some temporary relaxation for the sick and the elderly. For all those who are willing to commit to the monastic rule, there is no imaginable, desirable life outside the rule.

By virtue of this aesthetics of renunciation, the rule claims an essentialization of life into profoundly depersonalized communitarianism. Still better, depersonalization is rather the unrelenting task towards a full Christian persona. By making these rigors a warm habitation, an increasingly disciplined way of life immersed in an ideal of non-negotiable dispossession—total dispossession or nothing—must come into practice with no respite. Thus shaking up the world of owners, the rule becomes renunciation to the extreme Christological degree of self-sacrifice. The monk's individuality is never enough. Such unbearably individual lightness of being must persevere, after the imitation of the model of Christ, in the daily sacrifice of the *cenobia*. Faithfulness to this model must be cheerful. Cell-contained solitariness becomes *convivio*, or the ideal of Christian-life-as-banquet, and *conversatio*, or the ideal of commonwealth-as-uninterrupted fellowship, is of timely figural use in both Quiroga and More. A certain paradox must be highlighted here, an intense ritualistic synchronicity of privation of social intercourse paradoxically intensifies and gives hitherto unforeseeable new depth to an uninterrupted fellowship. The monastic fellowship is unavoidably universal. The ritualization of the mutual participation, or communion, is said almost to deliver the sublunary illusion of timelessness (or ahistorical illusion). It is as though only through an unbreachable commitment to dispossession, turning deprivation into a contented state of privation so to speak, that the monk may thus effectively bring about an acute awareness of unrestricted being together with other (wo)men (or fellowship). The monastic ideal operates with a paradoxically Christian logic of the more exiguous, the more meaningful. The monk embraces with sedulous obedience, humility and gratitude, the imperatives of the rule, until he finds delight in the concrete imperatives of the rule (the "sloth of disobedience" is the other darker side of the Benedictine ideal of observance or *devotio*). For a committed monk, the rule is no other than a gift. The rule is an endless, full-time mission for which he knows he will never be good enough.

Quiroga will seek the cooperation with the Franciscans, Augustianians and the less mendicant Jesuits, for his village-hospitals. This does not at all mean that there will be no tensions, quite the contrary at the legal table of negotiation of diocese jurisdictions. Monasticism will have a particularly strong incidence in sixteenth century Michoacán.[18] Among the most salient and general features of monasticism, which will find a way into Quiroga's rules, we may include the following: the breathtaking resilience of these rigorous social forms, the 1,500-year-old Benedictine rule, 1,600-year-old

Rule of St. Augustine, a breathtaking conciseness of formulation, oftentimes only a few pages, as regards the commonality of all goods and the total prohibition of individual property,[19] same-sex structuration of the secluded social realm, the increasing regimentation of the life in common, or *cenobia*, the social structuration in the *via negativa*, sexual renunciation or chastity, frugality in food and clothing, rotatory arrangement of social functions, compulsory manual labor, withdrawal from public sight and the orthodox framework of society, restriction of movement and cell confinement, a strenuous intensification of egalitarianism to a desirable impersonality, togetherness of living experience to the point of etymological distortion of "monk" by St. Augustine,[20] and the extremity of rigorous annihilation of the will via the total habitation of the explicitness of the rule. We are clearly in the historical antipodes of today's liberal format of dialogic, seemingly free-floating negotiation of social meanings.

The life-world becomes monastic life in the ritualization process of communal patterns of regularity and predictability after the explicit objective of social unanimity activated by charity (love is "treating with affectionate regard" in the etymological Greek sense). Charity is here an imperative towards the forging of an uninterrupted social continuum in careful balance of isolation and communitarian ritualizations. Unanimity will thus be constantly brought to the ritualized extremity of fusion of individual intentionality, thought and praxis (we may consequently try to imagine incipient early modern incursions of individuation into eminently pre-individualistic organizations with no generalized divisions of private and public).[21] The monastic rule intends no less than the extremity of individual annihilation from purpose, thought and action inside a largely pre- and post-individualist era. The paradoxical oddness, to us, of the juxtaposition of privation-as-need, or the virtue of dispossession, produces the monastic ideal of depersonalization, or *tabula rasa* which we will see explicitly articulated in Quiroga's *Información en Derecho* (1535), inside the strict regimentation of a synchronized collectivity constructed around the inflexible ritualization of the numeral (*mensura* or measure, *ordo* or *ordenanza*, *regula*, regulation or order). Early modern utopianism is unintelligible if detached from these notions. The larger early modern European expansionism into the Americas is unintelligible if dissociated from the urban *traza* or chessboard design, the clock-ticking *structuration* of indigenous labor and the inflexible prohibition of errancy or vagrancy (the Spanish language lends itself quite effortlessly into etymological adventures as regards the settlements or *asentamientos* of all despicable emptiness or *vacar*). Quiroga's early modern utopianism in the colonial world laid out open by these historical forces will be trying to construct a legal personality for the Tarascan-Purépecha communities very close to this indeed uncompromising monastic ideal of loss of inherited and personal attributes.

This Christian paradox spells out quite harshly that individual volition wants to destroy all that has supported its way up until the monastic moment. Its ultimate goal is no less than the annihilation of the self. The "fashioning of the [monastic] self," to use Greenblatt's language, is a drastic enterprise which "cuts" it into a sharp regimentation and secluded life for the promises of a radical metamorphosis. This unprecedented renewal must of necessity let go all the appurtenances which have been giving sustenance until that monastic moment. Individual volition wills not to be its own self, but an incomprehensible, inapprehensible other, conceptualized as sacred and always within the measures of the rule a-logically beyond all measure.

The 24 hours of the day and the 365 days of the year are thus scrupulously departmentalized into duties arranged by the unquestionable authority of the rule (Muriel has given us convincing descriptions of these rigors in Quiroga's hospitals). The monastic vision places the abbot in the role of benevolent and dutiful father to each monk. The abbot has absolute and undisputed authority. Everything must be carried out with his approval. In true cenobitic life, there is no excess of the abbot's law.[22] And there can't be excessive devotion to the horizon open by the good of the rule. The law/ yoke of the rule is transparent and lapidarian. The sedulous monk must follow to the letter of the rule and must also belabor to find delight in the scrupulous observation of the rule. Punishment of negligence is not to be neglected (physical punishment, restriction for communal lunch, separation from communal activities, even exile and excommunication).

The monastic construction of a desirable commonwealth represents the undisputed mono-vocal primacy of the faceless or pre-individualistic commonwealth. The letter of the law is the common welfare and the perfection of the commonwealth is its self-contended isolation.[23] The incorporation by Vasco de Quiroga's colonial reformation of the monastic ideal represents the historical paradox of the reinvention of old and resilient social forms in response to the incipient reconfigurations of primitive accumulation and money economy (we must remember the concept of money was a ground-breaking novelty in the Americas). Seclusion and self-sustenance respond to the expansionist crisis of the centralized state allocating tremendous colonial impositions of forced labor upon a majority of the indigenous population in the Americas. The aggravation of forced labor conditions will bring these populations in Quiroga's times close to extinction. The long-time achievement of legal exemptions regarding these colonial impositions for the populations settled in Quiroga's village-hospitals meets, however, with the rare occurrence of dispensation from internal monastic rigors. Monasticism, or the social aesthetics of cherished privation, inside the largely distressing early colonial configurations, constitutes no doubt a communal and radical sensibility to be seriously taken into account in relation to our main subject, if only in the strict and ritualized observance of a few good rules.

3. The Quiet Reformation of a Colonial World: Quiroga's *Ordenanzas*

We are perhaps now in a better position to move into Quiroga's rules and regulations as pertain to the two hospital-villages of Santa Fé de México and Santa Fé de Michoacán. Quiroga's colonial utopianism, I wish to repeat, cannot settle for the tiny rewards of literary irony. There is indeed very little playfulness in Quiroga's legal constructions, if any. Nothing is quite so foreign to Quiroga's vision as the contemporary celebrations of spontaneity and lawlessness, our likely predilection for chance operations or the apparent liberations of unstructured and seemingly unrestrained "free time" miraculously left alone by tentacular labor demands.[24]

Worlds apart from the festive *otium* for the happy few, Quiroga's utopianism represents a rather unpleasant kind of *negotium* against the surely unpleasant background of colonial genocide. In the shadowy fringes of hegemonic social forces which bring about the "colonization of the life-world" of the Americas,[25] Quiroga's reformation for the life of the majoritarian or indigenous populations is manufactured religously, repressively with no dispensations.

It is at the historical crux by the historical anomaly of the "I," the foundational gesture of the high state official, and the arresting cenobitic solicitations for the dissolution of all individual idiosyncracies, that we must place Quiroga's historical condition of possibility for the social experimentation commonly called village-hospitals (literally, "pueblos-hospitales"). It is crucial to highlight, taking the fork of the road as it were, that the early modern understanding of the notion of "hospital" is certainly far richer than it is today. We would like to risk the generic definition that an early modern hospital is the place where the eradication of poverty is expected to take place.[26] The early modern notion of hospital presses harder the also generic notion of hospitality towards the satisfaction of communal need. It is perhaps an unnecessary redundance to remark that poverty takes place among the most fragile social sectors (what today gets called "minorities"). In early New Spain, we must imagine the fat institutional neglect of the needs of the immense majority of the American population.

So, early modern hospitals theoretically aim at dismantling the greatest enemy of the commonwealth, poverty. Despite the generalized silence, we do not doubt that the international humanist Luis Vives (1492-1540),[27] is, side by side with the official father of the neologism of utopia, the English scholar Thomas More (1477-1535), also quite a strong influence for our *oidor*. Despite the missing link in the traceable sources for Quiroga,[28] we find it indeed difficult to believe that Quiroga was not acquainted, if only by hearsay with the most social dimension of Luis Vives's scholarship. I am thinking of the *De Subventione Pauperum* (1525).[29]

It is perhaps easy to see that these early modern notions of "hospital" and *subventio* do not quite lend themselves effortlessly to our contemporary notions of hospital and welfare system. In relation to our immediate context of New Spain, the generalized uneven and hierarchical allocation of one- or two-generation landowning possibilities by royal prerogative (*encomiendas*, *mercedes* and later *haciendas*),[30] the institution of the "hospital" appears to be mostly the brainchild of monasticism. Hospitals emerged historically in the Americas with the consent of early modern statism. And there were many.

We are not particularly interested in claiming immaculate originality for Quiroga's enterprise in relation to the Franciscans and Augustinians (this isolated claim strikes us as almost entirely banal and certainly ahistorical).[31] We are not interested in the opposite, in furnishing the dissipation of Quiroga's legacy amid the surely more encompassing forces of colonial monasticism (comparative task which, although quite plausible, surely exceeds the scope of this work).[32] We rather wish to make Quiroga, for the limited purposes of this work's format, representative of the historical possibilities for change, a valid synonym for utopianism, in the colonial context of early New Spain. The hospitality provided by colonial hospitals must be put historically together with this non-fictional institutionalization of early modern utopianism.

Yet we need to be cautious about either stretching too much the differentiation or the dedifferentiation of these monastic groups and the state apparatus, both of them expanding in the Americas, in a historical time which rather saw their profound collaboration and interpenetration.

The institutionalization of this collaboration, namely the *Patronato Real*,[33] made early modern hospitals a flourishing reality in New Spain.[34] Such hospitals, and Quiroga's fit into this official pattern almost perfectly,[35] allowed for some relatively strong possibilities for indigenous self-goverment, relative ethnic protection, tax-exemptions and some temporary or permanent dispensations from the generalized colonial practice of forced labor.[36] The structuration of tithes, inside the system of imperial taxation, obviously provided the regularity of income necessary for the maintenance and attendance of the hospital commonwealth. So, we must imagine Quiroga's collectivities inside a much larger, variegated archipelago of hospital communities under several religious denominations. Muriel's estimate follows upon Nicolás León's: the population was 30,000 for the hospital of Santa Fé de México alone.[37] We must consider it a peak number certainly fluctuating in the early colonial times of epidemics and privations.

It is safe to say that the colonial hospital tries to become a self-sufficient and, for the most orthodox early modern vocabulary, a perfect polity. The colonial hospital tries to become a relatively separated entity. Relative seclusion from a relatively underregulated and generally dangerous colonial world is the objective. This is done, as we will immediately see, by furnishing the hospital life with severe regulations which bind ethnic communities (the Tarascan-Purépecha to Quiroga's hospitals, for example). In the historical horizon of the hegemonic ideology of race purity (*limpieza de sangre*), the hospitals will tend to seal themselves off from the early teething troubles and whirling confusions of the colonial world around pre- and post-Hispanic ethnic ties.

This relatively secluded hospital settlement is tending towards the political ideal of perfection of relatively independent collective life-maintainance. Muriel remarks quite strikingly, "In relation to the *República del Hospital Real* de Santa Fé de la Laguna, there were no poor [people]" (my emphasis).[38] Strictly speaking, the hospital, under the umbrella terms of Spanish nomenclature, closely tries to resemble an indigenous commonwealth, with indigenous leaders often with Spanish-sounding names (at least in public documents). Muriel also mentions that the "first rector [of Santa Fé], following upon the dispositions of the *oidor*, was an Indian of royal Tarascan blood, called don Pedro [*sic*], who was a great support to the Quiroguian project."[39] Based upon these observations, the colonial "hospital" is thus clearly a momentary habitat constructed upon pitiable, random alms. Quiroga's hospital is mostly the new world translation of the humanist ruminations of More's fictional republic, but also—and we are here breaking into scholarly silence some tentative new ground—of Luis Vives's political proposals for the reformation of a commonwealth with no poverty. Early modern utopianism in the Americas will try to come close to this ideal of a relatively poverty-free commonwealth for selected pockets of indigenous peoples.

The qualitative jump is hence quite considerable, no doubt for us today, from Vives's exceedingly polite Latin ruminations in his exile in the city of Bruges (Belgium), passing through the Latin ironies of the English chancellor, to Quiroga's legal record often transcribed by *escribanos* in quite broken Spanish grammar inside the largely non-Spanish Americas. Quiroga's oral argument in his *ordenanzas* interpellate those who could not possibly have read them, the Tarascan-Purépecha communities in the vicinity of the new city of Valladolid (today Morelia).

We feel we must disagree with Zavala's classic pronouncement on the humanism of Quiroga.[40] We do not find entirely persuasive Pagden's suggestions either.[41] Following the path illuminated by M. M. Lacas,[42] we will not hesitate instead to state that Quiroga is first and foremost a man of state, of *hidalgo* social origin. Quiroga, trained in canon law, was never a professional writer and never intended to become one. His social profile is better understood in between the perhaps two leading social forces in the early modern period, absolutist state and monasticism. We are willing to accept that generic label for Quiroga of social welfare reformer, as long as we tie together some of the density of early modern notions of republic or commonwealth and *beneficencia*. If the imperial, expansionist design is never in serious question, political reformation needed the localized seclusion of hospital habitation for the most fragile social sectors, routinely called "Indians." Inside this hospital format, it is also perfectly possible to see subgroups of *cofradías* or *confraternitates*.[43] Let us now take a closer look into the harsh normativity of these social arrangements.

Within the historical landscape of allocation of lands and peoples into individual private and named ownerships, the hospital objective of gradual seclusion is modelled after a strict prohibition of ownership. The internal cancellation of individual proprietorship appears initially structured upon a diligent application to manufacturing and the mechanical arts. Quiroga's rules and regulations (*reglas* and *ordenanzas*)[44] start off by emphasizing the encomium of utilitarianism, the prohibition of idleness ("otros [oficios] vanos, inútiles y viciosos"), inside a strict and silent, guild-like regimentation of mechanical labor and social function (weavers, mine diggers, carpenters, construction workers, blacksmiths). Quiroga's *ordenanzas* initially convey to a contemporary reader the illusion of a rather silent and non-traumatic landscape of hard-working and efficient laborers.

Yet, within a nameless egalitarian frame, the fundamental social activity will be, already since childhood, agriculture. Within the horizon of agrarianism, the hospital construction of social egalitarianism will mean synchronized and measured application to the compulsory labor of agricultural duties. Attending to the lowest and fundamental human denominator of need, the biological imperative of eating so to speak, the political mobilization of the rule attends to the fulfillment of the biological and proclaims the "two or three days of work from sunrise to sunset per week" ("podrá salir a dos, o tres días de trabajo de sol a sol en la semana"), which translates into a total of six working hours ("seis horas del trabajo en común"). We only need to remember the official stipulations by the *Laws of Burgos* (1512-1513),[45] the *New Laws* (1542-1543)[46] and Hernán Cortés's *Ordenanzas* (1519-1520),[47] to see the glittering impact of the number six. Centuries later, the English working schedule was no lighter load.[48]

Toil for life will be sharply distributed to everyone within the boundaries of moderation ("poco, fácil, moderado"). Agricultural activity, truly the most encompassing activity in the period, becomes the fundamental social grammar inside Quiroga's commonwealth, much in the same way that Christian doctrine is the sole official text to be taught. Early modern utopianism in the Americas has no traffic with tolerance in relation to the belief system. No exceptions are tolerated in relation to both the measured rigor of labor and Christian rituals. Theoretically, and in marked contrast to More's vision, there is no slavery inside Quiroga's hospital precincts. Supervisors, the *Rector* (or he who "sets the social straight"), and *Regidores* (they who conduct the social straight), will be appointed periodically and they will be obeyed with no hesitation ("en todo obedeceréis y acataréis en lo justo, y honesto, y conforme a estas *ordenanzas*, y en lo tocante a ellas, sin resistencia, ni contradicción alguna desacatada [*sic*], ni maliciosa").

In strong contrast to the expected agrammaticality of the *cédulas*,[49] we find here a pervasive grammaticality of political reform exclusively in the Castilian language. Against Cortés's indeed brutal series of "hordeno [*sic*] y mando," readers will find in the *ordenanzas* an attenuated seriality (the "*que* +(no)+subjunctive" construction). In both cases however, we are dealing with a prescriptive textuality which demands the rather severe regimentation of the polity.

Quiroga's differentiation is not done without internal tensions. His recorded insistence on being diligent in responding to imposed rules points in the direction of some internal other of the rule—or misrule—that must be kept under control:

> [A]sí lo hagáis y obedezcáis y cumpláis según vuestras fuerzas, y con toda voluntad y posibilidad, y ofreciéndoos a ello, y al trabajo de ello, pues tan fácil y moderado es, *y ha de ser como dicho es*, y no rehusándole, ni os escondiendo, ni os apartado, ni excusando de él, vergonzosa, perezosa y feamente, *como lo soléis hacer* salvo si no fuera por enfermedad. (my emphasis)

Following a monastic inspiration, dispensations as to the rigors of the rule will only be granted exceptionally to the sick and the elderly. The thorough construction of sameness of production, identical agricultural toil for six hours' work, finds the other side of distribution of wealth according to need so that need, once it is annihilated and satisfied, may not have a place in the commonwealth. As stipulated by the Augustinian rule following the Biblical inspiration of the first Christian community (Acts, 4.35), "provided no one is denied what he needs," Quiroga's utopianism targets on social fundamentals,

> [Que] se reparta entre vosotros todos, y cada uno de vos en particular aeque [*sic*] congrua [*sic*], cómoda y honestamente, según que cada uno, según su calidad, y necesidad, manera y condición lo haya menester para sí, y para su familia, de manera que ninguno padezca en el Hospital necesidad.

Placing a greater emphasis on the production of wealth, rule stipulations as regards the distribution appear to have been neglected (the archaism *congruamente* is surely left to the supervisors' interpretive skills).

The regulated usufruct of social wealth, or *common*-wealth, is strictly circumscribed to an unambiguous delimitation of the territory and the permanent residence in it of its citizens for the generations to come. Restricted traffic and commerce with a hostile outside will be enforced:

> [S]olamente habeis de tener el usufructo de ello tanto cuanto en el dicho Hospital moraderes, y no más, ni aliende, para que en vacando por muerte o por ausencia larga hecha sin licencia legítima, y expresa del Rector y Regidores, se den a vuestros hijos o nietos, mayores casados pobres, por su orden y prioridad.

Bearing in mind the larger historical context of indigenous decimation, an almost monastic life-commitment to the narrow confines of the hospital territory, as well as scrupulous obedience to the established authority of the appointed officials, is an intertwined non-negotiable prerequisite for the timely care (or providence) of the needs of present and following generations. Usufruct of social wealth (the wide use of the archaism of *granjería* and *beneficios*), is thus constructed in the tight clockwork regulation of social obligations, restriction of traffic and travel, and solid submission to an unmistakably non-consensual patrilineal political centralization of the hospital commonwealth. If this colonial situation may be appropriately described as the formal agreement of a covenant, should we be allowed to use this notion in relation to the *ordenanzas*, it is without doubt a unilateral covenant (we have no way of knowing for certain any [formal] responses from the interpellated *vosotros*).

The good place and the non-place for the generational continuity of the Tarascan-Purépechas meets with the implementation of an inflexible social pattern of repetition and uniformity. Quiroga's prescriptive textuality, built upon an unrelenting, almost monotonous seriality, almost mimicks at another level the foundational disposition of the colonial Spanish grid for new settlements (the *traza* still perceptible in the colonial sections of most contemporary capitals in Latin America until to this day). It is not too difficult to notice the dry schematism of social construction in Quiroga's *ordenanzas*. It is also not difficult to notice an impatient, almost hurried quality in the prose, a desire for literalism.

Quiroga's colonial reformism abhors any legal relaxation into an amorphous social body (the "fomes" of sin in Aquinas). This reformed social body must of necessity pass through regimented and symmetrical patterns of demarcation and predictability: sameness. Our present distaste might have perhaps been the delight of the men and women in the sixteenth century. Social spontaneity was a non-issue, was not a choice.[50] This adjusted social geometry appears to be particularly true for colonial utopianism.[51] The construction of a strict spatialization and timely coincidence, or synchronization, which may strike contemporary readers as restrictive, if not altogether asphyxiating, must always be put in relation to the official awareness of the precariousness of the colonial norm, at least by the mid-sixteenth century. We must imagine Quiroga's desire for social predictability within a generalized unpredictability or criminality. Synchronism may be an early modern approximation to the abstract and utopian ideal of social standardization or egalitarianism. In this sense, the construction of a space for the indiscriminate and faceless usufruct of the "social good" needs protectionist measures *via negativa*:

> [D]e manera que cosa alguna, que sea raíz, así del dicho Hospital, como de los dichos huertos, y familias, *no* pueda ser enajenado en el dicho Hospital, y Colegio de Santa Fe, para la conservación, mantención y concierto de él, y de su hospitalidad, *sin* poderse enajenar, *ni* conmutar, trocar, *no* cambiar en otra cosa alguna y *sin* salir de él en tiempo alguno, *ni* por manera otra alguna que sea, o ser pueda, por cuanto esta es la voluntad de su Fundador. (my emphasis)

The hospital is thus constructed in the form of the island-like fortress, which negates, or tries to, exchange and transaction in the ocean of hegemonic proprietorship rights and the circulation of money. Quiroga's *negative* legalism always tries to keep the land-wealth of the hospital undividable for the centuries to come. Tena Martínez, as we already mentioned, extends the legal extinction of the Colegio de *San Nicolás de Pátzcuaro* until the late date of 1872. *The Universidad Michoacana de San Nicolás de Hidalgo* claims the vitality of this legacy until today.

In this reformed agrarian culture, no single "good," movable or not, circumscribed to the supposedly utopian terrain is allowed to be exchanged in any economic transaction without the approval of the appointed supervisors. A fierce sense of belonging and attachment to land, as though life depended on it, is unmistakably in place in Quiroguian repressive diction. Inside the true maze of *Indian Law* semanticization of newly acquired territories and peoples, hospital boundaries must be constantly supervised ("que visiten a lo menos una vez en el año los términos y tierras del Hospital, y remueven los mojones de ellas, si fuere menester, conforme a la Escritura de amojonamiento de las tierras, y términos del Hospital"). It is as though the utopian neutralization of the verosimilitude of private interest ("apropiandolo cada uno para sí lo que pudiese, y sin cuidado de sus prójimos, como es cosa verosímil que sería,…procurar lo propio, y menospreciar lo común que es de los pobres"), necessitates the non-ambiguous delimitation of a truly vital space. Quiroga's long-time juridical fights, which we will comment on later on, will precisely come into being as to the delimitations of boundaries and jurisdictions.

Quiroga's rules make a certainly excessive claim: to manufacture the extinction of social need ("donde vivais sin necesidad, y [con] seguridad, y sin ociosidad, y fuera del peligro e infamia de ella"). In this imaginary effort for the satisfaction of need, a tension in the very process of signification must no doubt occur: If the repressive quality of the law flourishes in an explicit construction, Quiroga's rules will coexist with intermittent future-oriented allegories of social satisfaction.

This historical contradiction has it that the non-negotiable rigidity of the good law, say, the concreteness of six working hours, simultaneously produces the excess of the law in the occasional fracture of literal signification into time-honored and patristic levels of interpretation. In relation to excessive allegory, we may call these levels of interpretation qualities of abstract signification. This signification process may be said to be the following: the colonization of the life-world is repudiated in a prescriptive textualization which targets on a clear desire for a strict political regimentation; this chimerical, almost untenable political regimentation must however thin out into a higher level of abstraction:

> [F]uera del peligro de las tres fieras bestias que todo en este mundo lo destruyen y corrompen, que son soberbia, codicia, y ambición de que os habeis, y os deseamos mucho guardar y apartar, quitándoos lo malo, y dexándoos lo bueno de vuestras costumbres, manera, y condición, como en toda buena policía.

The ideal commonwealth (the archaism of *buen policía*), must hence fight off against the three depolitized beasts of ambition, pride and selfishness. Occasional allegorical contortions will take Quiroga's corsetted diction, and his otherwise quite tangible reformist polity, into the thin air of a still insufficiently verbalized and abstract possibility:

> [Q]ue de nuevo se hay de dar a personas semejantes, que de ella y de prudencia tienen tanta necesidad, como vosotros teneis, se debe hacer, y conviene se haga, que es, y ha de ser conforme a la calidad, y manera, y condición de la gente a quienes se da, y según sus faltas, calidad, y necesidades, y capacidad, conservándoles siempre lo bueno, que tenga, y no destruyéndolo, ni trocándoselo por lo que no les cuadra, ni conviene (según suerte, y manera de vivir, entendimiento, estado y condición) y les sea a ellos más dañoso, que provechoso, y a su buena Cristiandad, y principios de ella, que conviene mucho sean buenos y bien concertados, ordenados y encaminados, sobre prudencia Cristiana, y que no vayan a dar en despeñaderos de almas, y cuerpos, como en algunas partes van, y se suele hacer, que es quitarles lo bueno, que tienen de humildad, obediencia, paciencia, y poca codicia, y la buena simplicidad, y dexarles, y ponerles lo malo, y contrario de ello.

In this above Manichaean design, figurations of vices and virtues fight over this view of "a kind of huddling of destitute bodies together for warmth"[52] over the "precipice of bodies and souls" waiting for the coming of "Christian timeliness" (providence) to deliver regimentation ("bien concertados, ordenados y encaminados"). Quiroga's diction in the *ordenanzas* must remain for some reason abstract, but only intermittently. In the middle of these rather colorless lists of regulations, the temptation to allegorical implosion of signification must have been strong for our high official (as a kind of necessary drinking excess and following hangover in the middle of round-the-clock bureaucratic paperwork). But it is kept restrained for the most part. We'll have to return to this restraint soon.

The regulation of the reformed social polity does not seem to have any internal clear-cut boundaries. Generalized panopticon visibilty cuts across unlikely hospital divisions of the private and the public spheres. The strong suggestion is, on the contrary, that everything is political and that everything is a public matter. As in More and Campanella,[53] Quiroga's rules pay close attention to a strict regimentation of social patterns of reproduction. The still recent, by 1565, Western importation of life-long monogamic and heterosexual coupling will be the inflexible norm inside the hospital confines. Although structured in larger family-units, the monogamic coupling is the exclusive legalized channel for social reproduction. It is as though the central maker of social manners in the colonial world, the *hidalgo*,[54] who suffered expulsion from the medieval institution of the *mayorazgo* in the old world, could not or did not want to remove himself from the same restrictive pattern of social wealth in the new colonial world. Theoretically everlasting monogamic arrangements, become the official conductors of private property in the colonial world. These arrangements become with little doubt an internally structural condition of imposition for social reproduction in Quiroga's communities. Yet, there is no private property in Quiroga's hospitals. It is no doubt a matter of curiosity why Quiroga's normativity would subscribe to this narrowly defined blood-related genealogy inside the hospital confines when there is no need—it is in fact impossible—to make any claims to individual property.

Yet, with no exceptions in Quiroga's Santa Fé commonwealths, all teenagers, of ages fourteen for males and twelve for females, must be socially distributed in life-long couple arrangements with slight regard for their preferences. In similarly repressive fashion, a seemingly idyllic kindergarten for the learning process of children is instituted. A gender divide applies since, despite the commonality of the hours of Christian doctrine, the males learn the office of agriculture two days per week, one or two hours per day in a leisurely way ("ésto a manera de regocijo, juego y pasatiempo"), the females learn womanly duties ("oficios mujeriles"), such as weaving.[55] Biological parents must supervise their progeny in the diligent application to all social duties. Should they be declared inefficient supervisors, the *Rector* and *Regidores* will replace them with better supervisors preferably within the larger family structure.

The hospital commonwealth is structured according to the logic of patriarchy and seniority. The eldest male sits in the most prestigious "chair" of social conductor ("el más antiguo Abuelo será el que en la familia presida, y a quien han de acatar, y obedecer toda la familia"). Quiroga's rules construct a hierarchical gender-based structure of obedience: children must obey their biological parents, women must obey their husbands, and all parents must obey theirs in an all-encompassing social group, or family, structured around a restricted male-lineage configuration formed by a total of ten or twelve married men. The hospital hierarchization of social roles takes care of the enforcement of the rules and the punitive dimension of neglicence ("la línea recta...dar razón de los excesos y desconciertos"). A surveillance of the enforcement of the rule and the punishment of possible relaxations of social duties are constantly enforced. Like the abbot in the monastery, the Father of the family, or the appointed substitute, is generally exempted from agricultural work in order to fulfil supervisory duties ("para que no sean perezosos en la labor del campo"). The Father figure, who is to be a model, will be encouraged to work in the fields. If the rigors of discipline relax, fatherly supervision will be replaced.

A strict distribution of the population inside the hospital precincts and tight controls of travel into the surroundings are to be enforced. There is a distinction between urban and rustic families. Whereas the former units stay closer to the center of the hospital, the latter appear to operate more like satellites. Yet, all the families rotate periodically. Every two years, four or six married persons ("cuatro casados o seis"), have to live in the more distant or sentinel posts, while the concentration of the population remains in the hospital commonwealth proper. There is a rotation every two years for those who may wish to leave back and settle among the urban families in the Hospital. These more rural enclaves are also regularly supervised by appointed personnel (or *veedores*).

In prevention of possible years of scarcity ("porque siempre os sobre y nunca os falte"), a centralized crop-raising plan is carefully set in place. The implementation of sedentary agrarian culture means a desirable abundance of all kinds of Castile poultry, and all kinds of domestic animals such as sheep, goats, cows, and pigs. Oxen appear to have been particularly welcome since they are not very expensive, and the hide, the meat and the fat can be all put to good use. A profitable usufruct may therefore be produced (the *granjería* of the *esquilmo* in the original language). A faceless landscape of measured and efficient farming activity in small land portions (or *huertos*) is also sanctioned by Quiroga's rules.

In the utopian goal of the domestication of chance operations, strict numeral precision regarding social wealth is crucial. In clear fascination with the number two, every two years, double production of what is needed, or a third of the ordinary production, will be the official goal. Almost incorporating the inflexible regular patterns of the monastic ideal, the hospital commonwealth will turn into a rotatory mechanism of season-imprinted agriculture. The utopian goal will be the domestication and prevention of all the unpredictabilities and uncertainties proper to agrarianism.[56]

Quiroga's rules provide these hospital communities with a succinct plan for the synchronized socialization, or ritualization, of measured toil for life. Patterns of regularity and predictability also apply to the restricted commerce and traffic with the hostile outside. The surplus of accumulated wealth is not to be sold to some dystopian locations under any circumstances, unless there be true signs of a fertile year coming:

> [L]o cual nunca enageneis, ni vendais, ni os desagais de lo que así sobrare en los años fértiles…después que esteis seguros que el año próximo siguiente no puede faltar por ciertas conjeturas naturales, que de ello tengais, podais vender el dicho depósito con toda fidelidad, y buen recaudo, depositar en su lugar que se hubiere por ello debajo de fiel custodia, con todo lo demás, que se hubiere en común.

Resisting an unconditional integration into an incipient economy of profit-making exchange, Quiroga's project is built upon the structuring of an equal participation in the production of goods and upon a relative neglect in the distribution of these goods. As in More, colonial utopianism thematizes an exaltation of use value, or almost instantaneous utility, over a relative deregulation of exchange value. In this land of presumably endless abundance, the problem of need appears easily solvable. It is the looming crisis of surplus, neglected by Quiroga,[57] which poses the main threat. Benefice is as dangerous as temporary loss and defeat politically, if there is no structure to regulate its flow.

Cortés's imposition of the social overseer, the *Fiel* figure, finds Quiroga's equivalent in the reliable safekeeping device of the *fiel custodia*. The prohibition of individual property finds the centralization of social wealth in the storage (or "deposito") and, straight from the official state documents, also in the everpresent figure of the chest with the three keyholes. The chest— objective correlative of this utopian providence of abundance (or *bastimento*) and the preservation of that which is precious and fragile, the wealth of communitarian practice ("la moneda del común")—will here need the triple supervision of the three officials or keyholders: the *Rector*, the *Principal* and the oldest *Regidor* of this utopian community. Ubiquitous is this chest in all reformist experiments, from New Spain to the resplendent Viceroyalty of Peru and the marginal lands of Paraguay; money (the quantifiable reification of human labor) must be kept out of any one pair of hands. With communal surveillance, the chest will keep money safe and concrete in the verifiable precision of numbers ("[que] tengáis vuestra cuenta, y razón clara y fiel").

A quite striking parallel to More's vision, it already appears beyond the reach of the early modern political imagination to envisage a desirable society which manages to do convincingly away with either slavery or money. The former, like need, is theoretically forbidden in Quiroga's hospital precincts. The latter, like two matches lit in the hands of a child with no concept of fire, is not to be let loose. The increasing social verisimilitude of market value is thus at least potentially kept at bay in what appears to be the utopian dream of reduction of most, if not all, social mediation to the primordial swift focus on social need. In the hands of efficient hospital personnel, the likely magnetism of the isolated figure of the chest—one is almost tempted to see it also as an allegorical figuration—is intended to provide for this unmediated satisfaction of social need: accumulated wealth automatically available for the needs of the people.Freedom thins out in this horizon of the rule and always yields to the non-negotiable necessity, always on the brink of indigenous extinction. Utopian freedom must therefore mean the ideally clockwork structuring of the cycles of collective necessity.

We might imagine, from the standpoint of these early indigenous generations, but only with much difficulty, the tremendous impact of money inside the largest historical picture of a barter economy and the colonial demands for the satisfaction of state tribute. In Hernán Cortés's texts, it is clear that money is the binding force among Spaniards. In Quiroga's rules, by contrast, money is instrumentalized as a protective device against a hostile outside. Money, already an inevitable shadow to all social transactions, sort of seals the hospital off from a hostile outside. Yet it is internally centralized in prevention of the unpredictable events which may come tomorrow. The chest contains the original legal contracts that provide warranty (*probanza* and *fé* in this epochal language) of the original ownership of the lands by Quiroga ("[que] tengan cofre donde tengan las Escrituras tocantes al Hospital"). Hence, unlike the no doubt firmer foundations of international social institutions, the Jesuits in Paraguay for example,[58] the communal experiment of the Hospitals of Santa Fé must account for the individual foundation of property rights, Quiroga's, for its partial successes and failures.[59]

Reformist desire towards more convincing forms of social standardization will structure a rigid imperative as regards utilitarian clothing. Against a background of official documents which prohibited a conspicuous luxury displayed by the Spaniards' clothing, surely most of them displaying the shamelessness of *hidalgos* turned into *nuevos ricos*, the monastic imprint is indeed here also clear in the ideal of restrained satisfaction of need as pertains to nudity. Quiroga's formulation proclaimed that a few good pieces of clothing for everybody are more than enough, and that nothing more than enough is to be tolerated. The utopian imperative regulates identical coarse pieces of clothing of cotton and wool, white, clean and plain without decorations ("de algodón, y lana, blancos, limpios, y honestos, sin pinturas, sin otras labores costosas, y demasiadamente curiosas. Y tales, que se defienden del frío y del calor, y de su mismo color si es posible, porque duran más, y no cuestan tanto, porque tienen menos trabajo, y son menos costosos, y más limpios").[60] As for the proverbial citizens in More's *Utopia* (1515), for whom, we are told, coarseness and fineness in texture is negligible detail,[61] utopian clothing in Quiroga's hospitals is also no doubt the figuration of a distinctly early modern reformist fascination for socially undifferentiated sameness.

We may envisage a social ocean of whiteness where individual idiosyncracies quite literally had no place. White, the a-chromatic object color of greatest lightness, may be said to bring sameness down to a zero-degree literalism. In musical terms, we may suggest the monodic mono-tone of Gregorian chant to emphasize this erasure of all differences. It is the principle of the same, with no fissures, which is the justice sought after by early modern utopianism on both sides of the Atlantic.[62]

The fascination with the number two continues as utopian generosity doubles the need to cover primal nudity. Two pieces of clothing are given to to every person, which no doubt gains extra historical meaning when put against the standard practice of the cloth-payment, oftentimes the mockery of payment, in the official retribution for the colonial imposition of forced labor. In a barter economy, clothing, like coca leaves, was a standard exchange element, when not a truly rare and desirable commodity.[63]

The strong social uniformity intimated by monocolor "back to basics," the no-color of whiteness and coarseness in texture, strongly suggests an almost biting and iconoclastic *tableau vivant* intolerant of idiosyncratic expressivity:

> o que si posible es, os conformeis todos en el vestir de una manera lo más que podáis, y de vestidos conformes los unos a los otros en todo, porque se causa de más conformidad entre vosotros y así cese la envidia, y soberbia de querer andar vestidos, y aventajados los unos más, y mejor que los otros.

Two sets of clothing ("dos pares de ellos") are distributed to all citizens. One is devoted to work and the other one is reserved for official festivities. This white habit, a kind of *tabula rasa* for a radically new society, makes the novelty and the cherished ideal yet to come quite simultaneous to the erasure and the straight deep cutting, in the carpenter's sense, of anything that might have preceded such reformist enterprise. Little, if anything, appears to remain of the Tarascan-Purépecha particularity in Quiroga's thorough reformism, at least according to these *ordenanzas*. Little dissonance, if anything, remains culturally meaningful at least according to the most elaborate *Información en Derecho* which we will analyze in the following chapter. Quiroga's millenarianism, incandescent formulation of Christian forms, is rather situated in a nowhere of Atlantic fusion. Inside the community precincts, there are no exceptions to this radical egalitarianism in clothing (we may remember Cortés's differentiation between *caciques* and others out of the pocket money of the latter). The archaism of "conformarse" (contentment in sameness and diligent obedience in the same tight knot, today we might perhaps translate into "compromise"), illustrates very well this monastic aesthetics that only anachronistically might we want to call *art pauvré*. By taking into account the totality of the social world inside these hospital confines, Quiroga's colonial utopianism certainly wants to eradicate all signs of superfluousness and detail ("vestiduras...sin pinturas ni labores de colores, que [no] sean muy costosas, ni muy curiosas"). Surely the archaism abundantly used in official documents of "so color de"—in the name of, under the pretext of—is never too far away.

This whitening of superfluous details is clearly to be understood in social terms. Early modern utopianism wishes to construct a rather faceless and anonymous commonwealth (we may only recall the art of portraiture in European courts to find a rather brutal contrast). Quiroga's legalisms are also dictating the suppression of useless professions, specifically lawyers and tailors. The only political roles mentioned in the rules are the *rector*, *principal* and *regidores* for the exclusive usufruct of the patrilineal cenacle of married men. Social mediation gets reduced to the timely care of these appointed supervisors. The rules neglect anything that is not social duty and we may translate this silence into social space deliberately untouched by centralist interference. Unmediated timely care for the most basic need—shelter, clothing, food...for everyone—is indeed the fundamental impulse of Quiroga's legalisms, which we have already equated with an iconoclastic white-covering impulse undelicate to any kind of intervention that is not profoundly social. In this abomination of any kind of curious costliness, or the extravagance of colorful figures of speech, except for the already mentioned occasional allegorical abstraction, Quiroga's repressive diction comes quite close to the Franciscan tradition of prohibition of interpretation and lapidarian literalism of the letter.[64] This literalism is no doubt the historical production of a social elite, the *hidalgo* versed in canonical law and also man of state who knows his way around the colonial world.[65]

Not all is a quiet bed of roses in Quiroga's prescriptive textualization. In visible tension against the egalitarian figuration of monocolor clothing, a rotatory male-centered political structuration is, as we have already seen, set in place. A patrimonial lineage is the fundamental political structuration of the Hospital communities. Every family unit, formed by ten to twelve married male representatives, elects the eldest male, the *Paterfamilias*, and all *Paterfamilias* are divided into four groups (or "cuadrillas"). Among these, in quite a close resemblance to the Castilian *Cabildo* structure, they select, by secret vote, the political stratification in the roles of *Regidores*, one Principal and, above him, one *Rector*. The *Rector*, the Principal and the eldest *Regidor* are the only ones, we should remember, who may have access to the chest of communal wealth. These will also be the magistrates of social interpretation.

To avoid the likely dangers of a tender commonwealth rooted in men's twig-bowing manners, according to Harrington's words, an almost inhuman and rather machine-like rotatory mechanism is socially set in place in Quiroga's hospitals. This mechanism arranges for the eventual participation of all these family representatives, all these are male it must be stressed, in the variety of social functions of representational politics and surveillance ("que estos se elijan cada año, y *de manera, que ande la rueda* por todos los casados hábiles," my emphasis). Three or four *Regidores* will be elected every year, the Principal and his superior, the *Rector*, will be elected evey three or six years following an implacable rotation. Their political service may be extended, however, if needed. The typification of the Principal is indeed fashioned after the father figure of the abbot in the monastery:

> [Q]ue sea buen Cristiano, y de buena vida, costumbres y exemplo, y esto por tres o seis años, o por todo el tiempo que conveniere y según aprobare... que sea manso, sufrido, y no más áspero, ni riguroso de aquello que convenga, y sea menester para hacer bien su oficio, y negocios del Hospital, y no consienta ser menospreciado de nadie antes procure ser amado, y honrado de todos como sea razón, más por voluntad y amor, que por temor, ni rigor.

After consultation with *Regidores* and *Rectores*, the Principal is the one who makes all important decisions. Disobedience to the dictum of the Principal is not a possibility ("a quien obedezcan todos...y no consienta ser menospreciado de nadie antes procure ser amado, y honrado de todo como sea razón, más por voluntad y amor, que por temor, ni rigor"). In the rotatory mechanism, an almost depersonalized and faceless conceptualization of time is instrumentalized in a seemingly most efficient observance of roles and duties. Unlike men's twig-bowing manners, this utopian commonwealth will be rooted in the movements of hands on a dial, the clock. Against the also clock-structured background of *cédulas* and Cortés's regulations, no social function in the hospital will escape this regimentation by the minute of the hour.

Colonial utopianism elevates the male-dominated political wheel of social duties to a desirable ideal. In excluding the female members, it is as though a more reduced and monastic male-binding monopoly of political supervision of the utopian community were set in place in sheer contradiction with the mono-color egalitarianism with no exceptions. If it is clear that the political figure of the Principal finds inspiration in the monastic molds of the pastor, in the etymological sense a giver of nourishment and sustenance to the community, it is also clear that Quiroga's description of the figure of this error-free Principal emphatically refuses to move away from the preconceived semantic territory of an allegorical language. The *Rector* in the hospital, very much like the abbot in the monastery, personify the goodness of the just law. Quiroga's rules will not move away from this axiom.

Utopian thematization of a contented seclusion from the surrounding coloniality lies in the repudiation of detail, an automaton-like absence of psychological instinct and a rather swift description of the social duties of all its members. The picture of a reformed commonwealth holds a convincing suspension of verisimilitude only in so far as those so-called utopian people remain silent, blank and free from any detailed description of its attributes and characteristics. No single face, no single name will be allowed to stick out. There are no prima donnas here. No dispensations. No whims. At the end of our reading, it is as though nothing had happened except the triumphant happening of an all-reaching tentacular normativity. Readers will slowly awaken to the shocking realization that there is here no plot. There is no mystery except the repressive structuring of the timely annihilation of social need. It appears that utopian literature, repressive culture in colonial Latin America to be sure, must behave very much like the proverbial donkey with blinders fixated upon the dangling carrot, not to deviate from this painful center of social need. The strong suggestion is that there is nothing else to say, that politically, the satisfaction of communal need among the most fragile social sectors is the end of the (hi)story. In Quiroga's case, an already sparse description thins out into the sole protagonism of this repressive imperative. As we will immediately see, the troubling thinning out of the warmth of narrative has to do with this repressive constitution. But, we may ask, how does one fight against repression if not with more of the same? Quiroga's *ordenanzas*, for all its hurried, contrived diction, do not wish to tell anything else except insinuate the satisfaction of communal need among the most fragile Amerindian sectors.

At the end of the document of Quiroga's rules, a civilizational stance for cleanliness, spiritual and corporal, is commended. And, at this point, a certain infantilization of the indigenous citizens is easily gleaned through. The Franciscan ideal of the *poverello* is no doubt also operating:

> [Y] no os vistais de vestidos curiosos, ni costosos demasiado [*sic*], como está dicho arriba, ni os imbixeis [*sic*], ni pinteis, ni os ensucieis los rostros, manos, ni brazos en manera alguna como lo solíades hacer, salvo si fuere por medicina, útil, y necesaria, porque así como es loable la limpieza, así es vituperable la suciedad, y andar sucios.

An unmistakable paternalism (who does not remember similar suggestions in the high school years?) is nonetheless intertwined with a truly egalitarian interpellation in the second person plural ("vosotros"), which is clearly not to be heard with today's ears.

Quiroga's prescriptive textuality does not shy away from the punitive dimension inside the Hospital confines. Mechanisms of social repudiation vary from occasional physical punishment to the extremity of expulsion. Despite Quiroga's earlier emphasis against it, there is plenty of room for interpretation:

> Que si alguno de vosotros, o de vuestros sucesores en este dicho Hospital hiciere cosa fea, y de mal ejemplo, por dó no merezca, ni convenga estar en él, y de ello se recibiese escándalo, y desasosiego, por ser revoltoso, o escandaloso, o mal cristiano, o se emborrachar [*sic*], o demasiado perezoso, o que no quisiere guardar estas *Ordenanzas*, o fuere, o viniere contra ellas, y fuere en ello incorregible, o fuere, o viniere contra el pro, y bien común de este dicho Hospital, sea luego lanzado de él, y restituya lo que de él se aprovechó, como ingrato del bien en el recibido.

All these empty signs, the "ugly thing" and the "bad example," the "scandal" and "restlessness," will of course be interpreted by the Principal. In an institution where obedience is the maximum virtue, disagreement with the Principal's view is not an option.

Quiroga's brief document of the rules and regulations ends with a most conspicuously direct borrowing from More's fictionalization: the big room where communal eating takes place. In a sharp five sentence description, the fundamental dimension of social nourishment is again allegorized:

> Hase de proveer el gasto de aquel del común, y conforme a sus manjares, y manera que tienen de ellos, y no muy curiosos, ni defectuosos, sino abundoso [*sic*], y muy alegre y el cuidado y el aparejo de esto sea de cada familia en las Pascuas de cada un año por familia el su día por su tanto, de manera que ande por todas las dichas familias, que lo sepan.

Time-honored four levels of interpretation could be easily applied to this monastic ritual of communal meal.[66] In this all too brief summary of More's account,[67] Quiroga's nervous style glosses over the obvious, the satisfaction of communal need in its most fundamental form of preservation, which is eating, but we dare say it is also not quite eating. A radically faceless construction of the need of the commonality ("el gasto del común") will be abundantly taken care of ("hase de proveer") in an abundant manner ("abundoso, [*sic*]," and "alegre") which is neither extravagant ("curioso") nor defective ("defectuoso"). There are no proper names in this dining hall. And one could go as far as saying that there are no proper names in these utopian dining rooms because there cannot be any. This digestive process must remain thus a strong insinuation of silent and anonymous satisfaction of human need.

Further details will not be provided by Quiroga's repressive diction. There is no information about the menu. An already familiar rotatory mechanism of one family to attend to the catering needs of the entire population duties will be established for an entire year. So will be the planning of the institution of the hospital within the hospital, the infirmary. Special attention will be paid to catering services during Easter holidays, which will also mark the rotation of the catering duties to another family. The imagination of these indigenous customers in the hospital refectory, truly the beggars' banquet, as though the easiest road to happiness were the stomach, could still be made more resplendent if we simply turn to the colonial norm of Hernán Cortes, the meager amount of bread and pepper and the standard dawn-to-sunset working load of the "Indian" distributed in *encomienda*.

Truly our dream today, these glittering good places and non-places of digestive satisfaction are to be situated, like the scattered hospital geography, inside the larger oceanic desolation of colonial hunger and criminality or official unpredictability in New Spain.[68] We may say, if only tentatively that the historical figure of Quiroga exemplifies the impulse to preserve and regulate that which is precious and fragile, the wealth of communitarian practice and the providence of abundance to need (*manjar* to hunger), which must no doubt acquire a collective dimension, or else be repudiated as negligible detail. Commonwealth is *benefiencia* and the figure of hunger or poverty is the greatest common enemy. Who would even bother about the satisfaction of any one individual? Eating, also in More, is envisaged far from the sorry picture of a solitary eater in any fastfood eatery, but as the occassion for "communal celebration" ("commonwealth," very much like "communal celebration" is perhaps a necessary redundance to bring, if only occasionally, to the hunger of historical memory). It seems to us that, within undeniable temptations to allegorical flights,[69] Quiroga's hasty enunciation still manages to communicate some of its original and undeniable seduction. This is particularly so at the crudest (should we say literal, even materialist?) level of eating, still to this day at the planetary level a dream for the many and a political challenge to all of us.

In this prescriptive textualization of the other of the colonial (mis)rule, Quiroga's regulations recreate the precarious, tense balance between the generalized prescriptive textuality of the law, which always wants to be taken literally, and the allegorical fall into momentary flights of fancy that try, but fail to grasp an (impossible?) enduring ideal of global human satisfaction (global at least within the hospital confines). There where the law wants the explicitness of the imperative and the repressive dictum, allegory will rather grow into the higher vapors of abstraction. It is as though the legal imposition, for all the combination of the positive and the negative, or the "do this and do not do that,"and for all the numeral precision, the six working hours for instance, does not, surely cannot, remain completely satisfied in them. The expressivity of allegory, bursting out ocassionally, signals that the fierce dictum of the repressive culture does not, cannot exhaust a seemingly a-historical utopian disposition.

Despite the figure of the chest, we advance that there is a fundamental lack of objective correlatives in Quiroga's vision. Quiroga's text is not quite a blueprint, not quite a do-it-yourself tool kit of an ideal commonwealth. Nor does it intend to be one. It is rather a succinct repressive thematization which exemplifies a historical disposition towards the ideal figuration of a much improved commonwealth for the most fragile, yet majoritarian social sectors in sixteenth-century New Spain. Despite some undeniable achievements, such as the glittering six-hour working period, there is rather a certain retreat from the concrete which may be said to signify an awareness of a historical impossibility for clarity of the vision regarding the global end-time satisfaction of social need within targeted indigenous populations. If production and distribution of wealth is no big problem in Quiroga's chimerical land of endless abundance, the enervation of social exchange, and the illusion of the stasis of surplus of wealth, is.

If need is ineluctably social need, and if need is unstoppably cyclical, in the sense that it will come to all of us tomorrow, Quiroga's historical tension will certainly increase in the hesitation as to whether legal technicism, or numeric precision, must win the day, or whether allegorical and poetic language, for all its expressivity, will be occasionally allowed to come to the surface, ruffle some feathers, blow some whistles and point in the imaginary direction of the other, even darker side of the repressive dimension. We wish to argue that the tension in Quiroga's regimentation of the polity is precisely built upon this unsolved dichotomy between the thicker layers of allegorical figuration and the number-centered thinning out into literalism.

It is important to insist that Quiroga's festivities do not amount to a free lunch for the indigenous hunger. With no concessions to the possibility of religious tolerance, holidays will have to coincide with the Christian year-round arrangement of saintliness, particularly in the observation of the foundational day of the Exaltation of the Cross (Sept. 14), when all stipulated permissions (*perdones* in the *Tabla* left unspecified in the rules), were granted by the Franciscan Bishop of Mexico City, Fray Juan de Zumárraga. Official permission for the hospitals was granted by *real cédula* of Nov. 13, 1535, confirmed by Viceroy Mendoza in Aug. 31, 1537, a letter of execution was signed Nov. 22, 1537, and finally later there was a *cédula* reiteration in May 12, 1551.[70] The Franciscan chronicler Beaumont confirms that Quiroga did not govern *in situ* ("entrar a gobernar [*sic*]"), the Michoacan bishopric until the rather late date of 1537.[71] The Franciscan Fray Juan de Zumárraga, Archbishop of Mexico, did not fail to commend the recent appointment of Quiroga to the highest institution of the *Consejo de Indias* (Feb. 8, 1537)[72] although he did so as a learned layman.[73] We will have to take these data into account for the most likely composition date of Quiroga's rules. The recreation of a fierce legal climate immediately before the consecration date of December 1538, and most likely in the last year of the *oidor* appointment in the *Segunda Audiencia* (1535), will help us protect our final hypothesis of Quiroga's strategic use of a prestigious legacy, that of More's scholarship, in the context of New Spain. It is important to emphasize that Quiroga's longest opposition, but not the only one, remained for the rest of his life the City Council of Mexico, already rebuilt upon the ruins of Tenochtitlán.[74]

Quiroga's rules conclude with a formal, yet hurried exposition of authorial intention. The final section of the rules invokes the social position of Quiroga ("*protestación* de la intención del Fundador...so toda la corrección debida," my emphasis of the rich legal archaism), as the seemingly sole legitimate foundation. If rules are formalizations of a disposition embodied by an institution, these rules circumscribe an indeed dry summary of quiet reformation of a hospital polity promoted by the individuality of a high state official. In standard construction of legitimation, the invocation of the signs "Monarch" and "God," bear witness to the still unnamed Hospital of Santa Fé and the Colegio de San Nicolás in the province of Michoacán, apparently not yet by 1535 fully made into a diocese.

Quiroga's prestigious social position forcefully comes to the fore, judge in the *Segunda Audiencia* ("siendo oidor"), in the last year of the appointment. Reinforcing this already elevated social position ("los buenos respetos"), the speaking subject, also sole maker of these rules, does not hesitate to waive in an ostensible manner a promotion into the ranks of the Catholic Church, perhaps the most effective invocation to authority in the unpredictable years of a highly corrupt centralized state. By the composition date of these rules, Quiroga carefully fashions his public persona in a transitional period. He is leaving state office and moving into a newly-created bishopric chair ("siendo Oidor, y en hábito de lego, como está dicho, y antes de ser electo Obispo, por los buenos respetos dichos arriba, y para los buenos efectos, que estas *Ordenanzas* han tenido, y con favor de su Majestad").

In claiming so promptly the coverage of ecclesiastical jurisdiction, it seems quite plausible that Quiroga, who remains unnamed in the rules except for this last-minute occurrence, tries to protect the early years of a foundation still in the making against a serious threat which has been legally channeled. By the end of our document, Quiroga wraps himself around with the sheep's clothing of a man of the Church on his way to a venerable Bishop's clothing ("sin autoridad de Obispo alguno, salvo para el decir de las Misas, como se requiere"), as though in an effort to immunize himself from further hostilities. A formal plea, quite close to a legal adaptation of the widely used rhetorical form of a *sermo humilis*, follows after this ("[los buenos efectos de las *Ordenanzas*] suplico siempre se les otorgue, y no se les niegue, quedando a salvo lo contenido en estas Ordenanzas"). The higher authority of the implied listener (the "suplico...a Vos," a proud individuality in the middle of the odd use of a *vosotros* against the officially sanctioned use of *Indios*), must also, for reasons quite unknown to us, remain unnamed. The patrons and supervisors ("patrones y defensores") of the various hospitals also remain nameless, which must mean that the *Patronato Real* was not yet officially sanctioned. And, still more strangely, we cannot find the names of the executors and beneficiaries, which we will only find in Quiroga's will. We must today blame the hastiness of the *ordenanzas* for this astonishingly nameless and quite unpredictable landscape. Surely there must be a political reason for this so hasty and indelicate a written record in matters so delicate.

In all the tentativeness of the final paragraph, Quiroga's foundational rules stumble into occasional ambiguity and certain imprecision of enunciation, when not in grammatical error ("[y] aunque si así no se guardare esta nuestra determinada intención, y voluntad, pueda volver a otros usos profanos, o píos, como nos pareciere [sic], y por bien tuviéremos [sic]"). The rules end in the middle of a political thinness of unnamed third person plural (a dangerously vague "ellos"), the supposed second generation ("Patrones" and "Defensores") of the Quiroguian legacy ("de él"). Hence, the formal declaration of dissent and objection of this rule-structured protestation wraps itself up with strategic silence, highly suggestive in the insinuation of ample numbers of influential patrons and allies, and thus perhaps even threatening to the hostile ears of those who might be present in court pressing charges against the possessions of the Quiroguian project. Quiroga's rules exemplify a thematization, truly a legal typology, of More-inspired desirable commonwealth. However, Quiroga's rules act out the typified legal function of a protestation, which we must carefully historicize.

We must contemplate the likeliest function of Quiroga's *ordenanzas*. A sedulous approximation to the, still to this day, prestigious site of utopian culture, the father figure of Thomas More, has perhaps something to do with the survival of Quiroga's rules until today. Despite the undeniable proximity to More's model, explicitly acknowledged in his most ambitious *Información en Derecho*, which we will analyze in chapter three, the name of the English scholar is not mentioned once in the rules (we have also mentioned the astonishing silence over Vives). It is as though Quiroga's plea for some international intellectual allegiance in the eyes and ears of the courtroom authorities, who were already most likely antagonizing the hospital enterprise, did not want to implicate others by their names.

The legalism of "protestation" entails Quiroga's public response with the almost intangible evidence (the "fe" and "probanzas") of the high, metropolitan culture and the good cause (the "buenos efectos") of the *ordenanzas*. Hence, the protestation technically operates in the form of an indirect affirmation, or as the typified duplication of the plea, which is also a formal denial, which is here desperately clinging to the prestigious site of utopian culture production (it must cling to it until this day to gain international visibility). Quiroga's rules, however, still give their model no proper name.

Quiroga's legalistic litigation makes use of More's fictionalization, already well known in lettered circles in New Spain, to make his already quite desperate case in the final repetition of a plea more persuasive and more winning (we may almost go so far as to fantasize a rather sophisticated *letrado* wink in the middle of the fierce litigation to some magistrates who might have been, if not knowledgeable, at least receptive to More's cultural capital). We may thus perhaps well envisage the historical situation that has Quiroga defending, by no other means than by literary allusion and by the written record, his social experimentation in front of a hostile judicial court. This will be the kind of social practice which Quiroga will have to engage in to no end from the early days of his arrival in New Spain.

Nicolás León has given us a detailed transcript of the secretive investigation ("residencia"), regarding Vasco de Quiroga's projects by the *oidor* Loaysa during the likely dates of the composition of the rules (Nov.

13, 1535, Feb. 4, 1536 and finally May 19, 1536).[75] But this is only one instance among many in the thick legal turmoil in the life of Quiroga, most often acting in the role of plaintiff. Beaumont has given us ample narratives of two notorious lawsuits over demarcated jurisdiction of bishropics and tithes: Vasco de Quiroga versus Fray Juan de Zumárraga (the big lawsuit, or "gran pleito,"1535-1584), and Quiroga versus Pedro Gómez-Marquer and Nueva Galicia (1551-1664).[76] García Icazbalceta also gave us a good account of the Zumárraga and Quiroga conflict, which the former lost.[77] Beaumont gives us a lengthy exposition of the lawsuit between Quiroga and the *encomendero* Juan Infante over neighboring *tierras baldías*, which the latter lost.[78] Tena Ramírez includes general references to another legal conflict between Quiroga and the Marquesado del Valle in the years of Cortés's son, Martín Cortés.[79]

Given these lasting and intricate legal cobweb entrapments, it does not appear strange that Quiroga, already a bishop of considerable presence in the political climate of New Spain and a man of venerable age, had good reasons to make a final trip to Spain from 1547 to 1554 (León, p. VIII), only two years before his death in Uruapán, New Spain in 1556. It is not at all preposterous to conjecture, taking into account Tena Ramérez's findings well into the nineteenth century,[80] that this trip made Quiroga's communitarianism enjoy the relative anomaly of municipal independence from established New Spain jurisdictions, the *Cabildo* of Mexico City for example. We may conjecture that the *Patronato Real* may have been secured during this trip. And it is no doubt this institutionalization which must have somewhat distanced the hospitals from the chaos of an incipient, yet intrusive Indian legalization growing out "a[n almost] permanent state of war" (Assadourian). In a largely colonial condition constructed upon the fierce imposition of tribute and labor upon indigenous communities, Quiroga's alternative communitarianism found its cornerstone in the exemption from tribute and labor, "prebendas" and "indultos" in the language of the period, for all the populations faithfully committed to the hospital life.[81]

Quiroga's rules are thus making an intervention into the legal machinery of an early colonial polity still radically in the making. In relation to these rules, shying away from the intricacies of canonical law, it does not seem out of place to imagine a performative reading, or better yet a declamation only later written down in this hurried prose. We may envisage a rhetorical strategy which desperately clings to the prestigious otherness of the English scholar, rather than the still shaky reputation of *converso* of Vives, in front of a jury that is about to incriminate the hospital projects (More's *Utopia* already circulating in New Spain as close to Quiroga as Zumárraga's personal library, as Silvio Zavala demonstrated).[82] Better yet, it is quite plausible that we may be perhaps dealing here with Quiroga's word as written in the legal proceedings by a third *letrado* party, most likely a low-ranking notary public. This might well explain the unpolished, a bit too synthetic and seemingly incomplete version of Quiroga's protestation in a rather meticulous man[83] (and this possibility also adds considerable weight to the profound orality of the document as found in the interpellations to the higher authority, the "Vos," and the "vosotros" of the purported audience of Indians).

This abbreviated protocol of repressive communication, Quiroga's *ordenanzas*, might just well be the colonial version of our contemporary courtroom shorthand transcription. Should this be plausible, we might be perhaps in a better position to understand Quiroga's guarded quality of enunciation, since the function of the rules is mostly working its final way into an unfavorable court decision against the hospital enterprises. Quiroga's apparent timidity of diction, even some of the convoluted constructions and errors, unless these be the misdoings of the notary public, may instead turn into Quiroga's weather-beaten awareness, even into a defense mechanism, in the middle of all looming complications ahead, legal and otherwise. Still better, the initial impression of readers as regards the timidity may turn into a rather savvy *oidor* tactfulness as soon as we are reminded of the standard formula, " I obey, yet I do not wish to comply" ("obedezco pero no cumplo"), which was perfectly intelligible to Spanish Indian Law, profusely used in the early modern period and set delicately in motion by these *ordenanzas* (inside the Spanish machine, this is as far as a state official could go).

We said earlier that Quiroga's thematization of the ideal commonwealth somehow needed to claim proximity to the *locus classicus* of More's highly respected humanist philology, self-described *sermo* after all. It is as though colonial utopianism needed to sap vigor and *converso*-free, clean pedigree from distant and metropolitan cultural artifacts. This culture of borrowing is thus conspicuously put in the middle of dry and plain legalisms, much like a delicate decorative British-born exotic flower by the side of the Spanish eating utensils (More is not named in the *Ordenanzas*, but only in the lengthiest *Información en Derecho*). Quiroga is thus translating the *sermo* of the ideal polity into the repressive culture of the ideal polity for indigenous communities under early Spanish colonization. These rules, clearly differentiated from *cédula* regulations or conqueror's *ordenanzas*, are first and foremost trying to inhabit the meaning-making protocols of legal rhetoric. They are mostly trying to make the case for the survival of his communities. The technical notion of "protestation" signals a rather unnerving courtroom conjucture for these communities. If this hypothesis holds, we may convincingly distance ourselves from apologetic excuses for the hurried coarseness of the *ordenanzas*. This protestation instead glitters despite and because of this non-belletrist making of More's subject matter serviceable on this side of the Atlantic.[84] Legal bureaucratization and belletrism are strange bedfellows and these *ordenanzas* prove it. The thematization of the encomium of utility belies our suggestion that Quiroga instrumentalizes this prestigious site of learned culture as a last-minute legal defense of his hospitals in the thick of courtroom litigation. Our ignorance is to blame if this claim has ever been made before in relation to the *ordenanzas*. We are also unaware of any responses to Quiroga's incomplete *ordenanzas*.[85] An unguarded response to Serrano Gassent's latest, most accessible edition of the *ordenanzas* (1992), is surely unwarranted as regards Quiroga's oral argument formally presented to a rather faceless audience almost 500 years ago in New Spain. This is due to the incomplete and fragmentary nature of the textual evidence we call *ordenanzas*. The lawsuit inside which these *ordenanzas* are meaningful has not yet been found. What we see in this colonial text is clearly not what we get, historically. And the whole truth of what we get, at least in this analysis, is mostly of a hypothetical or conjectural nature, at least until further evidence points in a contradictory historical direction.

4. Quiroga's Unsettling Moment of Final Truth: The Last Will

The contrast between these rules and Quiroga's terminal narrative, his *Testament* (Jan. 24, 1565), he died March 14, 1565,[86] highlights two fundamental moments of tension: first, there is an unambiguous endorsement of the official state ideology of race purity (or "limpieza de sangre"); and second, our Bishop of Michoacán appears to have benefitted from the usufruct of slavery. Let us take a closer look into these.

In his efforts to regulate the continuation of the already established hospital enterprise, an unambiguous delimitation of the property must take place,

[Y]o fundé en esta ciudad de Mechoacán [*sic*], en el varrio [*sic*] de Pásquaro, cerca de nuestra yglesia catedral de sant Salvador, el colegio de san Niculás, que aquí está fundado, por la gran falta de ministros de los santos sacramentos y culto divino, que aquí y en todo nuestro obispado de Mechuacán, a havido y ay.

The Colegio de San Nicolás, truly an official house of learning, acquires frontal textual stature in the apparent generosity of this private institution fundamentally devoted to the instruction of alphabeticization and Christian doctrine. The students officially enrolled at the Colegio are only Spaniards of the "right" kind, and these older than twenty years of age ("se reciban y crien estudiantes, puros españoles que pasen de más de veinte años"). In marked contrast with the monocolor monk-like clothing, these collegiate students are donned with a purple beret ("bonete de paño morado"), to be distinguished from all other students, indigenous inhabitants in the neighborhood, also Quiroga's servants, who are nonetheless also welcome to the Colegio education. All acquire for free an European-based knowledge of theology and language competence ("gratis todo").[87] An appointed President of this house of learning will be elected every three years. Interestingly, the President (the one who "sets it straight" or *retor*) is also the appointed reader and lecturer ("letor [de] sacramentos y cánones penitenciales [*sic*]"). Successful students form a lettered unit ready for a commitment to the Church ("para se hordenar de clérigos presbíteros"). The ideal of this international house is language learning ("y a deprender [*sic*] nuestra lengua, y a enseñar a los de nuestra nación la suya").

Yet, this language learning is certainly not innocuous. Subalternization of languages and students is formally set in place. To the pursuit of becoming "literate translators" (the notion of "clérigos lenguas" in the language of the period), the students officially enrolled will have to demonstrate the desirable scholarly attitude ("las calidades"), and a necessary honesty in answering all questions appertaining to prove the prerequesite of an unmixed birth-privilege ("así de limpieza de sangre como en lo demás que en tal caso es menester para ser hordenados de presbíteros para curas y pastores, y honestidad para lo que proceda la suficiente información y examinación que posible sea"). While insisting upon generational continuity (the insistence on the adverb "perpetuamente") nominal egalitarianisms as pertain to the intercultural process of language learning break down in this ethnic divide of the student population.

In the early reconfiguration of colonial estate structures, there is no doubt a foundational condition of relative wealth and privilege in the very production of a will. This formal pronouncement, a final form of communication, irreversible and truthful to the point of rigor mortis in the offing, was certainly not accessible to many in early colonial Mexico. The bequeathal of individual property implies that there is property to be handed down and that there is some knowledge as to how to do it. The letter of the will wishes to establish a perpetual form of payment to all the neighboring indigenous communities and their progeny:

> [E]n recompensa y satisfacción de lo que allí los yndios de esta ciudad de Mechuacán y barrios de la Laguna, travajaron, pues ellos lo hicieron y a su costa, sean perpetuamente en el gratis enseñados todos los hijos de los yndios, vezinos y moradores de esta dicha ciudad de Mechuacán.

In sharp contrast to the end of the will, a desire to fix a money-free contractual time and unlimited accessibility to learning practice for future generations is established in payment to a previous work commitment:

> [Y] ésto gratis como es dicho sin que para ello den ni paguen ni se les pida ni lleve cosa alguna, mayormente en la dicha dicha doctrina christiana y moral que les dexo impresa para ello en el dicho colegio e que han de ser enseñados gratis.[88]

Despite the racial division, the house of learning is here claiming to be a money-free haven of learning for indigenous communities, if they so desire to join in.

In the middle section of this convoluted last will, a narrative of the foundation of the hospitals and the necessity to protect clearly demarcated lines reads thus. The importance of this statement of belief justifies the length of the quote; length, which should also give us some of the incantatory quality of early modern legal writing:

> [D]os ospitales de yndios que intitulé de Santa Fee,[89] confirmado el título con la obra e yntención de ella, uno en la provincia de México e otro en ésta de Mechuacán, que es todo en esta Nueva España, a dos o tres leguas poco más o menos de las ciudades caveceras de cada una de estas dichas provincias, donde cada uno de los dichos ospitales está fundado y averiguado, con este orden, intento e voluntad que los constituye y disputé desde entonces para aora y desde aora para entonces que fuesen con todos sus términos, tierras, estancias e grangerías que nos les dimos, pusimos y compramos y les huve de su Majestad segund que al presente lo tienen e poseen y paresce por las escripturas de compras e merced de ello, para sustentación y doctrina, así espiritual como moral exterior y buena policía de yndios pobres e miserables personas.... Por ende en descargo de nuestra

conciencia declaramos lo susodicho ser e aver pasado asy en el efecto y
así aora aquí en todo y por todo e para el dicho efecto según y como dicho
es, lo declaro, ratifico y confirmo, todo con todo lo que así a los dichos
ospitales y a cada uno de ellos por mi les está dado y comprado y habido
de su Majestad, y tienen e poseen como dicho es y les está amojonado por
cédula y mandado de su Majestad como paresce por las escrituras de ventas,
merced y amojonamientos que dello tienen con más los batanes, molinos y
oficios de telares y ganados que allí después acá, ya muchos días y años a,
avemos acrecentado e multiplicado en que ellos también an ayudado y
ayudan encargándoles como les encargamos mucho y si necesario es
mandamos según que mejor podemos y devemos que todo lo que rentaren
los dichos molinos, batanes telares y ganados, que nos allí en ellos avemos
acrecentado e multiplicado y se hubiere dello, acudan con trescientos
ducados o su valor en cada un año perpetuamente para siempre jamás (pp.
294-295).

The contractual condition for this final pronouncement establishes an
approximate cartography of the wealth attached, by 1565, to Quiroga. The
will takes pains at the demarcation of the potential wealth ("términos,
estancias, granjerías," "amojonado[s] por cédula").[90] The blurring of this
geographical precision will be the occasion for all legal disputations. And
there will be plenty. Quiroga's contract with the authorities and following
hospital generations confirm that he bought the terrain upon which the two
hospital communities were constructed from the legal proprietor, the Spanish
Crown, in the *baldío* vicinities of the main urban centers ("a dos o tres
leguas poco más o menos de las ciudades caveceras [*sic*]"). The stated
purpose for the construction of these communities is the attendance of the
helplessness of the indigenous communities ("buena policía de yndios pobres
e miserables personas").[91] In prevention of possible disorders of property
transmission and administration produced by his inminent biological death,
the last will appeals to King Philip II to protect the stipulations of the contract
once the original buyer disappears ("compramos y les huve de su Majestad
segund que al presente lo tienen e poseen y paresce por las escripturas de
compras y merced de ello"). In the horizon of land-owning production of
wealth, no aporias are to be allowed, if Quiroga can help them, which would
have certainly destroyed the generational continuity of this experimental
communal enterprise.

The supposedly increasing production of hospital wealth is left however
surprisingly quite undefined ("molinos, telares, ganados" synthesized in
the "rentas"), by Quiroga. And yet, the historical shadow of our friend *Don*

Dinero already looms large here. Monetarization means that the multifarious hospital wealth (i.e., human labor) will have to be translated into the numeral precision of 300 gold coins or ducats (*ducados*) per year. The salaries of appointed officials of the two hospitals and the *Rector* of the Colegio de San Nicolás will come out of this total sum. The Crown, the official protector appealed to by the will, will have to provide this amount. Fifty ducats will be substracted from this total rent. These will be devoted to a monthly Mass celebration honoring the death anniversaries of Quiroga's parents and relatives interred in Madrigal de las Torres, Spain (the only testimony of Quiroga's birthplace), and also the arrangement of his departure ("para que ella se digan por nos después de nuestros días, en cada un año perpetuamente"). Two months before his death, Quiroga's will thus formalized this double symbolic bind with his ancestors in the Iberian peninsula and also with the following indigenous generations to reside in his New Spain hospitals (the generic ethnic name Tarascan-Purépecha is also missing).

Building firmly on the historical rights of individual property ("añadiendo derecho a derecho, dotación a dotación, donación a donación"), this last will wishes to close down all contracted debts ("en forma pura, mera, yrrevocable que es dicha entre vivos, de todo lo que es dicho y cada una cosa e parte de ello para el dicho hefecto...por dotados y constituidos como dicho es y a mí su poseedor en su nombre"). The historical irony has this utopian ideal of fiercely regulated money-free communitarian dispossession of the indigenous (i.e. "miserable") population inside the hospital precincts resting precisely upon this seemingly external dimension of privileged individual possession of individual property and deep legal acquaintance with Spanish law. It appears that this is historically the only social agent quite capable of securing a social contract with enduring effects upon the following generations in the Michoacán region. Unambiguous right to the individual possession of land in this surely violent agrarian world, where land is the ultimate horizon of wealth production, is no doubt a must for the continuation and survival of Quiroga's enterprise. His rules, as we have already noted, ironically intend to make individual property, as well as money, disappear from inside the hospital precincts. But outside these, privatization and commodification will gradually encroach upon all social energies and reign well until this day.

A vigorous monetarization of social energies, much like a historical symptom of collective fears to come, overtakes the last section of Quiroga's will. The two Principals of the two hospitals, who are selected every three years, must be proficient in languages. They must also be reliable and virtuous leaders ("sea virtuoso, ábil y suficiente lengua"). For their supervision, they receive a stipend of 150 gold pesos. Their meals of a moderate kind will be included in their wages ("pesos de oro de minas [*sic*] o su valor y más la comida moderada"). If they so need, they could have one or more assistants of the appropriate demeanor and dedication ("capellanes...clérigos de misa y de buena vida y exemplo"). These assistants must also be proficient in languages and receive a stipend of 100 *pesos* ("pesos de minas") and moderate meals. The responsibility for the election of the hospital Principal is already clearly structured by the rules: the president and main lecturer ("Rector and Lector") of the Colegio de San Nicolás is designated jointly by the *Audiencia* and the *Chancillería Real*. Quiroga's accummulated wealth, mostly coming out of the *oidor* wages ("quando los dichos ospitales fundava de mis salarios"), will be thus mostly channelled for the times to come through the regulatory patronage mechanisms of the absolutist state.

The final section in Quiroga's will includes the wish to his anonymous executors ("albaceas" and "testamentarios"), to comply with all payments in the shortest amount of time possible.[92] The names of Diego Pérez Gordillo Negrón and Francisco de la Cerda, two secular priests have been mentioned to fill this blank space.[93] An itemized list of money payments and named individual recipients is included. Quiroga's complete library of 626 volumes is donated to the Colegio de San Nicolás (this library is today sadly lost). A complete tabulation of all his movable goods is to be put up for auction ("se haga almoneda [de todo]" in the beautiful Spanish of the period). The money produced is to be given to the still incipient construction of the cathedral of Michoacán, its definite location a source of much disputation in the years to come. We know that one salient part of Quiroga's patrimony, the Colegio de San Nicolás de Pátzcuaro, passed to the already important patrimony of the young Society of Jesus (their arrival in New Spain in 1572). We also know that the Colegio was to be their second house in New Spain after Mexico City, which says quite a bit about the importance of the Michoacán region in the foundational period.[94] Besides the close proximity and collaboration with Franciscans and Augustinians, there is evidence that Vasco de Quiroga had requested, as early as 1547 and directly in letter-contact to the founder, the Spanish Ignacio de Loyola, the collaboration of the Society of Jesus for his hospital projects. This collaboration had to be postponed, however, due to the scarce numbers of Jesuits, until 1572.[95]

Yet, in the middle of this last contract, one final clause sticks out. In it, Quiroga announces the final gift of freedom to his slaves thus:

Ytem declaro y es mi voluntad que todos los sclavos [*sic*] que tengo, hombres y mujeres sean libres sin adición alguna porque ésta es mi voluntad.

There are no names and no detailed numbers. There is no explicit reference to age or ethnicity. For someone taking so many pains about a strict legal typology of slavery in his lengthiest *Información en Derecho*, there is no way of knowing whether Quiroga's slaves were of *naboría*, *tapia*, *de rescate*, etc. For someone who was so scrupulous as to have the bull of his nomination to the bishopric of Michoacán changed (Warren, p. 11), this rather concise carelessness is highly unusual. And yet, this written piece of evidence, inside a final document of the greatest importance, is telling us that the practice of slavery coexisted, and so did money, should we take the textualization of the rules in its face-value or thematic content, vis-à-vis the radical ideal of secluded clockwork egalitarianism of social duties until the termination of the biological life of the owner and founder.

We may speculate that biological death perhaps represented the only legal condition of possibility to set these slaves free from their social death. Perhaps there was no possibility of donation, no gift, no purchase, etc., as the fastidious stipulations which we may find in the New Laws, made it clear, at least theoretically, to change the legality of slavery into that of colonial subjectivities.

It appears clear that, despite the Crown's legalisms against slavery, these were never quite thoroughly implemented, and despite the silence over the phenomenon of slavery in Quiroga's rules, which we had interpreted as a swift form of eradication inside the hospital confines, the terminal condition of individual death appears to be here the last cut to some of these firmly implemented bonds of social subordination and degradation laid out against the historically (un)thinkable horizon of their negation. It had to be Quiroga's final moment of truth which did away with, or at least tried to, this rather unspecified form of slavery which was nonetheless part of his personal belongings.

5. Conclusions

Quiroga's *ordenanzas* do good to the commonplace that colonial literature is part and parcel of the hegemonic repressive culture. We've been proposing that Quiroga's *ordenanzas* exemplify the quiet, synthetic kind of political reformation (or utopianism) historically available to the early or foundational moments of the Spanish colonization of the Americas. Colonial utopianism thus historically means the theory and the practice within and against the hegemonic repressive culture of Spanish Indian Law (or *Derecho Indiano*), and the dutiful compliance with all necessary protocols for courtroom litigation.

These *ordenanzas* do not quite fit gently into the norm of early modern metropolitan utopianism. How on earth could they in the historical context of colonial Latin America? We do not wish to apologize for this unfittingness. We rather wish to recreate and expand it so that this norm may get a bit rarefied and relativized. If we focus on the subject matter of the *ordenanzas*, we find the construction of an indigenous commonwealth as politically desirable as early modern utopianism understood this adjective to mean: that is, monastic structurations of social duties, the chastisement of otium, drastic, harsh depersonalizations, timely and communal satisfaction of need, unconditioned prohibitions of money and slavery inside the confines of Quiroga's hospital-villages, etc. If we focus on the original maker of these *ordenanzas*, we find a Spanish *hidalgo* of the University *letrado* kind with a degree in canon law. The former student of law will be showing his true colors in relation to *Información en Derecho* (1535), which will take center stage in chapter three and *De Debellandis Indis* (1551), which we will analyze in chapter four. In sharp contrast to the two models of the professional metropolitan writer, More but also Vives, Quiroga reached the highest political position in the Americas, the office of *oidor* or judge in the *Segunda Audiencia* (1530-1535), and he also later secured the first chair of Bishop of the Michoacán region (1535-1565). It is surely this high political profile which has helped preserve this individuality from the erosion of the passing of time. But this has been barely so in relation to international early modern utopianism.

If this social origin helps explain the connections with the lettered elites in the European metropolises as well as the relative success Quiroga apparently enjoyed in the nitty-gritty litigation procedures, this social origin is also the most likely explanation for the partial successes and numerous limitations that, from our vantage point, we may today signal in relation to this hasty sketch of a better hospital world for Tarascan-Purépecha communities in sixteenth-century New Spain. But it is not terribly easy even for us today to imagine sustainable possibilities for change for the better for the most fragile social sectors in the early Spanish colonization of the Americas. If we focus on exclusion inside the *ordenanzas*, we find a political rotatory wheel of patriarchy and seniority, and we also find the intolerance of official Christianity towards anything which might have preceded its still recent, by 1535, arrival in the Americas. Yet, if we focus on the original social function of the *ordenanzas*, we run into the technicality of the "protestation," that is, the desperate double plea by our *oidor* for an almost lost cause in the public courtroom proceedings. We have been trying to elaborate how deeply orality penetrates the historical production of the piece of written evidence, most likely produced by a notary public, and how fragmented what today gets called Quiroga's *ordenanzas* has come to us. All these frustrations among contemporary readers are historically meaningful in relation to the meaning-making practices in the early modern repressive culture in the Americas. It is this heterogeneity that we have been trying to think about with care. And finally if we focus on Quiroga's will, we will immediately realize how intricately money and slavery were giving internal togetherness to the village-hospitals despite explicit repudiations to the contrary in the narrow and hasty textualization of the *ordenanzas*. This contradiction is not solely Quiroga's contradiction, and it would be silly to blame him for that. Rather, it exceeds the banality of his own individuality in a largely pre-individualistic era which nonetheless came face to face with the teething troubles of the historical arrogance of the "I." The *ordenanzas* are also caught in the midst of the official individual imposition from above and the monastic seductions of cloistered community. We have signalled how much of this tendency for social perfectability draws inspiration from monastic literalism.

We have also made it clear that Quiroga's political practice never intended a systemic eradication of colonial structures. This claim would be grossly anachronistic in relation to most, if not all public figures of the early modern period. The question of how to get rid of a generalized situation of domination was never anywhere in Quiroga's horizon in relation to the expansion of the Spanish Empire. His legal pragmatism rather took him in the direction of a localized intervention for the betterment of targeted ethnic groups such as the Tarascan-Purépecha. Quiroga's *ordenanzas*, in the antipodes of ethnographic accounts, do not dwell on the cultural specificities of these communities. The slippery notion of utopianism will historically translate into the institution of the hospital and the collaboration between the centralizing early modern state and the often most dynamic social forces inside the generic label of the Catholic Church; namely, the monastic forces.

Quiroga's repressive dictum however is neither comfortably located within the state dictum nor fittingly within the monastic 'religions' (as the Spanish had it in this period). Neither is it a proper state discourse since it claims both a differentiation from it and a strong desire for the long-lasting reformation of the pervasive state criminality, if only by negligence of the early moment of the colonization. Quiroga's *ordenanzas* are neither indigenous nor subaltern practices in these times when hegemony was constructed with tremendous precariousness. We don't think this kind of repressive practice was available to the indigenous populations, however cultured in Latin or Spanish in these early moments. We don't hesitate, however, to qualify Quiroga's *ordenanzas* using the term *indigenista* (or pro-Indian), with or without all the modifiers that we may today add to this rather general label.

Quiroga's communitarianism intended to construct an empty subjecthood modelled after a messianic Christianity. We have emphasized some of the rigors of a rule-dominated polity entirely carved out into a radiant novelty. It is perhaps for this reason that the Tarascan-Purepecha cultural component must of necessity disappear. Historical tensions, however, inform these *ordenanzas*. We have seen the centrality of the abolition of individual proprietorship and the firm implementation of an ideal of dispossession in this agrarian culture, and yet we also saw Quiroga's simultaneous defense of his property rights until his final days. We have seen the structural efforts towards an equal distribution of wealth ("the chest with the money of the people"), and yet also an almost suicidal carelessness about the surplus of wealth. We have marvelled at the inflexible ideal of monastic clothing, and yet we did not fail to notice the marginalization of women from political representation. We have rejoiced at the provision of six working hours per day, per person, and yet we run into the distressing clause in Quiroga's will which informs us that he held, if only in the eyes of the law, slaves until the end of his life.[96] We have certainly found delight in the anonymous satisfaction of social need, and we were not hesitant to quote the passage regarding the anonymous love-feast fellowship. And yet there was also our expression of distress in that there is no trace of anything which we might be able to call Tarascan-Purépecha in these *ordenanzas*. The perhaps distressing realization is that no cultural specificity is to be allowed in these *ordenanzas*, that these peoples must remain silent and faceless and anonymous, and that these communities could be from anywhere or nowhere. This nowhere was considered highly desirable for early modern utopianism and it is this unsettling heterogeneity with which we must today come to terms. We have also remarked how there is an inflexible centralization of social energies inside the hospital precincts and how the relative tax-exempt independence of the village-hospitals depended upon the institution of royal patronage (or the *Patronato Real*). Finally, we have mentioned the rather shocking coexistence of two modes of signification in this repressive document, the ineluctable, cut-and-dry number-centered explicitness of the rule and the much repressed expressivity and future-oriented flights of fancy of allegorical signification.

According to Quiroga's recorded *ordenanzas*, the construction of a desirable community in colonial New Spain is emphatically not a matter of choice. This eminently pragmatic document has no patience for the early modern pregnant notion of *albedrío* or the theologies of natural law and the law of nations (which we will analyze in chapter four). These truncated *ordenanzas* come to us with an eminent pragmatic outlook. We may also say that Quiroga's colonial version of Christian love, against the Bible's dramatization of the messianic vision, as in the Book of Psalms (2 and 110), is emphatically not a matter of individual choice either, but rather a historical matter of firm individual imposition upon a collectivity. Better yet, it is through this individuality that the Tarascan-Purépecha collectivity found social structures of hospitality. The love that gets articulated in these *ordenanzas* is perhaps the kind of love we today wish to know nothing about. But we need to take into consideration the historical surroundings, not to fall into sanctimonious pronouncements.

Against the colonial drama, Quiroga's colonial reformation had to take place in between the stipulated lineaments of the illicit and the licit, the unlawful and the lawful. In its theme and function, Quiroga's *ordenanzas* are stretching the social grammar of this foundational legalistic meaning-making polarity of official positives and negatives. Inside the grids of intelligibility of the Spanish Indian Law, this colonial reformation will be claiming the *indigenista* desirability of an-other place for the continuation of the life of the indigenous populations. In this utopian sense, colonial utopianism will be constructing a differentiated yet eventually legalized space for the possibility of life there where there is none yet (as the expressions "[no] habiendo lugar de derecho" and "[no] ha lugar" had it in the telling legal protocol of the period). Quiroga's fragmented *ordenanzas* make an institutional home for the Tarascan-Purépechas inside the early commotions of the colonial world. These rules do so in all compliance with legal protocols, yet they stand dangerously close to the edge of impropriety and presumptuousness (the "obedezco, pero no cumplo"), Taking into careful consideration the technicality of "protestation," these *ordenanzas* also stand quite close to being a lost cause. We must always remember Sempat Assadourian's notion of the "permanent state of war" as regards the standard criminality of foundational colonization. Against this impossible life-world of inter-generational living and partly living for the indigenous majority in the Americas, Quiroga's rules are proposing a quite remarkable heterogeneous regimentation of polity other than need, other than communal death, and other than the much despised outside of the law.

Portrait, included in *La utopía mexicana del siglo XVI: lo bello, lo verdadero y lo bueno* edited by Grupo Azabache (Printed in Italy, colección "Arte Novohispano," 1992).

Chapter III
ဆာ
The Legal Reformation of Colonial Subjectivities: Quiroga's Información en Derecho *(1535)*

1. Introduction

It is the initial suggestion that Vasco de Quiroga's lengthiest and most ambitious treatise, *Información en Derecho* (1535) constitutes an excellent opportunity for a historico-critical analysis of the repressive reformation, its possibilities and also limitations,[1] of subalternized or indigenous commonwealths in New Spain. We here wish to open up ourselves to this other foreign time and place, and propose that *Información en Derecho*, because of its uninviting, bureaucratic nature, may well represent historically the colonial cultures of repressive scholarship. Still better, this rather uncomfortable specimen of colonial literature may well qualify, in thematic content, structure of thematic content and social function, as a paradigm of the repressive practice of the alphabetic letter in a rather young, yet imperial romance language, Spanish in the early modern Americas. Quiroga's laborious treatise is however, for all its orthodoxy or historical normality, making a case for the reformation of social structures deemed quite explicitly largely criminal with respect to American populations. Our thesis: *Información en Derecho* represents within the modern dawn of the capitalist world-system the "traumatic belief"[2] in the reformation of this early Spanish colonization in the Americas. The proto-capitalist vehicle for this historical belief will be free wage labor. Free wage labor will however not be Quiroga's final word for the end of colonial history.

The following pages wish to work out in some detail the most salient characteristics of the reasonableness, but also the unreasonableness of this early colonial legality. Our critical analysis as regards the heterogeneity of this historically unsolved trauma will elaborate on Quiroga's egalitarianism (or utopianism), but also on the vertical structurations of "colonial" and "Indian" personalities. We do not wish to fetishize the legal record.[3] We are aware that the legal record is emphatically not the totality of the (hi)story-telling, yet we do not doubt that the repressive culture is a large, painful piece of the official story of coloniality.

Información en Derecho, an early *indigenista* intervention into Spanish Indian Law (or *Derecho Indiano*), develops three main themes: a) the efforts to provide a regulated contractual framework for labor relations (I dare call this frame reformist within proto-capitalist structures); b) the efforts towards a clear-cut reformulation of social typologies with a careful eye on the majority of the population ("pobrecillos macehuales, gente común"); and c) the occasional seduction of millenarianism and social delinquescence "with no content" or the desire for a post-Hispanic utopian moment of majoritarian contentment. These three main themes will unfold alongside Quiroga's six proposals for the change of the colonial state of emergency. These are: one, the relative seclusion of targeted communities under unambiguous colonial tutelage and the commitment to the self-satisfaction of indigenous need; two, the orderly and timely articulation of a social togetherness; three, the reconstruction of the rule of law (or *derecho de estado* [*colonial*]); four, the "wheel" mechanism of political representation; five, the strictly regulated contractualism of the toil for life by the mechanism of the clock or the post-colonial model of contractualism based upon free wage labor; and finally, six the repression of the social death of slavery.

To better illustrate these proposals within the imaginary horizon of Early Modern New Spain, we will be making abundant use of, even abusing the device of the typology. This is done, in the certainty that there is perhaps nothing, one may say at the outset, as explicit as this distinction, which will come to be discarded along the way, hopefully by the time most of its pedagogic potential has already been apprehended and transcended.[4] This chapter will conclude with a necessary abstraction or allegory, so that my readers may just discard its most tedious sections, tear out some illuminations and run away with them hidden in the backpocket.

2. The Traumatic Belief in the Reformation of Coloniality at the Dawn of the Modern World System

Información en Derecho represents the early modern repressive condition of possibility for political change, with its historical limitations, in the foreign horizon of the Spanish or early capitalist colonization of the Americas. In disagreement with those who do not welcome the notion of colonization in relation to Latin America,[5] this work wishes, following Quijano among others, to give it a greater critical depth, but also turn its negativity imaginatively inside out, almost like a dirty old sock, to thus potentially annihilate it if only in its future projection (de-colonization) for us today in Latin America and elsewhere.[6]

Early modern European expansion is obviously not happening in a historical and social vacuum. We wish to frame Quiroga within a world-system model, Wallerstein's global center-periphery model, Arrighi's emphasis on the mutation mechanism of migratory centers and the structural subordination or peripherialization of globalizing capitalism, and Dussel's emphasis on the no-good location of peripheral Latin America inside this global history.[7] We are here mostly understanding Spanish colonization as the historical emergence of capitalism in the Americas.[8] We risk the workable definition of capitalism as the historical penetration of free wage labor.[9] Quiroga's first-hand, first-generation attempt at the reformation of this unstoppable and systemic incorporation and subordination of the American populations to this historical novelty, will articulate a mixed array of contractualist free wage labor against the generalized colonial framework of forced labor. There will be obvious tensions in relation to his own design of six compulsory working hours for everyone and the prohibition of money in his village-hospitals as we have seen in the previous chapter.

It is in this early modern American horizon already penetrated by monetarized labor arrangements that we must situate *Información en Derecho*.[10] The social cost of this early modern globalization will prove tremendous.[11] It is this specific early or proto-capitalist imposition, and the analysis of historically structural possibilities for change, that mostly interests us here.

We are not alone in making this claim of Hispanic proto-capitalism in relation to the early historical coloniality of New Spain (Miño Grijalva[12] and Sempat Assadourian).[13] *Información en Derecho* will give us, we hope, concrete historical arguments for the pre-revolutionary repressive reformation of subaltern or "Indian(ized)" subjectivities already incorporated with no plebiscite into the early modern structuration of this globalizing system we haven't yet left behind). Within this work format, we wish to detail Quiroga's concrete proposals for the change of the mixed array of colonial labor. This colonial unfittingness or "paradigmatic loss" is the still valid commonplace for colonial Latin American Studies we here wish to address most concretely in relation to the early modern repressive political imagination.[14]

We are thus proposing the historical critique of the hegemonic logics set historically in place in the Americas. We will have to move uneasily between the Scylla of the (proto)capitalist economic logic and the Charybdis of the repressive culture of Spanish Indian Law, both historical forces triggering the embryonic conditioning of explicit or official coloniality, but also the future-oriented implicit or latent side of coloniality. We may wish to call this other side by the tentative name of colonial utopianism to differentiate it clearly from classic or metropolitan utopianism.

We must therefore imagine two symbolic moments, the Burgos debates together with the resulting Laws of Burgos (1512-3), and the Valladolid debates with the New Laws (1542-3), inside the big picture of the crises and transformations of a world-system, caught in the middle of a transition from the first (Genoese) to the second (Dutch) phase of accumulation.[15] This is the historical frame for Quiroga's Mexican years which will deliver his name to most encyclopedias. It is in the 1550s that we must imagine the core migration from Genoa to Seville,[16] from Seville to Antwerp, and already by 1559, from Antwerp to Amsterdam.[17] This capital accumulation will come to nest provisionally along the strip of the Rhine, the metaphoric battle line for the centuries to come. Thinking of the Rhine and the Michoacán regions together,[18] and strongly against Weber's excessive visibility,[19] we wish to stretch the chronology and the settlement of modernity with coloniality to thus cover the quite common neglect and brutal silence over the pre-Enlightenment Americas. The Spanish moment of global hegemony is the beginning of modernity. It represents the incorporation and the subordination of the periphery of the Americas to the teething troubles of the world economy. Spain will not become a semi-peripheral state until two centuries later, although signs of decline will start early.[20]

Arrighi has persuasively developed keen insights into the tremendous agility of capital, thinning out into high finance theology to gain some crucial distance from the trumpery of peoples, recognizable faces and datable events. It is as though at crucial moments capital accumulation calls retreat, simply "takes off," and "pulls surpluses out of trade and hold them in money form"(p. 230). The historical lesson appears to be that there is no intrinsic form to capital, that "anything goes" in the flexible combination of factors (be these centralized state, (de)territorialization, imperialism, (de)industrialization, any creed, language, "culture," etc.). The historical mutation of the by force supple mechanism of capital will abandon or recycle any of these factors, seize upon new ones, camp out momentarily and make business, but soon to let any of these factors go. Capital will always set to flight for destination unknown with no sentimentality toward any one permanent home. Arrighi's thesis is the rigorous homelessness of capital transformations. Capital, a migratory chameleon, is thus permanently *fuera de lugar* even when in place and always with restless feet and a quick mind for the next move. In looking into the mechanism of core and periphery combinations, Arrighi does not hesitate to situate the Darwinian cut-throat laws of the (market) jungle, less visible, more abstract and less datable, within the rather faceless centers of high finance (so much for Weber's suggestion of the pennypinching Puritan ethos as quintessential capitalism!). Another word for this mechanism of permanent mutation might be the abstraction, even the theology, of monetarization.[21] Monies, like mercenaries, are nobody's monies.

When contemplating the intercontinental human geography brutally transformed by money flows, the historical imagination must buckle up not to get giddy and forgetful. In historicizing Vasco de Quiroga, a re-framing of conventional narratives is needed, if only to give vitality, along with many others, to the intellectual emergence of the Americas ("emergence" in the dual sense of emerging to historical consciousness but also emergency or crisis exceeding intellectual life).[22] The horizon of the "first" sixteenth century, surely a heterogeneous horizon for all early twenty-first century inhabitants, represents, at least for us, the still precarious installation of the capitalist world system in the Americas. The myth of modernity proper begins here,[23] with the transatlantic globalization of distant spaces and disparate chronologies. This is the historical playground for Quiroga's measured reformism (whether he was fully or partially aware of these larger forces is immaterial). Yet, who is theoretically, historically in a good position to claim to know the matrix of capitalism at the global or local levels? How many ants are allowed to climb to a good observation point of the anthill of humanity? How many are allowed binoculars to foresee the arrival of the anteater? Varying degrees of awareness, but also unawareness or paralogism, are historical players in relation to Quiroga's project, and also our interpretation of it. Our conviction states that Quiroga's American utopianism is unintelligible without this early frame of modern capitalism. In dealing with this monstrous dimension, Quijano's original notion of coloniality allows our vision of the expanding world-system to run on two legs, conceptually. Coloniality will help us highlight some collective structures of domination and subordination operative during the sixteenth-century expansionism of civilizing capitalism (the language of Christian monotheism against barbarians could be thus decoded as the one and only triumphant march against which all other "cultures" will be relegated). If modernization is inseparable from colonization, we must follow the money: colonial modernity is our fundamental conceptual knot; and the study of pre- but also post-USA Americas, or colonial Latin American studies, often in the alienating home of the brave, must always face up to this tight knot, but always with a keen eye on its changes, since money-mediated modernity is never the definite purchase of any one nationality of the past or the present. Money changes hands, just like the upper hand of modernity, the making of this hegemonic nationality, etc. Glorifications, under the dusty name of Renaissance and Golden Age or any one national form of "literature," are here consequently out of place.[24] To the national pantheon of the "lettered city," we will not go gently for the main reason that it reads power and privilege.[25] With or without beautiful letters, early modern coloniality is the most resilient driving force in a transatlantic world made trans-Hispanic not by plebiscite.

This harsh logic of capital accumulation will deliver the Spanish "eccentricity" early in the dialectics between capital and the Early Modern state. There is apparent coincidence in the diagnosis of the "exhaustion of overextension,"[26] and also the "dissipation of their energies in the territorial conquest."[27] The size of continental America was simply too unwieldy and too unpredictable for the surely unruly Spaniards, capitalists in embryo whether they knew it or not, to exert an efficient and noiseless management of human labor. In Quiroga's lifetime, however, arms and high finance will go hand in hand in the alliance between Charles V and the Fuggers,[28] which will find the symbolic end to this "first" sixteenth century, when both superpowers Spain and France will declare themselves bankrupt in 1557. This turning point in the evolution of the European world-economy, 1556-7, will coincide with the official story of generational replacement: Charles V (1500-1558, accession in 1517),[29] holding the title of Holy Roman Emperor, will cede the Crown to his son, and retire to the monastic environs of Yuste (today, the headquarters of the *Academia Europea*).[30] His son, Philip II (1527-1598), will be the monarch of the unification of the Iberian peninsula and of the theoretical totality of Latin America for six decades.[31] This 1557 financial crisis will be the rather bitter pill for the new monarch Philip II already in his first year in charge of the always sun-lit empire (we only need to remember the astounding space-of-flows from Potosí-Veracruz-Seville-Antwerp-Genoa in the sixteenth century).[32] Other crises will follow: the European financial crisis of 1559, the collapse of the Spanish authority in the Netherlands in 1576 and the oft-mentioned defeat of the Spanish invasion of the British Isles, the *Armada* disaster, in 1588.[33]

Modernity is transatlantic flow and international exchange. It is not possible anymore, if ever, to divorce anonymous Indian labor in the Americas and the aesthetic splendor of the *Capilla del Condestable* in the Burgos Cathedral, subsidized largely by American gold, separate it from the magnificent architecture of the *Colegio de San Gregorio* in Valladolid, where Quiroga studied canon law and the Valladolid in New Spain founded by Viceroy Mendoza, or from the intensely delicate *plateresco* stone work of the facades of all palaces and public buildings in the Salamanca streets Quiroga must have been familiar with. We must no doubt include the most influential site for the production of juridico-political knowledge, the Washington of the sixteenth century, the University of Salamanca. The memory of the light and shadow sunset combinations in the stone facade of the Dominican Convent of *San Esteban*, where Francisco de Vitoria lived, is historically inextricably bound to the social forms of colonial life and death of the Indians on the other side of the Atlantic.

This "failure" to keep Spanish expansionism under some convincing form of centralized control needs to be unpacked socially a bit further. We may hypothesize the failure of the New Laws as the historical culmination of the "regalist" and the "seignorial" tendencies, with the alas! nominal victory of the former.[34] We may also wish to talk in terms of "winning" for the more open or coastal areas and "losing" for the more interior social geographies of Castile for the sake of the easy clarification of the argument which is basically one of expansionism of proto-capitalist structures in tension with centralizing state tendencies.[35]

We are willing to point out some social contradictions inside these centralizing tendencies, fundamentally promoted by the high nobility, the Crown and monasticism, which will nominally win, yet fail to hold together entirely the coordinated direction and purpose of settlement strategies inside the over-extension of the Americas. Mapping out this early modern human anthill, we must imagine the consolidation of the state bureaucracy,[36] and its patrimonialist tendencies, all the way down from the top level of the officially sanctioned political absentism (the figure of the *valido*).[37] No doubt, these tremendous social tensions permeated the politico-juridical enclaves constituted no doubt confrontationally.[38] The historical meaning of *pleito* (lawsuit) includes agreement, contract, but also feud, compromise, dispute, confrontation, war and big trouble. For a state official such as Quiroga, the official world, however corrupt, is the totality of the world and there is no desirable world outside officialdom.

Still, we may ask (Ortega's "pregunta a quemarropa"), what does all this barrage of dates mean to the immense majority of the Americas? On this side of the Atlantic, Raup-Wagner has already given us a vivid account of the tumultous oppositional atmosphere to state regulation.[39] García-Abasolo has provided us with a monographic account of Martín Enríquez's legal reform in 1568 in New Spain.[40] We also know of indigenous resistences to the point of near loss of the Empire, for example, the Zacatec-Nahuas and the Mitzón War.[41] It is during this early installation of this modernity/coloniality in the Americas, that the famous *New Laws* will be tried, unsuccessfully.[42] Epidemics grabbed native populations, and reduced them to one-third, while most regional forms of social control were changed from the contractualist tutelage of the *encomienda* to the surely imperfect and precarious patrimonialization of the *corregimiento* (1550-1575)[43] and the *congregaciones* (terminal phase in the first half of the sixteenth century).[44]

We may try to imagine the unimaginable, the demographic collapse of the indigenous populations during the first half of the sixteenth century, the dissolution (the logic of modernity) of the pre-existing social forms into new official forms (monogamic coupling, precarious wage labor for example), the reorganization of territories and labor power,[45] the generalized imposition of forced labor inside, or following Steve Stern, the installation of the "mixed array" of labor relations with the official hesitations and misgivings about the full legality of slavery,[46] the historical corruption of state bureaucracy and the surely changing alliances among high-level members of the Spanish state and the indigenous bureaucracy or the colonial institution of the *cacicazgo*.[47] Quiroga's village-hospitales must surely be imagined within these tumultous, profoundly unstable (un)official changes.

We must also imagine, but surely with increasing difficulties, the historical novelty and impact of the repressive jargon of (un)intelligibility, Spanish Indian legal culture (*Derecho Indiano*),[48] already the unavoidable regime of official truth for colonial Latin American literature,[49] with Spanish still the language of domination in most parts of the South American side of the continent to this day (although marginalized, but growing in the mostly hostile Northern part of the continent). This is the historical habitat for *Información en Derecho*.

We must understand Quiroga's thematization of the reformation of labor relations inside the social practice of the *letrado hidalgo* of the "middling sort."[50] Quiroga, a high state official and, according to most accounts, a scrupulous man of law, produced this repressive textualization most likely in the aftermath of the official exchange between the Dominican Matías Paz and the secular courtly figure of López de Palacios Rubios.[51] This exchange represents the prelude to the Valladolid debates and the famous offshoot of the New Laws. In relation to these two main fiddlers, Bartolomé de Las Casas and Ginés de Sepúlveda, we have to situate the less well known figure of Vasco de Quiroga in a neither-nor position, the no-good place of reformation. Why?

Quiroga is a secular man, a university-trained high official well versed in legal terminology and politico-juridical protocols. Yet he is also visibly inspired, as we have already seen in the previous chapter, by the severe regulated ethos of monastic communitarianism. He will become bishop of the important colonial diocese of Michoacán, not to relinquish but to invigorate this already quite prominent political profile. Politically, Quiroga, appointed by Charles V, is closer to the reformist Franciscanism of Antonio de Guevara.[52] It is within these official political venues that we must situate Quiroga's conceptual horizon for pre-revolutionary or early modern politics.[53]

Quiroga's political position in the Americas will aim at the transformation of the early atrocities of the colonial state. Philosophically, *Información en Derecho* means the attenuation of the Aristotelian natural servitude, and the endorsement of the official orthodoxy of the Thomist natural law and the law of nations. The conflict between these two conceptual levels of the law will deliver a rather thin line for the legality of slavery as we will see later. Quiroga is hence far away from Ginés de Sepúlveda, still in favor of the *encomienda* institution,[54] yet also relatively equidistant from the Dominican Las Casas.[55] In these political negotiations, I would see Quiroga closer, albeit in more modest legal platforms, to the sensibility of the also Dominican intellectual Francisco de Vitoria. It is the working hypothesis that Quiroga may constitute the Vitorian link to this politico-juridical thinking in the Americas, although empirical data of any direct contact between the two is yet to be found.[56] Still, I find an intellectual and emotional proximity which goes far deeper than generation, gender, geography and occupation. It is a common sensibility between these two men, Vitoria and Quiroga, for the invigoration, with all their hesitations, of the rule of law without which there is no polity but "tyranny."

3. Functions and Social Themes in Quiroga's Regimentation of Coloniality

We must reconstruct the specific social function of Quiroga's *Información en Derecho* (1535), inside the colonial repressive culture. We may sketch the totality of this social process by positing the theoretical beginning and completion of the legal process, the initial *demanda* (or citation) to the final *sententia* (or decision) of the judges.[57] So far, we do not have enough empirical evidence to reconstruct the entire process. *Información en Derecho* has come to us isolated, a single cog in a broken wheel so to speak, incomplete and insufficiently attached to Quiroga. This rather uncomfortable and tasteless treatise is not for the uninitiated. It is safe to assert that it would have been completely unintelligible in 1535 to the immense majority of the American populations. The distressing assumption is that this opaque quality is precisely the condition of possibility for the repressive production and social function of *Información en Derecho*.

This rather convoluted treatise is clearly addressed to a superior, while Quiroga was still *oidor*; yet the proper name of this superior has not been recorded, which is a little bit odd.[58] We are unaware of any direct or oblique responses to *Información en Derecho* by this hypothetical superior or by any other political figures of the day. Serrano Gassent makes the connection between this treatise and one *cédula* (Feb. 20, 1534), which reestablished the practice of slavery in the Americas (p. 65). She also pronounces *Información en Derecho* to be an anti-slavery treatise.[59] In the early colonial years, we wish to qualify this standard claim: the social process of slavery, like money, remains perfectly intelligible to the alternative world of *Información en Derecho*. Not even the English chancellor could fictionalize an ideal world of satisfied political desire without money or slavery! What Quiroga's repressive culture is after is not the dissolution of these apparently inevitable, and seemingly undesirable social forms (this appears to have been an unimaginable horizon for the early troubles of capitalist monetarization of social energies). Rather, *Información en Derecho* is proposing the repression of the redefinitions of slavery, and the strict contractual regulation of the new capitalist use of money, i.e. free wage labor, in the Americas with a wary eye on the weakest social sectors, the so-called indigenous peoples. Hence, we find the standard semanticization of

Quiroga's utopianism as anti-slavery erroneous and anachronistic. Quiroga, like Vitoria, found slavery perfectly legitimate and the use of money perfectly legitimate, despite their verbalized puzzlement and numerous hesitations. The reformist repressive culture operated not despite but because of these puzzlements and hesitations just as much as the overall politico-juridical structures. Neither the commotions of slavery nor the early fractures of money were understood by Quiroga. He did not hesitate to state his confusion. Yet this double para-logism remained historically unstoppable. Colonial utopianism will try to give some figure and rule of law to the early theologies of the capitalist use of money and try to chanel, if only theoretically, the brutally novel, potentially liberating social condition of free wage labor.

We have already mentioned the empirical impossibility which we face when we try to reconstruct the official social totality of the legal procedure surrounding *Información en Derecho*. We must be willing on the other hand to take into serious consideration the abundant typographical mistakes, the lapses and constant repetitions, the errors and the endemic sluggishness of this already Kakfaesque legal procedure. According to Kagan, the *cartas ejecutorias*, the theoretical termination prescibed by the legal procedure, did not amount to ten percent. Kagan's statistics, for the most important court of justice in the Iberian peninsula, the Chancillería of Valladolid, speak of 400 *cartas ejecutorias* for a hypothetical totality of 6,000 or 7,000 lawsuits (p. 93). Unfinished legal business appears to be not the historical exception, but the norm.[60] Fragmentariness is the early modern normal state of legal affairs.

According to Kagan, an "información en derecho" was an informative legal brief on a controversial issue.[61] The controversy here is the reformation of labor relations and the regulation of the historical novelty of free wage labor. The textual incompleteness of Quiroga's *Información en Derecho*, and we dare to generalize this phenomenon as the norm in colonial Latin American literature, will leave all readers with cold feet in the winter rain: there is no easy plot line, little nuance and no irony for humanists, no grandiose beginning and no explosive end, there are no recognizable protagonists with full names and no final heterosexual kiss to a happily conventional story. Instead, this colonial Latin American paradigm of repressive culture presents us with a historical heterogeneity formed by middle-brow Spanish, cluttered erudition, the imaginary plateau of the Fathers of the Church, and the insinuation of a social exchange populated exclusively by legal personalities with no face, name and apparently empty of all concrete (dare we say cultural?) content. These "empty signifiers" reach for the satisfaction of each other's needs as though all natural (dare we say cultural?) preconditions for exchange were immaterial or irrelevant. The structure of Quiroga's new social exchange appears to follow purely economic criteria. Quiroga's repressive fragment is thus a *media res* symptom inside a more complex and lengthier, most likely trying and aborted legal process for the most likely pursuit of simple exchanges of radical equality and harmonies of freedom.[62]

The social practice in the repressive culture is hardly ever *paños calientes* for those directly involved in it. We have already mentioned in the previous chapter how deeply our *oidor* was engaged in this colonial business of transatlantic courtroom litigation. He certainly knew first-hand about the unpleasantness of this confrontational plateau in a variety of legal roles, student and scholar, *oidor* and high state official, and most notably as plaintiff in the post-1535, post-*oidor* years. In a historical horizon dominated by the tyranny of the written record and the alphabetic letter in the middle of the illiteracy of the majority on both sides of the Atlantic, the public display of the image superimposed upon the authochthonous glyph culture and languages indigenous to the Americas, Quiroga's Spanish brief is orthodox *política de escritura* inside the social theater allowed by the repressive city.

The reconstruction of the totality of the legal procedure being upon empirical stilts, we must tease out the likeliest historical conditions of possibility of *Información en Derecho*. Quiroga's brief is of the learned kind and its length suggests that it must have been written, quite unlike the harried oral quality of the *Ordenanzas*, in times of some leisure for our *oidor*. *Información en Derecho* is neither concise, nor is it an elegant piece of writing. Its erudition in medieval canon law will choke the unguarded reader, who will most likely not digest it. Despite the explicit tribute to Thomas More, official father of utopian ironies, Quiroga's Spanish will release no humor, no irony (Kafka has taught us the rather unwelcoming effect of these two friends inside the repressive culture). Quite unlike Ginés de Sepúlveda, there is no humanistic dialogue. Quite unlike Vitoria, there is no abstract thinking about the ambivalent nature of the American populations. The issue of taste is radically a non-issue.[63] Here there is no romance, no single appeal to or use of sentimentality.[64] This representative piece of colonial literature did not at all wish to join the best-seller list. Quite the contrary, it must have circulated only inside selected circles and quite far away from the general public. The arid, unpleasant nature of *Información en Derecho* conveys, however, a rather strong historical feeling of late-night candle-burning, fastidious homework. Sacrificing style, *Información en Derecho* wanted to get some political things done fast. For all its long-winded early modern legalese, this manuscript still manages to convey a strong sense of historical urgency regarding the American populations who surely had no means of making any meaning out of its web-like intricacies.

Quiroga will not hesitate to call this legal brief hodgepodge (literally, "ensalada," p. 233). It is a fair self-description. The aridity of the prose and the burdensome weight of the bibliography, makes it highly unlikely for an oral argument. Readers are no doubt dealing here with a technical and genre-specific document, which is only intelligible, it is important to emphasize, to the very few with access to early Indian Law decision-making circuits. The *tlacuilos* (indigenous writers-painters) who composed the *Codex Mendoza* (1541) could not have made much sense out of *Información en Derecho*. The unintelligibility must have been mutual for Quiroga, had he been an eyewitness to the composition of the *Codex Mendoza*. We are today in no better position than Quiroga.[65] It appears thus safe to state that the most likely foundational condition of first-generation coloniality in New Spain feeds upon this mutual unintelligibility, between the *Codex Mendoza* and *Información en Derecho*, which surely benefitted those militarily most powerful, but perhaps not in the long run. The structural condition of walled-in unintelligibility for the legal culture did not, and still does not do it much harm, quite the contrary. Within this semiotic defense mechanism, colonial utopianism will be constructing internal mechanisms for social transparency, authoritatively.

Before turning to the concrete proposals, we would like to contextulize this representative piece of colonial literature. Serrano Gassent has given us some dates to remember: Quiroga, already nominated judge of the *Segunda Audiencia*, departs from Spain (August, 1530), enters Mexico City (January 9, 1531). The most likely foundation of the "village-hospital"of Santa Fé of Mexico, in the proximities of Mexico City appears to be as early as 1531; Quiroga arrives in Michoacán mid-1533. *Información en Derecho* is written in 1535, preceding in some years, but on the other side of the Atlantic, Vitoria's classic pronouncement *De Indis* (1539). We will find—we have Bernal's textual evidence—Quiroga in Spain participating in the Valladolid debates (1542-1543). The debacle of the New Laws, in what appears to be a settlers' victory (Raup Wagner), will be followed up by Quiroga's controversial *De Debellandis Indis* (1551, p. 14), which we will see in some detail in chapter four. Quiroga will die fourteen years later in Uruapán, México (March 14, 1565), according to Moreno (p. 17). If Dominican and

Franciscan monasticism, together with the *Segunda Audiencia* will form a common front against the settlers, this, according to most evidence, will be largely to no avail. *Información en Derecho* must be situated inside this common front, yet with some hesitations regarding the *encomienda* or tutelage institution for the most fragile and majoritarian indigenous social sectors. Surely there were no easy clear-cut solutions. It is high time to look closely into Quiroga's proposals for the reformation of Spanish coloniality in the Americas.

4. First Proposal: Towards a Local Self-Sufficient Indigenous Management or *Imperio Mixto*

Serrano Gassent's conventional interpretation of the notion of "imperio mixto," erroneously follows Quiroga: "proteger, tutelar a los naturales para, creando un régimen de policía mixta, temporal y espiritual, favorecer la cristianización y mejora en su civilización" (p. 27). But a social translation can take neither at their own words. These are Quiroga's words:

> [Y] porque sea mixta la policía, como esta tierra e Nuevo Mundo y la buena simplicidad, humildad, y obediencia y igualdad de él lo requiere...e asimesmo mire por razón desto también al fin supernatural, no por eso, a mi ver, se pierde ni destruye el fin temporal en tal arte e manera de república como ésta...porque [algunos] la ponen meramente evangélica y simplicísima solamente para el fin sobrenatural, y no adaptada para entrambos fines supernatural y temporal ni *mixto como es y conviene que sea aquesta desde Nuevo Mundo,* si se ha de cumplir con lo que la bula apostólica pone por cargo y manda que se haga en la conquista y pacificación de estas partes para la instrucción de los naturales dellas. (my emphasis, p. 236)

We wish to suggest the following: 1) the standard construction of legitimation for the early modern period as regards Spanish domination in the Americas will cling to papal sanction (*bula apostólica*). The historical alliance betweeen the Papacy and the theoretical protectionism of one strong national monarchy (the formula of the *De Translatio Imperii* is evidence of this).[66] This rhetoric will constitute the orthodox legal protocol for all discussions regarding the proper or improper possession of the Americas;[67] 2) *De Translatio Imperii* formulations, a sort of global mapping of political jurisdictions, will historically coalesce around the association between the centralized state and the Christian Church, most concretely in the institution of the *Patronato Real,* which will try to keep the strong opposition of settlers under control. It will not be easy. Quiroga's village-hospitales are to be understood at the crux of this association; and, 3) the sole attribution of the proprietorship of the expanding world to the Papacy, is the cause of the delegation of temporary proprietorship to the Spanish Crown, and also of the temporary patrimonialization of indigenous labor in the typified system of tutelage or *encomienda* system. Full-fledged citizens (or *vecinos*) will become responsible for the general surveillance of the commonwealth, or *proveedores del sustento* or *bastimento* of the structural needs of the colonial polity.

But there is still more historical content to the technical formulation of the "mixed polity" than meets the eye. We need to turn to the perfect example of early modern humanist, Juan Ginés de Sepúlveda (1470-1573), the opponent of Bartolomé las Casas in the Valladolid Debates (1550-51), to explain in further detail this political proposal of the "mixed polity." Ginés de Sepúlveda—international intellectual traveller, perfect embodiment of the humanist ideal of the *letras y armas,* trained in the prestigious center of Bologna under the supervision of Pomponazzi, translator of Aristotle, courted by the Medicis, Alexander VI, etc.,[68] chronicler of Charles V and advisor to Philip II—represents the harshest logic of modernity and the ardent rhetoric advocating the naturalness of the Spanish domination of the Americas.[69] We need to go into some detail to extricate the rhetorical structure of this logic, inside which the more concrete notion of "mixed polity" will make sense. This notion of "mixed polity," defended by Quiroga's *Información en Derecho,* will include some variations.

The polished, pedagogic dialogue in *Democrates Secundus* (1544),[70] written in the language of high culture, Latin, and showing formal resemblance to More's *Utopia* (1515), will be articulating the Aristotelian rationale for a "distributive justice"[71] as pertains to a time-honored hierarchical conception of human nature. Quite faithful to Aristotle,[72] Ginés de Sepúlveda, 1,867 years later, will give a rather sinister articulation of sameness and difference(s) as pertains to the early modern official understanding of what amounts to be human. The chain of equivalences, or sameness, of the *genus homo* effectively breaks down into various species or stocks with uneven enfranchisement and servitude obligations.

Aristotle's desire for the secluded and self-sufficient nation-state,[73] the relative quaintness and perceptible pettiness implicit in the intelligible political unit of the Greek household, with the naturalness of the exclusion from social goods of large sectors of humanity, women, slaves and foreigners, resurfaces with breath-taking historical resilience via Ginés de Sepúlveda's polished Latin. This time, however, the relative provincial quaintness of the Greek world emerges to an early modern "global village" of imperial possession. The Aristotelian notion of the social "good" is exclusively for the legalized minority of propertied citizens, whereas Ginés de Sepúlveda and Quiroga will historically come closer to the relative opening of 'good' into the totality of the existing world, the *encomienda* and *bastimento*, or commonwealth, albeit with unsolved or vertical tensions.

What amounts to "human" thus branches out for this sixteenth century Aristotelianism into a variety of uneven, asymmetrical forms. Consequently, there are various governmental structures established to control this almost unpredictable variety of human forms. Ginés de Sepúlveda, truly a strong intellectual candidate for the first Modern,[74] will construct an ontology of social exchanges based upon the rather perverse logic of "might is right." That is, this imperial Aristotelianism will break down unevenly the chain of equivalences or the sameness of humanity. But, for Ginés de Sepúlveda, humanity is a plurality of living forms ("varia hominum conditio"). This Aristotelian axiology ("might is right") proclaims that the perfect (human) form will effectively come to dominate the imperfect (human) forms. There will thus be a correspondence in the official arrangement which bespeaks of civil or royal government ("imperium civile, regium imperium"), also said to be akin to paternal care ("paternum imperium"), for men who are by nature free. That is, freedom means full humanity and adequate powers of cognition and intelligence. There are, on the other hand, those who do not qualify for this full-blown humanity, the proto-human populations or barbarians. We must highlight Ginés de Sepúlveda's strong repudiation of attention to detail; all American populations fit into this latter side of human degradation. This lack of curiosity for American specificity betrays the intellectual racism of this European ethnocentrism.

Early modern American barbarians are thus generally semanticized by Ginés de Sepúlveda as all those who are lacking cognitive discretion and trailing behind in the global journey of humanity.[75] Barbarians must be accordingly subjected to "paternal domination"("imperium herile"). The government of these inferior humans, who will not be left alone, is rather a rigid form of temporary patri-lineal subjugation: "heril" and "erus," or master, which is strongly related to the "paterfamilias" or "maior erus," and the second generation of the "minor erus" or young master. The authority-power (dominium-regnum-imperium) of this "erus" also brings to mind the strong suggestion of the man whom an animal-like man is accustomed to obey (should we wish to recall Pozzo and Lucky in Beckett's *Waiting for Godot*?). Ginés de Sepúlveda's Aristotelianism, enunciated from a historical position of force, or through Pozzo's blind eyes, faithfully sanctions the existing domination underpinning this social exchange by naturalizing or ontologizing it. *Democrates Secundus* constructs the conservative argument, "that's the way (human) things are" and the shrug of the shoulders.

Rather than attending to supernatural or metaphysical language, "imperio mixto" is thus here introduced as the supposedly temporary corrective measures for these proto-human populations. The American populations which Ginés de Sepúlveda never visited will correspond to the Aristotelian grid of intelligibility of human perfectability: barbarians are theoretically free, yet they will have to serve (forced labor) because of their depraved human nature. Thus, the historically expanding notion of humanity breaks down theoretically into the various stages of humanity. According to this logic of "might is right," the less developed humans will serve the most developed humans always already in a position of force. These servants deserve to serve at least temporarily due to their natural turpitude and precisely in order to achieve full humanity for themselves. When they will achieve this is unclear.

Yet all members of the *genus homo* are, despite this naturalized inequality, still theoretically free (Africans, for this humanistic vision, are quite beyond the pale of humanity). This nominal freedom does not, however, preclude the historical meaningfulness of social death or slavery as the most salient signifier to the contrary. The rather abstract political division of Spaniards and barbarians, the so-called "Indians," will become concrete in the "imperio mixto" which distributes the latter among the former. Two different political regimes will thus be institutionalized (the classic formulation of the "dos repúblicas"). Whereas paternal kingship is the naturalized ideal government for the Spaniards, the barbarians will be kept in a theoretically segregated state, the American reverse of the ideology of the *limpieza de sangre*, and thus in the theoretically temporary stage of mixed or paternal domination. During this presumably temporary stage, those serving the Spaniards will keep intact the legal condition of freedom ("conditonis liberae"), provided they comply with the typified formalization of the just war, namely the *requerimiento*. Those who refuse to comply, so the Aristotelian logic unfolds according to the Spanish humanist, will become, according to the law of nations, the social product, (slaves), of victory in a just war (this will be analyzed further in relation to Quiroga's canon-law intricacies in *De Debellandis Indis*).

This mixed domination will become concrete in the colonial institutions of tutelage and *encomienda* thus:

> [Y] a los bárbaros [conviene] tratarlos como ministros o servidores [servi seu mancipia], pero de condición libre [conditionis liberae], con cierto imperio mixto y templado de heril y paternal según su condición y según lo exijan los tiempos [barbaros istos tanquam ministros, sed liberos, quodan ex herili et paterno temperato imperio regendos et pro ipsorum et temporis conditione tractandos]. Y cuando el tiempo mismo los vaya haciendo más humanos [humanioris] y florezca entre ellos la probidad de costumbres y la religión cristiana, se les deberá dar más libertad y tratarlos más dulcemente. Pero como esclavos no se les debe tratar nunca et ut mancipia vero nulli tractari debent], a no ser a aquellos que por su maldad y perfidia, o por su crueldad y pertinencia en el modo de hacer la guerra, se hayan hecho dignos de tal pena y calamidad. (pp. 171-173)

Ginés de Sepúlveda's original Latin, which this Spanish quote is somewhat betraying, makes clear for us today this official logic of Spanish domination of the Americas (this or similar fragments must have been surely read aloud to Charles V and Philip II). The historical plasticity of the notion of humanity distressingly coincides with the mono-vocal enunciation of the official *letrado* in a historical position of force. Ginés de Sepúlveda will semanticize thus a heterogeneous American proto-humanity:

> Pero por otro lado tienen de tal modo establecida su república que nadie posee invidualmente cosa alguna, ni una casa, ni un campo de que pueda disponer ni dejar en testamento a sus herederos, porque todo está en poder de sus señores que con impropio nombre llaman reyes, a cuyo arbitrio viven más que al suyo propio, atenidos a su voluntad y capricho y no a su libertad y el hacer todo esto esto no oprimidos por la fuerza de las armas sino de un modo voluntario y espontáneo es señal certísima del ánimo servil y abatido de estos bárbaros. (p. 109-111)

According to this subalternizing logic, the Americas is the imaginary locus of the "not yet fully human," and the opposite of migratory European institutions of patrimonialization of social energies and legitimate kingship. Ginés de Sepúlveda naturalizes Spanish domination in the presumption that the American populations wanted their degraded world previous to the arrival of the Spaniards (the seed for individualism is implicit in this timid appeal to intentionality: Amerindians picked the wrong choice of barbarism). This "republic" of proto-rational populations dominated by passions, hence merits the domination by the Spaniards. According to this harsh humanism, whoever is historically on top is the perfect human form and thus endowed with all the right and the might to do accordingly.

The early modern criterion for human perfectability is thus established following the non-negotiable imposition of the monetarization of social energies, the repressive tyranny of the alphabetic letter in Spanish or Latin, the mapping out, parcelling out and distribution of these hitherto unknown territories, *soledades* and *baldíos*, the tabulation and codificiation of the still barely intelligible autochthonous social energies,[76] the maximization of labor and profit into free wage labor, which is compulsion by less visible means, the individualization of the working unit,[77] and the prohibition of idleness. We may see easily here the historical arrogance of the male "I," who posits himself without many hesitations as the measuring rod but also as the whipping post of entire collectivities in distant places (Ginés de Sepúlveda's scholarly axiology is situated in the antipodes of the existential claim to truth, such as Bernal Díaz del Castillo or Vasco de Quiroga, since he had no direct acquaintance with the Americas). No social unit will be allowed to remain outside these expanding structures. No social unit will be allowed to remain unintelligible. Ginés de Sepúlveda's unmitigated Aristotelianism of the "us v. them"of early modern civilization—the "us" of the literate people, humanists, Spaniards, Christianity, the use of the private property, the historical might of European expansionism, against the receiving end seemingly an empty signifier of "them" of American barbarism,[78] seemingly with no cultural 'goods'—exemplifies the harshest tendency to dissolve and destroy anything that may exercise a resistence to modern proto-capitalism. The theologies of proto-capitalism, combined with the prestigious jargon of authenticity (sixteenth-century Aristotelianism) thus provide the perhaps unconscious criterion, with or without Christianity considerably attenuated in Ginés de Sepúlveda, for the orthodox legitimation of the early coloniality of the Americas.[79]

To this rather oxthodox and courtly line of reasoning, Quiroga's *Información en Derecho* exemplifies the historical modulation of colonial utopianism. If the early modern political melody is sung by Ginés de Sepúlveda's tenor voice, Quiroga's colonial utopianism will represent the occasional or localized counter-tenor intervention. If Ginés de Sepúlveda's *Democrates Secundus* represents the official mainstream, against the early combative monastism, Quiroga's experiential knowledge will be aiming at the construction of a transatlantic commonwealth without ruptures from officialdom, yet with vocal discomfort. Specificially, our *oidor* will be working towards indigenous self-management and relative autonomy by clinging to the umbrella protection of the *Patronato Real* and the colonial institutions of tutelage, the *encomienda* system.

We must try to imagine, in relation to this historical dawn of the global village and the Universal Monarchy the construction of a trans-oceanic togetherness. Quiroga's argument would run thus: 1) we are all theoretically vassals to the Crown, the sole proprietor of lands and lives, as delegated from the Pope; 2) so it is true that with or without hesitations we are all human; yet, and this is the crucial Orwellian inflection, some are still more human than others. For the latter more fragile and yet majoritarian social sectors in the Americas, a system of social protectionism is needed. Using contemporary language, we may call colonial utopianism a kind of early modern system of social welfare.

Taking into painful consideration the constitutive authoritarianism of Spanish rule in the Americas,[80] the colonial notion of "Indian" personality will be stretching the early modern notion of humanity. It is as though the incorporation and the subordination of the newly incorporated subjects needed to recede into largely time-honored or medieval "lord-serf" vocabulary.[81] The sign "Indian" will precisely signal the incorporation of these human-resembling subjects into new political subjects under the sole sovereignty of the Spanish Crown. "Indian" will mark precisely those social agents in the below or subordinated, abject position in relation to the relative novelties, for the Americas, of incipient free wage labor, monogamic patterns of social reproduction, private property, the alphabet and the soon ubiquitous use of money.[82] "Indians" will have to serve ("mester, ministro, servicio"), but are not, theoretically at least, slaves ("servi, mancipia"). From a legal standpoint, "Indians," like children, adolescents or those with the label of mentally deranged in today's society, are located in an "in-between" stage between the unhappy marrriage of the freedom and unfreedom of potentially full social responsibility and rights. Coloniality is juridically this making of proto-humanity, which will cover the immense majority of the American population, which will get institutionalized into a neither-nor or ambivalent in-betweenness between freedom and unfreedom (slavery), forced labor and the looming wage labor. This will be the conceptual locus, a kind of no-place and potentially good place,[83] for Quiroga's intervention in *Información en Derecho*. We may slowly begin to understand the reasons behind Quiroga's firm repudiation of social ambiguity in New Spain since official ambivalences and hesitations don't appear to have been on the historical side of these "Indianized" communities.

Finally, there is still a bit more to the social and historical translation of this "imperio mixto" proposed by Quiroga to reform the early American coloniality.[84] Bringing the semiotic or communicational approaches to the historical three-dimensionality of toil for life (or labor), *imperio mixto* is then the sign which externalizes the secluded repression of the generalized colonial imposition of forced labor. The "mixed array" of forced labor will be caught, with no easy way out, in the "and" of feudalism *and* capitalism in the Americas.[85] Within the complexities of this global framework, current work on Latin America appears to emphasize the complexities and specificities of coloniality.[86] The authoritarian and para-logic condition of this *novohispano* contractualism is also, following Lalinde-Abadía's suggestions, no doubt related to Quiroga's defense of the *imperio mixto* (should we need to be reminded of the shamelessly distressing Chilean motto "por la razón o por la fuerza" to highlight this distressing marriage).

Against the monopoly of Anglo models for global contractualism, the Spanish language historically links the notions of *sisa* or *pecho* (tribute), and relates them to the Latin *pactum*, which according to the *Covarrubias Dictionary* (1611), means indistinctly *tributo o concierto*, both informing the double bind of social concert and punishment or *pena*. A careful diachronic exploration of this exceedingly rich semantic field associates the *derramas*, or the collecting of taxes and tributes, to the *heril* domain of the *dueño* or *amo*, who also happens to be the visible legislator of the rules of the social game. The lawmaker is thus the lord (by force) of a more or less clearly partitioned domain. The one-way circulation of the *pena* or punishment signals the social singularity who, always with power/knowledge, keeps collective energies under control, or *sujeta*, all those who will qualify under the oddly resilient misnomer of "Indians." The Indians thus become political subjects to the Spanish Crown by being subjected to a structural condition of domination or coloniality. It is only with great difficulty that we may imagine a sixteenth-century "Indian" trying to make sense of *Información en Derecho*, within and against the conceptual constellation of Spanish Indian Law (or *Derecho Indiano*). It is safe to say that the intricate, reclusive nature of this university-based knowledge/power and the brutal novelty of this jargon of authenticity in the Americas made this repressive paradigm for colonial literature an almost totally opaque textualization to the Indian majorities. This opacity, we have already stated, is historically meaningful. If the exercise of force/rule and the official magistrates of interpretation are historically in the same tight social knot, colonial utopianism was situated in the vicinity of these official enclaves.

Unintelligibility is, rather than a hindrance or a nuisance, a structural condition, or even a deliberate strategy for the (re)production of the repressive culture, but also for its reformation.

The legal technicality of the "mero o mixto imperio"[87] historically signals the exchange between the big guy (the Crown) and the smaller guys or *señor(es)* against the potential American wealth, tentatively regulated in the *feudo*.[88] This early modern vertical recognition, or non-egalitarian contractualism, makes the lord the ultimate judge for the full civil and criminal jurisdiction of the *feudo* ("mero mixto imperio" or "alta, baja [instancia]"). It is clear that the time frame and the depth of the cession are left at the discretion of the appointed officials, often knee-deep in the muddy historical waters carrying the monetarization and patrimonialization of public office (Tomás y Valiente). The cession must also have been no doubt penetrated by chance fluctuations and political contigency. As we have already mentioned, the chronic liquidity problem of the Spanish monarchy in the early modern period led to an increasing liberality ("prodigalidad") in the concession of these juridical rights. "Mutual love/bond of rights and duties [*pechos, derechos*] are formalized between these uneven, contracting parties."

We must conceive the possession and usufruct of land and human labor ("tierras, vasallos") in the Americas as the predominant definition of wealth (Quiroga's village-hospitals also exemplify the relatively insularized seeds of manufacture). This typified social exchange always has the donating party in the Crown, theoretically the sole proprietor of the totality of lands and responsible for the well-being of all the lives. The cession by this true proprietor ("enajenación, donación, merced") means the temporary possession ("tenencia") by an appointed party. Patrimonialism of lands and lives must be negotiated, at least theoretically by every single generation and intergenerational transitions will be extremely conducive to tension and conflict. Following upon the royal donation, the definition of this double patrimony of peoples and lands will take place always in the confrontational enclaves of and always according to the protocols of the repressive culture. Lawsuits, Quiroga's political bread and butter in his post-*oidor* Mexican years (1535-1565), will occur precisely in the contradictions over these jurisdictions. The social definition of the rights and duties of these "mero o mixto imperio"stipulations, will constitute the bone of contention in a multilingual, palimpsest-like superimposition of generational (dis)continuities destructured by, and also restructured under, a regime of coloniality which will be here to stay surely to the agony of the many.[89]

Following Maravall, we may thus imagine the historical tension between the statist or monism and fragmented pluralism. The political forcefield finds the polarization between the centralized or nomothetic regulation and the idiographic deregulation or the emphasis on the strongest particularity of this hegemonic authoritarian contract. The issue appears to be whether to singularize or pluralize the master-slave model. The mapping of New Spain was thus negotiated to include land demarcations, human labor, the customized concessions of social repression, or justice, and even the production of money. To compensate for this cession, the receiving party must pay taxes ("renta, tributo"), to the sole proprietor. It is not difficult to imagine how the liquidity problem and the chronic state bankruptcy must have broken down the initial transparency of these contractualist models into the production of false or underegulated money and an increasing liberalization in the concession of "empty lands" ("baldíos"), and how the endemic corruption of state officials against the early background of proto-capitalist structures in the Americas must have worsened the global situation. We may hypothesize, following Stern, the arrest of free wage labor in colonial Latin America and the long-lasting colonial bastardization with forced labor. We may go further and posit the slow penetration of the monetarized and equalizing social mechanism inside the repressive culture. *Información en Derecho* will attest to this effort in contradiction to the *Ordenanzas*. The challenge here will be to try to imagine the tremendous social impact of this historical novelty, free wage labor, in early modern Americas as a simultaneously destructuring market theology, but also a potentially liberatory restructuring force or process incorporating, with no plebiscite, an hitherto unimaginable and truly heterogeneous humanity under coloniality.

If according to the official (hi)story, the transatlantic commonwealth and the possession of the Crown must coincide, our state official will lean closer to statism. Quiroga's project will be striving towards a localized self-sufficient indigenous "imperio mixto." It is surely not too farfetched to suggest the most likely historical landscape: the overextension of the American colonial condition of being must have continued delivering impossibilities or illegalities, rather than yielding itself to any one complete repression or predictability.

5. Second Proposal:
La Buena Policía y Conversación

The hegemonic logic of modernity tells us that indigenous populations will not be allowed to be left alone (we have already mentioned the incorporation of the indigenous elites in the colonial institution of *cacicazgo*). Under coloniality, all American political communities will be made intelligible sooner or later. In the language of the period, human associations will be talked about in terms of *comunicación*, and even *conversación* and the pre-Hispanic forms, surely barely intelligible to newcomers like Quiroga, will be declared to be habitats where solitude, or *soledades*, grows disturbingly thick and wild (and we only need to summon the notion of *excomunicación* to feel some of the intensity of these political operations). We will soon see the harsh treatment of all those outside these newly formalized polities.

In the sails of the strongest Spanish forces for global reconfiguration, *comunicación* and *conversación* historically translate into the coloniality of the *encomienda* system, quite literally the task of entrusting someone with the provision of somebody or something (and this archaic use is still heard in Latin America today). Subalternized communities will be allocated to recognizable political subjects (mostly Spaniards, but not exclusively). *Feudo* becomes *encomienda* in the massive reconfiguration and allocation of lands and peoples, legally labelled "Indians." In years of almost permanent war conflict, this tutelage system is theoretically designed to provide the necessary substenance to the social totality or commonwealth. The *encomienda* is the colonial institution which theoretically caters to the commonwealth, i.e. provides the *bastimento* or *proveedor del sustento* to the expanding totality of Spanish vassals.[90]

Información en Derecho certainly participates in this aforementioned civilizational prejudice which attributes an almost ontological subaltern status to a radical heterogeneity. But there are also perceptible hesitations, Ortega y Gasset's tight knot of *creencia* and *duda*, as regards the self-appointed civilizational belief. In Quiroga's treatise, this subaltern status may also be, qua subaltern status and via the conceptualization of natural law, the desirable condition of possibility for something radically post-Spanish and new (millenarianism). The existential situation must not have been at all easy for Quiroga. We are dealing here with the first-time first-generation contact of a lettered sexagenarian and man of state face to face with a hitherto unimaginable, almost entirely unintelligible human dimension. Unintelligibility must have surely worked both ways (we may imagine a first meeting with aliens landing in our backyard: Should we volunteer a handshake? Should we address them in polite English? Offer them sweetened tea? Ignore the disagreeable hairs and bright colors? Do they understand our accent? Do we take advantage of their apparent weakness? Would they take advantage of ours? Should we ignore them altogether?).

Speaking from a historical, social position of relative force and privilege, Quiroga will be also articulating the belief/doubt regarding this early modern orthodoxy of the hierarchization of the human dimension. There is no easy solution, except for the early possibility of segregated racialized communities of the Spanish and indigenous republics under imperial Spain. Quiroga's legalistic mindset will not allow him to make drastic pronouncements in relation to the early modern globality. His plans for reformation of the coloniality will thus have to remain pre-revolutionary, *indigenista* but not indigenous, and necessarily local in the early modern or pre-revolutionary stage for politics.[91]

Quiroga's historical desire for the increased regulation of the commonwealth will, however, get complicated with a millenarian vision which mobilizes the political paradox of heterogeneity (the "us v. them") with a new twist against this aforementioned orthodox vision. *Información en Derecho* will be simultaneously saying that "they" (the indigenous populations), are backward or more primitive than "us," and, precisely because of this primitivism and backwardness "they" will paradoxically constitute the "stuff [Christian] dreams are made of" in relation to a colonizing "us" which is always already debased and corrupt, almost entirely beyond any possibility of redemption.

Seizing upon the Spanish moment of globalizing hegemony, *Información en Derecho* will intervene into the colonial world which is already upside down, and criminally so. The repressive culture will try to come to the rescue and thus reframe under the names of *buena policía* and *buena conversación*. To achieve this goal, the pre-Hispanic condition of human unintelligibility, for our state official, must be undone with no second thoughts:

> y viven derramados como animales por los campos sin buena policía, y se crían a esta causa malos, fieros, bestiales y crueles, perjudiciales, inhumanos e ignorantes e tiranos entre sí mismos, aunque no nos molesten a nosotros ni impidan paso ni nos tengan tomada cosa nuestra ni que nos pertenezca ni sean enemigos del nombre cristiano. Pues que basta vivir en notoria ofensa de Dios su Criador [*sic*], y en tiranía de sí mismos, como gente bárbara y cruel, y en ignorancia de las cosas y del buen vivir político, y sin

ley ni rey, como son estos naturales…[Q]ue nunca tovieron [*sic*] ni tienen ley ni ordenanza ni costumbre buena alguna ni ciencias donde lo puedan saber ni deprender [*sic*], sino que todo está puesto en ignorancia y bestialidad y corrupción de costumbres. (p. 93 & 98)

Quiroga proclaims, holding hands with Ginés de Sepúlveda and Vitoria on this one, that pre-Hispanic social forms have no meaning to be rescued for the post-Hispanic future. These incomprehensible and alienating forms are therefore to be repudiated with no ambiguous language. "They" constitute largely the abominable human formulation or "tyranny." Dispersion ("derramados") is visible evidence of this abomination for a classic Europe-based equation between humanity, city-dwelling civilization, always semanticized according to the prestigious jargon of intelligibility (Aristotle), with or without Thomist attenuations. The new barbarians are the American naturals which will be predominantly semanticized in a radical state of almost total dispossession (the seriality of the "without the good," the "sin" particle). They do not have "it," the "good" goverment, law and the true knowledge ("buena policía, ley, rey, en notoria ofensa de Dios"). Hence, indigenous peoples are backward or below the acceptable level of civilized humanity ("inhumanos, ignorantes"), albeit in a rather harmless, self-alienating way. But there is more.

We must still tease out Quiroga's historical axiology (or Ortega's "creencia-duda"). Following Aristotelian taxonomies, our *oidor* in the last year in office briefly sets out to qualify three good or "perfect" ways of arranging the human polity, which he will declare absent from the pre-Hispanic Americas (the "they do not have them" argument). There will also be three bad ways, one of which (unruliness of violence or tyranny), will describe "Motezuma's" rule.

The three good forms for the transcontinental polity ("unión y congregación de muchos perfecta"), are according to Quiroga monarchy, aristocracy and timocracy, which are defined as the best vehicles for the achievement of a commonwealth. It is thus not strange at all that the Early Modern fracturations of Spanish estate society will be advocating, almost nostalgically from official positions, timid forms of republicanism (aristocracy and timocracy), but only for the happy few of the propertied classes, in what is really a plutocracy. Yet, we will see how this prestigious formulation fares poorly in Quiroga's own reformulation of labor regimes and local governments.

The three bad forms for the transcontinental polity mean confusion and self-interested particularity under the names of tyranny, oligarchy and democracy. Quiroga's historical inability to come to terms with other non-Aristotelian forms for the human polity, makes him place the pre-Hispanic political pinnacle, "Motezuma," under this first category.[92] Quiroga despises what he ignores, politically. *Información en Derecho* makes pre-Spanish forms unlivable heterogeneity and arbitary rule of fear. "Motezuma" is the politically empty and yet "unnatural" sign to be repudiated. This pre-Hispanic American degradation of political life will have to change with the arrival and liberation by the Spaniards. These bearded Spaniards will be the chosen ones to deliver the goods (messianism), also according to Quiroga, but not necessarily for them. The Spanish hegemony is merely the vehicle for drastic transformations that *Información en Derecho* only dares touch obliquely, and always in relation to the rather generic legal nomenclature of *Indios*. Quiroga does not differentiate among the various communities. His early contact with the Tarascan or Purépecha communities in the Michoacán region must have surely helped him to gain a keener, more site-specific and fastidious vision of these *Indios* (the *Latinos* of the sixteenth-century Americas). We must therefore be more careful and relate Quiroga's repressive intervention, and the liberatory potential almost exclusively relate to the *Purépecha* communities in the Michoacán region, and certainly not to the totality of indigenous populations (Las Casas's interventions will generally operate at this more general level of politics).

We must therefore imagine the no-place and potentially good place of the Tarascan region in a transitional stage, never quite entirely subjugated by Aztec domination, but also never quite systematically rampaged by the early atrocities of Spanish colonization, except for the leader of the First *Audiencia*, Nuño de Guzmán.[93] Quiroga's reformation, coming from one of the four *oidor*es of the Second *Audiencia*, is hastily responding to the early institutional crisis of colonial state crime. And it is perhaps for this reason that Quiroga's legacy is still as much celebrated in Michoacán as that of the peace-maker or *pacificador* of the Tarascan communities (as the numerous commemorative statues of Quiroga in Morelia and Uruapán, or the central presence of Quiroga and More in the magnificent mural in the public library Gertrudis Bocanegra in Pátzcuaro, Morelia painted by Juan O'Gorman attest to this day). History does not of course stop here. It will be precisely the Michoacán region from where a significant leadership of the social forces (the figure of Hidalgo), will be claiming independence from Spain three centuries later.[94])

So, *Información en Derecho*, following the discursive decorum of state orthodoxy, will be largely proposing a clear-cut reconfiguration of social energies:

[Se ha de proveer] que haya buena y general conversión y bastante sustentación para todos, españoles y naturales, con conservación dellos y de la tierra; y esto que sea por tales modos, medios y arte y por tales leyes y ordenanzas que se ada[p]ten a la calidad y manera que ellos las puedan saber, entender y usar, y guardar y ser capaces dellas; y desta manera son las de mi parecer, sin los entrincamientos y oscuridad y multitud de las nuestras, que no las sabrán ni entenderán ni serán capaces dellas de aquí al fin del mundo. (p. 98)

The ethical imperative to reproduce human life (or *conservación*), forces our state official to endorse a legalistic reformation of the colonial state in the belief that the rule of law (or *estado de derecho colonial*), always *already* threatened by martial law (or Sempat Assadourian's notion of "estado de guerra permanente"), is better than nothing for the most fragile and indigenized populations in the Americas (racialization may be said implicitly or not to signal social fragility). Quiroga's early *indigenismo* will vindicate for this pragmatic reason the theoretical safety net of the Spanish Indian Law, always *already* with a wary eye on these majoritarian populations of the Americas, since the utopian goal of the disappearance of the bureaucratic machine of the law was already impossible for the sixteenth-century political imagination.[95] We are thus getting from an insider the political desire, which largely coincides with official verbalizations, for the change of the sluggishness and opacity of the bureaucratic legal machinery and for the reformation of a few good laws automatically intelligible, and thus immediately appropriated, by these most numerous social sectors most damaged by coloniality. Settlers and foot soldiers, Bernal Díaz del Castillo but also Ginés de Sepúlveda, would have surely been not happy with this radical suggestion, which puts Quiroga closer to the harsh accusations historically produced by Franciscan monasticism.

Yet, to achieve this historical goal of the reproduction of life, colonial utopianism must face the distressing realization that for these imported proto-capitalist structures there will be no "hit and run." There will be no going back. Money will not politely back off and apologize with a promise never to come back to the massive destructurations and restructurations of territories and peoples under coloniality. There is no pulling out the settlers, soldiers and lawyers from inside the centrality of Iberian expansionism, a fleeting, yet lasting and traumatic moment of the global historical process of expanding capitalism. Quiroga will be far away from Las Casas's extremist arguments, which may be said to be in the historical minority.[96] And precisely for this reason this prophetic voice is today the main point of reference for the theology and the philosophy of liberation.⁹⁷ Quiroga's quiet reformation, on the contrary, does not, cannot wish to acquire in mode and mood the global proportions of these messianic denunciations.

One possible historical lesson may tell us that Quiroga's partial reformation, carried out by the tremendous impetus of early modern capitalist expansionism, must necessarily have come from within (the repressive culture is always part of the official (hi)story). A second possible historical lesson for these pre-revolutionary times may suggest that the survival of these village-hospitals depended necessarily upon self-disciplined seclusion. Its establishment will have to operate within the racial mechanism of social differentiation of the *limpieza de sangre*, but the other way round, that is, the social differentiation of the pro-indigenous, most specifically Tarascan empty signifier. We must imagine the long-lasting Crown failure to discipline completely the distant overextension of American human geography, the background of the official policy of the two republics and Quiroga's repudiation of social ambiguity:

> Porque tengo por muy cierto para mí, qiue sin este recogimiento de ciudades grandes que estén ordenadas y cumplidas de todo lo necesario, en buena y católica policía y conforme a la manera de esto, ninguna buena conversión general ni aun casi particular ni perpetuidad ni conservación ni buen tratamiento ni ejecución de las ordenanzas ni de justicia en esta tierra ni entre estos naturales, se puede esperar ni haber, atenta la calidad dellos y della, ni con esta buena policía y estado de república, dejarlo de haber todo muy cumplido y aventajado y abastado [*sic*] [abastecido]. (p. 103-104)⁹⁸

Quiroga's repressive culture exemplifies this political impulse towards the reformation of coloniality following the tic-tac dictum of early modern technique (we may remember Ortega y Gasset on Charles V's fascination for watches in the Yuste monastery). The explicit goal is the symmetrical arrangement (or *recogimiento*) of human togetherness so that the reproduction of human life (*conversación, conservación*), may fall within political rule. Without the former cause, the latter consequence is not happening, and with the former the latter is barely happening by 1535 when *Información en Derecho* was written.

Yet, Quiroga's political imagination will not stop there. It will hit the target of (political) survival, by surpassing it in the rendition of (political) contentment. Already encroached by maximizing economic profit, Quiroga's vision will be announcing the communal contentment only in abundance ("cumplido, aventajado, abastado") among those social agents always on the verge of extinction. Quiroga's utopianism thus wishes to construct repressively "las Indias mejores" (the expression is from Las Casas),[99] where only misery and death are present. There is in Quiroga no call to arrange a plebiscite for the "natives" to decide what to do. There is here also no concrete reference to any (wo)man, no reference to any singularized ethnicity, no specific geography. *Información en Derecho* gives us an arresting, unnerving, almost unbearably cold place for a better society where singularized choice is a non-issue. *Buena policía* (or good government), will come to be produced solely with zero-tolerance as to possible deviations from these non-negotiable regulations (*ordenanzas*). It is as though political reformation must seize the historical day created by Spanish expansionism, and yet must keep it under some kind of localized predictability before it is already too late and goes permanently out of control under generalized colonial misrule.

Inside the lettered-city walls of official regulation, Quiroga's repressive mechanism will try to implement a localized, also more strict horizon of regulation (so that "politics" subsumes under "policy" in this pre-revolutionary vision of Spanish *política*). Quiroga's reformation may be said to be a homeopathic method operating in a localized area of the generally malfunctioning and deteriorating political body. Early modern colonial utopianism will not be able to think beyond this hegemonic horizon of the repressive culture and the tyranny of the alphabetic letter. For Quiroga, there is no outside to this rule-dominated horizon. Yet, the achievement of a certainly frightening predictability and social symmetry will not be the fulfillment of Quiroga's political desire. In a refreshing moment, our man of state is telling the Emperor, and most, if not all of his delegates, that they are all naked, politely. That is, law-making in the colonial situation has, by 1535, been a rather sloppy job and officialdom stands on the brink, if only by negligence of institutional crime. Quiroga does not hesitate to bring theological language to add some additional angularity to his denunciation: Spanish Indian law is by 1535 a "sin" (p. 201). This is how Quiroga develops his cavalier, yet firm critique of early Indian law-making:

> [N]o dejaré siempre de decir cuánto mejor, e más sin pena e menos trabajo, se hace y corta la ropa a la voluntad de su dueño, que es Dios y el Rey, que no de estas piezas y remiendos con que se atapa [*sic*] un agujero y se hacen ciento, como son estas piezas y remiendos de leyes y ordenanzas, que ordenando nunca acaban de ordenar cosa que baste; antes, por atapar [*sic*] un agujero, hacen ciento, y por deshacer una gotera hace cuatro, y por no acertar bien una vez en el camino y errarlo, rodean y le andan

muchas veces y nunca le acaban de andar ni llegar a la posada ni reposo que desean; y por cortar un inconveniente nacen siete o ciento, como cabezas de hidra. Y acontece en aquesto como cuando para hacer un bueno y dulce son y dulce música, toman en las manos la vihuela muy quebrada y destemplada, y trabajan y mueren por la templar y concertar. (p. 201)

The rule of law is, according to this high state official, the misrule of law. The self-appointed magistrates of the rule of law (or *estado de derecho indiano*), do not, cannot keep it together. The colonial reality is, according to Quiroga, the permanent fracture of the rule of law, or martial law, in these Americas turned upside down. Which is another way of saying that the early modern state has lost, according to its own language, its legitimacy. Quiroga's delicate figures of social destruction put on the imaginary table the leak in the roof of the household, an awkward-looking patchwork in the knitting, a conspicuous hole in the wall, a straight road to shelter not taken, and a small, sorry-looking sixteenth-century guitar (*vihuela*), out of tune. Following repressive protocols, the denunciation is unambiguous. Those who follow Maravall will not be looking for Che Guevaras among state officials in the early modern Americas. Yet, Quiroga's polite political critique is, I would like to suggest, as far as the global critique of political structures was allowed to go officially, in an already transatlantic early modern horizon for humanity.

6. Third Proposal: The Restoration of the Rule of Law, or the Utopian Desire for Social Transparency

In agreement with metropolitan utopianism, Quiroga's reformation will be advocating an inflexible transparency of social structures. Inside Quiroga's contractualist framework, there are two main clauses: the unalienable right to the universal freedom of all social agents, and the "no" to the permanent condition of alienated labor, or slavery, which includes one significant fineprint—the social product of winning a situation of open confrontation, or "just war" (p. 137). Quiroga's critique will be directed against the greatest enemy under coloniality, the equivocation created by the always *already* strongest social sectors.

[L]os conquistadores o pacificadores de estas bárbaras naciones…según e cómo e de la manera que les tengo dicho que les van a requerir y persuadir o, por mejor decir confundir e enredar y enlazar como a pájaros en la red, para dar con ellos en las minas y espantarlos y escandalizarlos, de manera que nunca osen fiarse ni venir de paz, porque haya más lugar su deseo que es éste de poblar las minas: rapiñas, robos, fuerzas, opresiones, tomas e violencias, tomándolas, talándolas y comiéndoles y destruyéndoles lo que tienen, y casas e hijos y mujeres, sin ellos saber ni entender ni aun merecer por qué; y demás desto, la miserable y dura captividad en que nosotros los españoles los ponemos, no para mejor aprender la doctrina y servir en nuestras casas, con que allá los malos informadores untan el caso e quiebran el ojo, sino para echarlos en las minas, donde muy en breve mueran mala muerte, y vivan muriendo y mueran viviendo como desesperados, y en lugar de aprender la doctrina, deprendan a maldecir el día en que nacieron y la leche que mamaron. (p. 116-7)

This question, "How does one deal with the rule of pervasive abuse of force?" may circumscribe Quiroga's historical dilemma in the horizon previous to the private-public bourgeois departmentalization of political life (the "private" sphere of feelings, opinions and beliefs is a non-issue for *Información en Derecho*). Quiroga's proposals will pass necessarily through the restoration of the rule of colonial law towards whatever the future might deliver. The political denunciation is quite explicit in the emphasis on the superlative diminution of the civil life: "reputados en nada, muertos vivientes" (p. 142 & 154). And this social nothing ("la miserable y dura captividad"), tragically signals every Spanish equivocation (the blind Pozzos "untanx el caso e quiebran el ojo"). If Spaniards are mostly the ones to participate in this damaging, contradictory hypocrisy ("color e ilusión de engañador, Satanás,"and "contradicción y repugnancia entre las obras y las palabras," pp. 192-193), this early modern desire for reformation must somehow pass through equivocation towards a rigorous transparency of indigenous life continuum:

[A]sí españoles como naturales, sin armarles buitreras para dar con casi todos ellos en la sepultura de las minas, como se las arman, y sin volver al vómito, que ya una vez tan sancta y católicamente había cesado por la provisión revocada. Por donde, de necesidad, estos naturales, o la mucha mayor y mejor parte de toda la suma dellos, han de ir de necesidad a parar a la buitrera del hierro de guerra o de rescate, como dicen de cangas o de mangas, y de ahí consumirse en la sepultura de las minas, como tengo dicho, sin embargo de todas las ordenanzas sobre ello hechas, que todos quedan cojos y cortos y llegan muy tardíos o nunca, si las ocasiones y raíces, de donde tantos males y pestilencias que los acaban nacen, no se cortan. Porque sin esto, en esta tierra, todo otro remedio y toda otra ordenanza es imposible y es dar ley solamente a las palabras; porque en las obras, permitida una vez la cosa y dada la ocasión, hay imposibilidad en el cumplimiento de las justificaciones, modos, maneras, condiciones e limitaciones con que se permite, y mucha licencia y facultad y atrevimiento y soltura en las tiranías, fuerzas y robos y agravios y malos tratamientos, que a causa del grand derramamiento de los indios y de estar así como están por los campos solos, donde no les dejan de hacer males y daños, robos y violencias, y tomas de tamemes y comidas, y de hijos y mujeres, sino solamente el que no quiere, porque el que quiere, que son casi todos los españoles, bien sabe que no tiene de qué temer. (p. 122-123)

Quiroga's muscular language spells out the figures of colonial destruction: the vultures in the minefields, the vomit of death in life, the pestilence of the hot-iron branding of the legal slaves. This self-reflective language is nonetheless painfully aware of the fearful distance between words and deeds ("las palabras y las obras"). If modernity is, we dare generalize, the desire for expanding regulation, and yet also the official awareness of the precarious bridging between facts and regulations, modern reformation is the unambiguous desire for the complete subsumption of the former by the latter, and also for the sun-lit installation of the global polity firmly within the official horizon of the rule.[100] The apparently fragile rule of law will only find vigor in its inflexibility with no exceptions ("permitida una vez la cosa…hay imposibilidad en el cumplimiento"). Against endemic official hesitation ("ya una vez…revocada"), Quiroga's reformation had to respond unambiguously to this rather Brueghelesque landscape: the non-ambiguity of intense populational decline, the standard horror of the unregulated branding of the slaves in faces and thighs (pp. 188, 210), the Crown involvement in the "asiento" and "hierro real"(pp. 251-2)[101] and the legalized slavery, booty in a just war (pp. 189, 211, 222). Quiroga felt a severe reformation was needed to respond to this sorry upside-down state. Quiroga will semanticize expanding early modern humanity as the meager, stale, foreboding "thing" which must be necessarily substracted from the world market and which cannot be made "alien" permanently ("para que no se mude el estado de la cosa [humana]," "su natura es inajenable," pp. 143, 148). In legal parlance then, the unlivable coloniality (the no-place under no circumstances) is the social exchange conducive to the irrevocable labor exchange of the most fragile social sectors. This is the "injury" Quiroga will be fighting against by promoting the novelty of free wage labor. Too early in history to even consider a generalized compensation (Las Casas's "retribución"), Quiroga needs first to return the necessary protocol to the collective rule of law in order to later turn convincingly to these surely multiple indigenous "injuries." Global health is no longer for our *oidor* foreseeable in the near future. Millenarianism will provide an imaginary antidote.

To guarantee the constant dynamism of the "unalienable human thing," and this is Quiroga's ontological axiom, the watchful eyes of a police state are needed:

> Y de aquí por ventura debe proceder que se requieran en este contrato tantas solemnidades, condiciones y requisitos como de derecho se requieren, porque faltando alguno dellos, no se podr'a arguir dolo [or "injuria"] ni consentimiento contra el vendido ni la buena fe que se requiere por parte del comprador. (p. 149)

The concrete meaning of this legal wrong, or "injury" is the "maximum civil diminution" of irrevocable labor transaction (p. 158). Against this generalized state, *Información en Derecho* must no doubt historically cling to the colonial protocols of the law[102] as one inevitable step towards some desirable, if murky new form of global polity yet to come.

7. Fourth Proposal:
The City of Equals in the New World

Drawing inspiration from the social experimentation already taking place in Santa Fé de México, Quiroga narrates thus a possible social alternative to coloniality. The importance of the quote merits its length:

> [U]na ciudad de seis mil familias, y cada familia de a diez y hasta diez e seis casados familiares della, que son sobre sesenta mil vecinos, sea tan bien regida y gobernada en todo como si fuese sola una familia, así en lo espiritual como en lo temporal. E de manera que dos religiosos puedan en lo espiritual dar recabdo [*sic*] bastante a más gente que agora, así como están derramados sin buena orden de policía, dan e pueden dar ciento, e todo sin dar ni recibir las pesadumbres y trabajos que estando así derramados como están se reciben…de manera que cada familia tenga su padre e madre, de familia a quien teman e acaten e obedezcan los de cada familia a los suyos, e que sean tales de quien reciban ejemplo e castigo e doctrina, e den cuenta cada cual de su familia y familiares della que esten a su cargo, e otros que han de ser como jurados de treinta en treinta familias, que han de ser a cargo de cada uno de estos jurados, a quien todos los de su juradería [*sic*] e parroquia obedezcan e acaten, e con quien se junten a proveer en todo lo necesario; sobre los cuales presidan e han de presidir

los regidores de cuatro en cuatro jurados, que han de ser a cargo de cada uno de los dichos regidores; demás de éstos ha de haber dos alcaldes ordinarios e un *tacatecle* [*sic*];[103] todos los susodichos indios elegidos por la orden que más largamente pone el parecer de la república, que no será de los peores, sino la mejor de las mejores que yo he visto; e sobre todos, un alcalde mayor o corregidor español puesto por su Majestad y esta Real Audiencia en su nombre. (pp. 234-5)

This ideal polity thus described is possibly the most eloquent tribute to More's *Utopia*.[104] We fully agree this time with Quiroga's words: this previous quote is a rather verbatim account ("a la letra lo saqué") of the metropolitan model, which, despite some slight differences, is putting together More's city of equals and the subaltern Indian category. The transcontinental stretching from Quiroga's perspective is quintessentially early modern. We must however always bring the abstract notion of subalternity, i.e. the overwhelming sixteenth-century majority of the American population, to historical concreteness.

This system of coloniality, we've been arguing, is early modern Spanish capitalism in the Americas. And "Indian" signals all those social agents structurally subordinated by this embryonic and chamaleon-like system. Quiroga's normative design is an alternative tending towards the well-being of these "Indianized" social sectors. Quiroga is thus going against the early irregularities of global coloniality, locally.

Yet, it is meaningful, and perhaps distressing to some, to witness that Quiroga's political operation does not, or perhaps cannot, deviate much from the official grid of intelligibility (*estado de derecho indiano*),[105] and rarely, if ever does it display an emphasis on "Indian" particularities (surely the biography of the individual is not entirely unrelated to this "oblivion").[106] *Información en Derecho*, largely a treatise on labor relations, is more often than not explicitly de-emphasizing particularity or ethnicity (we may wish to suggest that racialization is a constant, implicit source of unexplored tension). These would not operate, in Quiroga's vision, as outsides to the expanding system. *Información en Derecho* does not wish to create any kind of outsides to the system. His *indigenismo* may be said to operate, perhaps paradoxically by "indianizing" proto-capitalist structures by de-emphasizing "Indianness." This colonial utopianism does not believe in the desirability of outsides to the system. Quite the opposite, for Quiroga, assimilation to the still no doubt fragile or nominal sameness generated by the expanding proto-capitalist colonial system, i.e. Christian civilization, is the only way to go. Heterogeneity or segregation do not appear strong enough to reach the level of politics and thus lose the battle from the start. This utopian operation inside officialdom will strive to make habitation for American populations underneath politico-juridical nomenclature and inevitably work towards the improvement of life conditions of Amerindian populations (or "las Indias mejores"). The inner logic is that one must at least use the legal frame and assert the "miserable" condition of Indians to reap the theoretical fruits (or *privilegios*). All the elements which may qualify for cultural differences remain unintelligible, politically in Quiroga's vision. Our *oidor* is clearly not a cultural relativist, and the branding of this praise or accusation to most, if not all political figures in this period, would be anachronistic. Quiroga's utopianism is rather firmly constructed upon the implementation of nomothetic legislation with an emphasis on the continuity of Indian life and the attenuation of labor. In other words, *Información en Derecho*, the brainchild of a former student in canon law in Valladolid, has nothing to say about cultural differences, and, quite unlike Las Casas, little about the self-government potential in the orthodox formulation of the law of nations.[107] We wish to interpret this silence as the erasure of all differences or singularities and his desire to follow a "reductive" model of political life. One might wish to add that this was necessarily so, historically. Political life boils down to labor policies and little else seems to matter to Quiroga in this treatise, which most often will shy away from grandiose political statements. The historical lesson of this colonial utopianism appears to be saying, quite in agreement with classic or metropolitian utopias, that the achievement of sameness for the commonwealth is the early modern horizon for global justice, and that the construction of this desirable sameness among the most fragile social sectors is indeed a very fragile construction which always will have need of an explicit repression. Quiroga's utopian operation is thus "going for sameness all the time," so to speak.

We would like to ask, why this explicit tribute to More when the Spanish political model available for local government is undoubtedly closer to Quiroga's community of interpreters of *Información en Derecho*? We have already mentioned tangentially in chapter two some of the most likely reasons for silence on Luis Vives. Should we see a *letrado*'s strategy dusting off his university robes and displaying his bookish culture to thus better persuade a superior who might have been acquainted with More's prestige, if only by hearsay? It is as though the appeal to More, one literary figure among many others, is needed against the competing supremacy of Vitoria's Thomist rationalism or Ginés de Sepúlveda's fiercely humanist Aristotelianism. It is as though the foreign titillation of More's prestige would allow some elbow room to Quiroga inside this official constellation. How does Quiroga's city of equals relate to the expanding maze of global and regional governments, if not as the utopian "floating island" which, after the official clearing of the geography of New Spain, cuts itself off as it were from all local jurisdictions, and pleads for the unmediated protection of the highest political structure, the Spanish Crown?[108] Quiroga's regalism will have to remain firm.

Much like More's moon-shaped *Amaurote*, which is two hundred miles at the center,[109] Quiroga's rendition of the indigenous polity, thus laid out in the following diagram, appears to be asking from us to remain alert and perceptive to its numeral concreteness. The most likely humanist ploy in More's fictionalization will have to remain less certain in *Información en Derecho*.[110] More's micro-level is formed by forty persons, men and women, and two bondsmen. These two bondsmen are absent in Quiroga. One goodman and one goodwife are the general managers of the general household or family. Thirty farms or families form one distinguishable political unit (Quiroga's level one), with the head ruler called *Philarch* (or head bailiff). Approximately twenty members of the family are responsible every year for agricultural duties. Every tenth year, all families change their dwellings by lot. Every thirty families, or farms, choose a magistrate yearly, who's called *syphogrant* in the old language and *philarch* in the new language (approximately, Quiroga's levels two and three). The *syphogrant* will supervise agricultural work and he is exempt from such work. All *syphogrants* (approximately 200), will select four *tranibores*, out of the four quarters of the city, who will select in secret procedure one lifetime superior or *prince*, who will not be deposed except in the case of proven fraud (Quiroga's levels four and five). All *syphogrants* meet with the *prince* every three days. Informal political meetings are strictly forbidden. In More's polity, high political positions (*tranibores*, *prince*), must be *letrados*. Priests, also exempt from direct involvement in agricultural work, are also supposed to enforce general supervision. More's design has nothing to say about a multiplicity of cultures. Quiroga's model inserts the indigenous peculiarity (*tacatecle*), following the standard mechanism of patrilineal seniority.

We have already dwelt in relation to the schematic *Ordenanzas* on this equalizer of the female-free wheel as regards political representation. We have also mentioned the other great equalizer of clockwork agricultural labor with no exceptions. We must now enrich this latter dimension. *Información en Derecho* will give us a more detailed and articulate design with regard to labor. Let us take a closer look into this utopian conditioning for the human toil for life.

Diagram: Quiroga's City of Equals in the New World

(from top (King) to bottom or totality or ideal city)

> **1.** The Spanish Crown (Charles V)

> **2.** The Viceroy (Antonio de Mendoza), the Archbishop of Mexico (Juan de Zumárraga) and the four judges or *oidores* in the Supreme Court in the Americas or *Segunda Real Audiencia* (Alonso Maldonado, Francisco Ceynos, Juan de Salmerón and Vasco de Quiroga)

> **3.** 1 Mayor (or *alcalde mayor*) or 1 Spanish main manager (*corregidor*) nominated by the Crown or the Supreme Court

> **4.** 2 ordinary deputy mayors (*alcaldes*) and 1 indigenous leader (*tacatecle*) and the general supervision of 2 men of the church

> **5.** 4 jurisdictions under 1 governing manager (*regidor*)

> **6.** Each jurisdiction (*jurados, juradería* or *parroquia*) is formed by 30 elected families. The four jurisdictions amount to 120 elected families.

> **7.** Each distinguishable political unit or "family," is formed by 10 to 16 married couples (*casados familiares*). Each political unit has a dual leadership of the father and mother ("padre" and "madre").

> **8.** The totality of the political entity (or city) is formed by 6,000 families, or 60,000 neighbors (the smallest political unit is thus formed by these 10-member "family" units). The correspondence between indigenous individuality inside the family unit on this side of the Indian Republic and "vecino" on the other segregated side of the Spanish Republic is not clear.

8. Fifth Proposal:
The Reformation of Colonial Labor

Quiroga's legal reformation of early modern coloniality in New Spain must surely go down radically as the social mechanics of labor. The crucial question will be, how does the repressive culture and the toil for life intersect in relation to the satisfaction of majoritarian need? Quiroga's proposal is for the non-ambiguous contractualism of all labor exchange, the surveillance of a third party, the non-ambiguous construction of a social typology based upon incipient free wage labor and the repudiation of the category of "the irrevocable." This category will, however, remain alive and intelligible in Quiroga's millenarianism.

If the *Ordenanzas* gave us the equalizer of the six-hour labor arrangement, *Información en Derecho* will give us instead the reformulation of labor exchanges based upon the relative historical novelty of free wage labor, the utopian archipelago inside the early modern ocean of forced labor for the periphery of the world-system.[111] Quiroga will be proposing the strict regulation of all the social agents involved in this colonial labor exchange. Strong emphasis is placed upon the most fragile or indigenous parties of the labor exchange, which will be taken to the abstract or generalized dimension of working individualities with no particularizing features. If the category of ethnicity or race may be said to signal the rights of peoples historically marginalized, this category will here remain distressingly underdeveloped, almost entirely marginalized. Quiroga's proposals for the abstract contractualism of non-differentiated individuals in wage labor transactions must do away with all distinctions, in what might have been, if only initially, a potentially liberatory gesture for already subjugated peoples.

Quiroga's designs formalize the theoretical egalitarianism of wage labor. Thus he is aiming at the eradication of the standard colonial practice of forced labor, social pattern which will prove historically tremendously resilient, pliable and long-lasting for colonial Latin America. The individualized working unit with no recognizable attributes other than the expenditure of labor and energy within a stipulated time-frame, will have however the final say in the conditions informing the contract (nature of the duty and the payment and the time-frame):

> [Y]...por ser unos hombres y naciones de gentes mejores de servir que otros y por tener como tienen las gentes muy diferentes maneras de servicios

y servidumbres entre sí y muy extrañas unas de otras, a lo que pienso procede y debe proceder la prohibición y vedamiento [*sic*] que hay, que no se puedan vender ni transportar las semejantes personas, obligadas a semejantes servicios, que no pierden ingenuidad (como son los hijos que venden los padres en tiempo de necesidad y otros semejantes), en gentes extrañas, como son la gente de nuestra nación española, muy extraña. (p. 130)

Información en Derecho does not shy away from the two-way circulation of social heterogeneity. *Extrañeza*, another word for unintelligibility, must have surely worked historically both ways and Quiroga's prose highlights this historical fact in the shadow of the early penetration of theology of free wage labor of money-free environments. Hence, this structural miscommunication as regards societal exchanges ("servicios y servidumbres"), finds here the alternative measure of its official repression. Quiroga gives force to a legalized prohibition: the contractualized exchange between the party who offers the labor force, the *alquilado*, and the party who will benefit from the expenditure of this time and energy, the *alquilante*, will not mean, and this is the crucial clause, the automatic and permanent loss of freedom (or *ingenuidad*), of the former. This prohibition will remain an axiom for Quiroga's alternative construction of a social architecture. It is as though, given the everpresence of force in the early structuration of coloniality, Quiroga is ready with the whistle keeping a quick eye on the abyss of permanent social death (or slavery), which is theoretically marginalized under this colonial legality. Differences in historical modes of social reproduction ("servidumbres extrañas [en] gentes extrañas"), are thus, according to this inflexible legal repression, filtered, and surely radically impoverished, through the uninvited, mysterious guest, free wage labor.

Quiroga's repressive reformation thus constructs a social grammar of negation as pertains to its central, most encompassing social category, labor. We may imagine the mechanics of the legal recourse, in a pre-individual age, in the use of the typology. It is as though the neglect of all other possible categories (race, nationality, gender, etc.) was somehow for our author less damaging, and therefore less central in the social exchange, which must necessarily pivot (so *Información en Derecho* is suggesting) around the satisfaction of communal need (by 1535, "Indian" need means the permanent dissatisfaction of need, or death, and colonial utopianism emerges from within these historical ruins). To address this majoritarian need, Quiroga's legal repressivity is constructed around a double, emphatic negative: no labor transaction is irrevocable not even with the willingness to do so on the part of the *alquilado* living under unbearable circumstances. Quiroga's early modern legal reasonableness antecedes all contemporary approaches to psychologized, privatized choices (all "right to privacy" claims would have remained here unintelligible and anachronistic). Quiroga's legalism maintains, however, some elasticity as it incorporates, if only conceptually, that which most likely admits no regulation, the satisfaction of need. This abstract need, which is no doubt quite close to Las Casas's "precepto común para bien común," we must imagine historically circled by the two contracting parties, the official referee and the looming shadow of *Don Dinero*. The monetarized exchange of human time and energy is succinctly semanticized so as to suggest the mutual satisfaction of the needs of both contracting parties. A crucial differentiation is still needed, however, to Quiroga's design:

> [Por esta razón] que el hombre libre no es mercancía, y [esta] otra [razón], que el hombre libre no es dueño de sus miembros, parece que son las mismas en el hombre libre e ingenuo que sufre ser vendido para tener parte en el precio, no siento por qué deba hacer en él diferente disposición, pues que no hay culpa ni poquedad ni voluntad libre, sino constreñida de la necesidad...ni paciencia que dañe donde concurra extrema necesidad que no tiene ley, sino la mesma, que es que no pierda libertad ni ingenuidad, salvo solamente en caso que concurran las calidades y condiciones que el derecho requiere, [dicho contrato debe cumplir con] seis condiciones: edad de veinte años arriba en el vendido; en el vendedor que sepa que vende libre; y otro tanto en el vendido, que sepa y no ignore su condición de libre, y así tengan mala fe; y en el comprador, que lo ignore y así tenga buena fe, creyendo que compra siervo; y en el vendido, que demás [*sic*] de lo dicho, no se engañe ni yerre en la condición de su estado, sufra ser vendido para participar del precio; y que en hecho de verdad lo participe y lo reciba y goce. (p. 134)

The theoretical contemplation of extreme need, that which, according to Quiroga's legalistic mindset, is clearly against the good-intentioned faith in all laws, highlights the fundamental predicament of Quiroga's alternative framework. The proposals included here for the generalized social negotiation in New Spain must unambiguously separate two units, free man and merchandise. The world of intersubjectivity is thus made entirely, radically heterogeneous from the early global world of the transatlantic market. Yet, money signals that there must be some traffic between these two worlds, the human and non-human worlds. Commodificiation is already in the offing. The intersubjective contractualism, with regular supervisions on the good faith of all participants, will thus follow rigidly the aforementioned conditions. "The human thing" will not entirely enter to play permanently in the playground of buying or selling since the utopian measure of time will theoretically break these bonds open ("man" is in essence here movable good always with an expiration date for the purchasing party). This is done so with an initially paradoxical repression. According to Quiroga, patrimonialization is forbidden: no man owns himself, the energy in his limbs cannot be entirely left at his discretion, and therefore no man may legally sell the energy and the time generated by his limbs for work permanently. The crucial legal clause rests unambiguously upon the negation of this final adverb, *not* permanently.

We must thus come to terms with the following historical paradox. This negativity, quite far from debilitating the already weakest social sectors at first glance, may instead hold them to political life more firmly. The argument that, "I do not own my own body just as much as you do not own yours," puts the two agents, the colonizer and the colonized, theoretically within the same horizon of legal dispossession. Quiroga tries to do something outrageous: suspend patrimonialization inside a profoundly communal consideration of debt (or owing). We may see again the "historical eccentricity" of Quiroga's utopianism in the activation of the two-way or reciprocal mechanism: I owe to the commonwealth the same toil for life as you and we will get from the commonwealth the same provisions for life that we need. Firmly upon this structure of sameness, Quiroga's juridical reformation thus finds in this prohibition of permanent possession its foundational moment.

With the protectionism of social dynamism in Quiroga's contractual model, the sign "money" may well signal the catalyst as well as the equalizing factor which, almost entirely out of the blue, might well have provided the colonial polity with money pockets and suitable conditions for impermanence and change. At least theoretically, this societal model above illustrated is closer to Marx's aforementioned vision in *Grundisse* than Hegel's master-slave model. The early fracturations of the capitalist use of money may have potentially set some master-slave contractualism loose. This is however no free lunch. Quiroga's early *indigenismo* makes this indigenous party historically and politically meaningful only in so far as there is the abstract potentiality for assuming, like any other social agent, a convincing working condition.

If *Información en Derecho* is a historically convincing prefiguration of modern proto-capitalism in the Americas, and this is the strong claim of this chapter, the reformation of this expanding life-world system must present no faces, no names, no races, no genders, no languages, no geographies, as though already trying to catch up with the unsentimental demands of the transatlantic world-market constantly moving on its own foundation. The foundational placelessness of mutational capitalism meets here with the abstraction, or necessary reduction, of what amounts to be human, i. e. the toil for life (or labor). Humanity, that is, the marriage of historicity and plasticity of anything which may qualifiy as human, thus remains fixed on the basics, the toil for life and the annihilation of the toil for life (the political donkey with blinders looking at the dangling carrot). Quiroga's legalized personalities are fundamentally working units and fully human in the Marxian sense of transcendence of their individual needs and the social engagement with each others' needs.[112] This content-free humanity is exclusively predicated in the vicinity of collective need and its utopian satisfaction. Quiroga's early modern political medicine here appears almost exclusively to enforce, if only initially, the repressive thinning out of all social forms into individualized labor units radically with no cultural baggage of any kind. It may be possible, if only tentatively to call this abstract dispossession freedom, if only against the surrounding negativity of unregulated colonial unfreedom:

> [Q]ue el hombre libre no es señor de sí, ni de su ingenuidad ni libertad para las enajenar, y que el hombre libre no puede ser vendido...ni cae en nuestro comercio...ni recibe estimación...[como el lugar sagrado o público tampoco se puede enajenar, p. 145], ni es señor de sus miembros...y es porque, como dicho es, no tiene en sí poder ni facultad ni voluntad de derecho para se lo quitar así mesmo, ni perjudicarse en ello, como cosa prohibida por derecho enajenarse por ningún pacto ni consentimiento que sea; y también, porque como el que venda de natura del contrato se obligue a entregar, que consiste en hecho, y no a dar ni a pasar señorío de la cosa vendida, que consiste en derecho, en las obligaciones de hecho subcede la obligación solamente al interese [*sic*], el cual pagado, de necesidad ha de quedar libre el que es vendido, como lo es y era de antes, pues que de derecho, por paga de aquello que se debe, se quita toda obligación. (p. 136)

We would like to repeat that Quiroga's post-colonial contract will gives us two agents in a seemingly face-to-face exchange, theoretically equal, both of them called "free men," yet both of them always of necessity empty of any concrete, singularizing content. The strong suggestion is that this vision for the transatlantic commonwealth ("bien común"), must necessarily be semanticized in a negative minefield of formal dispossession irrespective of the content and the extent of the moneyed exchange. Quiroga's ideal commonwealth emerges from within the money system of equality and freedom, the realization of which is here only incipient inequality and unfreedom in the sense that it is not possible for the attentive reader to see a full-dress semanticization of the pre-capitalist mode of production or "compulsion," and its disappearance in relation to the relatively compulsion-free wage labor. And it is also quite impossible to see the chance fluctuations of interest and profit. If readers will not see here the logic of capital accummulation, it is also impossible to see what these workers will do with the money they make. In Quiroga's social exchange every day appears to be a new day, and there is an apparently decontextualized timelessness in this drastic discontinuity. The "no" and the "ni" series construct these "empty" human signifiers, while the "Indian" adjective slips away under the economic carpet. If the individual is here merely the individuation of money, then money—the mechanism of market sameness—here already represents the extinction of all distinction.[113] In the shadow of these historical forces, early modern justice is imagined to be social sameness in dispossession around collective need and Quiroga's colonial utopianism, in all historical coherence, will have to repudiate the permanent patrimonialization of human energies (monetarization will be the Trojan horse of (permanent) patrimonialization in this social model). In other words, Quiroga's apodiptic argument will run as follows: if neither party owns anything, neither party may therefore sell, forfeit or relinquish *permanently* what is by the rule of law not theirs; *accordingly* all parties owe everything to the social totality or commonwealth, which includes their most fragile, precious human feature, their needs. The social mechanism of freedom will be here predicated upon the extinction of need, and it is the vision of the historical fragility of this humanity disentangled from need which must thus necessarily cling to the destructurations and restructurations of the money economy. Quiroga is already proposing by 1535 a reformation of New Spain based upon the generalized suspension of the historical plausibility of property and the strict mechanism of free wage labor, precisely during the centuries of rampant patrimonialization of geographies, lands, official state responsibilities, etc. This is already no small feat. And yet as we have already made clear, it is unambiguously an authoritarian, yet potentially post-colonial or liberatory feat. But it is clearly not the end of history as Quiroga himself made it quite clear.

We may use, albeit cautiously, the tokenized language of individual choice in the predominantly pre-individualistic setting of the Americas. These quotes give further depth to Quiroga's ideal form of social contract:

[P]ero si de su espontánea y agradable voluntad permitió ser vendido al comprador de buena fe que pensaba que compraba esclavo, y siendo el vendido mayor de veinte años y recibiendo el precio y concurriendo los otros requisitos que se requieren de derecho y pudiéndose entregar, aunque no dar, porque es hacerse del señorío del comprador y recibiendo el precio y concurriendo los otros requisitos que se requieren de derecho y pudiéndose entregar, aunque no dar, porque es hacerse del señorío del comprador, que esto ni lo puede ni es obligado a lo [*sic*] hacer, porque él no es señor de sí ni puede pasar en otro el señorío que él de sí mesmo no tiene, ni la natura del contrato le obliga a ello hácese esclavo, pero de manera revocable. (p. 137)

Y es así también de la natura del contrato de buena fé de venta, que es contento con la paga del interese, cuando la cosa vendida no está en poder ni señorío del que la vendió para la poder hacer el que la compró ni darle el señorío della, antes de su natura es inajenable y tal que no cae en nuestro comercio, como no cae la cosa sagrada ni pública, en quien también vale la venta que della se hace para pagar el interese al comprador, pero no para que se mude el estado de la cosa. Porque ninguno se obliga a lo imposible ni da lo que no tiene ni cae en su poder para lo hacer de otro ni en comercio nuestro para se poder enajenar irrevocablemente; y así lo entrega, puédese revocar y restituir al estado primero, como de entrega que se hace de cosa inajenable, y tal, que entregándola, no se puede pasar el señorío della. (p. 148)

Quiroga's repressive coherence, gaining here some distance from Lalinde-Abadía's repressive para-logism, does not shy away from constructing an ontology thus: No one may own somebody else's time and energy permanently, because the "human thing," unlike merchandise, cannot change its unalienable state irrevocably (Quiroga's vision is precisely oppossing these two adverbs of the denial of time, permanently and irrevocably). It is thus impossible (or rather illegal), for this "human thing," to change its unalienable, sacred or public nature (nobody's possession), into unchanging alien status. This repressive axiom about human nature always situated in a world economy cannot change despite the occasional individual willingness to do so. The appeal to "will" or "choice" is the sanctioned mode to enter into the agreement of this economic transaction but cannot do violence to the aforementioned axiom ("[la] espontánea y agradable voluntad" or *albedrío*, cannot alienate itself permanently into somebody else's possession, not even willingly following the demands of need). Thus, *Información en Derecho* locates, if only theoretically the fragility of the "human thing" outside the vagaries of the market. We must no doubt see Quiroga's proposals as radical, ground-breaking novelty in the sixteenth-century Americas: Indian subalternity is having some actual say, while being subjected to the irresistible violence of historical individuation, to the conditions of the social contractualism. The subaltern can here at least theoretically speak to arrange temporarily his or her working conditions. No adjectives will however give concrete faces to the buyer ("comprador") and seller ("vendido"), in this one-to-one, face-to-face transparent transaction ("de buena fé").

In trying to change the early criminal state of the American coloniality, *Información en Derecho* de-emphasizes the semiotic or communicational complexities of New Spain, "the cultural baggage" we may wish to call these, and mostly seeks into the gradual, surely uneasy mutation of forced labor into free wage labor. It is quite telling that the ideal contractual situation includes only rarely standard Christian language. Quiroga articulates a concrete social definition predicated thus: a) the official imposition of the suspension of private property ("señorío"), makes all people in their dispossession free and equal; b) the enjoyment of somebody else's time and body energy, will have to be carefully arranged, so that all stipulations (or debt relation), are fulfilled for the contracting parties; c) the party who, forced by need, is willing to give some of his time and energy to a second party cannot do this permanently, whether willingly or not; d) the offering party remains irreversibly free and equal to the receiving party, and both parties cannot claim ignorance about this legalized condition of negative repression as pertains to their binding, formal equality, and e) if all subjects are theoretically free men, i.e. all *ingenuos*, all contracting parties will be subjected to an unambiguous labelling of time and labor following the still novel destructurations and restructurations of wage labor. This is the arrangement which will take the center of the dance floor in *Información en Derecho*. The future society will have to go through this model, willingly or not. If Quiroga's most ambitious treatise represents the proto-individual world of singularized working units, it is also true that this repressive culture is largely unwilling to psychologize the mindsets of these contractual parties. *Información en Derecho* is the theater of law situated firmly within the early modern horizon of proto-individual, yet pre-psychological and pre-bourgeois American world.

We may imagine *Información en Derecho* intervening into a colonial world so soon structured around the looming "theology" of wage labor, if only precariously. It will take centuries for its unquestioned hegemony. Quiroga's repressive proposals aim at categorial and social simplification following upon labor demands (in a sense the early modern utopian desire is the cry, "Off with the cultural baggage, off with cultural specificity!"). Following Steve Stern's "mixed array," unquestionably related to Adorno's "paradigmatic loss" and Mignolo's "colonial semiosis," we must imagine a rather slow and laborious site of changes and inter-penetrations of under-regulated forced labor in uneasy marriage with poorly structured wage labor, but also a rich variety of compulsive mechanisms, more or less visible structures of subordination and social death, abundant multi-lingual (mis)understandings, endemic corruption of state officials, etc. (Stern's "approximations of wage labor, complicated tenancy, share and debt credit, forced labor rafts and slavery"). *Información en Derecho* signifies however the theoretical dissolution of the rather obscure distinction of *esclavos de naborías*,[114] which would have been hurting the stipulated fifth or *quinto* allowed to the Crown. It also signifies the legal marginalization of slavery as presumably an exceptional state of being and the relative maintainance of *cacique* property (pp. 251-3). We must thus try to imagine that which is not easy, the mutation of a transatlantic world from pre-money to post-money-as-capital, if not in the short-run of Quiroga's lifetime, certainly in the long-run globality of human history. Coloniality does not disappear in these global complexities, it is important to emphasize, but rather changes its mask according to the historically stronger dictum of monetarization. There are no words in *Información en Derecho* about the minefield labor requirement or *mita* and no suggestions about alternative patterns such as the voluntary or *minga* minefield laborers as delineated by Stern. The insinuation of categorical simplification, or social egalitarianism, is latent but remains largely underdeveloped and not without tensions. Against the strict equal patterns of money-free labor for Quiroga's village-hospitals in the *Ordenanzas*, *Información en Derecho* proposes instead the general pattern of wage labor for the global reformation of coloniality. It is still an early date in relation to these later hybrid developments of colonial labor, yet the seeds of another better time and place had already been planted.

The economy and the law constitute an uneasy marriage, historically: the repressive culture and proto-capitalist economic demands and needs will deliver the rather anti-Aristotelian juridical formulation of universal *ingenuidad* or the catholicity of vassalage, and also the chance fluctuations or more subtle compulsions of free wage labor as delineated in relation to the individualized working unit. In the early horizon of modernity/coloniality for the global regulation of social energies, law and fact ("derecho" and "hecho"), must also go hand in hand trying to keep the vagaries of the use of force socially at bay, if only temporarily. Fittingly, the repressive culture of colonial utopianism, firmly within the horizon of modernity/coloniality, wishes the reestablishment of the rule of law. Quiroga's Mexican years will face the likeliest historical scenario for New Spain of martial law or state of emergency. The invigoration of the rule of law, drastically in a trans-national or international setting, is a necessary step, if only initially for the protectionism of the political life among the most fragile American populations.

9. Sixth Proposal: The Repression of Slavery

Contrary to the commonplace of anti-slavery for Quiroga's treatise, slavery remains here historically intelligible. And it must be put, no doubt uneasily, within the general configuration of free wage labor above summarized. It might appear at first sight that Quiroga's societal contract, defending the unalienable right to freedom ("inajenable libertad," p. 137), would have logically done away with unfreedom or the social death of slavery. Neither notion, freedom nor unfreedom, is transparent, but historically mediated.[115] Slavery will have a long life well into the nineteenth century.[116] There is a fine print to Quiroga's social contract which makes the sign "true slave" automatically functional in the theoretical contemplation of the non-contractual situation of force or war:

> [Y] para ser y poder tener por esclavos verdaderos los que de estos naturales a nuestro poder vienen, por vía del hierro de rescate, como nosotros los queremos y hacemos, venidos a nuestro poder, aunque ellos no lo sean en el suyo, habían de tener entre ellos la misma condición que tienen de derecho los verdaderos esclavos que es la ya dicha. (p. 142)

Legally sanctioned unfreedom, or slavery, is thus reincorporated into Quiroga's proposals for the reformation of coloniality. The truth of legality versus the falseness of its illegality regarding the social phenomenon of slavery in proto-capitalist societies under colonial domination is thus built upon the theoretical situation of the suspension of the rule of law, i.e. the formalization of open conflict or war. The social product of winning a "just" war is "true" slavery,[117] and all these social bodies will be typically branded with hot-iron. Quiroga's repressive construction of this truth of slavery is historical orthodoxy in perfect agreement with Francisco de Vitoria.[118] With or without official hesitations, the Crown will also historically profit from these standard operations (the institution of the *asiento*). Quiroga's contractualism previously delineated appears, if only occcasionally, to break open in the coexistence between the political "us v. them" dialectics and the underdevelopment over ethnicity, which most likely signals the "they" of the political equation (Indians, Africans). Yet, this is not explicit but rather implicit in *Información en Derecho*. Just when we thought we would have idyllic labor contracts, we all of a sudden start seeing Pozzos and Luckys struggling in an environment of open conflict and survival of the fittest!

The historical contradiction, slavery and contractualism, is clear in *Información en Derecho*. Inside the agrarian horizon, tentatively open to the intrusions of the manufacture in the Michoacán region, our *oidor* is nonetheless holding firm to the orthodoxy of his historical day: the legality of non-subjects, the human product of winning a "just" war, also defended by the two main schools of thought, Dominican Thomism (Vitoria) and Spanish Aristotelianism (Ginés de Sepúlveda). Slavery, so the political orthodoxy stated, is the logical product of the law of nations, which goes against the theoretical egalitarianism of all civilized peoples under the natural law. This historical contradiction vastly exceeds the individuality of our *oidor*.

In the theoretical recuperation of the notion of slavery, there is an intense legal contradiction which creates a hybrid of man and thing, which is precisely the dichotomy Quiroga wanted so carefully to maintain in his previously delineated free wage contractualism. There is, we must say it again clearly, no repudiation of the category of slavery inside a largely barter economy of the indigenous practices already penetrated by 1535 by the capitalist use of profit and money. There is perhaps no historical possibility for a firm repudiation of this systemic, increasingly confusing subalternization given the relatively scarce presence of money and the slow emergence to the American reality of the novel theology of wage labor.[119] *Información en Derecho* will be clinging to the theoretical severity and repression of this contractualism if only to keep the early destructurations of indigenous communities under some form of official control. Yet, the theory of the legality of war leaves the door open for a major commotion of this design for change.

The legal notion of the slave thus strikes us as an emphatic contradiction, the "not quite a human thing yet" asking for the breakdown of sameness and the colonial system of tutelage. This historical contradiction coexisted with official hesitations, and also with the theoretical freedom for all indigenous peoples set up later by the *New Laws*. Around this repressive and progressive monument, early coloniality means the fragile enforcement of the rule of law. The criterion of perfectability is most commonly introduced, also occassionally by Quiroga, to try to ease out this contradiction into an unforeseeable future which will be most likely like waiting for Godot. This conceptual ambiguity—it is crucial not to miss this point—did not prevent the operativeness of the subaltern sign. Quiroga's fastidious legalism warns the reader about the historical complexities of the notion of (true) slavery: "Y allí en cuanto dice que son esclavos, de buena guerra, entiéndelo con la debida proporción: en diferentes circunstancias, [en] diferente manera" (p. 259). The word "slavery" is corrupt, he says. It is very different from ours. They don't know what slavery among us really means. They misuse the word. These are often repeated statements in this self-consciously repetitious treatise.[120] Money-free exchanges are already quite an unintelligible source of wonder for our *oidor*. We may in fact entertain the opposite distressing assumption, that this ambiguity over social death (or slavery) made it grow more resilient and plastic according to the needs of the times. We may also try to imagine, not without difficulties, the mixed array of forced labor and slavery. Quiroga will give us his puzzlement thus:

> [Y] en éstos, en los desta tierra, semejantes a estos alquilados a perpetuidad, haya otra y muy diferente manera y diferencia de la que hay *y ha de haber* en la condición dellos, pues que vemos y nos consta que no pierden entre sí estos que se alquilan y vender sus obras a perpetuidad, que nosotros decimos que son esclavos, entre ellos no pierden libertad, familia ni ciudad, ni hijos ni mujeres ni casa ni hacienda ni ajuar, de necesidad se sigue que digamos que son especies y diferencias de hombres libres ingenuos en quienes como dicen los derechos alegados, muchas diferencias hay, y no de siervos ni esclavos verdaderos, en cuya condición no hay ni puede haber diferencia alguna, según los derechos que dichos son. (my emphasis, p. 143)

Indigenous slavery is here semanticized as those who have been perpetually hired ("alquilados a perpetuidad"). And this social practice is to be differentiated from the legalized condition of the "true slaves," who constitute the human booty of a just war. In this landscape of early coloniality, i.e. the mixed array of labor, Quiroga's candid lines register no small confusion about the apparent happiness among the "indigenous slaves," since always according to our *oidor* they do not lose what the Spaniards have already learned to treasure (freedom, household, city, family and property). There is some visible incongruence since the orthodox statement was that American populations did not have the concept of private property

(Ginés de Sepúlveda). Allegorically, monetarization and patrimonialization are already firmly in place in the Americas, if incipiently so.

So it appears that "they" must have some sort of social arrangement after all, which they do not relinquish when they become slaves to other indigenous subjects, as opposed to Spanish subjects. This ambivalence goes through *Información en Derecho*, the admiration at social forms seemingly more benign and orderly, as well as the occasional, blunt denial, following Aristotle, of the political condition to the American communities ("they did not have laws but paintings," p. 161). By seizing pre- and post-Hispanic forms of social exchange, Quiroga's repressive culture of moneyed contractualism is forced to question its own faulty terminology.

Información en Derecho historically emerges in the official middle of this categorial confusion. Quiroga's reformation had however to make some clear meanings inside this expanding structural ambiguity. His proposals, four years after his arrival in New Spain, carve out a social space for pre-Hispanic social conditions against the expanding Spanish legal grid of intelligibility. This operation is done largely by neglecting cultural specificity (we may say it is internally dedifferentiating pre- and post-Hispanic social groups). This assimilation is however taking place with a keen eye on the "radical diminution of citizenship, of those reputed nothing, and like the dead, without volition" ("la máxima disminución de ciudadanía y reputados por nada, y como muertos, sin tener querer ni no querer," p. 142). If Quiroga's reformation is constantly trying to reduce this hell of living and partly living, it is also true that his imagination is mainly incapable, or unwilling to eradicate this degrading social practice once and for all. The expanding coloniality of Spanish capitalism in the Americas will always bring it back: the presumed exceptionality of the "just" war situation may have well been instead the rather normal or foundational condition of expanding coloniality during Quiroga's lifetime.

Yet, against seeds of egalitarianism, a sub-basement of undifferentiated human condition, that is, all those with the freedom (or "ingenuidad") suspended, if only temporarily due to explicit conflict ("guerra justa"), remains thus historically intelligible to Quiroga's reformist vision. The category of slavery remains perfectly operative under the theoretical condition of exceptionality (not however in Quiroga's village-hospitals). This intelligibility clashes with the contractualist framework of proto-wage labor arrangements for the Indian totality in the Americas. In legal terminology, the possibility (*hay lugar*) for the effective suspension of rights inside the articulation of a system of rights and duties exists. Or in other words, the positive and the negative notions of freedom and unfreedom always go hand in hand, explicitly or not. Slavery is not a *fuera de lugar* however globally, historically in the Americas according to the official (hi)story of Quiroga's repressive culture. Mixed or hybrid labor patterns in colonial Latin America (Stern), will be slowly, historically breaking open the abstract and expanding gulf between the two extreme notions of free man (or "hombre libre"), and true slave (or "verdadero esclavo"). Almost twenty years before the official, if seemingly unenforceable, ban on Indian slavery by the *New Laws* (1542-3), *Información en Derecho* already gives us an early conflation of these two social categories, inside which the immense majority of the American population will come to be officially situated, whether they liked it or not. Coloniality is not ever a matter of plebiscite.

10. The Imaginary Flight out of Colonial History: from Hot-Iron Branding to Wax Melting

What would be the point of reconstructing historical subjectivities if not to gain a keener understanding of humanity as historicity and plasticity? What would be the point of reconstructing early modern subjectivities if not to make our contemporary identities terminal? What could we do today with Quiroga's axiom of the suspension of patrimonialization (you do not own yourself and your limbs are not yours, p. 134), in the sails of monetarization always *already* within the horizon of capitalism? What damage, if any could these historical Indianized subjectivities do to our privatized, psychologized selves? In the pre-bourgeois era, doesn't typology arrest somewhat the banality of individual voluntarism and the (false) dichotomy of the private and the public? Isn't the juridical subject one of the most severe and penetrating constructions of subjectivity we must all inevitably deal with?[121]

The contemplation of historical horizons other than our assumed or imposed (sub)conscious belief system may help us to defamiliarize, and thus deliver keener insights into our habits. It may also energize if only momentarily our current historical dissatisfaction. The close contemplation of heterogeneous arrangement of social energies may help us also relativize our own position in relation to changes which will surely come to us. In the Mexican periphery of proto-capitalist personalities, *Información en Derecho* should also help us realize that the self-presentation card of the law, its reasonableness, is inexcusably historically mediated, but most importantly, that such reasonableness is, should we all follow Lalinde-Abadía's suggestion of *paralogismo*, quite undistinguishable from the Kafka-before-Kafka scaffold structure of prejudice, hesitation, flaws and errors, dilatoriness and incompleteness (after all, Quiroga explicitly calls his most ambitious treatise *ensalada*). Does the denunciation of incoherence or contradiction necessarily always hurt the repressive mechanism? Or, is the cry, "But the emperor is naked!" always hurting the reputation of the emperor? I would say, not necessarily. Lalinde-Abadía has been calling for a "sociological" and "paralogic" understanding of the historicity and change of the repressive culture. I would argue that this general model applies quite fittingly to Quiroga.[122] We must substantiate historically casuistic particularism and serial jurisprudence with no "concrete" or graspable subject of rights.[123] Quiroga's treatise is, at least for us, a good early modern beginning for the historical triumph of the rights of the individual over collective rights.[124]

After all the reader's pain and travail, *Información en Derecho* may turn out to be a magnificent example, never quite pleasurable or comforting, of an unsolved historical contradiction, the repressive reasonableness of the contractualism of free wage labor, streamlined social taxonomies as pertain to labor and the dissolution of all taxonomies in the dream-like annihilation of labor. I wish to call this latter radical tendency, millenarianism (we may imagine Chief Justices Earl Warren or Rehnquist making these claims from the Supreme Court benches to open up to Quiroga's predicament!). It is thus possible to see in Quiroga's occasional millenarian expressivity the perhaps permanent crisis of the repressive culture and its contractual logic.

Could it ever be doubted that during this early modern coloniality subjectivities were much altered and destructured, discarded and forgotten, but also transformed, improved or degraded? Could it ever be doubted that coloniality represents the permanent fracture of the rule of law (or *derecho de estado*), the normalized crisis of the state of emergency which we haven't yet left behind as the contemporary Chilean motto still reminds us ("o por la razón o por la fuerza")? The historical lesson would still vindicate human plasticity mostly in the historical roads not taken. This is but one vision of post-colonial humanity as similarity, uniformity and monotony:

Por do algunas veces me paro a pensar en este grande aparejo que veo, y me admiro, cierto, mucho conmigo, porque en esta edad dorada desde Nuevo Mundo y gente simplecíssima [*sic*], mansuetíssima, humildíssima [*sic*], obedientíssima [*sic*] de él [*sic*], sin soberbia, ambición, ni cobdicia alguna, que se contenta con tan poco y con lo de hoy, sin ser solícitos por lo de mañana ni tener cuidado ni congoja alguna por ello que les dé pena, como en la verdad no la reciben por cosa de esta vida; que viven en tanta libertad de ánimos con menosprecio y descuido de los atavíos y pompas de este nuestro, en este infelice siglo, con cabezas descubiertas y cuasi en el desnudo de las carnes, y pies descalzos, sin tratar moneda entre sí y con grand [*sic*] menosprecio del oro y de la plata, sin aprovecharse del uso ni aprovechamiento dello para más de solamente andar galanes en sus fiestas, hasta que los españoles vinieron, que por tenerlo ellos en tanto, ya lo van teniendo estos en algo; y en verlos dormir como duermen en el suelo sobre petates y piedras por cabecera por la mayor parte, y no tener ni querer ni desear otro ajuar en su casa más que un petate en que duermen y una piedra en que muelen maíz y otras semillas que comen y pagar con tanta simplicidad y verdad y buena voluntad, lo que deben y lo que ponen, y cómo convidan...y en fin, de verles cuasi en todo, en aquella buena simplicidad, obediencia y humildad y contentamiento de aquellos hombres de oro del siglo dorado de la primera edad, siendo, como son por otra parte, de tan ricos ingenios y prompta [*sic*] voluntad y docilísimos y muy blandos y hechos como de cera para cuanto dellos se quiera hacer. (pp. 226-7)[125]

It is impossible not to see in this exceedingly beautiful passage, Quiroga's self-loathing operation or inferiority complex of the superpower. The subalternized *gente*, early foreigners arriving in this new world system, represent the possibility of other horizons, the semiotic site of the potential, superlative change. Giving another twist to the standard official messianism, López de Palacios Rubios (1450-1524) for example,[126] the political dichotomy of "us v. them" spins around: the "us" precisely because of its historical power and privilege is not what "we" desire. This wish exceeding all political reason, Quiroga is quite explicit in this double estrangement and unintelligibility (his amazement has still for us today a genuinely engaging child-like quality). It is a kind of, what others do, I do not understand, and they appear to be in their apparent dispossession much happier than us who claim all knowledge. This hatless, shoeless anonymous bodily nudity is for Quiroga the historical moment of unadorned truth for the future: the gratuitous or moneyless social exchange will have to pass through the looming of free wage labor and patrimonialization. We are tempted to call by the name of lyricism this accusatory, teeth-grinding sense of the historical lesson of privation and of political happiness yet to come. *Información en Derecho* is abruptly lyrical in this precise sense.

To the reformation of these American communities, there can't be any pyschologized melodrama, sentimentality or euphemism. It is precisely for this severity of countenance that *Informatión en Derecho* may well make a claim to represent, at least to us, amid the wasteland bureaucratic dryness, a timid April-rain seduction, slowly inviting to the more or less likely play of "pre- and post-individual singularities or non-personal individuations" (Deleuze), of "[pre- and] postindividual collective relationships around the absent center of birth a new subject to come" (Jameson). The rather unglamorous, non-visual, cumbersome legal erudition is precisely for this reason historically meaningful (the onion of the alphabet letter hides the more recondite repressive layers). Is it all too ridiculous to give some consideration, if only for a fleeting moment, to the juxtaposition of these "empty" personalities and the "we" of Rigoberta Menchú as one possible strategy among many? I wouldn't say so.[127]

Quiroga's intermittent millenarianism, in the middle of this deeply uncomfortable brief, signals a deeper fracture in his historically modulated legal rationality. This fracture, the sharp contrast between the hot-iron branding of the slaves and the figure of wax melting cannot be emphasized strongly. There is no transition from one stage to the next. There is no easy or visible communication. Readers do not quite know how to get there from forced labor, or even free wage labor. Yet this deliquescence of social typologies is where this lyrical prose wants us to go (not in vain we have the recurrent utopian figuration of the floating island detached from all *tierra firme*). The colonial nightmare suddenly vanishes, and almost like a hot tornado coming from nowhere, takes away all social differences, public and private distinctions collapse and all singularizing differences melt down. Millenarianism toys around with this imagined terror of undifferentiated delinquescence (the pliability of human wax, the stuff dreams are made of). These post-colonial, post-capitalist presences are radically with no attributes and the rather strong suggestion is that they cannot and will not leave this emptiness as freedom. These utopian personalities will not leave a faceless, speechless anonymity.

Figures of historical dissolution, what Quiroga terms "the golden age" or the "new or true Church," will be exclusively for these *macehual* creatures: "los verdaderos pobladores...estos miserables, como rebaños de ovejas, han de ser herrados...digo a aquestos pobrecillos maceoales, que son casi toda la gente común, que de tan buena gana entran en esta grand cena que en este Nuevo Mundo se apareja y guisa (p. 67)." Franciscanism is round the corner in this lyricism of careless, happy birds of gratuitous existence (we may bring to memory the character of Toto in Pasolini's *Uccellacci e Uccellini* (1965)). It is never a naive or ignorant celebration. It is the celebration in the thick middle of the historically surrounding genocide.

This is the unambiguous meaning of "New World" in Quiroga's vocabulary, the accusatory millenarianism wishing, inside the repressive culture of peripheral protocapitalism, a radical change. The strong medicine of millenarianism, if only imaginatively is thus responding to the colonial nightmare of history. How else to cope with the sixteenth-century dimension of Indian toil for life if not with the flattening out of all legal forms of typological classification? Does not the joy come from the irrational belief in the end of history, the annihilation of all labor?

11. Conclusions: Five Allegorical Pages to Tear Out and Run Away With

It is time to synthesize. Let us do it allegorically. One possibility of a narrative will go on like this: Once upon a time, a long time ago, in what's now called the West, in the early modern beginnings of the system we now live in, capitalism, somehow this mysterious thing grew stronger, more intrusive than ever. Although it is not at all easy for humans, and I am one, to see the whole process, we must try to imagine pre-existing social structures gradually releasing the seed of their own destruction. For example, the *mayorazgo* institution let loose a mass of propertyless *hidalgos* who had no option but to go for the truly unpredictable American adventure. Money mediation became ubiquitous and that mysterious thing, which is not a thing but a process, released the mechanism of the free wage labor (who would have believed it?) to eventually steal center stage. Soon, monetarization and patrimonialization started playing catch on both sides of the Atlantic. This story will tell that an unstoppable expansionism of these originally European structures took place. In the sails of this strange thing, money-as-capital, a whole realm of novelties arrive and settle in the Americas: the alphabetic letter, Latin and Spanish, *Derecho Indiano*, Christianity, horses, iron, private property, monogamic heterosexual couple arrangement, etc. These novelties mixed with authocthonous habits, pre-money arrangements, indigenous languages, money-free or ritualized exchanges, and produced many headaches for state officials and others. Yet it is clear that there was domination and destruction of people by people. Which is why we have proposed the notion of colonization to better understand the early modern human horizon in the lands which got called *Indias Occidentales*, or continental America. Much against the commonplace, which places true capitalism and true modernity in latter timeframes and nationalities, the Iberian peninsula was the first location to deliver these proto-capitalist forms outside Europe. Other capitalist hegemonic forces would later come from inside and outside the strict geography of the Americas until today.

No one really quite knows how or why, but a mindset fixated on the endless increase of money and profit finally settled in. Official policies were designed accordingly. Modernity means the institutionalization of the total regulation of social energies inside this money system. Coloniality means the structural subordination of people by people in the Americas based upon the new regulation of this money system. If modernity means the desire for the rule of law (but also the misrule) coloniality in the shadow of modernity means martial rule or the rule of force. Some of these early modern political measures were reasonable. Some were unreasonable. Yet there is little doubt they were mostly designed to provide for the purse of all the big political guys. Since there was much confusion, and people did not really understand each other, these big guys often disguised the novel trappings of wage labor with compulsive labor. In the meantime, the system was indeed much more elastic and unpredictable than everyone might have predicted. It changed its colors, like a chameleon, not to be easily recognized, every one hundred and fifty years or so. Patrimonialization and monetarization could not quite catch up with each other, and all political turmoil and conflict would come out of this uneasy marriage. There was never enough money in the official purse. Bankruptcy was more common than uncommon. It was as though some deity pulled the invisible strings to all participants on both sides of the Atlantic telling them what to do and not do, albeit in a language no one could really understand.

The main protagonist of these pages, Vasco de Quiroga was one of these *hidalgos* but also a relatively important, university-trained man, a *letrado* who could make convincing existential claims to knowing the Americas or *indiano*. He was well acquainted with the legal literature of the period and the repressive protocols. Following orders, he had to go to the Americas in the sixteenth century in the prestigious position of judge or *oidor*. A rather scrupulous man, his political position was always clear from the beginning: he would push for the monism or statism against the plurality or fragmentation of social interests which appeared to be hurting American populations the most. Quiroga is credited until to this day with the firm implementation of manufacturing in the Michoacán region, which some say is a transitional stage between agrarianism and industrialism, although there are some disagreements on this suspicious linearity.

"Tata Vasco," a highly visible representative of the repressive culture, attempted a quiet reformation of some of these expansionist structures in the Americas. *Información en Derecho*, Quiroga's most ambitious piece of writing, is historically intelligible inside the big picture of early historical capitalism, and the smaller picture of the repressive culture in peripheral New Spain. This legal bill is proposing some changes to the early abuses of the Spanish colonization. Against what others might tell you, there is indeed a sixteenth-century Spanish-manufactured utopianism in the much forgotten lands of the early modern Americas. We have learned by now how to make this (un)intentional oblivion a good source for restlessness and unpredictability.

The one thesis of these many pages is that *Información en Derecho* represents the traumatic belief in the reformation of early Spanish coloniality in New Spain. Quiroga proposes the self-sufficient management of indigenous communities, the strict structuring of collective energies, the restoration of the rule of law as the first necessary step to the improvement of living conditions for the indigenous majority of American populations, and the "wheel" or circular mechanism of representational politics, but mostly for males. *Información en Derecho* also develops, most importantly, proto-egalitarian proposals: the establishment of mutually satisfying exchanges among seemingly unbounded and propertyless individuals based upon the novel mechanism of free wage labor. This difficult treatise finally proposes the repression, not the abolition of slavery, which was to be legally the human booty of winning a just war. Most people thought this was just the right, normal thing to do. And Quiroga was no exception.

Indian subjectivities came to be produced during these distressing colonial times. Against those official speakers who promoted the denial of the simultaneity of all members of the human species, Quiroga constitutes an ambivalent example of an early modern *indigenismo*. His civilizational prejudices were juxtaposed, often contradictorily to a genuine preoccupation with the most fragile social sectors. *Información en Derecho* proposes severe contractualist measures appertaining to the historical novelty of wage labor. It is possible to see here the beginning of an individuation process and the dawn of intentionality. But there is also the coexistence of the exciting desire for the social deliquescence, or millenarianism, which imagined an unprecedented potentiality among these social sectors most severely punished and almost entirely destroyed by the colonization of early capitalism. If on the one hand Quiroga wanted the careful labelling of all social forces, on the other hand, his millenarianism wanted the melting down of all typological orderings. The satisfaction of collective need is the goal. With or without biblical resonances, such millenarianism or the deliquescence of wax, surely inspired by colonial Franciscanism, will not hide its repugnance for the complex processes of individuation and patrimonialization that were historically taking place. The arrest of the typology thins out thus into the simplification or the formal egalitarianism of free wage labor with no content. Yet we must face the historical "failure," the mixed array or paradigmatic loss, of the permanent state of emergency and long-lasting generalized combinations of compulsive labor. Quiroga does not hesitate to confess his confusion and amazement at this mixed array of pre- and post-Hispanic social relations. His most memorable pages, the fresh vegetation in the colonial desert of the Spanish law, will intimate the inevitability of the collapse of all methods for social classification, and the affirmation of human plasticity towards a more tight, warm integration of a trans-Atlantic, Indianized totality. There were of course no easy ways out of these collective dilemmas and struggles which, vastly exceeding the banal individuality of our *oidor*, we have been here exploring.

Mural (fragment) by Diego Rivera entitled "Mexico: De la conquista hacia el futuro," in *Diego Rivers: Los murales del palacio nacional.* (Américo Arte Editores, S.A. de C.V., Instituto Nacional de Bellas Artes, 1977. ©2000 Banco de México Fiduciario en el Fideicomiso relativo a los Museos diego Rivera y Frida Kahlo. Av. Cinco de Mayo No. 2, Col. Centro, Del. Cuauhtémoc 06059, México, D.F., reproduction authorized by the Instituto Nacional de Bellas Artes y Literature, México)

Chapter IV

ॐ

The Early Modern Literature of Spanish Rule in the Americas: De Debellandis Indis *(1552) and the* Juicio de Residencia *(1536).*

1. Fragmented Textualities of the Repressive Culture in a Para-Print World

No reader with a slight regard for the imaginary site of colonial Latin America will ever touch Vasco de Quiroga's *De Debellandis Indis* (1551),[1] not even with a ten-foot pole. We are willing to recall Buñuel's *Andalusian Dog* (1928), the famous scene with the absent-minded youth toying around with the mutilated hand lying on the pavement, to emphasize that not many readers with some regard for Latin America will ever suffer, if they can help it, a thorough reading of *Indis*. This is not unfortunately our case. This bureaucratic piece of repressive scholarship demands full-time hard work. There are here no moments of happiness, no flights of fancy, and no gossipy salaciousness. Those unhappy few who will dare after all will not expect to come out of the enterprise smelling of roses. *Indis* is a badly damaged and incomplete, uninviting and shoe-flavored legal textualization of a subject matter which provides theoretical grounds for the early modern domination of people by people. This rather depressing subject matter, to say the least, will surely try the patience of most contemporary readers mostly, and not exclusively at the formal level of repressive rhetorics of domination. Formally, *Indis*, originally articulated in the early modern vehicle of high culture, Latin (and Quiroga's Latin is rather barbarous), is modulated according to the discursive protocols of rationality proper to Thomist essentialism. This early modern orthodoxy of legitimation of Spanish colonization of the Americas (*De Translatio Imperii*), will surely represent a challenge to our historical imagination, in both matter and manner, while offering no easy reward. We must engage with this repressive rationality if we want to strive towards a round vision of our main figure Vasco de Quiroga.

Quiroga's deeply unentertaining scholastic *quaestio* heightens a strong sense of historical heterogeneity. *Indis*, this "little monster," at times firmly trespasses the threshold of readability or intelligibility, which is another way of saying that it is we who fail to come to terms satisfactorily with this repressive rationality. We are fortunate in that René Acuña is our scholarly precedent, who also felt the need to muster his best spirits along the way to wrestle with this unpleasant "little legal thing" ("tratadillo latino," pp. 7, 13, 23, 49). Holding thus all impatient moods on a short leash, we wish to argue in the following pages for the early modern meaningfulness of this legality in spite of, but also because of, the all too strong persuasion to the contrary. After all, it is axiomatic that unpleasantness is part and parcel of the repressive culture, let alone the repressive culture under colonial conditions of production. Giving up on entertainment then in relation to this historical production of this legal industry, the following pages propose a close-reading of the problematic textualizations and the main themes of *Indis*.

The question is, how should we today come to terms with this quite unreadable "monster"? Because there is no hiding: we are here dealing with a resisting text of rather confusing style (Acuña's "estilo enmarañado," pp. 11, 34). The barely twelve sheets (or more properly *folios*) of the original *Indis* contain no less than fifty names and more than one-hundred references, explicit or not in relation to the politico-juridical formulations of medieval canon law. In this rich storehouse of knowledge still prestigious for this early trans-Atlantic modernity, the citation is often implicit or abbreviated, at best traceable, at worst approximate, and not uncommonly misleading. *Indis* exacerbates, for Acuña, the "incoherent mobility [*sic*] of Quiroga's thinking" (p. 11), and the profoundly "contingent, bureaucratic nature of [his] writings" (p. 34). There is apparently no way around the "homework" quality of this exercise of Latin letters in our colonial times, which will not allow us to make grand pronouncements about human nature. *Indis* will not let us give ourselves to champagne celebrations about the felicity of expression of the individual genius.[2] These repressive *letras coloniales* do not allow for *prima donnas*. Instead, we are to imagine this resisting textualization, never for the many, and with no apologies, in the historical coherence of the early colonial repressive circumstance. This is the trans-Atlantic stretch to our historical imagination.

Given the impossibility to claim literary merit, or canon status for *Indis*, we wish to risk the following generalization: *Indis*, dressed in a downright unpleasant, seemingly disheveled attire, exemplifies a mainstream textualization of the repressive culture *in* the Americas in both matter and manner. And perhaps the preposition, the "in," is a little bit misleading in this historically inevitable "in-between" or "trans-" Atlantic world. Designed to bridge at least two sides of the expanding world under Spanish rule, this chapter will deal with Quiroga's quite disparate *Indis* (1552) and *Juicio de Residencia* (1536). In relation to the former, what we wish to indicate is that *Indis* exemplifies, quite beyond the mere background or thematic referentiality "about" the Americas, the structural impulse to bring "American" populations under the hermeneutical modes of the Spanish repressive culture, inside which Quiroga's social role must always be imagined. Our early modern example of legal culture of scholarship with an Americanist preoccupation must include all its fragmentariness and heterogeneity. *Indis* is historically meaningful not despite, but precisely because of such ahistorical accusations of fragmentariness, unstable authorship and apparent unfittingness which still need to be historicized rigorously.

The continental novelty of America, still *Indias Occidentales* well after the reference date of 1552, emerges to the collective consciousness of the repressive culture as the "problem" which must be of necessity manufactured and solved always according to early modern grids of intelligibility. The historical unpredictability of the Americas must be, surely by all those social agents operating in these repressive circles, tamed and brought down to intelligibility and predictability. The predominant grid of juridicial intelligibility was, in these high spheres of official decision-making, Thomist rationality which, almost three hundred years after Aquinas's death (1224/5-1274), was in the middle of a strong revival in sixteenth-century Spain. The Dominican Francisco de Vitoria (1486-1546), was the one to deliver this repressive Thomism, with or without hesitations, for the Spanish colonization of the Americas. *Indis*, which coincides perfectly with Vitoria's *De Indis* (1552), will not let go of the empty signifier of "America." Quiroga's rather incoherent treatise represents the lackluster attempt to incorporate such novelty into officialdom.

Indis thematizes the official orthodoxy of the Spanish colonization of the Americas. Specifically, the legal commonplace of the *De Translatio Imperii*. That is, its content bespeaks the imperial mission in the Americas as historically ineluctable and desirable *carpe diem* for collectivities on both sides of the Atlantic. There is no pulling out of the troops (in the previous chapter we developed the expansionism of the world-system). There is a sense of duty and mission among state officials, and this is also perceptible in Quiroga's literature. At the level of social function, *Indis* is probably the most intricate piece of repressive erudition formally attributed to Quiroga (we will soon explore the dilemmas of this attribution). At the formal level, what has reached us today from this "only ideally complete" repressive textualization constitutes a rather succinct section out of a tripartite scholastic treatise which (according to scholarly evidence that we will also analyze soon) most likely passed through many important hands inside and outside the Spanish court circles. There is little question that Acuña's hypothesis, which we will endorse, of the historical circulation of this treatise is due to the debatable attribution to Quiroga, who would not have worried too much about writing for social venues other than the repressive circles (we will soon see the likely candidates for the multiple paternity of this repressive writing). The close reading of this intricate repressive text will give us, we hope, concrete information about Quiroga's likeliest political position. The contrast between these two repressive situations, *Indis* and *Proceso de Residencia* will constitute, we also hope, a good panoramic view into some of the historical complexities of the repressive constellation over the early modern Americas. According to most scholars, the original context for this "anonymous, fragmented and disorderly manuscript" (p. 25) is the famous Valladolid Debates (1550-1551).

Indis constitutes a relatively belated and quite deferential, yet unsolicited scholarly intervention into the juridico-political debates which had been taking place in the Spanish court, Valladolid (we may wish to recall the foundation of the new Valladolid, today city of Morelia in the neighborhood of Quiroga's village-hospitals in the Michoacán region by the Viceroy Mendoza in 1541). To imagine this historical situation, we may dwell a bit longer in the most likely historical meaningfulness of the excruciating difficulty of *Indis*. If, according to Acuña's words, *Indis* is truly Dante's *ombra* in the almost happy purgatory of libraries, what kind of meaning should we make of this? How should we ignore what is not possible to ignore, and what seems to be the last straw breaking the camel's back, the highly debatable authorship (the unsolved tentativeness, the "puede ser [de Quiroga]" (pp. 7, 12, 27)? Does not this unresolved issue, particularly so for a contemporary sensibility, put all the castles in the air of thick doubt? Who would bother with an impossibly difficult and boring legal text of depressing content from the periphery of New Spain (today Mexico), with no agreed-upon author? Who would bother with a deformed, incomplete ugly "baby" thrown out of the bathtub into in the suburbs of history with no good credentials and no parents? We have again no choice but to make all these unpleasant circumstances, the suspension of authorial certainty included, historically meaningful so that some of these may somehow, if only subconsciously, bore some holes into the defense mechanism of the likely contemporary boredom. But early modern textualities do not come easy.

1. 1. Filling in the Historical Blanks: Acuña's Detective Story

We may initially propose the format of a detective story to raise the following questions: In relation to *Indis*, who did what to whom, who was directly involved, where, when, how, what's the payoff? We must anticipate that the scholarly reconstruction will not be able to provide all of the answers. The non-existing satisfactory answer to "Who's done it?" will have to take us to the slippery issue of early modern authorship. We will historicize and thus attenuate the "scandal" of this slipperiness inside the repressive circles. The fragmentariness of *Indis* will have to force us to speculate among its most likely historical possibilities. We will sometimes be facing a wall with no good answers, and we will have to address these sincerely. We are lucky we will be able to turn occassionally to Acuña's precedent. Hardcore empiricists have it tough in this repressive neighborhood.

We are not alone in the "failure" of satisfactory answers difficult to come by, since other scholars, considerably more knowledegeable than us, have already admitted to some of these structural, i.e. historical, blanks. Yet, rather than looking the other way, or mindlessly at these sour grapes, it is crucial to carry on with the interrogation of this "failure." We need to take a closer inspection of the historical condition of such "failure." What follows is a close reading of Acuña's interpretive close reading which analyzes the traceable evidences in relation to *Indis*. What follows is the critical analysis of this textual materiality at the closest, crudest, most unavoidable level possible. Always in dialogue with colonial scholars, this is thus mostly a historiographic re-evaluation.

So, the detective story goes on like this: Most sources will tell us that Quiroga was in Spain during 1547-1554 (p. 21),[3] and most specifically in the then unimportant city of Madrid, judging by the always tentative composition date of *Indis* (1551). We may only speculate what Quiroga might have been doing in the little enclave of Madrid. There is a letter (April 23, 1553), signed by Quiroga and addressed to Bartolomé de Las Casas. This letter, which is printed by Acuña (pp. 19-21), requests from the towering Dominican friar some comments in relation to a little treatise entitled *Indis*. There is no absolute certainty, but it is most likely that this *Indis* is the one Acuña, in his own cautious words, rescued for us. In this letter, the former *oidor* portrays himself as an old and sick man, yet always quite deferential towards the Dominican friar who clearly appears a man higher in office or prestige ("no sé cómo lo ha tomado," p. 21). Against this background of the Valladolid Debates, where legitimacies were being contested, it is not at all implausible to imagine *Indis* as a rather ill-digested follow-up by Quiroga on some of those discussions. We have no evidence of any direct response from Las Casas to Quiroga's request. Had it happened, it surely had not been sympathetic or suave. The main formulations in *Indis* are quite anti-Las Casas, if not in scholastic manner, clearly in political matter.

Acuña provides the dates for the two sessions of the Valladolid Debates (August-September 1550 and April-May 1551),[4] and the complete names of all participants, no more than thirteen high magistrates of political interpretation.[5] The name of Vasco de Quiroga, against Bernal de Castillo's record mentioned in the preceding chapter, is not included among these. *Indis* is hence, we must be willing to speculate, a rather last-minute attempt to get a decent hearing from the main figures present in Valladolid, as to the whys and the hows of the Spanish colonization of the Americas. It is mostly for convenience sake that we will split these magistrates into two main groups, gathering around the pivotal figure of the Dominican Bartolomé de Las Casas, advocate of some degree of self-determination for the Americas, and the courtly intellectual Juan Ginés de Sepúlveda, advocate of the Aristotelian logic of might is right. *Indis*, according to Acuña, reached both leaders.

If the Valladolid Debates thus constitute the likeliest historical framework for the production of *Indis*, Quiroga, clearly a second fiddle, pictures himself amid numerous disclaimers closer to experiential or first-hand knowledge rather than the lettered knowledge ("más de experto que de *letrado*," p. 20). Quiroga's *captatio benevolentia* rings quite true in his lack of knowledge ("inhabilid/ad"), not fully deserving Las Casas's attention ("[que] vuestra Señoría no se canse de leerlo, que es letra menuda y le cansará," p. 21). Most contemporary readers will agree no doubt with the accuracy of Quiroga's self-presentation.

1. 2. The Good Guy, the Bad Guy and the Long Hair in the Soup

Early modern textualities are hardly ever the easy, unproblematic, ahistorical creatures of human practice and imagination contemporary readers will instantly apprehend effortlessly. The textualization of social struggles, so unlike breathing for a non-smoker, is never, we dare say, a natural, spontaneous, painless thing. The textualization of social energies, cleary not a thing, is instead most often a fragmented series of fragmented, even unreliable and unsettling processes, historically. The historico-social process of textuality is, without the paratextual oceans of experience and imagination, hardly ever the complete story. Unfortunately, textuality, perhaps the naturalized habitat for the colonial scholar, is hardly ever romantic love at first sight, or a given. Textuality is instead, almost always for the colonial scholar, a big problem which, like a scandal in the family, is not easy to negotiate.

It is not difficult to call *Indis* a nuisance, but the historical condition of such nuisance is less easy to come by. We will give it a try. If *Indis* is available to us today with the historical status of archival evidence, scholarly librarianship is to blame. In the long shadow of these two strong early modern individualities, Bartolomé de Las Casas and Vasco de Quiroga, *Indis* has reached us today because of the exploration of the monumental maze of Las Casas's papers (p. 25). There is, however, no recognizable signature in *Indis*, although the doubtful paternity of this "bastard son" will signal Quiroga. There is no need to run helpless to the interpretive tactics of deconstruction to try to historicize the most likely conditions of production of this manuscript: Acuña's paleographic facsimile edition, which preceeds our efforts by eleven years, has already done for us most of the heavy work.[6]

Acuña's scholarship is also not hanging from thin air. His erudite, good-humored work also draws material and inspiration from a dialogue with preceding scholarship, which originally dates back to the eighteenth century. Acuña mentions the name of Juan Bautista Muñoz (1745-99), at the *Real Academia de Historia* (Madrid). The Mexican scholar will be following Muñoz's words. We are here following Acuña's: "[*Indis*] puede ser del

Obispo de Michoacán, don Vasco de Quiroga" (p. 27). There are some troubling questions: Should we take this slippery likelihood at face value? Or what should we do when we appear to be dealing with non-falsifiable situations? But is this so? Yet, there are still other unsolved issues, and more hands left yet unmentioned, in relation to this deeply uncomfortable early modern legal manuscript.

If Muñoz catalogued his doubts for posterity, with Acuña following suit, the original assembler or *adicionador* of *Indis* was apparently, according to the latter, no other than Las Casas (pp. 27-28). There are, however, at least three more scribes of uncertain identity who left their "ink footprints" in the textual materiality of *Indis*. We need to take a look at these ghosts of uncertain presence. Addressing subject number one, corresponding to the handwriting of the totality of the treatise, which is *not* Quiroga's, Acuña says, without further comments, that it "does not matter" (p. 29). Addressing the subject number two, one who made a single marginal note and who will also remain unidentified, our Mexican Sherlock Holmes says, again without further comments, that he was "someone who participated in the Valladolid debates" (p. 29). As regards subject number three, the one who left several marginal notations on several sheets of *Indis*, this is, always according to Acuña, no other than Las Casas's arch-rival, Juan Ginés de Sepúlveda. Acuña harbors no doubts about this latter attribution of identity (p. 30).

So, at least we must take into account four, if actually not five early modern fathers for the composition of the *Indis* Acuña edited eleven years ago: the anonymous *letrado* of the majority of this copy of *Indis*, the "original" is considered to be lost, the anonymous Valladolid participant and Ginés de Sepúlveda, with both leaving marginal annotations, the attribution to Quiroga according to Acuña, and finally Las Casas, since Acuña found *Indis* in the spectacular library of the Dominican friar, fact which justifies the material preservation of the manuscript until to this day. To this exclusive male plateau of repressive scholarship, we could easily add the names of Juan Bautista Muñoz and also, of course, Acuña.

We thus have the intriguing situation that *Indis*, despite its compact, almost impenetrable legalese, or precisely because of it, somehow managed to circulate inside the privileged circles of politico-juridical interpretation, and that it reached the two main contenders of the Valladolid Debates. The careful consideration of the historical materiality of *Indis*, historically circumvented by the already existing print culture, disavows claims to any single paternities.[7] No doubt the name of Vasco de Quiroga, surely recognizable for sixteenth-century men of state, allowed for *Indis* to make its way into decision-making centers of power and privilege ("escribió de su propia cuenta, sin ser invitado a hacerlo," p. 49). There must have been something in the name of the former *oidor*. Still surprisingly, the sorry shape of *Indis* coming from the closet of the dead reaches us today with nagging questions: how could this have survived for so long? And, does it deserve its longevity? This surprising survival may perhaps hide something of some interest after all.

The foreign horizon of early trans-Atlantic modernity thus presents to us this proto-individual textuality, essentially a bureaucratic work in progress inside the largely unaccessible, male-dominated enclaves of the repressive culture. Scholarly efforts have been so far mostly devoted to trying to dispel the pending uncertainty of the anonymity of this profoundly uncomfortable treatise. Inter-generational scholarship on *Indis* has historically been nagging at this bone without yet having reached its marrow. We would like to suggest that perhaps there is not one. Perhaps the naturalness of the singularity of authorship is an anachronistic red herring we should all learn, if not to forget entirely, at least to relativize historically.

In fact, we would like to propose that it might just be more historically fitting to try to imagine instead a succession of male pens (re)inscribing, sometimes merely scribbling, repressive meanings into this document, truly a palimpsest, which struggles to become a persuasive legal brief to thus have an impact upon transatlantic configurations of the American polity. With all its limitations, the preliminary stages of bureaucratic work in public policy, or the repressive culture, are thus asking for our heightened sensibility towards the collective participation in the meaning-making process in an early modern horizon which must have found most likely the notions of single version and single authorship, if not something utterly incomprehensible, clearly a weird-looking couple of strange bedfellows, and a historical eccentricity. In this early modern horizon, *Indis* is thus a historically collective work in progress only marginally penetrated by the accelerated demands of the mechanical reproduction. This rather invisible American repressive industry, *Indis* inside the Valladolid Debates, quite far away from orchestrated exhibitions and ephemeral architectures of imperial eulogy, will be left largely ignored by the print culture. If it is clear that the interpretive task of *Indis* is also communal dialogue and collaboration among different generations of colonial scholars, it is also clear that the choral quality of composition of *Indis* must include, with or without doubts, the name of Quiroga.

Muñoz's discreet librarian ghost comes thus from the dead, invoked by Acuña, to enjoy its five minutes of public exposure. Muñoz is the main source for the attribution of the third, hasty pen to Ginés de Sepúlveda ("sobre la marcha," p. 30). *Indis* thus circulated, despite its self-described imperfect quasi-*letrado* from hand to hand among magistrates of abstruse legal interpretation in the vicinity of the Valladolid officialdom. It is clear that Acuña's date of the manuscript, 1552, is only one tentative point of reference. Copies of this version must have surely circulated and are now lost in the Spanish archives (pp. 31-32).

Still, this exclusive male forum of elite cultures of repressive scholarship will not let us abandon the imaginary territory of historical speculation and conjecture. Circumstantial evidence points in this direction of the likelihood of the association between *Indis* and Quiroga (Acuña's tentativeness of the "puede ser," p. 30), and also of the likelihood of *Indis* being a somewhat belated 1552 response (the Valladolid Debate took place in August-September 1550 and April-May 1551). Acuña feels the need to respond to the early article by the French Hispanist Marcel Bataillon,[8] amid verbalized disagreements with Zavala regarding the paternity issue of *Indis*.[9] There is a history of early disagreements between Zavala and the tandem of O'Gorman and Fernández as regards Quiroga's *Rules*,[10] which must be put against the classic disagreement between Marcel Bataillon and Edmundo O'Gorman over different understandings of historiographic endeavors.[11] Kripper-Martínez's most recent overall re-evaluation of Quiroga chooses to follow Zavala's doubts on *Indis*.[12] We are here following Acuña, not so much in the solving of the paternity issue, but rather in the pursuit of the historical concreteness and the collective orthodoxy of the repressive culture inside which Quiroga lived.

Bataillon, despite losing much of the discursive field to O'Gorman, displayed an enviable accuracy as to Quiroga's political position at a time when *Indis* was not yet known. Acuña's fastidious scholarship on *Indis* reinforces, in our opinion, Bataillon's early speculations: Quiroga comes quite close to Ginés de Sepúlveda and gets far away from Las Casas. That is, Quiroga legitimizes the Spanish colonization of the Americas, and the no longer *oidor* but the first Bishop of the Michoacán region will argue in favor of the *encomienda* system for the most fragile and also majoritarian social sectors (today we might wish to call these "minority groups").[13] *Indis* thus provides intellectual argumentation for the *justos títulos*. We will have to look closely into this argumentative texture of this repressive argument.

So, in light of this imperial theme, it is quite plausible to conjecture that Las Casas's response to *Indis*, which we do not have, might have been quite critical of these *De Translatio Imperii* formulations or *justos títulos*. If Las Casas is today for many the good guy who defended the Indians, and Ginés de Sepúlveda is the truly ugly, but also truly modern in the unrepentant Aristotelian hierarchization of early modern human reality, and also the impassive and unattenuated articulation of the right to conquer, Quiroga's political position in *Indis*, in general theme or subject matter but not in manner or form, comes quite close to the latter humanist figure. We do not wish to shy away from historical uncertainty: whether the treatise is Quiroga's original creation or not remains as yet undecidable. Perhaps most importantly, there is a building cornerstone of certainty which most scholars will endorse: the spirit of the letter in *Indis* is very much congruent with Quiroga's axiology or worldview as far as we can gather from the Rules and *Información en Derecho*. Quiroga's belief, with all its hesitations, is very much the official ideology of an impassable opportunity, but also a moral imperative for the Spanish regulation of the Americas. To regulate means, for him no doubt, to modernize, with or without Thomist phraseology, and we strongly need to transcend the liberal trap of the authorial intention: the early modernity of novel and brutal capitalism in the Americas was not going to be stopped by some politico-juridical deliberations. Colonial utopianism, also for *Indis* with all evidence to the contrary, is to be understood as the formal or official intervention into these modern vehicles for human experience and imagination.[14]

If the juxtaposition with Ginés de Sepúlveda, the humanist version of the early modernity of capitalism,[15] arguably quite uninviting from the early modern American standpoint,[16] paints the customary white clothes of Quiroga a bit black, there is no need, with Bataillon, to apologize. There is also no need to re-paint them white. Historiography is, for us, not quite the game of name-calling among black kettles and pots. Nor are we claiming whiter colored clothes today. Our concern is instead the round understanding of the historical and social role of Quiroga in relation to the historical concretization of the notion of utopianism in the Americas. We do not quite agree with Bataillon when he talks, in relation to Quiroga, about a "*criollo* feudalism" (p. 279). We do not quite see the qualification of humanism, let alone of humanitarianism,[17] in relation to our state official, despite some necessary corrections of Zavala's commonplace on Quiroga by Anthony Pagden.[18] Rather, we see Quiroga as the historical effort toward the official reformation of proto-capitalist structures mostly inside politico-juridical enclaves. We see in *Indis*, never quite a disguised sheep in orthodox wolf's clothing, the tensions, with or without uncomfortable Thomist rhetoric, proper to the reconfiguration of these politico-juridical structures that are historically trying to catch up with the teething troubles of early modern capitalist expansionism. Fitting into the repressive colonial utopianism we have already seen in relation to *Información en Derecho*, *Indis* will also provide rhetorical legitimation to this larger early modern globalization.

Yet, some further scholarly pains will have to remain with us. Acuña has drawn our attention to a long hair in the soup, the unsettling connection between *Indis* and one little piece with an identical title by friar Miguel de Arcos, the chief responsible for the Dominicans in Seville and an intimate acquaintance with Francisco de Vitoria. Hanke and Millares-Carlo's 1943 text, fundamental background for the historical orthodoxy of *Indis*, includes this rather succinct text.[19] The trouble comes from the fact that Arcos's presumably synthetic summary of Quiroga's *Indis*, does not mention the latter by name. Already quite predictably, an invisible *letrado* hand is also at work. This repressive document attributed to Arcos has reached us with a notorious blank space ("vide un tratado del Obispo de_____ [*sic*]," p. 3). There will be no names about the author of *Indis* who will be nonetheless qualified as conscientious and acquainted with Indian customs ("hombre de zelo…que tiene experiencia de la manera de los Indios," pp. 6, 7). In spirit, however, Arcos's summary endorses the official thesis of the legitimation of the colonization ("los títulos de justa guerra").[20] In the meantime, Acuña pulls a little bit on the ears of the eminent American Hispanist Lewis Hanke, who also speaks of the possibility of Quiroga's paternity (p. 34-36). Acuña defends that the copyist of Arcos's pages (technically, a *parecer*) "did not know very much about the business in the *Indias*," in Bataillon's words.

Following Bataillon, Acuña will state that the nagging blank of ignorance included in the little piece preserved by Hanke and Millares-Carlos is the fault of the anonymous *copista*, and that this synthetic copy must relate to a previous text, today lost, written by Quiroga when he was still *oidor* of the *Segunda Audiencia* (1531-1535). In this early modern forest of elusive textualities, we must learn from intelligent squirrels not to jump all too easily to the missing trees of comfortable conclusions: Folowing Acuña, Arcos's version of *Indis*, which has been copied by somebody else, is technically a stated opinion (a *parecer)* which is, at least in format if not in subject matter, quite different from the *Indis* produced by the *oidor* Quiroga. This early product is still not the *Indis* associated with the Bishop Quiroga retrieved for posterity by Acuña's laborious scholarship. The essence of Acuña's discrepancy with Hanke is mostly chronological disparity. The apparent similarity in these titles is misleading: there is just not one *Indis* but many visible and invisible textualities so called. According to Acuña, we are dealing with at least two different textualizations separated by almost twenty years. Quiroga's *Indis* discovered by Acuña has nothing to do ("nada que ver") with the substance of the treatise (1532-35), which, mostly preserving Arcos's opinion, was published by Hanke and Millares-Carlo. This latter version is the one which includes the baleful omission of Michoacán ("Obispo de _____ [*sic*]," pp. 34-45). One wishes one could rub this blank, like Aladdin his lamp, to see emerge the words "Michoacán"! But it is not quite possible.

Acuña, however, will not hesitate to state that he is quite happy about this invigorated likelihood of the attribution of his *Indis* to Quiroga. He does not hide that he is dealing with the "copy," and not the "original," placed today in the *Real Academia de Historia*, Madrid (p. 50). He is also careful to point out his relative disinterest in "demonstrating [Quiroga's] authorship [of *Indis*]" (p. 69). Almost like a fox saying he is *not* big on sour grapes, Acuña confesses to be mostly interested in the recreation of the historical climate regardless of Quiroga's most "plausible" paternity of *Indis* (pp. 69-70). Acuña will go quite beyond the pale for any sane doctoral candidate: he will describe his own careful edition as glamourless and "thesis-less" (pp. 70, 72). Following his example, we are thus also willing, in the middle of this rather lengthy detectivesque story of patrimonialist paternities, to propose the most likely historical plausibility of anachronism for the singularity of authorship inside these male-dominated precincts of the repressive culture. We have to deal with the negativity of missing pieces and incomplete sources. Like Marianne moore, "we too dislike it." Like Acuña, we are not fully committed to the clarification of the singularity of the paternity of *Indis*. We wish instead to explain some of this bewildering dance of traceable and ghost textualities that are not entirely warm and easy. Our goal is the convincing recreation of the historical texture of colonial legality that makes all these confusions historically meaningful.

2. *De Translatio Imperii* in the Americas: *De Debellandis Indis*

The expanding totality of the Christian Republic in the Americas, or Vitoria's "universal community of the faithful," was not to allow for drastic social resistances or alternatives outside the official vision of this expanding totality. There will be no exceptions, or unintelligibilities, left untouched or outside this rule of legitimation which will officially rest upon Papal sanction. Modernity will thus incorporate the hitherto unimaginable human landscapes of belief and praxis repressively. Official messianism is never far away from this historical vision in the sails of global power and privilege (we have already mentioned in the previous chapter the courtly figure of Juan López de Palacios Rubios).[21] Inside competing legal codifications, Natural Law and Law of Nations primordially, there will be in *Indis* no shadow of a doubt about the legitimacy transferred by the institution of Papacy to Charles V (accession in 1517, cession in 1557), despite the overwhelming corruption of Alexander VI (1431-1503), the representative of the Borgian family who, together with Ferdinand the Catholic, would become the role models for Machiavelli's ideal prince. The discursivity of the *justos títulos*, or *De Translatio Imperii* formulations, will remap universal boundaries of political sovereignty, and it will do so typically for one generation. We must remember that Charles V held the title of "Emperor," but not his son Philip II (1527-1598). We may imagine the early colonial model of the *encomienda* system reproducing locally in the Americas this global model of temporary ownership for one or two generations. We may imagine the fight for power and privilege in the official formalization of this temporal time-frame. With all its legal orthodoxy, *Indis* out-Herods Herod in its renewed pledge to the institution of the Papacy. The Pontiff's proclamations will be the axiom scrupulously left untouched by most early modern intellectuals, Quiroga among them, and this is particularly true within all those intellectually influential social circles which we may synthesize as monasticism (Las Casas will be an early exception to this rule of obedience). In the no doubt painfully slow transference from ecclesiastical to civil or lay use of possession and control of wealth, almost like the folding and faulting of tectonics, the early modern period will deliver the collaboration of both institutions, monarchy and monasticism, in the *Patronato Real*,[22] no doubt with blurry boundaries inside the still quite invisible historical tendency towards secularization.[23] The strong insinuation here is that Quiroga's village-hospitals must have been institutionalized closely following the shadow of these formulations, already tried in newly seized territories such as Granada,[24] and the North African city of Oran, Algeria. Biographical accounts of Quiroga situate him in training *in partibus infidelium*, possibly in the service of the archdiocese of Granada, already acting as the judge of the *Residencia* Process of the *corregidor* of Oran, *Licenciado* Alonso Páez de Ribeira and, also quite fittingly, drawing up a peace treaty with the so-called Tremece, a Moorish state bordering on Oran.[25]

Indis, with all its slippery fragmentariness and incompleteness, "shameless" multiple paternities and barbarous Latin, constitutes for us a rather quintessential candidate for repressive scholarship. This intractable legal document by a public official in the Americas, trying to veer the transatlantic polity towards a greater unification,[26] may thus well qualify, for all these "wrong" reasons, to represent the early modern state culture of legal scholarship in a colonial world. Persuasiveness in these narrow historical circles of repressive signification, it is quite clear, does not follow the rules of our liking.

2. 1. Doing Repressive Things the Dry, Scholastic Way

We wish to restate that *Indis* will give legal voice, or *justos títulos*, to the Spanish colonization of the Americas. *Indis* thus constitutes the Latin vehicle in the early modern Spanish house of imperial design, for the historical invigoration of time-honored formulations of *De Translatio Imperii*. To attend to this larger vision, the manuscript literature of *Indis* emerges from a rather bureaucratic, juridico-political context with little or no patience for issues of individual taste. Acuña does not, however, shy away from castigating with gusto the Latin of *Indis* ("Latín de jurista mal avenido, incómodo con los clásicos, [de] deficiencias inexclusables [y] vizcaínas licencias), "much coarser than the Latin from the indigenous pupils from Colegio de Santa Cruz Tlatelolco" (p. 51). The orthography fares no better, yet Acuña looks the other way in order not to embarrass this demure lady further (p. 51). Quiroga is not entirely to blame for these irregularities, since this *Indis*, we have already mentioned, is not the original version which is now considered lost (p. 51). Worlds apart from the stylistic heights of Juan Ginés de Sepúlveda, Francisco de Vitoria or Elio Antonio de Nebrija (1441/2-1522),[27] the 870 lines of *Indis*, which will hardly move the reader to tears of joy, will however treasure, always according to Acuña's edition, the rather heavy erudition merchandise of fifty-eight references to authors, mostly Fathers of the Church, and twenty-three references to medieval works, which are not uncommonly obscure, or even long lost for the general public. Taking the reader's breath away, the twelve *folios* of *Indis* quite shamelessly register ninety-two quotes from canon law and thirty-nine quotes from civil law (p. 55), most often in a maze of abbreviated references of almost purely cryptic language (Acuña's edition of *Indis* includes 44 pages and 249 endnotes which shed light, if not always clear light, on these references). If Quiroga's legal erudition is thus loaded, it is alas also oftentimes misplaced. Acuña does not hesitate a bit to speak of the bombastic quality and the undigested name-dropping of this Latin legalese ("mero relleno indiscriminado, oropel jurídico de segunda mano," p. 52), charges which no young academics will hear without trembling knees. Acuña will not back off from charging the saintly figure of "Tata" Vasco with some ignorance and certain malice in the simplification of medieval sources (p. 190, 214). *Indis*, rather unconspicuous and quite forgettable a literary piece for all its political orthodoxy, includes "little novelty" in either substance or form, and quite a few "theological insufficiencies" (p. 61). With these precedents, our readers will rest assured that we will not be making big claims for the grandeur of *Indis*. Quite the contrary, we wish to defend, for quite other historical reasons, the unconspicuousness of *Indis*. We will continue arguing, with quite another mindset of expectations, for the need to go deeper into the historical significance of the thematic content of these textual irregularities. What the following pages will offer is the dramatization of some salient historical incongruities intrinsic to the repressive culture we haven't yet left entirely behind. The rather unconspicuous quality of *Indis* comes from its full embrace of historico-political orthodoxy, i.e. the endorsement of the official ideology of the *justos títulos*. *Indis* is, for us, the rather modest repressive garb of this imperial design.

Indis formalizes the tripartite scholastic form of the *questio* scholastic form, the initial "negative" arguments, followed by the *responsio*, which tends to represent the main thesis or the authorial intention, and the conclusion or the *confutatio*, which quite symmetrically presumes the demolition of the initial or negative arguments. We may imagine, initially at this narrow or merely formal level, two conflicting historical sensibilities, the humanistic dialogue and the scholastic treatise. Formally quite in the antipodes of the polished humanistic sensibility of the dialogic format,[28] and we may recall More's *Utopia* (1515), Ginés de Sepúlveda's *Democrates Alter* (1550), Juan de Valdés's *Diálogos* (1530),[29] and the well-known nutshell by the Franciscan Antonio de Guevara's *El Villano del Danubio*,[30] our unfortunately uncomfortable scholastic treatise presents a rather less personable, if incomplete architecture of legal argumentation. Having little of the fearful symmetry and disciplined exhuberance of Aquinas's *Summa Theologica* (1265-1272), there can be no doubt that *Indis* is the slovenly, relatively unpretentious and decidedly bureaucratic "bastard son" of Thomist rationality.[31]

There are missing sections at the beginning and also at the end of the remnant *Indis*. The initial "negative" arguments are mostly missing. The conclusion is also incomplete. Acuña's *Indis* is thus formally mostly the middle section, or the *responsio*, and the almost complete conclusion.

Making sense of this early modern repressive textualization, the original twelve *folios*, or the thirty-seven pages in Acuña's bilingual Latin and Spanish edition, is not at all easy, despite the wealth of information provided by the Mexican scholar. Due to the abbreviated concentration of medieval authors and sources, predominantly from the Fathers of the Church, this early modern jargon of repressive authenticity opens up for the contemporary reader an almost impossibly bridgeable gulf of foreign heterogeneity.

Separating the thematic core from this off-putting legalistic husk will release the meaning of the *justos títulos* thus: it is perfectly right and proper for the Spaniards to seize the Americas since the sole site of global legitimation, the Papacy, has so declared quite unambiguously, ceremoniously. I quote from the Spanish translation provided by Acuña:

> [L]os predichos nuevos pueblos descubiertos novísimamente por los hispanos participan con nosotros del Derecho Natural...se consideran ovejas de Cristo (p. 145, 142)...desde el advenimiento de Cristo toda jurisdicción, dominios y principados fuéronles sustraídos a los infieles y transpasados a los fieles. (p. 147)

Around this semantic gist, *Indis* does not neglect the protocols of the coronation of the Emperor, the ceremony of the unsheathed sword and the oath exchange between the pope and the emperor (pp. 152-3), as though bearing in mind the non-figurative quality of meaning of the ceremonial precepts in the Thomist rationality[32] (we must bring to memory the Játiva-born Rodrigo de Borja y Doms, later Alexander VI (1492-1503), who will be the original purveyor of these original bulls). The male genealogy of Abraham, Moses, Christ and Peter settles for *Indis* the rock solid legitimacy of the seizure of the Americas ("transferre imperium," p. 154). This transference has, by 1552, long been fulfilled completely ("transpaso consumado y total,"p. 159). The future of the American possessions is left up at the discretion of the Emperor ("la ambulatoria voluntad del testador," p. 157). The situation is however far from being this easy, historically.

Indis settles thus quite formally the "monstrous doubt," O'Gorman's expression, as to the political ontology of the American populations. These American populations are said to participate of the Natural Law, yet all jurisdictions are said to be suspended following upon the new undoubtable point of reference, the birth of Christ. Christ's successors, the institution of the Papacy, have with absolutely no doubt universal jurisdiction, and thus possess the perfect legitimacy to delegate jurisdiction to the most dependable monarchies.

What historically amounts to be fully human in this sixteenth-century trans-Atlantic horizon, is thus sealed off metaphorically by this expanding official totality of humanity united in Christian belief. The axiom is that catholicity is universal, yet it is also expanding and cannot be any less than universal and expanding simultaneously (the official chronicler, the Franciscan Guevara, will dedicate his texts to his intended reader, the "sacra, cesárea, católica magestad" [Charles V], anything less than this would be an offense). Within this forcefield of hegemonic Christian belief, we must however imagine competing social agents, mostly grouped under the umbrella term of monasticism. Within this theoretical sameness of Natural Law and charity (*caritas*), there is a historical obligation according to *Indis* towards Christ's sheep on both sides of the Atlantic. In this non-negotiable Christ-centered theorization, the incorporation (*reino* and *dominio*) of the Americas is perfectly legitimate (p. 147). The pope, Christ's successor, is the sole proprietor of the totality of the world. Again, the axiom is that the pope has total authority over this global property. In other words, nobody owns anything, or everybody owes everything not to each other, but to the pope:

> debido al traspaso hecho por Cristo a favor de Pedro, los infieles no tienen principado, ni trono o dominio alguno (*principatum, thronum, dominium*), y que no hay hombre ni raza que posea hoy [1552] el imperio, a no ser el Papa y la iglesia universal Católica en cuyas manos está toda potestad (*potestas*) tanto espiritual como temporal. (p. 149-151)

For the official messianism inflexibly thematized in *Indis*, the social institution of the Church is the *locus* of all appeals to legitimation (*mater imperii...totius orbis*, p. 151). For this official discourse, the early modern totality of the life-world, or commonwealth, is already out of joint without taking into consideration the brutal novelty of the Americas, which will of necessity have to relate to the Christian *fontano lugar*. The ground-breaking impact of the *novum* cannot be here underestimated. To incorporate this looming continentality of mostly unintelligible human forms, the trans-Atlantic world will break uneasily down into the smaller political units of the *regna* and *dominia*, which Acuña translates respectively into "sovereignty" and "relations of ownership and debt" (p. 190). Whereas the general argument offered by *Indis* is clear, i.e. the papal sanction, the *fontano lugar* of legitimacy beyond reasonable doubt, proclaims that the seize of the Americas is the only right thing to do, it is clear that the specification and reconfiguration of these global jurisdictions will be a bit more problematic.[33] The formal configuration of levels of political domination, the *distinctio dominiorum* (pp. 190, 211), will be the thorny issue in *Indis* precisely in the uneasy repressive theorization of the Natural Law and the Law of Nations:

> Todo esto junto, lúcidamente demuestra que, pues el imperio y toda jurisdicción están en manos del Papa, al obtener de Alejandro VI, pontífice entonces felizmente reinante, la ón y gracia apostólicas de aquellos nuevos reinos de Indias donde no se reconocía la Sede Apostólica, ni al Emperador ni a príncipe católico alguno, debe concluirse que los gloriosísimos reyes de España fundandos en esa concesión apostólica, legítimamente y a justo título (*legitime et justo titulo*) se apropiaron para sí y sus sucesores de aquellos reinos de Indias (p. 153-5).

Let us take a closer look into this uneasy argumentation.

2. 2. The Uneasy Marriage of Natural Law and the Law of Nations

Rather than blaming the dead with the charge of ethnocentrism,[34] these pages wish to deal with some of these conceptual entanglements in relation to the repressive culture. It is not an easy thing to do.[35] Inclusions and exclusions of social agents from political goods will be formally established upon the recognition and compliance with the official, unquestionable belief in the Christian doctrine (no doubt, historical worlds apart from the inclusions and exclusions in the liberal content-free formalism as pertains to a consumer society). Conceptually, we must try to distinguish these levels of legal reasoning in *Indis*: Natural Law (*Ius Naturae*), Law of Nations (*Ius Gentium*) and Civil Law (*Ius Civile*). We should also provide the Spanish translation (*Derecho Natural, Derecho de Gentes* and *Derecho Civil*). Confusingly, these conceptual boundaries are quite blurred. *Indis* will provide no easy ways out of here.

We appear to be dealing with several levels of abstraction in this rather formal and even formulaic thinking process. Natural Law has to do with the primary and indemonstrable judgments about the teleology of the repressive action, whereas Civil Law has to do with the actual, concrete implementation of the repressive culture ideally in agreement, but not necessarily with the not so transparent postulates of the Natural Law. The Law of Nations is situated uneasily in an intermediary position between these two.[36]

Indis will build a split inside the notion of the Law of Nations: primary or more abstract and ineluctable; and secondary, more concrete and less coercive formulations (pp. 167, 171). The former "level" cannot be in all fairness contradicted, whereas the latter "level" could well revolt against the most abstract tenets of the Natural Law (as in "God is good"), as in the generic case of war. If there can be no possible contradiction inside the repressive culture of the primary tenets of the Law of Nations, the secondary tenets are quite often disregarded, even violated. From the most general to the most municipal or concrete structures, principles are thus said to "live" among humans in the form of precepts, rules and decisions. These principles are theoretically intelligible to all fully rational human forms; yet, and this is the catch, these are not transparent, so mediation is needed. They appear to be arranged in a cascading correspondence, yet there is also potentially conflict but only at the lowest, most concrete levels of repressive application. If Thomist rationality is built upon the axiom which will assert that the first principles are indemonstrable, the legalization of war, or "just war," further complicates the derivation, or correspondence, from the most general to the most concrete repressive formulations of any polity. Thomist rationality, due to its intimate cohabitation with conflict, or war, is thus far from being satisfactorily global and entirely self-sufficient. Legalism and paralogism go hand in hand historically.

If orthodox *Indis* semanticizes the Natural Law as the abstract principles which must, of necessity, apply to the totality of humanity ("omnia erant omnibus communia," p. 167), these primary tenets of the Natural Law do not, however, have the force of compulsion. In other words, *Indis* debilitates, if not trivializes the referentiality of the Natural Law. For this concrete repressive horizon of early modernity, the sameness of universal egalitarianism, or human togetherness, breaks down to smithereens: the gradation of the category "human." This "natural" communitarianism, or pre- or proto-capitalist moment of repressive truth, appears to have been left behind already by 1552, when *Indis* was produced. Instead, the secondary precepts of the Law of Nations are historically in full force against the Natural Law, which we could semanticize, using a more contemporary language, as all the social goods needed for the satisfaction of human needs and the sustainability of all human forms. In legalese, coloniality of power is the early modern hegemony of the Law of Nations over the Natural Law. In other words, *Indis* makes the Americas the site of illegitimacy. That is, early modern Americans initially appear quite unintelligible to the strictly European sources of legitimation, i.e. the papacy; and yet *they* own and owe among themselves illegitimately. The historical paradox of this illegitimacy, from European sources of legitimation, puts them closer to the more abstract, yet empty tenets of the Natural Law. Also for *Indis*, it is a double-blind situation since the undisputable, yet not enforceable truth of global communitarianism is out of place ("fuera de lugar"), historically. Accordingly, since the Law of Nations is not handcuffed by the Natural Law ("ius gentium secundarium (…) contra rationem naturalem," p. 167), *Indis* constructs the Americas, from the standpoint of repressive Thomism, as the grim-looking realm for the dominion of the Law of Nations, or the logic of might is right. Early modern Americas is, for *Indis*, the *locus* of disorderly irregularities, open conflict and war (pp. 167, 171 & 173). This colonial fracture, also for repressive Thomist discursivity, coincides with Sempat-Assadourian's formulation of the "permanent state of war," mostly for the early colonial Americas.

So, *Indis* will endorse that all political possessions in the Americas prior to the arrival of the Spaniards are the result of "unjust titles." If the Papacy is the only manufacturer of titles (*justos títulos*),[37] the bull sanction will leave no doubt about the American illegitimacy and, the Spanish legitimacy. The Law of Nations, inside which the logical possibility of the "just war" must be conceived, emerges conceptually precisely from this attributtion of illegitimacy to all pre-Hispanic American polities. The colonial situation of domination, or rather *servidumbre*, is mainly the product of the secondary prescriptive tenets of the Law of Nations: namely, the rule of force of the strongest (pp. 167 & 175). If it is axiomatic that the primary tenets of the Law of Nations cannot be derogated, this is not the case for the secondary ones which appear to take us all in the direction of structural violence. *Indis* will give us the imaginary landscape of an impoverished, debilitated God who does not wish for, yet cannot do anything against the domination of men by men:

> Razón de la razón áes que la adquisición de bienes particulares (*acquisitio rerum particularium*) está permitida a todos los hombres…mas la adquisición de reinos y principados (*regnorum et principatuum*) no está permitida a todos por presumirse fruto de la violencia, a no ser que conste de la elección de su principado, o de que éste se obtuvo por sucesión de predecesores que lo adquirieron de manera legítima…. Tanto más, cuanto que, por tal elección en el principado, se impone al pueblo una forma de servidumbre (*servitius inducitur*), servidumbre que Dios no introdujo al crear el mundo (*servitutem in creatione mundi non introduxit Deus*)…. No creó [Dios] al hombre, empero, para que estuviera sometido a otro hombre (*non autem creavit hominem ut homini subiieceretur*). (p. 172-3).

Thus paradoxically, the enfeebled God, invisible manufacurer of the often violated Natural Law, will however finally, almost obliquely become the terrifying force of the Old Testament God. Quiroga quotes the terrifying lines from Isaiah: 45:

> "Estas cosas dice el señor Dios a mi ungido Ciro, cuya diestra he tomado yo para subyugar ante su faz a las gentes y doblegar los lomos de los reyes, ante el cual abriré las puertas y ninguna se cerrará: "Yo te precederé y humillaré a los gloriosos de la tierra, las puertas de bronce derribando y quebrantando las barras férreas y darte he tesoros recónditos, etc." (p. 156-7)

> "Thus saith the Lord to his anointed, to Cyrus, whose right hand I have holden, to subdue nations before him; and I will loose the loins of kings, to open before him the two leaved gates; and the gates shall not be shut; I will go before thee, and make the crooked places straight: I will break in pieces the gates of brass, and cut in sunder the bars of iron: and I will give thee the treasures of darkness and hidden riches of secret places, etc."[38]

The Law of Nations will thus open the historical door to the rule of force.[39] Inside the castle of power and privilege which is the repressive city of letters, *Indis* says that the Spaniards, blessed by the Pope, represent after all God's will in the Americas. This official messianism, everpresent in official chroniclers since López de Palacios Rubios, was the historical orthodoxy to which our former high state official surely had to subscribe, at least officially. So does *Indis*, paying fastidious attention to all protocols of intelligibility.

It is this above rendition of the Law of Nations which will mostly give theoretical grounds to the official discourse appertaining to the Spanish expansionism into the early modern Americas. If there is no acceptable excuse to be made against the non-negotiable univocity in and of Christian belief ("los referidos nuevos indios jamás pudieron ni podrán excusarse de creer en un solo Dios creador del cielo y de la tierra, lo cual es fruto del Derecho Natural," p. 181), it is also true for *Indis* that Christ's birth quite radically suspends and reconfigures all political jurisdictions, except for one exclusive monarchic representative. *Indis* already makes some distinctions inside the public and private dichotomy: no infidels will be in all legitimacy allowed to hold political jurisdiction, yet these infidels will be allowed to hold to their private possessions, only in so far as they comply with official Christian formalities of communitarian belief (we saw this in Quiroga's *Regulations* in chapter two). The disobedience of the formalized repressive mechanism for the first encounter, the *requerimiento*, will constitute the "perfect crime":

> De modo que, habiendo los referidos indios no solamente omitido obedecer el dicho requerimiento de los hispanos de recibir la ley de Cristo antes habiéndose alzado en su contra...su delito es y fue perfecto. (p. 179)

Thus in this early modern situation, shot through by the American *novum*, *Indis* tries to create typological venues of social predictability. The social behavior in this permanent state of war structured according to the *requerimiento* procedure will be considered proper to this permanent state of irregularity. Disobedience to the *requerimiento* automatically generates the typified situation of a just war, which appears to be what the strongest party wants anyway. To bring some of these conceptual tensions back to our life, we may say that the sameness of the Natural Law must contend with the proliferation of differences corresponding to the Law of Nations. Against the unenforceable "quality" of the former, what holds the Law of Nations together is the rule of force (Quijano's notion of "coloniality of power"). Civil Law will constitute the concrete or specific implementations of these differences. Whereas the naturalizing regulation will emphasize the forces of integration and continuity, most commonly using the language of Christianity, "national ethnicities" will pull in the other direction of greater independence and autonomy among all those creatures situated in the vicinity of the category of "human," never a historical given (of course, the mutational mechanism of three-dimensional proto-capitalism in the Americas will also energize both tendencies, equally). We may thus say that the Natural Law follows a nomothetic model and the Law of Nations, an idiographic model in the production of knowledge.[40] There is of course no permanent resolution either way, and contradictions will come to be produced. Against the theoretical commonality of the Natural Law, i.e. we are all potentially perfectible humans, vassals and Christians, the historical emergence of political differences, the "us v. them" of politics, will be established following explicitly the language of the Law of Nations (we may imagine the conflict between the level of humanity, the genus *homo*, and the political level, the "us v. them"). According to *Indis*, the formalization of the transatlantic commonality in the Christian belief is the only permissible legitimation. *Indis* will not provide an explicit racialization of social energies. In other words, there is no other explicit repressive argumentation in *Indis*, quite unlike *Información en Derecho*, other than the religious argument. Less visibility of any other possible categories (class, race, gender, language, etc.), does not necessarily mean that these may not be there historically operating, but perhaps intermittently or subconsciously, in between this dense, if fractured, Latin.

The Natural Law, or the sign "God," means, at least in our reading, the utmost level of generality or abstraction; namely, historicity or the inter-generational continuum of the genus *homo*. Accordingly, the Law of Nations may instead operate, momentarily borrowing from the biological sciences, at a lower, more localized level of the recognizable collectivities or ethnicities. Finally, the Civil Law brings "it all home" at the lowest level of the particularity or the recognizable families (this mediation may be said to be like the faces in the photo album, the names in the historical newspaper, or the "facts" in the historical record). Whereas the highest level of abstraction deals with the most-encompassing and presumably unchanging categories of the universals ("ius immutabile," p. 166), the more tangible articulations of the repressive culture, the Law of Nations and the Civil Law, enter by contrast the real game of historicity and are thus subjected to change and transformation. Taking into account these mechanisms of differentiation, *Indis*, we are willing to assert, pushes in the direction of dedifferentiation of ethnicities, because of the attraction for the highest (impossible?) level of abstraction, or Natural Law. The repressive articulation of the official messianism of *Indis*, no doubt an imperial ideology always inside the time-honored formulas of *De Translatio Imperii*, appears to have been, in all historical likelihood, much to the advantage of the always *already* historically more powerful. So, for all the elaborate architecture of this Thomist rationality, patient readers will finally have to face the rule of force as the non-verbalized motor of history, global justice which ultimately will always coincide with the will of the God of the Old Testament. We are all equal, yet some are more equal than others "por la razón o por la fuerza," historically. These tremendous lines are quite explicit:

> [E]l principado introduce la servidumbre del hombre mediante la opresión del más fuerte... Y hay que concluir asimismo que los príncipes y reyes de España asistidos por la autoridad apostólica … legítimamente pudieron desplazar a los príncipes de las Indias y hacer propios sus principados (*legitime ammoveri, eorum principatus sibi ipsis appropriare*)...conforme al Derecho de Gentes, un pueblo libre no reconoce superior [y] puede declarar guerra a otro pueblo libre, aun si el tal pueblo es libre, siempre que lo haga para buen fin para regir y gobernar bien a aquel. (pp. 174-5, 177)

In Cold War language, there are no "doves," just "hawks" in this early modern political landscape, also for *Indis*. The codification of the "just war" means the perfect legitimacy of the open conflict in the Americas as enunciated from the socio-historical position of force of the repressive culture. Thirty years after the seize of Tenochtitlán by Hernán Cortés in 1521, *Indis* will not provide an ethnographic account of American specificities. *Indis*, quite unlike the *Regulations* and *Información en Derecho* does not exercise the legitimacy of experiental or first-hand claims to knowledge. Instead, doing the homework in Canon Law and the Fathers of the Church, and Aristotle is conspicuously absent here, the systematization of social agents on the American side will thus be articulated in quite insidiously simple and straightfoward terms: these new Indian populations and the Spanish will be together in the Natural Law, yet these will be quite distinct according to the other darker side of this typical Renaissance rhetoric, the jargon of authenticity of the Law of Nations. Within these unsolved conceptualizations for social (de)differentiation, *Indis*, formally as well as thematically, constitutes the rather disturbing scholarly account for the minority of literate men of Early Modern law, quite firm in the belief in the legitimate seizure of the Americas. *Indis*, precisely for not having bright imported clothes, may well constitute a valid paradigm for the critical analysis of an Early Modern textualization which is more than just thematically related to the Americas. *Indis*, the incomplete copy of doubtful paternities, with all its bureaucratic, rather unpleasant nature, constitutes the Thomist argumentation for the time-honored *locus* of the *justos títulos*. Humanist dialogues—we analyzed Ginés de Sepúlveda in chapter three—although also "hawkish" in imperial theme, constitute a rather exotic extravagance inside these repressive precincts. There can be few doubts as to the thesis that *Indis*, with or without paternity dilemmas, with or without crises or doubts, rigidly textualizes thematically, but also formally, Quiroga's belief in the legitimate Spanish seizure of the Americas. Following Ortega y Gasset, this belief was historical, collective and subconscious and thus vastly exceeded the repressive (mis)doings of this no doubt powerful individuality.

3. The Theater of Colonial Law: Quiroga's *Juicio de Residencia*

Our historical imagination must now cross the Atlantic waters from the metropolitan side to the peripheral side of early *novohispano* repressive coloniality of power. If *Indis* was most likely produced during Quiroga's sojourn in the Iberian peninsula (1547-54), the *Proceso de Residencia* (1536),[41] quite a different repressive textualization in its radically collective choral quality, came to be produced while Quiroga was absent from the American territory. Worlds apart from the rather abstract early modern political theorization of *Indis*, the eminent pragmatism of the *Residencia* will give us textual pretext to look closely into the legal construction of the official truth around the "empty subject" of our post-*oidor* stepping down from office.

The *Residencia*, historically the formal mechanism instituted by the Spanish empire to investigate how the previous administration had behaved, will not ruminate about expanding human nature. It could not care less about conducting these sorts of philosophical investigations. Instead, this theater of the repressive culture wishes collectively to get the bureaucratic job done, more or less effectively. The subsequent report of this *Residencia* (we are about to look closely into León's pages) was commonly used to determine if the individual under investigation should be promoted, retired or imprisoned. It is in the always fragile, inter-generational transitions inside the bureaucratic machine that the *Residencia* came to be produced, always on the brink of criminalization. The point was to try to give verifiable substance to the record of the individual who had just left office.[42] León's selective edition of this *Residencia* constructs a clean record for Quiroga, whose best defense is to not be present in the process.

This is *about* the official construction of the legal personality of the *oidor* Quiroga without Quiroga's active participation. Quiroga will thus remain the absent cause or referentiality to the entire *Residencia* process. The truth of this bureaucratic paperwork, inside the essential performativity of the repressive culture for a world of illiterates on both sides of the Atlantic, what we wish to call "theater," speaks unambiguously of the excellence of Quiroga's political legacy. In sharp contrast to the rather cumbersome scholarship of Indis, we will try to see into the various modulations of repressive writing in this colonial theater of social energies. In looking at the historical performativity of this repressive textualization in the colonial world, there is again no novelty claim. We wish to activate a critical evaluation of the social text of *Residencia*, already discovered by León's classic scholarship. We wish here to historicize the horizons underpinning the sheer materiality of León's record and hopefully fill in his blanks convincingly. The *Residencia* is without doubts one significant part of Quiroga's official record, the record he himself couldn't have written. Firmly moving away from issues of single paternity, this empty center, the "about" Quiroga, will thus take center stage repressively. Let us look closely into how this is accomplished, historically.

León's forty-four-page document, the so-called "section IX," already a selection of the total *Residencia* file kept in *Archivo de Indias* (Seville, Spain),[43] is titled "*Residencia* del Señor Quiroga." It is initially dated 1577, twenty-one years after Quiroga's death in 1556. There are no reasons for this confusing dance of internal dates. There are, however, historical reasons for this dance of almost blind dates. We need to look carefully into the always problematic conditions of production of this colonial textuality.

We must deal with the historical complexities of this repressive time machine carefully. We have first the date of Nov. 13, 1535 for the initial *cédula* announcement which will trigger the whole process within the official timeframe of sixty days (p. 41). Two more dates follow: four months later, Feb. 24, 1536, which is the proclamation of the original *cédula* in Mexico City, and May 19, 1536, which is the official conclusion of this investigation (technically, the *residencia, pesquisa, información secreta*, or *sentencia* (pp. 41, 83). The four-month-long *Residencia* is thus officially not complying on paper with the original *cédula*-allowed time frame of only sixty days. We do not know the reasons for this tardiness in fulfilling the official deadline. This item of repressive bureaucracy will sleep in the dust of the historical archive quite undisturbed for centuries. It will take centuries, 363 years to be precise, for a selection of this bureaucratic manuscript to emerge to the light of book publication. These pages of mine follow León's 1940 scholarship fifty-nine years later—the excuse again, the name of Vasco de Quiroga.

The lacunae of this distinctly early modern colonial textualization will not go easy on literalist or textualist approaches. These strategies for decontextualization are here not welcome. This textual ground for the repressive theater, *Residencia*, will provide numerous headaches to contemporary readers. But then again, popular readership is not a concept the main *escribano* of this *Residencia*, Antonio de Turcios, had in mind. Textualization for this largely para-print repressive culture, side by side the more elitist print culture, is instead largely an inevitable bureaucratic nuisance, which must always follow prescribed protocols.[44]

The *Residencia*, the textualized, evidential record of a profoundly aural dramatic process, will provide abundant moments of a calculated irregularity, even carelessness. This document is sadly incomplete, profoundly asymmetrical, uncomfortable and arcane, deliberately hasty, precariously fragile, monotonous and repetitious, largely uninviting to the surely limited sixteenth-century community of readers and interpreters and, with little doubt, to most contemporary readers. This textualization, historically designed *not* to be a culture of mass entertainment, visibly demands the almost old-fashioned interpretive skills of a miniaturist artisan. It is also safe to assert that it was surely not experienced this way, historically. The theme is again unpleasant: the public routine of surveillance and timely punishment for possible wrongdoing. There will be little or no comfort for the contemporary reader. Yet, I would like to suggest a bit stubbornly that some surprises will eventually emerge.

In working with León's "Quiroga highlights" of the complete *Residencia* file, still unpublished, in what is already a heavily abbreviated *escribano* account of the repressive *Residencia* theater, issues such as copy and original, private and public, and also individuality, if not singularization, appear quite banal and misleading, seriously anachronistic inside this sunlit theater for the interplay of collective energies. This colonial repressive environment, puzzling and disturbing to be sure, forces our historical imagination to open up to its changes and instabilities through the protocol structuring of linear time.

In this *escribano* script, the issue of the signature is worth noting. No individuality is here taken at his word. The banality of the isolated pronouncement of each individuality will, however, find the repressive mechanism of individuation in the rather long list of depositions which comprise the main textual body of the *Residencia*. In fact, individuality is here nothing but the singularization of traceable evidence or the eye-witness account with the formalized ratification of the signature. But, *Residencia* includes abundant irregularities. Wrapping up, however, this individual fragility, the official record will need a choral plurality of witnesses. The signatures of the original *cédula* are three: the royal stamp of the Monarch, the Monarch's mother's first-name, Juana, and the official secretary, Juan de Sámano. There is still a little chorus which attests further to the legal truthfulness of this repressive document. Readers will find at least five abbreviated names, most likely attesting to Sámano's reliable craftmanship ("la hice escribir por su mandado—Fr. Gz., cardinales seguntinus.—El doctor Beltrán.—El doctor Bernal.—Registrada, Bernal de Arias, por canciller, Blas de Saavedra," p. 43).

Playing catch on this side of the Atlantic, the new *oidor* and *licenciado* Loaysa will be appointed the ultimate responsible of all the necessary investigation procedures ("todas las incidencias, dependencias, anexidades [*sic*], conexidades [*sic*]," p. 42). Loaysa will have to be present during the

Residencia proceedings ("ante vos personalmente," p. 41). He alone will evaluate the political meaning of the possible wrongdoings ("pecados públicos," p. 41), as regards the official policy of the conversion of the indigenous populations to the Christian faith, the handling of finances and punishments ("conversión, hacienda, penas, cámaras, fisco," p. 42). The original *Residencia* process however extends to all four *oidores* of the *Segunda Audiencia* (1530-1535); that is, Salmerón, Maldonado, Zeynos and Quiroga, who are all automatically stepping down from office once the *cédula* is read aloud in the main square in Mexico City (Feb. 24, 1536). The *cédula* is the formal cause of the *Residencia*. In sharp contrast to arcane *Indis*, these *Residencia* protocols will take place in broad, holiday afternoon daylight in the main square of Mexico City. Challenging our historical imagination, Turcios's written record, rescued from the archival dust by León's colonial scholarship, will attest to this historical event.

Loaysa's sentence, as recorded by the *escribano* Turcios, will construct a clean record for the *oidor* office of Vasco de Quiroga. Again, here there is nothing but the public persona (the whole "right to privacy" mindset is here historically quite meaningless). This final pronouncement by Loaysa, the main judge of these *Residencia* proceedings, will however have to be accompanied by the necessary chorus: the *procurador* Alonso de Paredes bearing witness, "el cual dijo que lo *oía* [la sentencia pronunciada]" (my emphasis, p. 84). Loaysa's signature ("consta por lo haber *visto*," my emphasis), is also accompanied by the signature of the *escribano* Turcios, the official manufacturer of this *Residencia* record. The multirelational construction of this signature process of formal statements, bearing multiple witnesses upon bearing witness as it were, is indeed quite rigorous. Truth will emerge officially from the coincidences, even insistences or repetitions, in these depositions.

The summarized account of thirty-five depositions, and not thirty-nine as is promised by the preceeding list of witnessing names, will constitute the thematic center of this *Residencia* (one is a juridical subject as long as one cuts the historical figure for a credible witness and vice versa). The depositions of four important witnesses, among these the Franciscans Juan de Zumárraga, Francisco de Bolonia and Juan de San Miguel are, quite surprisingly, missing. With the *escribano* Turcios surely looking over their shoulders, these remaining thirty-five witnesses will have to sign Turcios's summarized account of their version of things. Some will not hesitate to confess that they cannot do it, because they cannot read or write (p. 59). Juridical truth, clearly the homogenization of dictions, will thus emerge in this colonial world from the mono-lingual interconnectedness of all these serialized depositions exclusively in the novel, yet imperial, romance language in the Americas (just imagine a bunch of newly-arrived "foreigners"ceremoniously conducting repressive business in this intricate jargon of authenticity in the center of your hometown!).[45]

The original *cédula* gives permission to Loaysa to arrange for an abbreviated account of the proceedings, should this be at all necessary (p. 41). The *escribano* Turcios will eagerly take full advantage of this prerogative: the evidential core of this *Residencia*, the complete list of thirty-five depositions, is quite strikingly not verbatim. Expediency wins the day of this *Residencia*, which will fail to fulfill official deadlines, at least in its written record! Besides not having a copy of the list of questions presented routinely to these witnesses, contemporary readers may speculate, perhaps convincingly that the non-verbatim account by Turcios represents a safe or non-problematic case for Quiroga's political profile in this radically non-textualist repressive culture ("reading" Turcios's *Residencia*, filtered by León's scholarship, does historical violence to the three-dimensional performativity of the *Residencia*). Contemporary readers have thus no valid excuse not to try to imagine the entire process building upon this fractured, incomplete textual materiality, which is all that we have so far available.

Always according to León's incomplete document, these thirty-five witnesses are asked an apparent maximum of thirty-seven questions. We only have partial access to the last four questions. Individualized accounts vary in quantity, detail and relevance to Quiroga's *oidor* profile. These accounts are *never* verbatim. With one only exception, they run from a couple of lines to a full two pages. As uneven and irregular as this repressive textuality is, readers will have to parse out the not so unfrequent agrammaticalities of Turcios's barbarous romance language in order to get at a rather general comment about Quiroga, typically appealing to some experiential knowledge of his office-holding and general reputation. With not one negative deposition, Quiroga had no reason to fear.

Historical access to this repressive forum is not predominantly afforded through secluded, silent, indoor, individualized readership.[46] This colonial theater lies no doubt in the historical antipodes of our contemporary world of privatized, psychologized, traumatized selves. So, these repressive *letras coloniales* will manufacture the timely performativity of a broad daylight main square city hearing. On the first day of the *cédula* proclamation (Feb. 24, 1536), the repressive machine is set in motion in the early hours of the evening with the *señor licenéciado* Loaysa, *juez de residencia* (or appointed

chief justice) bearing witness. He is not, he cannot be left alone. Juan de
Montilla, *pregonero público*, will be the appointed reader of the *cédula*
instructions calling witness to testify in favor or against the former judges
of the former High Court ("a altas e inteligibles voces dichas...y en presencia
de mucha gente que a ello se halló," p. 44). With the *escribano* Turcios
inevitably bearing witness, the site for the repressive culture will be thus
established in the public building of the judicial houses all holidays from 2
p.m. to 3 p.m. and for a maximum timeframe of sixty days (we have already
noticed how this inital timeframe will not be respected). More witnesses
will be summoned to this repressive protocol. Turcios mentions Alonso de
Contreras, the Mayor of Mexico City the *alguacil* Melchor de Trujillo, the
alguacil-escribano Martín Herrera, the merchant Andrés de España, and
Juan López.

Turcios's repressive language gives away historicity quite eloquently,
"la Audiencia Real se hace" (p. 44). That is, performativity is really what
"makes" this colonial world and this colonial world is made official only
repressively. In a trans-Atlantic world of majoritarian illiteracy, officialdom
needs performativity, its chiaroscuros of visibility and opacity, and vice
versa. The tyranny of the alphabetic letter, or textualization in the impetuous
romance language, albeit traceable material evidence attesting to the historical
vagaries of the ephemeral theater, remains nonetheless relatively
marginalized on the American side of the Atlantic. On the Iberian side
however, the final magistrates of interpretation will have to form their final
decisions inevitably based upon the information provided by their two
intermediaries Loaysa and Turcios. I am not aware that this ratification exists.
There is no indication that there was a follow-up on this *Residencia*
proceedings.

The non-negotiable *cédula* communication is aired in sunlit main squares
also in neighbouring populations. The town crier, Tomás de Rixoles, will
be the one to deliver the news. It is a multi-lingual proclamation, Rixoles is
called "lengua intérprete" (p. 44). Radiating almost web-like from the main
square in Mexico City, information ("mandamientos"), is sent to other
jurisdictions inside the historically expanding colonial geography of New
Spain but also outside to Guatemala, Jalisco and the minefields ("las minas").
The explicit goal is for this official message to reach the ethnic lords ("indios
principales"), even in the most distant areas, who might have had something
to say about the *oidor* role of Quiroga. Thanks to this natural and wireless
system of communication, witnesses will be able to attend the *Residencia*
proceedings. They will come from Mexico City but also from the

neighbouring city of Tlaxcala, the Michoacan region, the city of Tecuzco [*sic*] and the region ("provincia") of "Guaiocingo [*sic*]." Although Turcios's annotation of new Spain geography is at times profoundly hasty and erratic, we may confidently state that at least seven witnesses will come from the region of Michoacán. Among these, there will be several indigenous witnesses who will declare themselves to be residents in Quiroga's village-hospitals.

Still, preceding these thirty-five depositions, Turcios provides a rather succinct summary of only one charge against Quiroga. Its vagueness appears to suggest that it does not amount to too much: some contractual miscommunication regarding duties and payments for construction work done in the hospital between Quiroga and the rather faceless and nameless indigenous residents:

> [S]e quejaban los naturales de esta tierra y que a causa de no tener adobes los de México para llevar al dicho edificio deshacían sus casas para llevar a él, y ansí lo dijo don Pablo al dicho licenciado Quiroga e que desde esta ciudad al dicho lugar de Santa Fe que hay dos leguas muy grandes, llevaban los indios a cuestas los adobes, piedra y cal para el dicho edificio, y alguna madera e que si no fuera porque era el tetúan [*sic*] no le hicieran la obra por el precio que se la hicieran, y que se concertaron primero con él, y que le dijeron que no tenían materiales que los buscar. (p. 45)

We will have to get back to this charge in a few pages. Yet, we may well ask, who are these seemingly voluntary witnesses? Turcios's material, according to León's selection,[47] releases the strictly male choreography of thirty-five legal personalities. With Quiroga absent from his own *Residencia*, these thirty-five depositions about Quiroga will be constructing the political record of his *oidor* years (literally, "dar fé"). The features of these witnesses are put down hastily and quite irregularly: identification will include a Spanish name, oftentimes incomplete, profession, procedence, age and nothing else. The essentially early modern fragmentariness of the official record gives us the strictly male plateau of thiry-five speaking subjects: seven low state officiales (three *corregidores*, one *alguacil*, one *escribano*, two *bachilleres*), six settlers (literally, *vecinos*), ten men of the Church (mostly Franciscans), and four indigenous leaders, half of these with the explicit "indio natural" from the Michoacán region. Among these thirty-five witnesses, a considerable portion, concretely eight witnesses, will remain unspecified, with absolutely no information about who they are and what they may do for living. Sometimes, the name is simply the first name. As already stated, the initial list fails to deliver all complete depositions (did León neglect some of these witnesses, even the more famous ones?): four witnesses in the original list will be absent from the series of depositions. The ages will vary from twenty-five to fifty-five "or more," as the document will not uncommonly add. The juridical protocol of the signature will almost always bring formal closure to every individualized deposition.

The repressive dramatization of this colonial collectivity will have to place verbalization under the limelight. These speaking subjects will release a profoundly non-psychological and a rather matter-of-fact account of Quiroga's public office. This *Residencia*, with all imaginable paralogisms, operates quite irrespectively of the witnesses' individualized belief system. The world view of any speaking subject, Chief Justice Loaysa included, is quite immaterial and banal to the intolerant *Residencia* belief mechanism which will have no option but to manufacture in the eyes of superiors in office the official truth, repressively. It is the collective repressive making of an official belief on Quiroga that counts, and little or nothing else.

Individual intentionality, never entirely self-reliable and never self-sufficient, is a rather paltry, almost negligible *thing* in this collective enterprise. There are here no embellishments, no wisecracks, no inclination to irony, no humorous release of social tension. Turcios's account describes dryly the series of existential claims to official truth with no value judgments. Abstaining systematically from any pronouncement, depositions and credibilities will be weighed confrontationally, exclusively for Loaysa to interpret. In this bureaucratic arena which must manufacture social truth officially, these witnesses will not be quoting Aquinas, Vitoria or Aristotle. Unlike *Indis*, this is not a lofty discussion on the goods and ills of *justos títulos*. Instead, this *Residencia* mechanism of surveillance and control for state officials, will be mostly concerned with the rather unglorious task of making sure that the *oidores* of the Second High Court did a good job while in colonial office. The task is rather modest, and Turcios's document will release no dramatic outcome in the serialization of "been there, done that" claims and also not unusual hearsay accounts ("I have been told, I have heard, people say"). The *Residencia* witnesses will be using both types of claims. Contradictions will have to be ironed out or ignored altogether. In facing this collective jigsaw puzzle of sayings, Loaysa will not be able to afford the luxury *not* to make a final pronouncement. His final decision, as we will soon see, is not a lengthy extrication of judirical reasoning as pertains to scholarly sources. Quite the contrary. Quite close to Acuña's hypothesis on Ginés de Sepúlveda's pen in *Indis*, Loaysa's final sentence appears to have been issued "on the run" ("sobre la marcha," p. 30). Fragmentariness will not cease to bother contemporary readers who will have sometimes to infer in between these highly irregular *escribano* agrammatical lines. But again, agrammaticalities, rather than their pretentious city cousins, the *cultismos*, are everpresent actors in this repressive drama, not scripted but thus textualized by Turcios.

The *Residencia* is structured to prove or disprove the validity of these rather generic irregularities about Quiroga's public office. The performativity of the repressive circumstance will put these witnessing speaking subjects[48] thus: what you are as qualified witness, theoretically under no compulsion, is what you say you saw or heard, and therefore know, about Quiroga's *oidor* office and the larger enterprise of the village-hospitals. This collective making of a repressive personality will allow exclusively for these rather baleful agonies of expressivity. Little to nothing else is to be tolerated here. No witness will endorse the one initial charge against Quiroga. In the following pages, we wish to highlight some of these depositions.

Juan Seciliano, witness number three, who lives in Mexico City, forty years of age, states the most repeated account on Quiroga's political life. Recorded typically in indirect free style by the *escribano* Turcios, it reads,

> [E] que ha visto allí muchos indios e indias que les enseñan en la vida cristiana, e ha tenido e tiene allí un religioso fraile que los enseña y dice los divinos oficios e que es verdad que allí se curan los enfermos y entierran los muertos e tornan cristianos e acogen muchos peregrinos y hacen otras buenas obras, que este testigo tiene la dicha obra de Santa Fe por lo que ha visto, por muy buena obra e santa e que redunda en much utilidad e provecho de los naturales de aquella comarca. (p. 47)

The deictics unmistakably give away the two locations: the "here" of the repressive place of the colonial *Residencia* proceedings and the "there" of the Santa Fé hospital, where some "good" is done, presumably. This deposition is the semantic essence of Quiroga's early modern utopianism according to most scholarly accounts. The "there" is, according to Seciliano, the good place, which is *not* here, for the indigenous populations. And "good" means Christian life, the cure for the ailing, the burial for the dead, the shelter for pilgrims and free food for hungry visitors. The tone of these depositions is in general rather neutral and descriptive. The diction is rather simple, almost entirely devoid of any tension or emotion.

Martín de la Horra, witness number five, about whom we only know that he is forty years of age, deepens thus the existential claim to legal truth:

[E] que ve que los dichos hospitales e pueblos de Santa Fe están diestros en las cosas de la fe, tanto como los que más lo están y hay entre ellos personas que predican a los otros a las cosas de la fé, con tanto fervor, que parece que ya contraen alguna envidia entre las personas que entienden en la conversión de los naturales y aun querían deshacerlo por ver que la obra ha ido siempre mejorando e que allí se casan e acogen personas miserables como este testigo (es testigo) [*sic*] de ello…pueblo principal…que el dicho licenciado [Quiroga] ha tomado a su cargo, ha visto este testigo que ha gastado en ello casi todo su salario e la mayor parte que tenía de su majestad por *oidor*…que allí lo echaba todo, a más los favorecer con comida como en dalle vestuarios y hacerles iglesia casas y otras cosas que son necesarias, y compralles tierras de personas que las tenían en la comarca para que siembren, como en ornamentos y otras cosas de libros y en avesallos a cantar para que oficen una misa…a este testigo le parecía que el dicho licenciado tiene allí todo su afición y esperanza y lo estima en tanto como una cosa muy estimada. (pp. 49-50)

With not much legal room for speculative hesitations, Turcios's *escribano* pen impatiently summarizes the gist of the oral exposition. The "unembellished matter-of-fact bureaucratic account of political matters as pertains to Quiroga's *oidor* office will semanticize the village-hospitales as the eating places for the "miserable."[49] These are said to be not for profit. But, what is really happening in these hospitable places according to the *Residencia* record?

Witness number eight, the succinctly put "Bartolomé," presently a low-ranking official or *alguacil* from Mexico City, will state the following:

[E] ha dormido en él muchas veces e les ha visto a los indios rezar sus horas e maitines en tono de noche y de día en el dicho hospital de Santa Fe, e les ha visto comer como españoles con mucho concierto e allí les muestran a leer y a escrebir e contar e la doctrina cristiana, como de buenos cristianos que es tan santa obra como ha habido en estas partes e este testigo un día que allí estuvo vió bautizar por el prior de San Agustín más de cuatrocientas e quinientas [*sic*] ánimas con sus candelas encendidas en las manos e este testigo siendo corregidor seis leguas de allí, los dichos indios de Santa Fe fueron con este testigo a buscar los ídolos que en aquella comarca había e se los buscaron e trajeron a este testigo e los envió al licenciado Quiroga e los quemaron…hay mucho recogimiento e doctrina como dicho tiene e no se dice deshonestidad ninguna e se hace con tanta limpieza que es maravilla. (pp. 52-3)

Most witnesses will reinforce this official contentment in the civilizing mission: the candlelit ritualization of Christian belief, the restrained propriety of social arrangement, the structuration of collective readership, the satisfaction of the most basic needs for the continuation of life, that which is historically not a given, etc. It is with this sudden realization, certainly with some embarrassment, that "life" comes as the doubtless "ground" for our philosophical preoccupations.[50] Bartolomé's deposition officially makes a case for this most inevitable need, "eating," i.e. that which we cannot do without.[51] So is shelter, which is also not historically a given in early New Spain, as witness number twenty nine, Rafael de Cervantes, makes it clear: against the "here" of the repressive surveillance and coloniality, it is *there* where the poor find warmth ("e se acogen muchos pobres e allí se abrigan los que poco pueden," p. 76). This claim to repressive truth is made first-hand and can only be made first-hand ("I have seen it," "I have been there," and less convincingly "I have been told"). In the early years of permanent breach of social contract, Quiroga's village-hospitals appear to respond, at least according to these *Residencia* depositions, to the early erosion of American commonwealth by giving shelter and food to the disenfranchised. It is however not a free lunch: the novelty of Christian belief is, historically with no second thoughts, intolerant *in partibus infidelium*.

Quiroga's early modern *and* colonial utopianism, the good place and non-place of these village-hospitales, is here repressively semanticized as the civilized, clean and honest place. Again, monasticism is the strong ideal social model which almost all *Residencia* witnesses will invoke to defend Quiroga's case. Turcios's non-verbatim hastiness in this romance pen appears to strongly insinuate that there is no case. So, against the shameless idolatry of pre-Hispanic nudity (p. 76), these so-called village-hospitals will represent honest living in its tight monastic collectivism. Almost all witnesses will emphasize the strict ritualizations of prayer and religious ceremony (pp. 56, 57), the abundant church singing (p. 69, 70), the nun-like honesty in feminine clothing (pp. 55, 59), and the indigenous compliance to monogamic, heterosexual life-long arrangements (p. 55). The juridical construction of official hospital belief is radically in the official singular form of Christian belief. Idols are burnt and idolatries are extirpated (pp. 58), apparently with no coercion, at least according to witness thirteen, someone called quite simply, the illiterate Suero Esturiano of more than thirty years of age:

[Q]ue lo que este testigo [Suero Esturiano] ha visto le ha parecido en el dicho hospital mucha honestidad y mucho recogimiento e que este testigo se espanta de tanto como tienen no siéndoles por fuerza mandado...y ansí es de creer porque no parecen sino monjas en su honestidad...y sabe este testigo según ha visto que en el dicho hospital se acogen muchos naturales perdidos así huérfanos como de otras calidades e se acogen en él. (pp. 58-9)

Quiroga's village-hospitals are thus unanimously, according to these depositions, the *lugares de acogida* or charitable locations,[52] often state-sponsored and routinely supervised by appointed individuals within monastic "religions," as the sixteenth-century romance idiom had it, most commonly Augustinians and Franciscans.[53] In the beginnings of the individuation or the privatization of the totality of life, this rather faceless corporate contentment is also corroborated by some of the explicitly racialized witnesses. There are only two witnesses with the redundant race category of "indio natural." These are the witness number sixteen, Alonso de Avalos, and the witness number eighteen called Don Francisco, both from the region of Michoacán. Besides the high number of unspecified witnesses with incomplete names, we may extend the list of non-Spanish witnesses to five, if we include the witness number eleven already mentioned, the *naguatato tarasco* Francisco de Castillejo. We would have to add witness number seventeen, simply called Ramiro "principal de el pueblo de Mechuacan y del barrio de Páscuaro de más de cincuenta años (p. 62), and the witness number nineteen, a second unspecified Don Francisco, who is said to be related to some local chieftain in the Michoacán region (p. 65). We are forced to read in between Turcios's sketchy and fractured lines, yet it is quite plausible that these legal personalities with incomplete Spanish-sounding names who are said to come vaguely from the Michoacán region may well qualify for the indigenous input to these depositions. There is no explicit indication that these indigenous pronouncements carry more or less weigth or importance. There is also no explicit indication that they do not carry any weight or importance at all.

Quite possibly of Tarascan-Purépecha extraction, the initial "Don" signals, at least for two of these indigenized depositions, the social status of *cacique* positions in the early colonial structures for local government.[54] These "Indian" statements are equally praiseworthy of Quiroga's political role. Alonso de Avalos, "indio natural de la provincia de Mechuacan [*sic*]" (p. 60), will also formally rejoice at Quiroga's civilizing mission:

[P]orque ahora según que dicho tiene están quitados de mil bellaquerías e vicios enormes que tenían de manera que siguen todo lo que les predican ahora y más ahora que está el dicho hospital de Santa Fe hecho que es mucho buena [*sic*] porque allí se acogen los que tienen motolinean [*sic*] que quiere decir pobreza e allí los visten e les dan de comer e sierven a Dios e que saben que van a las dichas oraciones y horas del día much multitud de gentes e los siguen e que viendo este testigo que hay en la dicha provincia que no lo sabía esplicar [*sic*] segund está porque en servicio de Dios e obedecen ahoraú que nunca [*sic*] a su majestad. (pp. 61-2)

Turcios's paratactic Spanish language, worlds apart from entertaining belletrism, will remain quite unruffled and value-free about this generalized praise. There will be no asides. There will be no one expression of disbelief or surprise in the entire document, as though the performance of the repressive culture in early New Spain was the most natural thing to do. Or historically also, the most boring and bureaucratic thing to do. Inside these utopian communities, the encomium of monastic obedience is followed with docility. Outside, the obedience to the monarchy is reinforced accordingly, according to Avalos. Quiroga's colonial utopianism is thus historically not explicitly subversive of imperial structures. Modelled after Antonio de Guevara's official criticism of imperial structures, there is no historical reason to believe it was so implicitly.

Deposition number seventeen by the succintly called Ramiro, *principal* from the "village" of Michoacan and the "neighborhood" of "Páscuaro [*sic*]" gives us a good account of the historical collaboration between Quiroga, Tarasca-Purépecha and Chichimec communities:

[Y] sabe que el dicho licenciado Quiroga fué a la dicha provincia e los llamó a todos los principales de la dicha comarca e les habló e les dijo un parlamento mucho bueno [*sic*] diciendo que dejasen todas las idolatrías y siguiesen en las cosas de Dios Nuestro Señor e que se casasen con una mujer sola e no con muchas como ellos hacían de antes e que después de lo dicho tiene todos le obedecieron e pusieron por obras el sermón porque luego le dieron al dicho licenciado muchos diablos hechos de piedra e de palo e delante de muchos de los dichos principales delante de este testigo los quemaban y quebraban...e que plega a Dios Nuestro Señor que se lo agradezca e le dé su gloria pues tanto fruto ha traído en la dicha provincia y asimismo sabe que el dicho licenciado hizo cerca de la ciudad de Mechuacan un hospital bueno el cual lo labra pues que en él se recogen muchos indios naturales de la dicha provincia e de otras partes e que sabe que por saber nuevas del buen tratamiento e de las cosas que en él se predican e hacen e cómo acogen a los pobres en él y se han venido mucha gente de los chichimecas e de cada día se van poblando más viendo las cosas tan buenas como son. (pp. 62-3)

The timely gathering of this repressive *Residencia* mechanism, every holiday witnesses will be heard from 2 p.m. to 3 p.m. in the *Audiencia* buildings in Mexico City, will construct for the historical record this apparently peaceful *extirpación de idolatrías*. Similarly, witness number eighteen, the one called Don Francisco, explains how the hospitals were built in the empty landscapes of Michaocán in the preceding two years (p. 64). The theme of insular indigenous contentment emerges, no doubt always with the Christian language of historical authenticity still strongly influential for this early modern horizon. According to witness number twenty-nine, Rafael de Cervantes, the *provisor* or bishop-like religious administrator from Mexico City, this happiness is semanticized as "mass chanting, quietude, honesty and cleanliness" (p. 76). According to the Augustinian friar Juan de Sant Román, "These orphans come from the most faraway lands and languages" (p. 81). In this pre-typewriter era, Turcios's indirect, non-verbatim style, heavily cut by León's classic scholarship, will have little patience for these indigenous specificities. His pen will however attest to this theme of the ideal city thick in the middle of social struggle and repressive surveillance in this manner and its narrative will not go beyond this point.[55] This is the rather dry and standard account of Quiroga's legacy which is not short of veneration and some eccentric gestures.[56]

The serialized witness performativity of this experiential truth will necessarily manufacture the "commonplace" on the *oidor* Quiroga. Juridically, the coincidence of these assertions is called the official truth, which historically will only come out of Loaysa's mouthpiece. There is no such thing as a non-official record and this official domain must of necessity be falsifiable, concrete and existentially-based enunciations. Brushing away the frequent agrammaticalities, which must remain profoundly significant inside the monolingual record of this official Spanish *Residencia* language, the likely irregularities and contradictions will be treated exclusively at the level of diction. In this "epoch of misery" (p. 79), the *escribidor* Turcios is quite mechanically doing the recording, and Chief Justice Loaysa will do the sifting of this wealth of information. As though holding a kaleidoscope, Loaysa will have to get one, and only one, official "truth-figure" for his absent superiors to see on the other side of the Atlantic, verified exclusively in this written *Residencia* record. The comparison and contrast of these depositions will have, of necessity, to generate the singularity of the official truth. This time, it will be Quiroga's clean record. But Loaysa's deliberations, should these at all exist in print form, are not included in León's selective *Residencia*.

The last witness included in León's incomplete list, the number thirty-five, is the Augustinian friar Alonso Borja (perhaps related to the Spanish branch of the powerful Borgia family which managed to put at least two of his members in the political pinnacle of the Papacy, Calixtus III and Alexander VI?). Borja's will be the final words before Loaysa's final sentence. León's succinct one-page rendering of Alonso Borja's deposition speaks of the ideal of *apartamiento* and welfare service to the indigenous commonwealth. Poverty, and not coloniality, is Alonso Borja's main concern as the most imposing threat to this early colonial society:

> [D]ijo que lo que sabe de la dicha pregunta es que este testigo porque reside en el dicho hospital de Santa Fe cómo se acogen en él muchos pobres nescesitados indios que se entierran los muertos y vienen de diversas partes otra gente e se curan los que están enfermos y les dan todo lo que han menester ansí de comer como vestir e sabe que se casan los huérfanos allí e a bendición como lo manda la Santa Madre Iglesia y se bautizan los infieles y se dotrinan y enseñan los indios inorantes [*sic*] en las cosas de la fe y todo lo toman muy bien y con tan entera voluntad que apenas se podría hallar de los naturales tan buenos cristianos como en ellos parece y lo muestran y que esto sabe de este pregunta y no más. (pp. 82-3)

In this historical milieu where Christianity was officially undistinguishable from full-blown humanity, Christian ritualization flourishes in Quiroga's village-hospitals according to the resident Friar Borja. There is no explicit talk in the entire *Residencia* about labor conditions inside the village hospitals. We do not know whether the *Rules and Regulations* which we have developed in the second chapter of this work were here implemented. We cannot know either if these utopian residents were allowed to participate in the proto-capitalist contractualism we have developed in the third chapter in relation to Quiroga's lengthiest *Información en Derecho*. Instead, this Christian *locus amoenus*, or official forest of social happiness, inside this tight *Residencia* format, will quite simply not allow readers to see any concrete trees as pertain to specific labor relations. These thirty-five *Residencia* depositions routinely bypass this unentertaining theme of colonial labor altogether as though the Christian jargon of authenticity was always enough authenticity for the goodness of this hospital polity. If the condition of production of the *Residencia* has nothing to do with Juan de Grijalva's chronicle we included in chapter one, the message regarding Quiroga's village-hospitals is basically identical: these constitute idyllic social gardens of Indian Christianity.

This repressive mechanism, despite the apparent lack of explicit self-reflexivity, still develops the conceptual marriage of *beneficio* and *commonwealth* in the Aquinas's tradition. It is also Vitoria's. That is, the political ideal for the early modern coloniality is here also enunciated collectively as the self-sufficient restraint from traffic and intercourse, the *mojón*-signalled boundariness of seclusion (*apartamiento* and *recogimiento*), the rigid and timely measure of duty and need, the repudiation of *otium* and the encomium of manual labor,[57] the ritualistic structuration of collectivities around Christian belief and duty, the unyielding obedience to established authority, the ideal of shawl-covered, even nun-like honesty in demeanor, chastity and monogamic patterns of social reproduction and, finally, the welfare system for the satisfaction of need among those most needy. This monastic ideal was once again to be left untouched by this bureacratic *Residencia* making of the official truth.

The *Residencia* process, that which is not historically simply a text, closes down with Loaysa's pronouncement, which is also, quite shockingly, summarized by Turcios's hasty *escribano* pen. There is however a previous irregularity we should not neglect to mention. There is a quick mention of twenty-six charges ("en cuanto a veinte e seis cargos"), once again in reference to the hospital-village of Santa Fe. Yet, Turcios's consistently lazy *escribano* pen at the end of the *Residencia* proceedings this time surprisingly copies verbatim the only succinct and unspecified charge he himself wrote at the very beginning of this document. The pettiness of the charge is thus left to stand repeated again at the end of the document as brought to life by León,

> [E] que de esta ciudad [de México] al dicho lugar de Santa Fe que hay dos leguas muy grandes llevaban los indios a cuestan los adobes cal y piedra para el dicho edificio y alguna madera e que si no fuera porque él era el tatuán no lo hicieran la obra por el precio que se la hicieron e que se concertaron primero con él y que le dijeron que no tenían materiales que los buscase[n]. (p. 84)

This insinuation of overworked, unpaid Indian labor will be falsified by the official record of the *Residencia*. Following upon this unnecessary, exceptionally verbatim redundance, and with no signs of punctuation, Loaysa's conclusion abruptly continues:

> [E] que del dicho cargo e de que todo lo que tenía en él daba e di por libre e quité al licenciado Quiroga pues la obra es de Dios y para él se hizo y en

su servicio está empleada y ha sido y es muy provechosa y necesaria para los naturales desta tierra donde Dios Nuestro Señor es muy servido y loado y ansí se averigua por los descargos que el dicho licenciado Quiroga da e ansí mismo consta por lo haber visto. (p. 84)

So is the final juridical production of freedom succinctly pronounced: There is no sustainable charge with which to criminalize Quiroga's *oidor* office. Following the main textual body of thirty-five pieces of evidence, Loaysa's signature is correspondingly registered. Should we entirely "blame" Turcios's pen for laziness and discharge León's altogether? It wouldn't be entirely fair to say so until further verification of the documents by and on Quiroga held in the *Archivo de Indias*, already patiently catalogued by Escobar-Olmedo, takes place. With what we have so far available however, the pettiness of this *Residencia* charge is without doubts dismissed, since there is not one single deposition giving it here any credence. Missing the original *cédula* schedule by two months, these four-month *Residencia* proceedings are finally done with. Loaysa's and Turcios's final signatures at the end of the *Residencia* proceedings keep company to the (for us) distant, final date of this repressive theater of colonial law, May 19, 1536. There is a third party in the background, Alonso de Paredes, representative or *procurador* of all the *oidores* who is also bearing witness ("el cual dijo que lo oía," p. 84). His signature appears to be unnecessary. We are not aware of any repercussions to the tardiness of this *Residencia*. It is also quite impossible for us to infer anything about Loaysa's final sentence as regards the three remaining *oidor*es Ceynos, Salmerón and Maldonado,[58] also formally summoned by these public repressive proceedings.

4. Final Conclusions

This fourth chapter has allowed us yet two other dimensions to the early modern literature of Spanish rule in the Americas. Always in relation to our central historical figure, Vasco de Quiroga, we have looked at the repressive construction of colonial subjectivities as it pertains to two very different processes which reach us today via these two fractured textualizations. One has been the rather uncomfortable and shoe-flavored *De Debellandis Indis* (1552), of still doubtful paternities, despite Acuña's intense scholarship. The other, León's selective edition of Quiroga's *Juicio de Residencia* (1536). This chapter has been seeking to highlight the sharp contrast in the repressive making of social reality, or truth, by these two very different colonial textualities: whereas the former constitutes a convincing, yet fractured example of orthodox political theorizing originally produced in Spain, the latter is an outstanding, while also incomplete testimony of the eminent pragmatic performativity of the repressive culture in early New Spain. Against the historical background of the Valladolid debates, *Indis* thematizes the Thomist naturalization of the *justos títulos*; that is to say, the legitimacy of the Spanish colonization of the Americas via the alliance between the Spanish monarchy and the papacy. Sixteen years earlier, the *Residencia* proceedings for surveillance and control of state officials in the Americas, exemplify the ritualized collective makings of juridical and bureaucratic truth "about" the *oidor* role of Quiroga. So, chapter four displays these two rather different examples of early modern "deaths of the [singular] author."

We propose the sign "text" as the perhaps convincing shorthand form for social "process." In relation to these two "texts" then, we have defended these two main theses: One, a rigorous acquaintance with *Indis* must of historical necessity refute the rather naturalized tendency to look for, and even want, authorial singularity, be this Quiroga or anybody else. And two, a detailed reading of the *Residencia* performativity must also of necessity negotiate profound textual deficiencies without which this early modern repressive process cannot be properly understood historically. In these interpretive endeavors, we felt we had to have a dialogue with the international culture of scholarship about Quiroga. René Acuña is inevitable for anybody who wants to struggle at his or her own risk and patience with *Indis*, and Nicolás León is also inevitable for anybody who wants to come to terms with the *Residencia*. Neither has the definite word. Nor are mine final either. Yet we think that this chapter four offers further insights not only in relation to Quiroga, but also in relation to the *novohispano* theater of the repressive culture at two different levels. We have been looking at the rather abstract political theorization and also at the rather boring and bureaucratic job to get things done more or less efficiently. Plans for further archival research in Spain and Mexico will have to contextualize and substantiate this rendering.

Finally, we would like to emphasize that we still need Ortega y Gasset's vision of the essential historicity of human nature. One is almost tempted to naturalize the historicity of human nature. Yet, looking at social energies from the impossible standpoint of *genus homo*, we would like to argue that we still need Ortega's formulations for the radical intersubjectivity of "all that is" ("todo lo que hay"), and all that matters. As in Abbas Kiarostami's *Taste of Cherry* (1997), we are all in it together, even if it is only to drive around the deserted city and arrange your own suicide: life is thus inter-generational inter-subjectivity. The naturalness and plasticity of anything human does require that the social and historical circumstances not fall into the trap of idealism, or the trap of mental laziness. We may be at times guilty of this charge, too. Putting the social clothes to this natural nudity, we hope to have done at least some harm to the standard American idiom with the paltry history of heroes, of winners and losers, baseball and nostalgia, west and the rest, etc. We hope to have produced unsettling questions about historicity, or heterogeneity, since it is the threatened generational continuum of humanity that is at stake. We do not wish to give up this grand narrative, or bewildering horizon, of the permanent crises and transformations arranged by collective belief systems or subconscious rationalities. It is our final claim that practitioners of colonial Latin American studies, and others, need this stretch to the historical imagination and also highlight misery of intelligence as regards the surely presumptuous efforts to comprehend "life," the unavoidable ground, yours and mine, inevitably changing according to places and circumstances, realities and possibilities, fears and dreams. That's why we've been suggesting for this "life" the good places, the bad places and the non-places. We have done so in relation to the historical figure of Vasco de Quiroga.

But we must always historicize most concretely. This work has wanted to come to terms, without timidities or false pieties, with the repressive circumstances of life, the unavoidable juridico-political ground historically situated in the periphery of the early modern world system. We have wanted to look at the good places and non-places for the commonplace of early colonial law which a keen eye on the reformation of coloniality. To this objective, we chose the second fiddle of Quiroga. We already said that the notion of utopianism was mostly intended to be the whipped cream covering the knotty literature of the repressive culture, truly a bitter green spinach we cannot do without socially or historically in the rather strict chronological frame of this work.

The bureaucratic moment of official truth was the *lugar*, the *locus* we wanted to explore more than thematically. The repressive culture has so appeared to us to be the historical collective confrontational forum of relative but changing global power and privilege. Quiroga's history is no doubt "history from above," yet one always needs to explain how this historical matrix may come about, and how some of the internal differences and specificities get played out, and why this is so and not otherwise. We get the feeling that it has not been possible sometimes to assert things unambiguously, and have not hesitated quite a few times to elaborate on these moments pregnant with doubts and silences. The early modern record, we would say, is particularly, almost historically "naturally" conducive to this. In this confrontational forum of the repressive culture, the expressivity of all speaking subjects is, to put it mildly, much regulated and rather slim. This is the place where inclusions and exclusions of people by people from goods, needs and duties get structured formally, always on the brink of criminalization. Protocols and technical languages are inevitably needed, historically. The repressive arena is the social space where the flare of jargon will take occasional flights of fancy with surprising combinations of visibility and opacity. Far from entertaining, naturalness in demeanor or diction is here historically not a virtue, but ignorance, and optimism in the thick of lawsuit uncertainty or legal debate is mostly the optimism of the uninformed. The changes and the transformations, the reformations and the failures to reform, do not historically form part of the bookish culture of entertainment in early New Spain. Alas! The repressive place is not the most idoneous habitat for social romance, nurturing didacticism or nurse-like healings. Here there is precious little warmth or shelter. The early modern law, or today's law for that matter, is never light literature, no *locus amoenus*. The repressive culture is the *there* where there is little delight, abundant teeth-gritting uncertainty and breath-taking anxiety (Ortega's "encogimiento de la holgura"). We have been arguing that the repressive culture constitutes the social circumstance for the formalization of larger social landscapes of insolidarity and misery. Yet, we have been also arguing that the repressive colonial culture may have also functioned, for someone like Vasco de Quiroga, as the historically available conditions of possibility for the sustainability of collectivities and the implementation of an incipient egalitarianism.

In our efforts to build scholarship on the demonized hole of Hispanic utopias, we felt we've been walking away from the whipped cream of utopianism and closer and closer towards the green spinach of the repressive culture. We feel we have been looking for the salt sometimes in vain. The repressive circumstances have appeared to us—it could not have been otherwise—as the inter-related, inter-subjective or inter-dependent kaleidoscopic human world of protocols for surveillance and control of social energies. In this rather ghastly place, speaking subjects constitute themselves as such as long as they keep on speaking within the more or less explicit stipulated boundaries of the repressive game. Legal truth is, with little doubt, produced antagonistically, fought against and written downoften confusingly amid much paperwork largely destined for the dust of the archival record, and for the perusal of following generations of academic historians.

But, again *not* to philosophize, early modern utopianism cannot be reduced to a nimble metropolitan Latin textualization with the warm theme of the city of equals. Utopia, an early modern neologism, together with "relox" (or clock), is historically not just the metropolitan Latin pen against the wallpaper background decoration of the Americas. Historically, the ideal city is rather the clockwork regulation of collective duties and responsibilities: utopia and "relox" are thus tied together in the same tight early modern knot (we also mentioned Ortega y Gasset's vignette of Charles V's retirement in Yuste surrounded by clocks and mechanical toys). From this marginalized location of the Americas, and again the plural form is as inevitable as it is desirable, and not exclusively for scholarly exercises in colonial Latin America, the American human experience also produced, as it could not have been otherwise, utopias. Yet, these utopias are not calm beds of roses or hammocks and free time in the backyard of the West. Within our chronology of the early modern period, the manufacturing of utopias is historically done, as we have suggested in the preceeding chapters, inside the precincts of the almost always unpleasant repressive culture. Imagining human plasticity within these repressive circumstances, we have turned to the historical figure of Vasco de Quiroga. We have here studied four textualizations "by" and also "about" him: *The Rules and Regulations for the Good Government of the Village-Hospitals* (1532), the *Información en Derecho* (1535), the *De Debellandis Indis* (1552), and the *Proceso de Residencia* (1536).

In the critical analysis of this early modern repressive literature in the colonial world, we have developed four main themes: one, the ideal city or the city of equals, two, the proto-capitalist contractualism and free wage labor, three, the *justos títulos*, and four, the making of the public record, a clean one, for the *oidor* Quiroga. The language of these four textualizations has been the romance, yet imperial, language, Spanish, in all these textualizations, except in the all too doubtful *Indis*. Yet, this early modern Spanish is no piece of cake: this written Spanish is for the most part *escribano* Spanish, that is, abundantly agrammatical, yet fresh, almost consistently careless and quite intimate with a profound orality. It is also early modern legal Spanish deeply entrenched in the early modern protocols of still prestigious medieval Canon Law language and with no easy concessions to a more general readership. Quite in the antipodes of the bourgeois novel, the sheer quantity of textual production is here rarely an issue. This historical heterogeneity, at the crudest level of a quantitative approach to textual materiality, will have to say that *Información en Derecho* is, in Serrano-Gassent's edition, Quiroga's lengthiest and most ambitious piece of writing, i.e. this textual culture of repressive scholarship is simply 197 pages long. The *Rules*, also according to Serrano Gassent, amount to a breathtakingly succinct body of twenty-three pages. *Indis*, in Acuña's bilingual edition, is no more than thirty-six pages. The *Residencia*, in León's selective edition of "Quiroga highlights," is a mere body of forty-four pages. We need to be very careful, however, to dismiss this paucity of textual record for two main reasons: first, these are references which make sense mostly in a print or book culture, and the early modern repressive culture is eminently para-print culture. And second, Escobar-Olmedo has catalogued quite literally thousands and thousands of manuscript pages having to do directly with Quiroga's courtroom litigation. We have mentioned how León's synthetic edition of the *Residencia* on the *Segunda Audiencia* is useful, yet incomplete and a misleading piece of evidence since these forty-four "pages" are presented severely denaturalized from the proceedings involving all four *oidor*es (Escobar-Olmedo's catalogue speaks of 638 "hojas en tres piezas," which is considerably thicker than the bulk of this work). Once with this complete document, we will hope to be in much better shape. Until that moment however, it appears safe to say that Quiroga did not ever wish to become an author or a writer, let alone an intellectual, as we today tend to understand this notion, when we do not dismiss it or banalize it altogether, not without embarrassment in public settings outside and also inside the academy. *Indis*, we have so illustrated, is early modern legal academic practice, whereas the collective performativity of the *Residencia* is clearly not.

In these repressive circumstances for political change, we have also explained the social function of these "texts." A comparative summary might do some good. The *Rules* is technically a "protestation" inside an unspecified courtroom drama. *Información en Derecho* is a legal brief addressed to an unspecified superior for the reformation of colonial labor in the Americas within the two symbolic moments of the Laws of Burgos (1512-3) and the New Laws (1542-3), and, should we wish to provide a big narrative, also inside the global transitions from the first (Genoese) to the second (Dutch) phase of capital accumulation (Arrighi). *Indis*, on the other hand, is a fragmented Thomist tripartite rationalization for the *justos títulos* against the background of the Valladolid Debates. And the *Residencia* is the rather careless *escribano* record of the collective theater of surveillance and control of state officials in New Spain after they step down from office. Inside this already inevitable transatlantic world, the original location of production of these "texts" is New Spain for the *Rules, Información en Derecho* and the *Residencia* proceedings, and Spain for *Información en Derecho*. Mapping the historical cartography of this toponymy and legal textualities in the vicinity of Vasco de Quiroga, the early colonial world is inseparable from this early modern world. Consequently, the early modern world will remain unintelligible without the still largely neglected colonial dimension of pre-USA continental America. In historicizing reform projects (utopia), our emphasis has always been to suggest that the association between modernity and coloniality is not derivation, causality, not even the inversion of Eurocentric causality. Rather, our desire has been to try to describe as critically and accurately as possible, the already historically inevitable hierarchical inter-dependence and uneven co-existence of trans-Atlantic repressive locations in a still unfinished modernity.

To illustrate this, Quiroga has been my excuse. Quiroga has been the red thread for the readers to follow to put at least some of these preoccupations together. The issue of paternity, historical dawn of intentionality, has inevitably come up explicitly at least once. Yet, we have seen the "by" Quiroga and the "about" Quiroga. The *Rules* and the *Residencia* give testimony to a rather hasty *escribano* pen. The *escribano* to the former record will remain unnamed. The latter is Antonio de Turcios. The convoluted *ensalada* of *Información en Derecho*, Quiroga's appropriate self-definition for his most ambituous scholarship, is doubtless by Quiroga, whereas *Indis* may be tentatively attributed to Quiroga. In the fragmented *Indis* manuscript closely studied by Acuña, there are however at least three different handwritings, Bartolomé de Las Casas, Juan de Sepúlveda and an unidentified third party. So, multiple paternity of this profoundly uncomfortable repressive textualization has been my preference. Zavala and Acuña are still, in this scholarly paternity lawsuit, the two main contenders. In this largely para-print social neighborhood of the repressive culture, orality is indeed a significant factor in both the *Rules* and the *Residencia*. Yet, orality is considerably attenuated for the candle-lit, late-night scholarship of *Información en Derecho* and *Indis*.

The critical analysis of Quiroga's political change in the early modern periphery of a colonial world effectively took the best of these endeavors to the rather unpretentious *letrado* practice inside the repressive culture. This was quite an unplanned mental trip which, we must confess, we had not imagined quite like this at the beginning of the work process. The *letrado* culture turned out to be closer historically to dry, bureaucratic paperwork than belletrism and fun. After this travail however, we firmly believe that the detailed emphasis upon the historicity of at least some of these so-called textual insufficiencies and irregularities, may help energize our historical imagination so that it opens up to a distinct foreign historical horizon, which includes all of us, if only negatively. Against the all too frequent silences in relation to early modern American utopias, our efforts wanted here, in relation to the name of Vasco de Quiroga, to rekindle the still warm ashes of egalitarianism or utopianism. We have found convincing proto-egalitarian dispositions, but also limitations, contained in Quiroga's colonial literature. Our historiographic endeavors for the making of heterogeneous landscapes of social egalitarianism have always been against what is, and what is not, or not yet, and what might be in the near future. Quiroga's serious efforts for serious change in a colonial world, we hope it is clear by now, could not have been light literature. Belletrism and fun, when they exist, are clearly a rather small part of the colonial literature in the new world which includes all of us.

Nunc iners cadet manus.
Durham, North Carolina, March 1999
and San Carlos, California, June 2000.

Notes

Chapter I

1. Against antiquarianism and nostalgia, J.A. Maravall's inspirational program is found in *Los Factores de la Idea de Progreso en el Renacimiento Español* (Madrid: Real Academia de la Historia, 1963).

2. For the historicization of the social mechanisms of normativity and repression, or the law, not unacquainted with authoritarianism and violence, see the panoramic *Iniciación Histórica al Derecho Español* by Jesús Lalinde-Abadía (Barcelona: Ariel, 1970).

3. This inspiring definition of happiness as collective labor and solidarity is originally taken from the Peruvian sociologist Aníbal Quijano, in *Modernidad, Identidad y Utopía en América Latina* (Lima: Sociedad y Política, 1988).

4. For some of these reproductions of statues, public places and news of official commemorations, see Rubén Landa's *Don Vasco de Quiroga* (Barcelona: Biografías Gandesa, 1965).

5. *Crónica de Michoacán* por Fr. Pablo Beaumont (México: Talleres Gráficos de la Nación, 1932).

6. *Juan O'Gorman: Arquitecto y Pintor* by Ida Rodríguez Prampolini (México: Universidad Nacional Autónoma de México, 1982).

7. *Los Murales del Palacio Nacional. Diego Rivera* by Raquel Tibol, Víctor Jimnez, Itzel Rodríguez Mortellaro, Juan Coronel Rivera and Carlos Fuentes (Milán, Italia: Grupo Bufete Industrial, SANLUIS Corporación, 1997).

8. For further images of Quiroga, see the lavishly illustrated *La Utopía Mexicana del Siglo XVI: Lo bello, lo verdadero y lo bueno* (Italy: Grupo Azabache, 1992).

9. For this rather crippled automatism of the historical imagination, see the classic edition, including an introduction by Eugenio Imaz, *Utopías del Renacimiento: Moro/Campanella/Bacon* (Mexico: Fondo de Cultura Económica, [1941] 1993). There is a rather curious example of a panegyric scholarship about utopia on occassion of this publication, see "Letras de Utopía: Carta a Don Alfonso Reyes" by Zavala and also "Utopías del Renacimiento y Renacimiento de la Utopía by Pedro Gringoire" in *CA* (2/Marzo-Abril 1942, Año I, Vol. II): pp. 146-158.

10. The rather excellent research tool, *The Oxford Encyclopedia of the Reformation* (Oxford: Oxford University Press, 1996), includes information about Vasco de Quiroga's nephew, Gaspar de Quiroga, Cardinal Inquisitor-General of Spain. For the family tree of the Quiroga family, see Fintan B. Warren's *Vasco de Quiroga and his Pueblo-Hospitals of Santa Fé* (Washington: Academy of American Franciscan History, 1963): pp. 8-12.

11. Coloniality, originally Aníbal Quijano's term ("colonialidad [del poder]"), or historical situation or structural system of domination, which surely exceeds the narrow frame of the pre-independence or "colonial" world. See "Colonialidad del Poder y Experiencia Cultural en América Latina," *Pueblo, Epoca, Desarrollo: La Sociología de América Latina* (Caracas: Nueva Sociedad, 1998), and "Colonialidad del Poder y Democracia en América Latina," in *Le Future Anterieur: Democratie et Exclusion en Amerique Latine* (Paris: L'Harmattan, 1994).

12. We are making an argument which takes into account the notion of referentiality, or the "here" and the "theres" of inclusions and exclusions which are also instrumental to utopianism. Spanish adds an intermediary third element to these deictics ("aquí, ahí, allí"). Antonio Machado's terrible line is not entirely misplaced here, *"Castilla* miserable desprecia cuanto ignora." For a classic inspirational dealings with these "points of reference" or "grounds," see Ortega y Gasset's attack on Toynbee's profession of a certain internationalism, in *An Interpretation of Universal History* (New York: Norton & Company, 1973): pp. 15-25.

13. We have in mind Giovanni Arrighi's periodization of capital accumulation included in *The Long Twentieth Century* (New York: Verso, 1994). Arrighi's four stages, from early modernity to our contemporaneity, include the first Genoese or Spanish moment, the second Dutch moment, the third British moment and the so far fourth and final American moment of capital accumulation thus in linear mutation approximately every 150 years. Chapter three will provide a brief development of Arrighi's panoramic vision of the modern world system which will help us frame Quiroga's lengthiest treatise *Información en Derecho.*

14. For the articulation of some skepticism as to the impact and commotion of modernity in Latin America, see three references among many: Aníbal Quijano's *Modernidad, Identidad y Utopía en América Latina,* ibidem, and Enrique Dussel's *The Underside of Modernity: Apel, Ricoeur, Rorty, Taylor, and the Philosophy of Liberation* (New Jersey: Humanities Press, 1996), and Walter D. Mignolo's *The Darker Side of the Renaissance: Literary, Territoriality and Colonization* (Ann Arbor: The University of Michigan Press, 1995).

15. Looking for some fresh air, we may be reminded of Ortega y Gasset's disconcerting definitions of modernity: the beginnings of illegitimacy and deconsecration, but also the distemper at the tremendous enrichment and openness from "I" to "you." This inter-subjective openness is also an injury, through which we have come to understand the unpredictable variations of

human plasticity. My edition has been the English version, *An Interpretation of Universal History*, ibidem, pp. 160-169.

16. For the rigorous historicization of the notion of humanism and the *Studia Humanitatis* (or the humanities), the early modern revivalism of Latin as the vehicle for the radical transformation of society (Nebrija), and the slight regard for barbarous *letrados*, see "Un prólogo al Renacimiento Español: La dedicatoria de Nebrija a las Introduciones Latinas (1488)," by Francisco Rico, in *Seis Lecciones Sobre la España de los Siglos de Oro: Homenaje a Marcel Bataillon* (Sevilla: Universidades de Sevilla/Burdeos, 1981): pp. 61-85.

17. We are reminded of the dictum "I am myself and my circumstance and if I do not save it ("salvar"), I do not save myself." We take "salvar" to mean to contextualize, to historicize. My edition has been a classic one: Ortega y Gasset's *Meditaciones del Quijote* (Madrid: Publicaciones de la Residencia de Estudiantes, 1914).

18. The connections between the two men are beyond doubt. Quiroga constitutes the early evidence of Morean influence in the trans-Atlantic Hispanic world. Yet there is still plenty of work to do about these negotiations and exchanges. See, "El 'Tomás Moro,' de Fernando de Herrera," by Royston O. Jones in *Boletín de la Real Academia Española* (Madrid, 1950, Tomo XXX, Cuaderno CXXXI, Sept.-Dec. 1950): pp. 423-438; and also Jones in "Some Notes on More's 'Utopia' in Spain," *MLR* (Vol. XLV, Oct. 1950, Num. 4): pp. 478-482. See also Francisco López-Estrada's "Un centenario humanístico: Tomás Moro (1478-1978)," in *Seis Lecciones Sobre la España de los Siglos de Oro*, ibidem, pp. 11-38.

19. Many names could be mentioned in relation to the rebelliousness of these [American] provinces. We will see some of these names emerge in crucial moments in the argumentation of early modern and colonial utopia in the following chapters (Enrique Dussel, Walter D. Mignolo, Edmundo O'Gorman, José Ortega y Gasset, Aníbal Quijano, etc.). One possible origin is with no doubt Leopoldo Zea. We have in mind, *Discourse desde la Marginación y la Barbarie* (Barcelona: Anthropos, 1988), *Latinoamérica en la encrucijada de la historia* (México: Universidad Autónoma de México, 1981), *Convergencia y especificidad de los valores culturales en América Latina y el Caribe* (México: Universidad Autónoma de México, 1987), *Descubrimiento e Identidad Latinoamericana* (México: Universidad Autónoma de México, 1990). For a recent re-evaluation of some of these debates, see Santiago Castro-Gómez's *Crítica de la Razón Latinoamericana* (Barcelona: Puvill Libros, 1996).

20. Two rather dramatic examples of this no-place of pre-USA and post-USA Americas for the political imagination are Samuel P. Huntington's *The Clash of Civilizations and the Remaking of the World Order* (New York: Simon & Schuster, 1996), and Francis Fukujama's *The End of History and the Last Man* (New York: Free Press, 1992).

21. *The Dictionary of Imaginary Places* by Alberto Manguel and Gianni Guadalupi (New York: MacMillan Publishing Co., 1980).

22. *The Recent Encyclopedia of Utopian Literature* by M. E. Snodgrass (Santa Barbara: ABC-Clio, 1995).

23. *Utopian Thought in the Western World* by Frank E. Manuel and Fritzie P. Manuel (Cambridge: The Belknap Press of Harvard University Press, 1979). Frank E. Manuel also edited the volume of essays entitled *Utopias and Utopian Thought* (Boston and Cambridge: Houghton Mifflin Company and The Riverside Press, 1966).

24. *The Principle of Hope* by Ernst Bloch (Cambridge: The MIT Press/3 Volumes, [written in the USA 1938-1947, revised 1953-1959, originally published as *Das Prinzip Hoffnung* in 1959], 1986).

25. *Utopics: Spatial Play* by Louis Marin (Atlantic Highlands, NJ: Humanities Press, 1984).

26. *Realistic Utopias: The Ideal Imaginary Societies of the Renaissance, 1516-1630* by Eliav-Feldon (Oxford: Clarendon Press, 1982). We found one extra essay, "Secret societies, utopias, and peace plans: the case of Francesco Pucci" (*Journal of Medieval and Renaissance Studies*, 14: 2, Fall 1984, pp. 139-58).

27. There are two utopian bibliographies put together by Glenn Negley: *the Duke University Library Utopia Collection* (Issued by Friends of Duke University Library, Durham, N.C. 1965), and the book version *Utopian Literature: A Bibliography with a Supplementary Listing of Works Influential in Utopian Thought* by Glenn Negley (Lawrence: The Regents Press of Kansas, 1977).

28. In this conference, our participation made it into the print culture. See our "Jesuit Proposals for a Regulated Society in a Colonial World: The Cases of Montoya and Vieira," in the important anthology *Un Reino en la Frontera*, edited by Sandra Negro and Manuel Marzal (Quito/Lima: Abya-Yala & Universidad Católica, 1999).

29. For this typical non-inspirational non-presence of the Americas, see the latest slim *Utopistics, or Historical Choices of the Twenty-First Century* by Immanuel Wallerstein (New York: The New Press, 1998). Chapter three will make abundant references to Wallerstein's major historical research and center-periphery conceptualization of the capitalist world-system.

30. We must state however that we tried to address this systematic blindspot in *The Society for Utopian Studies-1997 Annual Conference*. Krippner-Martínez, whom we will meet later, joined our efforts, under the panel heading of "Iberian Utopias in the Sixteenth Century World." His presentation was entitled, "Paternalism and the Colonial Utopia of Vasco de Quiroga (manuscript)."

31. Raymond Trousson's work is emblematic of this persistent forgetfulness where early modern Americas has no place in the imagination of ideal places, *Historia de la Literatura Utópica: Viajes a Países Inexistentes* (Barcelona: Ediciones Península, [Original French Edition, *Voyages aux pays de nulle part. Historie littéraire de le pensée utopique,* 1979] 1995).

32. *Utopian Thought in the Western World*, ibidem, pp. 14-5.
33. The More section includes the following lines: "A few decades later a Mexican judge, Vasco de Quiroga, introduced a Utopian constitution into a network of Indian hospital-villages in Santa Fe, with common ownership of property, alternation of rural and urban emplyoment, the six-hour workday, and distribution of goods according to need," *Utopian Thought in the Western World*, ibidem, p. 148.
34. Robert Ricard's *La Conquista Espiritual de México* (México: Editorial Jus/ Polis, 1947): pp. 302-3.
35. This utopian team is formed by: More, Eberlin von Gunzburg, Rabelais, Patrizi da Cherso, Anton Francesco Doni, Gasparus Stiblinus, Campanella, the unidentified I.D.M. Gentilhomme Tourangeau, Johann Valentin Andreae, Robert Burton, Francis Bacon and Ludovico Zuccolo (pp. 15-30).
36. Following the rules of the game of politeness and propriety, Stelio Cro is to be credited with the findings of the anonymous *Sinapia* (XVIII century). See, *The American Foundations of the Hispanic Utopia (1492-1793)*. (Tallahassee, Florida: The DeSoto Press, 1994). Volume one deals with Sinapia and the Discourse on Education and volume two deals with the Jesuit republic in the Guarani territories. In this late chronology, there is also the notorious "monstrous" scholarship by Antonio de León Pinelo, *El Paraíso en el Nuevo Mundo*, edited by R. Porras Barrenechea (Lima: Auspiciado por el Comité del IV Centenario del Descubrimiento del Amazonas, 2 Vols., 1943).
37. We must acknowledge Walter D. Mignolo's dealings with this historical unfittingness (or "saberes fuera de lugar"). See the important elaboration "El Metatexto Historiográfico y la Historiografía Indiana" in *MLN* (96/No. 2, March 1981): pp. 358-402; "¿Que clase de Textos son Géneros? Fundamentos de Tipología Textual?," *Acta Poética* (4-5/1982-3): pp. 25-51; and also "Los Cánones y (Más Allá de) Las Fronteras Culturales (¿De Quin es el Canon del Que Hablamos?), *Lecturas. Separata*. The original English version is, "Canons a(nd) cross-cultural boundaries (or, whose canon are we talking about?)" in *Poetics Today* (12:1, 1991): pp. 1-28.
38. We find Aníbal Quijano's work persuasive as regards the production of knowledge. He will use the phrase "the crisis of the Euro-American identity," which is of course a certain America and a certain Europe not to be mourned universally. Latin America is thus the heterogeneity to this crisis and historical condition of possibility for the invigoration of experience, in *Modernidad, Identidad y Utopía en América Latina*, ibidem, and "Colonialidad del Poder y Experiencia Cultural en América Latina," published in *Pueblo, Epoca, Desarrollo: La Sociología en América Latina* (Caracas: Nueva Sociedad, 1998).
39. *Before European Hegemony: The World System A.D. 1250-1350* (New York and Oxford: Oxford University Press, 1989).
40. See the excellent treatment by Elizabeth McCutcheon, *My Dear Peter: the Ars Poetica and Hermeneutics for More's Utopia* (Angers: Moreana, 1983).

41. See Helen F. Grant's "The World Upside Down," in *Studies in Spanish Literature of the Golden Age, Presented to Edward M. Wilson*, Edited by R. O. Jones (Madrid: Tamesis Books Limited London, 1973).

42. Coloniality is a historico-social phenomenon. That is, structures of domination are subjected to crises and transformations. That's how I understand historicity, "always on wheels." In relation to early modern languages, Latin is the unquestionable international language of high culture and prestigious knowledge production, Spanish follows next superimposed over Amerindian languages. Coloniality is historically not necessarily monolingualism. Neither is Nebrija in a Castilian-only position, neither is Philip II staunchily advancing monolingual policies. Coloniality could historically be articulated in one or many languages or fluctuating between these two poles. Distressingly perhaps, neither Machiavelli nor Quiroga had anything to say about languages in conflict. For the early modern political thinking, language management was a rather marginal, even a non-issue. See Rico, ibidem; but also the exceedingly interesting *Aislados en Su Lengua (1521-1995)* by Antonio Blanco-Sanchez (Madrid: Anejos del Boletín de la Real Academia Española, Anejo LIV, 1997), and Silvio Zavala's *Poder y Lenguaje desde el Siglo XVI* (México: El Colegio de México, 1996).

43. *Historia Crítica del Pensamiento Español. Tomo 1: Metodología e Introducción Histórica* (Madrid: Espasa-Calpe, 2edición, [1979] 1988), and *Historia Crítica del Pensamiento Español: Tomo II: La Edadde Oro* (Madrid: Espasa-Calpe, 2edición, [1979] 1986).

44. *Oposición Política bajo los Austrias* (Barcelona: Ariel, 1972).

45. *Utopía y Contrautopía en el Quijote* (Santiago de Compostela: Pico Sacro, 1976). There is English translation by Robert W. Felkel, *Utopia and Counterutopia in the "Quijote"* (Detroit: Wayne State University Press, 1991).

46. *Utopía y Reformismo en la España de los Austrias* (Madrid: Siglo XXI Editores, 1982).

47. There is the recent more modest and in my mind less convincing work by Fernández-Herrero, *La Utopía de América: Teoría, Leyes, Experimentos* (Barcelona: Anthropos, 1992), prologued by Abellán, which essentially repeats the same vision. Fernández-Herrero focuses on the Jesuit experimentation in the relatively marginal and frontier Guarani territory during the late colonial period.

48. For the continuum of this myth of renewal, quite close to the celebration of hispanicization, see the *Utopía de la Nueva América: Reflexiones para la Edad Universal* by Ignacio Hernando de Larramendi (Madrid: Mapfre, 1992).

49. "[U]na honda convicción…la de que América es tierra utópica, o mejor aún, que América es la Utopía [*sic*] por excelencia. Y así frente a una Europa envuelta en una triste política, donde las ambiciones y la corrupción se disfrazan con el contradictorio y absurdo nombre nombre de "guerra de religión," y donde el eje de acción gira en torno a la maquiavlica razón de estado, América

aparece como la Utopía salvadora, como la Tierra prometida que esperaba impaciente la vieja y podrida Europa," *Historia Crítica del Pensamiento Español. Volume 2*, ibidem, p. 391.

50. See for example this Spanish locus classicus in Domingo Ynduráin's *Humanismo y Renacimiento en España* (Madrid: Cátedra, 1994).

51. *Diálogo de la Dignidad del Hombre por Fernán Pérez de la Oliva*, edited by J. L. Abellán (Barcelona: Es de Cultura Popular, 1967).

52. *Diálogo de las Cosas Ocurridas en Roma por Alfonso de Valdés* (Madrid: Editora Nacional, 1975).

53. *La Idea de América: Origen y Evolución* by J. L. Abellán (Madrid: Istmo, 1972).

54. Juan Gil's *Mitos y Utopías del Descubrimiento: 1. Colón y su Tiempo* (Madrid: Alianza Editorial, Sociedad Quinto Centenario, 1989), and *Mitos y Utopías del Descubrimiento: 2. El Pacófico* (Madrid: Alianza Editorial, Sociedad Quinto Centenario, 1989).

55. See the section "A New World Paradise," in Kathleen Ross's *The Baroque Narrative of Carlos de Siguenza y Góngora: A New World Paradise* (Cambridge: Cambridge University Press, 1993).

56. See Pedro Henríquez Ureña's *La Utopía de América* (Caracas: Ayacucho, [1978] 1989).

57. We have written a study about this theme, "An Early Modern End of the World in the New World: Passion(ate) Narratives by Motolinía and Mendieta" (*Mexican Studies/Estudios Mexicanos*, forthcoming). We will see the poorly repressed latency of Franciscan millenarianism in Quiroga's *Información en Derecho*.

58. Our characterization of the early modern period in explicitly political terms is indebted to Maravall. We share his reticence in the delicate insinuation of complete change or "revolution," for our timeframe, as though the subject had to be broached tangentially. Maravall will use this notion only once in relation to the Castilian opposition to Charles V's early years, or the *Comuneros* movement. See the *Las Comunidades de Castilla: Una Primera Revolución Moderna* (Madrid: Revista de Occidente, 1963).

59. See Marvall's inspiring article, "Interpretación de la crisis social del siglo XVII por los escritores de la época," included in *Seis Lecciones sobre la España de los Siglos de Oro (Literatura e Historia). Homenaje a Marcel Bataillon* (Sevilla/Bordeaux, 1981): pp. 113-158.

60. "Como la obra de los conquistadores era todavía somera, un trastorno de tal naturaleza era posible todavía en la época en que los utopistas concibieron su empresa: *América, país de la utopía*. Claro está que que no fue éste el resultado conseguido, pero un hilo utópico quedó incorporado a la figura de América desde aquel momento. Y por repercusión, también en esa Europa que lo había fabricado" (my emphasis), *Utopía y Reformismo en la España de los Austrias*, ibidem, p. 11.

61. *Utopía y Reformismo en la España de los Austrias*, ibidem, p. 112ff and *Los Factores de la Idea de Progreso en el Renacimiento Español*, ibidem, pp. 13-15, 29-30, 92-94.

62. *Utopía y Reformismo en la España de los Austrias*, ibidem, p. 4.

63. We have in mind the generalized, almost unconscious commonplace of "world history" as illustrated by the *Lectures on the Philosophy of World History. Introduction: Reason in History* (Cambridge: Cambridge University Press, 1975): pp. 124-151, 162-209. This is the resilient narrativity, or rationality, where pre-USA America is nowhere to be seen. Against this commonplace, Hegel and Weber's "Protestan ethic" of quintessential capitalism, chapter three will build upon Arrighi and Dussel around Quiroga's *Información en Derecho* (1535).

64. Always in the shadow of Las Casas, Maravall, who also follows Zavala, has some rather generic and tangential words for Quiroga's "New World" conceptualization, included in *Utopía y Reformismo en la España de los Austrias*, ibidem, pp. 129, 162, 170-172. We will see this millenarianism inside the repressive culture, which Maravall somewhat neglects, in greater detail in chapter three.

65. *Utopía y Contrautopía en el Quijote*, ibidem, p. 26.

66. For a vast panorama into historical transformations, see Maravall's "Dos Términos de la Vida Económica: La Evolución de los Vocablos "Industria" y Fábrica," in CH (Madrid: Octubre-Diciembre, 280/282, 1971): pp. 632-661.

67. "La utopía es cualquier cosa menos una fantasía ineficaz, inoperante," in *Utopía y Reformismo en la España de los Austrias*, ibidem, p. 3.

68. To challenge the ahistorical notion of "modern" in the American vernacular, we may turn to Maravall's rather idiosyncratic definition: "Llamamos moderno no a lo que en el tiempo cae cerca de nosotros y que a nosotros está inmediatamente ligado, sino a la época nueva, cualquiera que sea la distancia a que queda de nosotros y cualquiera que sea también su relación con nuestra situación actual," *Utopía y Contrautopía en el Quijote*, ibidem, p. 38.

69. The first date, 1529, signals Charles V's imperial reign and the official ideology of reformation according to his chronicler Antonio de Guevara, who is close to Quiroga. The second date, 1605, is the date of the publication of the first part of Cervantes's most famous work during the reign of Philip III, no longer with the imperial throne, *Utopía y Contrautopía en el Quijote*, ibidem, p. 18-19.

70. See "Interpretación de la Crisis Social del Siglo XVII...," ibidem, pp. 131-145.

71. Maravall has documented the early modern geography of money circulation with special attention to its scarcity in Spain during 1575-1578. The theatrical pranks of the *gracioso* about *Don Dinero* must be imagined historically side by side the poor circulation of the volume of money, avalanche instead of slow irrigation, the ocean of low productivity loan policies by *mayorazgo*

primogenitors and some islands of proto-industrial manufactures, "Interpretaciones de la Crisis Social," ibidem, pp. 139, 144.

72. We are refering to the essay "The New World in Eschatological and Utopian Writings of the Sixteenth to the Eighteenth Centuries," included in *Studies in the Colonial History of Spanish America* (Cambridge: Cambridge University Press, 1975): pp. 206-238. We haven't been successful in finding the original Spanish version.

73. As the anthropological preservation of some of these ritualizations in the contemporary Peruvian context as showed to us. See Manuel Burga's *Nacimiento de una Utopía: Muerte y Resurrección de los Incas* (México: Instituto de Apoyo Agrario, 1988), and Alberto Flores-Galindo's *Buscando un Inca: Identidad y Utopía en los Andes* (La Habana: Casa de las Américas, 986).

74. See for example, Beatriz Pastor's *Discursos Narrativos de la Conquista: Mitificación y Emergencia* (Hanover: Ediciones del Norte, [1983] 1988), and *El Jardín y el Peregrino: Ensayos sobre el Pensamiento Utópico Latinoamericano 1492-1695* (Atlanta: Rodopi, 1996).

75. For example, Isaac J. Pardo's *Fuegos bajo el Agua: Invención de la Utopía* (Caracas: Ayacucho, n/d).

76. Following Zavala, Góngora provides a brief synthesis of the rules of the village-hospitals. There is also a brief paragraph, which appears to be second-hand information also from Zavala, on the so-called "Judicial Report," the *Información en Derecho*, which we will see in detail in chapter three, "The New World in Eschatological and Utopian Writings...," ibidem, pp. 129 & 232-234.

77. "Vasco de Quiroga y Bartolomé de las Casas," included in *Estudios Sobre Bartolomé de las Casas* (Barcelona: Península, 1965): 267-351 [273].

78. *Enciclopedia de México* (México, 1988): pp. 6822-6826.

79. *Vasco de Quiroga y sus Pueblos de Santa Fé en los siglos XVIII y XIX* (México: Porrúa, 1977): pp. 162-173.

80. *Crónica de la Orden de N.P.S. Agustín en las Provincias de la Nueva España, en cuatro edades desde el año de 1533 hasta el año de 1592* (Mexico, Imprenta Victoria, [1624] 1924). We have polished the grammar and we have modernized the spelling. We have also added missing punctuation to this rather unstable romance language which quite explicitly treasures the rough texture of the monastic cloth ("veían los vestidos con jerga gruesa, el hábito estrecho, y sencillo, que parecía más cilicio que vestidos, unos crucifijos en las manos y tan grande olor de santidad que se andaban todos tras ellos," pp. 37-8). In Spanish "jerga" (or "jargon") refers equally to clothing and discourse. All pages refer to this edition.

81. Beaumont speaks of 60 Spanish families and 9 religious persons allowed by the official *ejecutoria* to populate the Michoacán region, which cost not one "drop of blood" for the Spanish Crown (p. 177). The Franciscan friar mentions

the 30,000 vecinos for the city of Valladolid (1542) founded by Viceroy Antonio de Mendoza, and again 30,000 for the hospital of Santa Fé. Perhaps the two locations being historically almost quite interchangeable, Beaumont appears nonetheless to use numbers quite approximately, as included in *Crónica de Michoacán*, ibidem, III Volume, pp. 41, 149.

82. See for example Elsa Cecilia Frost's *Este Nuevo Orbe* (México: Universidad Nacional Autónoma de México, Centro Coordinador y Difusor de Estudios Latinoamericanos, 1996): pp. 105-116.

83. These are the "first successful missions [among the Tarascan Indians around Lake Pátzcuaro," or "a cooperative commonwealth" influenced by Thomas More's *Utopia*," and "he laboured diligently on behalf of the welfare of the natives, seeking their temporal as well as spiritual salvation." Two corrections are in order: Quiroga was never a Dominican and there is no verification as to a "volume of sermons" (Lars Mahinske, Britannica representative, personal communication, Oct. 29, 1997).

84. *Enciclopedia de México* (México, 1988): pp. 6822-6826.

85. The web-site version of *Mexico: Biography of Power (A History of Modern Mexico, 1810-1996* (washingtonpost.com/wp~srv/style/longterm/books/chap1/). The access date was: July 29, 1998.

86. *El Descubrimiento de América que todavía no fue* (Barcelona: Laia/El Barco de papel, 1986).

87. *Memoria del Fuego. 1-Los Nacimientos* (España: Siglo XXI, 1982): pp. 152-153. There is English translation: *Memory of Fire. 1-Genesis. Part One of a Trilogy*, translated by Cedric Belfrage (New York: Pantheon Books, 1985): p. 132.

88. *Teatro Eclesiástico de la Primitiva Iglesia de la Nueva España en las Indias Occidentales* (Madrid: José Porrúa Turanzas, 1959): pp. 161-173.

89. Information included in Gregory A. Banazak's *The Ecclesiology of Vasco de Quiroga* (Roma: Pontificia Universitas Gregoriana, Facultas Theologiae, 1991): pp. 2-3.

90. *Vasco de Quiroga: La Utopía en América* (Madrid: Historia 16, 1992).

91. *Vasco de Quiroga: De Debellandis Indis. Un Tratado Desconocido* (México: Universidad Nacional Autónoma de México, 1988).

92. *Fundamentos de la Historia en América* (México: Imprenta Universitaria, 1942): pp. 21-28. There is a seminal exchange with Marcel Bataillon in which O'Gorman pulls the carpet floor to his side, *Crisis y Porvenir de la Ciencia Histórica* (México: Imprenta Universitaria, 1947). O'Gorman's major work is *La Idea del Descubrimiento de América: Historia de esa Interpretación y Crítica de sus Fundamentos* (México: Centro de Estudios Filosóficos, 1951). See a recent brief critique of O'Gorman in Neil Larsen's *Reading North by South: On Latin American Literature, Culture and Politics* (Minneapolis: University of Minnesota Press, 1995): pp. 110-116.

93. *Santo Tomás More y "La Utopía" de Tomás Moro en la Nueva España* (México: Alcancia, 1937).

94. *Vasco de Quiroga and his Pueblo-Hospitales of Santa Fe*, ibidem.
95. See Warren, ibidem, for the tremendous difficulties and material-textual holes of these incomplete, when not isolated and decontextualized or lost sources (pp. 35-6).
96. We have had access to Moreno's so-called facsimile edition on occasion of the *Primer Congreso Indigenista Interamericano, Reglas y Ordenanzas para el Gob de los Hospitales de Santa Fé de México y Michoacán* (Pátzcuaro: Secretaría de la Economía Nacional, 1940), also the *Historia General de Michoacán. Volumen II: La Colonia*, edited by Enrique Florescano (Morelia, Michoacán: Gobierno del Michoacán/Instituto Michoacano de Cultura, 1989), and the latest lavishly illustrated *El Michoacán Antiguo: Estado y Sociedad Tarascos en la Epoca Prehispánica*, coordinated by Brigitte Boehm de Lameiras and including essays by ten authors (Michoacán: El Colegio de Michoacán/Gobierno del Estado de Michoacán, 1994).
97. Our edition has been Leoncio Cabrero's *Relación de Michoacán* (Madrid: Historia 16, 1989).
98. Zavala's literature on Quiroga has been reprinted numerous times: *La "Utopía" de Tomás Moro en la Nueva España y Otros Estudios* (México: Antigua Librería Robredo, de Jos Porrúa e Hijos, Biblioteca Histórica Mexicana de Obras Inditas/4, 1937), *Sir Thomas More in New Spain: A Utopian Adventure of the Renaissance* (London: Hispanic & Luso-Brazilian Councils, 1955), *Recuerdo de Vasco de Quiroga* (México: Editorial Porrúa, 1965), and *La utopía mexicana del siglo XVI: Lo bello, lo verdadero y lo bueno*, with Silvio Zavala, Miguel León-Portilla and Guillermo Tovar de Teresa (Italy/Mexico: Grupo Azabache, 1992).
99. See "Topografía de una Utopía: De la *Utopía* de Tomás Moro a los Pueblos-Hospitales de Vasco de Quiroga," by Pablo Hermida-Lazcano (Madrid: *Revista de Indias*, Depto. de Historia de América "Fernández de Oviedo," Centro de Estudios Históricos, Mayo-Agosto 1995, Núm. 204): pp. 357-390.
100. *Documentos Inéditos del Siglo XVI para la Historia de México* (México: Porrúa, 1975). There are minor pieces: the biographical rendering of Quiroga (p. xxviii), Zumárraga's endorsement of the appointment of Quiroga for the Bishopric of Michoacán (p. 74-6), and several communications with state officials like the Viceroy Luis de Velasco (pp. 244-5, 328, 333).
101. *The Ecclesiology of Vasco de Quiroga*, ibidem.
102. *Collision of Utopias: Vasco de Quiroga's Mission to the Puerhepecha-Chichimec of Michoacán, México, 1537-1565* (Harvard University, Divinity School, Ph.D. Thesis, 1990). Through the University Microfilms International (UMI-Work Information Service), I have had however access to the abbreviated version of this work. The book version, just reached me while proofreading *Michoacán and Eden: Vasco Quiroga and the Evangelization of Western Mexico* (Austin: University of Texas Press, 2000)
103. *La Acción Pastoral de Don Vasco de Quiroga* (Mérida, Yucatán, México:

Mons. Manuel Castro Ruiz, Arzobispo de Yucatán. México [Univ~~~~~~~~
Navarra, Spain, Ph.D. Thesis, (1987), (1988).

104. *Don Vasco de Quiroga: Oidor of New Spain* (Loyola University of Chicago, PhD Thesis, 1940). We have had access to the microfilm version of this thesis kept at Brown University Library.

105. *The Politics of an Erasmian Lawyer, Vasco de Quiroga* (Malibu: The Center for Medieval and Renaissance Studies, University of California, Los Angeles/ Undena Publications, 1976).

106. *Don Vasco de Quiroga (Protector de los Indios)* (Salamanca: Kadmos, 1993).

107. *Erasmo y España: Estudios Sobre la Historia Espiritual del Siglo XVI* (México: Fondo de Cultura Económica, second edition 1966), arguably a touchstone among global histories of religion in the early modern Hispanic world. The final chapter explores the trans-Atlantic impact of this European intellectual in the historical context of New Spain. That Erasmus was widely read among lettered circles is beyond question, but one may wonder about the concrete impact among *letrado* courtroom practices.

108. See "La utopía cristiano-social en el Nuevo Mundo," by Stelio Cro in *ALH* (Vol. VI, Núm. 7/1, 1978): pp. 87-129. Unlike Eliav-Feldon, Cro, following quite close Maravall's classic pronouncements, speaks of the three *locus classicus* of early modern American utopianism: the "empirical utopia" of Las Casas, the "elective theocracy" of Quiroga and the Jesuit kingdom in the relative colonial marginality of Paraguay. There is no question that we are dealing with real social models for social experimentation of various proportions and impact. There is no question that Christianity is the hegemonic or official forcefield, also horizon or condition of (im)possibility, in which all these historical creatures lived.

109. Ceballos-García reproduces from R. Aguayo Quiroga's official proclamation of the establishment of the Bishopric of Michoacan ("Decreto de Erección del Obispado," 1554). The similarities between this formalization and the Ordinances for the Good Government of the Village-Hospitals (the *Reglas y Ordenanzas para Buen Gobierno*), are certainly striking, pp. 125-139.

110. We would suggest that Banazak misreads Bernal Díaz del Castillo's narration of the Valladolid Debates. Banazak dispues that Quiroga might have been on the *encomendero* side: we answer with a resounding "no." Tata Vasco was on the side of the poor and exploited Indians who, as he was wont to say, were used by the Spaniards until the last drop of blood has been bled from their bodies. Yet it was his ambiguity or incompleteness in joining their side that led some people—like Bernal Díaz del Castillo—to believe that he was on the side of the exploiters; and it was the ambiguity of his life that was reflected in the ambiguity of his thought," p. 72). This crude polarization in the makings of saintliness is symptomatic of Banazak's mode of thought. We will see in chapter three the likeliest historico-political positioning of Quiroga also in relation to Bernal Díaz del Castillo.

111. *El Episcopado Hispanoamericano. Institución Misionera en Defensa del Indio* (1504-1620) (Cuernavaca, México: Sondeos, Núms. 32-38, 7 vols., 1969-1970) and *El Episcopado Hispanoamericano. Institución Misionera en Defensa del Indio* (1504-1620). *Apéndice Documentales, Tomos 1 & 2* (Cuernavaca, México: Sondeos, Núms. 71-72, vols. 8-9, 1970).

112. Dussel's philosophy of liberation is corroborated by Gutirrez's theology of liberation as regards the explicit valorization of Quiroga's historical importance. Gutierrez also speaks of Quiroga as modellic example of peaceful Christian mission, only second to Las Casas's "excessive" or prophetic vision. See, *En Busca de los Pobres de Jesucristo: El Pensamiento de Bartoloméé de las Casas* (Lima: Instituto Bartolomé de las Casas/IEP, Núm. 124, 1992): pp. 402-3, 604-5.

113. The Franciscan Pablo Beaumont constitutes a mostly reliable source as regards this colonial *locus* of legality ("ha (o no ha) lugar"). Readers have access to the colonial mapping of the Michoacan region, the legalization of *tierras baldías*, the attribution of *tierras realengas* for one or two generations and the early and sudden monetarization of social energies and resources. Beaumont highlights the relative condition of exceptionality (privileges and immunities) for Quiroga's hospitals, to alleviate, as it was commonly said, the helpless "imbecility" and "misery" of the Indians. See, *Crónica de Michoacán. Tomo III*, ibidem, pp. 172-296.

114. Dussel develops the problematic collaboration of the Crown patronage of Church structures in the Americas, see *El Episcopado Hispanoamericano*, ibidem, (No. 33, v. 2 (1969), pp. 134-192). We will see in following chapters some details of this historical association as pertains most concretely to Quiroga.

115. For the mapping of New Spain, see Peter Gerhard's *A Guide to the Historical Geography of New Spain* (Cambridge at the University Press, 1972). For the mapping of the hospital institutions, see Josefina Muriel's *Hospitales de la Nueva España. Tomo I: Fundaciones del Siglo XVI* (México: Instituto de Investigaciones Históricas, Serie Historia Novohispana, Núm. 12, 1990).

116. Dussel's maths are taken from Borah and Cook's speculative estimates. There are severe fluctuations: 1524-1548, a diminution by 85%, epidemic heights in 1546-7 and 1580, 37% growth in 1560, with internal indigenous migrations, away from *encomendero* irregularities and First *Audiencia* corruptions, to the *sierras* and Quiroga's Santa Fé de la Laguna, a neighborhood by the Lake of Patzcuaro, "despite its regulated severity." See *El Michoacán Antiguo*, ibidem, pp. 116,142-4. Santa Fé de la Laguna has been defined "rectoría de clérigos" affiliated with the Cathedral *Cabildo* in Mexico City. The population during for Santa Fé during Quiroga's lifetime is the rather modest figure of 4,000 Indians. In 1571, the hospital had 340 taxpayers ("tributantes"). For further mostly post-Quiroga information on numbers, see *Partidos y Padrones del Obispado de Michoacán (1680-1685)* by Alberto Carrillo-Cázares (Zamora, Mich.: El Colegio de Michoacán/Gobierno del Estado de Michoacán, 1996).

117. The region of Michoacán is covered by *El Episcopado Hispanoamericano*, ibidem, (v. 5, pp. 111-130).

118. Dussel writes that the Diocese included ·puebios tarascos, otomies, mexicanos, cuitlatecas, piringas y otros, no olvidó por ello a los guerreros chichimecas, nombre genrico de varias tribus rebeldes." This is said to be the ideal of the primitive Church which is also new in the New World (v. 5, p. 128). We will see some of these millenarian moments, what Dussel also calls the prophetic potential of the [permanent] invention of the charity, in chapters two and three.

119. "Vasco de Quiroga y Bartolomé de las Casas," ibidem.

120. "Fuentes Patrísticas, Jurídicas y Escolásticas del Pensamiento Quiroguiano," in *Textos Políticos en la Nueva España* (México: Universidad Nacional Autónoma de México, 1984): pp. 158-171.

121. See Anthony Pagden's "The Humanism of Vasco de Quiroga's Información en Derecho," included in *The Uncertainties of Empire: Essays in Iberian and Ibero-American Intellectual History* (Aldeshot, Hampshire: Variorum/Ashgate Publishing Company, 1994).

122. *El Humanismo en el Nuevo Mundo: Ensayo Histórico y Perspectivas Contemporáneas* (Mexico: Miguel Angel Porrúa, 1997), prologued by Silvio Zavala.

123. *Conquista y Conciencia Cristiana. El pensamiento indigenista y jurídico-teológico de Don Vasco de Quiroga (+1565)* (Quito: Abya-Yala, 1990).

124. *Vasco de Quiroga y sus Pueblos de Santa Fe en los Siglos XVIII y XIX* (México: Porrúa, 1990).

125. *El Real Colegio de San Nicolás de Pátzcuaro* (Cuernavaca, 1967).

126. This chapter is included in the following work, *Images of Conquest: Text and Context in Colonial Mexico* (University of Wisconsin-Madison, PhD Thesis, 1993). We have had access to the early manuscript version of this chapter.

127. *Mexico: Biography of Power: A History of Modern Mexico, 1810-1996*, ibidem.

128. The website address: www.mexicodesconocido.com.mx/hipertex/quiroga.htm. The access date is May 9, 1998. The access date for following website references is also May 9, 1998 unless otherwise indicated. All quotes come from the quoted printouts unless indicated otherwise.

129. There is also a website which tries to associate quite confusingly this locality with the name of Quiroga. The website address is: www.ccu.umich.mx/mich/morelia/iglesia-1.html.

130. The website address is, according to the full information in the printout: www.altavista.digital.com/cgi~bin/query?pg+q&stq=10&what=web&kl=XX&.

131. The website address is: mexico.udg.mx/cultfolk/Tianguis/tianguis.html.

132. The website address is: www.mex.desco.com/colonial/1510.htm.

133. The website address is: www.cam.org/~tlahuic/patze.htm.

134. The website address is: www.onr.com/consulmx/october97-3.html.

135. The website address is: members.home.net/quiroga/quiroga.htm.

136. The website address is: www.fore-tech.com/casamaya/history.html.
137. The website address is: www.ccu.umich.mx/mich/morelia/iglesia-1.html.
138. The website address is, according to the full information in the printout: www.altavista.digital.com/cgi-bin/query?pg+q&stq=10&what=web&kl=XX&.
139. The website address is: www.anuies.mx/anuies/revsup/res039/txt1/htm.
140. The website address is: http://jupiter.itesz.mx/simorelos/guia/anterior/97-11-16/001.html.
141. The website address is: www.rcs.it/riotta/98-03-28/19.htm. The access date is 12/8/98.
142. *Santo Tomás More y "La Utopía" de Tomás Moro en la Nueva España,* ibidem. We tend to read these rather idiosyncratic objections more as an early reaction against Zavala's "humanizing" white-washing of Quiroga's political profile.
143. The website address is: www.mexconnect.com/mex_/history/jtuck/jtuckbio.html. The access date is 12/10/98.

Chapter II

1. We must explain the reasons for this rather controversial word choice. The traditional notion, inside the Hispanic tradition, for early modern political experimentation is "reformismo," which we take from J.A. Maravall. We have specifically in mind his following works: *Utopía y Reformismo en la España de los Austrias* (Madrid: Siglo XXI, 1982), but also of *Carlos V y el Pensamiento Político del Renacimiento* (Madrid: Instituto de Estudios Políticos, 1960), and *La Oposición Política bajo los Austrias* (Barcelona: Ariel, 1972). We must also include J. A. Abellán in *Historia Crítica del Pensamiento Español. Tomo II. La Edad de Oro* (Madrid: Espasa-Calpe, 1986). The notion "reformism," which sounds a bit odd in English, is eclipsed by the centrality of the notion of the "Protestant reformation." We feel we must use this naturalized notion, and try to unsettle it, if only a bit. By so doing, we hope to bring into consideration the severe underrepresentation of the "Spanish moment," and also the "Latin American moment" in relation to early modernity, and beyond. We must also note that the notion of "reformación," today an archaic usage, was commonly used among sixteenth-century figures, Bartolomé de Las Casas, for example.

2. For a summary view of the early colonial collapse of the population, see J. I. Israel's *Race, Class and Politics in Colonial Mexico, 1610-1670* (Oxford: Oxford University Press, 1975). See also Gruzinski's *The Conquest of Mexico* (Cambridge: Polity Press, 1992): pp. 80-81 and 193-195. Sempat Assadourian does not hesitate to use the expression "permanent state of war" for the early period of colonization. Although he uses it in the immediate context of the Andes, we find it perfectly applicable, at least in the foundational years, to our context of New Spain. For a detailed account and its relations to genocide, see chapter one, "La Gran Vejación y Destruición de la Tierra: Las Guerras de

Sucesión y de Conquista en el Derrumbe de la Población Indígena del Perú," in *Transiciones hacia el Sistema Colonial Andino* (Mexico: El Colegio de Mexico, 1994).

3. *Recuerdo de Vasco de Quiroga* by Silvio Zavala (Mexico: Porrúa, 1965): p. 16.

4. *Vasco de Quiroga and his Pueblo-Hospitals of Santa Fe*, p. 26.

5. Unless otherwise indicated, chronological data in relation to Vasco de Quiroga is taken from Fintan B. Warren's *Vasco de Quiroga and His Pueblo-Hospitales of Santa Fe* (Washington: Academy of American Franciscan History, 1963). Occasional references will be taken from Rubén Landa's *Don Vasco de Quiroga* (Barcelona: Grijalbo, 1965).

6. *Vasco de Quiroga y sus Pueblos de Santa Fé en los Siglos XVIII y XIX* (México; Porrúa, 1990): p. 162.

7. Fintan B. Warren, Quiroga's most reliable biographer, says the following, "We know only that he held a licenciate in canon law but not in sacred theology. In the bull of his nomination to the bishopric of Michoacán, he was designated as a licenciate in sacred theology but, with a lawyer's scrupulosity for exactness in official documents, he asked the Holy See that this error be corrected, since his licenciate was in canon law. The correction was made in an apostolic brief, 'Exponi nobis,' of July 8, 1550" (ibidem, p. 11).

8. Maravall gave numerous formulations to the vision of "the sixteenth century as one of the periods most loaded with utopian potential ("carga utópica") in the modern history of Europe." One of the most well-known articulations is "Utopía y Primitivismo en el Pensamiento de Las Casas" (Revista de Occidente, December 1974): pp. 311-388.

9. In his day, Maravall wrote, "How is it made compatible an attribution to the spirit of the bourgeoisie with a class-inflected political consciousness and unambiguous class-defined behaviors and attitudes, with the insisting defense of the principle of communal property, and with the appellation to coercive forms of traditional societies that we may find in More, or with the attitude against the use of money in the "modern" sense clearly against the corresponding mercantile use of the money-driven economy?" in *Utopía y Reformismo*, ibidem, p. 69, my translation). See the self-conscious role-playing and unresolved dilemmas of the humanist intellectual at the table of the aristocratic great in Stephen Greenblatt's *Renaissance Self-Fashioning* (Chicago: The University of Chicago Press, 1980): pp. 11-73. See also, Richard Halpern's account of More's devotion for the moral economy of use value against the destructiveness of aristocratic expenditure, in *The Poetics of Primitive Accumulation* (Ithaca: Cornell University Press, 1991): pp. 136-175.

10. See, "La Concepción del Saber en una Sociedad Tradicional," and "Los Hombres de Saber o Letrados y la Formación de su Conciencia Estamental," in *Estudios de Historia del Pensamiento Español* (Madrid: Ediciones Cultura

Hispánica, 1967): pp. 203-260 and 347-380. We may see the state-sponsored lettered intervention, with all its historical impatience and dynamism, slowly breaking down a more traditional (i.e. feudal) notion of monumental knowledge and the cognitive attitudes of antiquarian preservation and pious reverence. See also Walter Mignolo for a panoramic view of the colonial specificity of the *letrado*, in *The Darker Side of the Renaissance* (Ann Arbor: The University of Michigan Press, 1995): pp. 289-296.

11. See the detailed family reconstructions by Miranda Godínez, *El Real Colegio de San Nicolás de Pátzcuaro* (México: Cuernavaca, 1967): pp. 3-16. See also, Warren reconstructions, still with some obscurities, like the precise date of Quiroga's birth. Due to lack of documentation, there is still missing an account of the early life in Spain, yet it appears beyond doubt that Quiroga, the second son to a petty nobility pedigree, became a member of that corps of *letrados* who during the reign of Ferdinand and Isabella replaced the greater nobility in many of the duties of the court, in *Vasco de Quiroga and His Pueblo-Hospitales of Santa Fe*, pp. 8-13.

12. The foundational diocese of Michoacán was blurry and expanding and considerably bigger than today's state of Michoacán. It encompassed the states of Guerrero, Michoacán and Colima, its boundaries went all the way to the south of Tamaulipas, the totality of the actual size of Michoacán and included a fairly good portion of today's Guanajuato, Jalisco and San Luis de Potosí. For a mapping of the colonial diocese in a later, post-Quiroga date, see *Partidos y Padrones del Obispado de Michoacán*, 1680-1685 by Alberto Carrillo Cázares (Zamora, Michoacán: El Colegio de Michoacán/Gobierno del Estado de Michoacán, 1996).

13. *Hospitales de la Nueva España. Tomo I: Fundaciones del Siglo XVI*, by Josefina Muriel (Ciudad Universitaria, México: Universidad Nacional Autónoma de Mexico/Cruz Roja Mexicana, Instituto de Investigaciones Históricas, Serie Historia Novohispana, [1956] 1990): pp. 65 & 73.

14. For a rather synthetic, yet persuasive account of these historical developments, see *Historical Capitalism* by Immanuel Wallerstein (London: Verso, 1984).

15. See Fredric Jameson, chapter four, "Of Islands and Trenches. Neutralization and the Production of Utopian Discourse," in *The Ideologies of Theory. Essays 1971-1986. Volume 2. Syntax of History*. (Minneapolis: University of Minnesota Press, second repr. 1989).

16. J. I. Israel gives us some numbers for regular clergy, 2,000 in the 1650s, 250 Franciscans and Augustinians in the mendicant province of Michoacán, total number of ecclesiastical personnel in Mexico City in the mid-seventeenth century, 1000 nuns, more than 2,500 in Valladolid, capital of Michoacán, secular clergy in Michoacán, some 300 in 1640s, in *Race, Class & Politics in Colonial Mexico*, footnotes 93-95. See also Gruzinski's reading which tells us of a displacement, later in the sixteenth century, of mendicant orders from a dominant position and the hegemony of secular clergy, the canons of new

cathedrals and the Jesuits. Regular clergy increased from 800 to around 3000 individuals from 1559 to 1650, while the secular priests in the archbishopric of Mexico alone grew from 158 to 451 between 1575 and 1622, in *The Conquest of Mexico* (Cambridge: Polity Press, 1993): pp. 193-194.

17. For a historical view of the monastic rule and some specificities and insufficiencies of the monastic rule, see *The Rule of St. Benedict* (The Liturgical Press, 1981): pp. 79-151, 168, 180 and 434.

18. For a panoramic view, we suggest the classic account by Robert Ricard, *La Conquista Espiritual de México* (México, Editorial Ius/Polis, 1947).

19. It is important to differentiate, however, that the foundational repudiation of personal property at the individual level does not necessarily preclude the management of property at the communal or institutional level. It is almost redundant to say that the conditions of management and transmission of property in same-sex institutions is outside the ethics of the heterosexual couple made more or less standard and hegemonic practice until to this day. There is evidence of state interest in the restriction of the orders' growth. It is possible to find *cédulas* restating the prohibition of property owning, which then almost instantaneously make these institutions into idoneous social mediators in a world of owners and entrepeneurs. See, Richard Konetzke, for state intrusions into ecclesiastical institutions, *Colección de Documentos*, pp. 273,388, 395, 435, 495 & 507. It is plausible to give the "criollización" of ecclesiastical institutions in New Spain as centuries advance, see Mantilla, Luis C, "Criollización de la Orden Franciscana en el Nuevo Reino de Granada," in *Actas del II Congreso Internacional sobre los Franciscanos en el Nuevo Mundo. Siglo XVI*, in La Rábida, 21-26 Septiembre 1987 (Madrid: Deismos, 1988): pp. 685-727, and, Morales Valerio, Francisco, in "Criollización de la Orden Franciscana en Nueva España. Siglo XVI, in *Actas del II Congreso Internacional sobre los Franciscanos en el Nuevo Mundo. Siglo XVI*, in La Rábida, 21-26 Septiembre 1987 (Madrid: Deismos, 1988): pp. 661-684.

20. See the historical orientation to *The Rule of St. Benedict* (The Liturgical Press, 1981): pp. 61-63.

21. Enrique Dussel has convincingly spoken about the historical arrogance of the strong individuality, the phenomenology of the "I conquer" in relation to Hernán Cortés, as the legitimate precursor of Descartes's *cogito*, *The Invention of the Americas: Eclipse of "the Other" and the Myth of Modernity* (New York: Continuum, 1992).

22. Take chapter 68 in the Rule of St. Benedict, "If it should happen that burdensome or impossible taks are imposed on one of the brethren he should indeed accept with complete calm and obedience the command of the one who so orders, but if he sees that the weight of the burden quite exceeds the limits of his strength, he should quietly and at a suitable moment explain to his superior the reasons why he cannot do it, not in a proud way nor with a spirit of resistance, or contradiction. But if after his explanation the one in authority

remains firm in requiring what he has ordered, the junior must understand that this is what is best for him, and let him lovingly trust in God's aid, and so obey."

23. Thomas Aquinas's *Summa Theologica* (1266-73), inside which is the *Treatise on Law*, is possibly the most influential single point of reference in the early modern Christianization of Aristotle. The Dominican Francisco de Vitoria (1485-1546), at the University of Salamanca constitutes the most influential presence in the Spanish revival of Aquinas and Aristotle in the sixteenth century. *Treatise on Law* is quite eloquent about the ontological reasonableness of the law as indistinguishable from the commonwealth. The law is teleologically for the common good and violence is anything which diverts from it. Quite eloquent about the monastic ethos, Aquinas speaks of the darker side of the law as the "fomes" or formlessness of sin. My edition has been, *Basic Writings of Saint Thomas Aquinas. Volume 2* by Anton C. Pegis (New York: Random House, 1945): pp. 742-978.

24. See Greenblatt's and Halpern's accounts, ibidem, for some of the association between writing, political reformism and playfulness in relation to Morean fictionalization of an ideal commonwealth. Quiroga's vision, although undoubtedly inspired by the English scholar, has indeed none of the attributes of *jeu d'esprit*, the "textual excess" of a whimsical dream (Halpern, p. 175), or the "self-conscious [authorial] role-playing" and deliberate construction of "opacity" and "absurdity" (Greenblatt, p.33 and 15). In fact, our main reading of Quiroga is quite the reverse. Some of these differences might well help us concretize, if only initially enunciated as differences in tone or mood of enunciation, the historical specificity of colonial reformism in the foundational period in relation to the contemporary counterpart of European or metropolitan reformism.

25. The phrase "colonization of the life-world" has been taken from Enrique Dussel in *The Invention of the Americas*, ibidem. See also the recent compilation of essays in English for a good panoramic view of Dussel's philosophical work, *The Underside of Modernity: Apel, Ricoeur, Rorty, Taylor and the Philosophy of Liberation* (New Jersey: Humanities Press, 1996).

26. "Vasco de Quiroga en el ambiente misionero de la Nueva España," by Pedro Borges, in *Missionalia Hispanica* (Año XXIII, Núm. 69): pp. 297-340.

27. See Abellán's *Historia Crítica*, ibidem, for a valid general presentation of Luis Vives (pp. 108-132).

28. See the section "Fuentes patrísticas, jurídicas y escolásticas del pensamiento quiroguiano," included in *Textos Políticos en la Nueva España* by Carlos Herrejón Peredo (México: Universidad Nacional Autónoma de México, 1984): pp. 159-171. See also René Acuña's prologue to the laborious edition, *De Debellandis Indis: Un tratado desconocido* (México: Universidad Nacional Autónoma de México, 1988), for additional information regarding Quiroga's erudition.

250   *Good Places and Non-Places in Colonial Mexico*

29. My edition, *Del Socorro de los Pobres (De Subventione Pauperum)*, in *Obras Completas*, edited by Lorenzo Riber (Madrid: Aguilar, Editor, 1947): pp. 1355-1411.

30. For a convincing mapping out of the Pacific section of the colonial Michoacan diocese, see the following articles by Elinore M. Barrett, *"Encomiendas, Mercedes* and *Haciendas* in the *Tierra Caliente* of Michoacán" (*Jahrbuch fur Geschichte*, 1973): pp. 71-112; and also "Indian Community Lands in the Tierra Caliente of Michoacán" (*Jahrbuch fur Geschichte*, 1974): pp. 78-120.

31. Fintan Warren, O.F.M., does precisely this to highlight the singularity of the individual. Besides his major autobiography, see also "Vasco de Quiroga, fundador de Hospitales y Colegios," *MH* (): pp. 25-46. [incomplete reference] Muriel, *Hospitales*, ibidem, also appears to signal somewhat the primacy of Quiroga, yet she is quick to point out the geographic and temporal proximity of foundations of hospitals by Franciscans and Augustinians and how blurred and changing these overlappings were, pp. 57-115.

32. Pedro Borges, O.F. M., "Vasco de Quiroga en el ambiente misionero de la Nueva España," ibidem, does precisely this. See also Manuel Merino, O.S.A., "Don Vasco de Quiroga en los cronistas augustinos," *MH* (): pp. 89-112. [incomplete reference]. See also Fidel de Lejarza, O.F.M., "Don Vasco de Quiroga en las crónicas franciscanas," *MH* (Año XXIII, Núm. 68): pp. 129-244.

33. See *King and Church: The Rise and Fall of the Patronato Real* by William E. Shiels (Chicago: Loyola University Press, 1961).

34. The inevitable classic reference for a panoramic vision of the institution of the "hospital" in the specific context of New Spain is Josefina Muriel, ibidem.

35. Nicolás León has given us the complete collection to this date of all official *cédula* documents appertaining to Quiroga's communities. We have the formal adjudication of "empty" lands, the official proclamation of the royal protection of these lands, the permission to Quiroga to nominate all necessary religious personnel, and the final acceptance by the institution of the Monarchy of the Patronage (*Patronato Real*). These are included in *Documentos Inéditos Referentes al Ilustrísimo Señor Don Vasco de Quiroga Existentes en el Archivo General de Indias* (Mexico: Antinua Librería Robredo de José Porrúa e Hijos, 1940): pp. 1-35.

36. For a panoramic vision of this historical landscape of colonial labor, see the disagreement between Immanuel Wallerstein and Steve Stern. See by the former, the classic *The Modern World-System: Capitalist Agriculture and the Origins of the European World-Economy in the Sixteenth Century* (New York: Academic Press, 1974); and by the latter, "Feudalism, Capitalism and the World-System in the Perspective of Latin America and the Caribbean," AHR (vol. 93, Núm. 4, Oct. 1988): pp. 829-872). A rather tense exchange between the two is found in the following pages of this same issue (pp. 873-897).

37. Muriel, ibidem, p. 61.

38. Muriel, *Hospitales*, ibidem, pp.67-9.
39. Muriel, *Hospitales*, ibidem, p. 68. Muriel makes a little mistake in the page reference to the León document: it is rather the document IV, entitled "Patronato Real de los Hospitales y Colegio de San Nicolás" (1551), which includes the name of a "Pedro de Yepes tesorero de la santa catedral de el dicho obispado de Mechuacan en nombre del deán y Cabildo de ella sede vacante y del letor y retor del colegio de San Niculás [*sic*] que el reverendo en Cristo padre don Vasco de Quiroga, primero[*sic*] obispo de la dicha provincia de Mechoacan [*sic*] difunto dejó fundado en la dicha ciudad de Páscuaro [*sic*] y de los dos hospitales de Santa Fe (pp. 30-35, 34). This document IV is an official communication ("carta ejecutoria") from Philip II sanctioning already in September 10, 1565 Quiroga's last will delivered by the aforementioned Pedro de Yepes, Royal Tarascan Indian if we believe Muriel's words, to the members of the *Tercera Audiencia*. We will see in close detail Quiroga's last will in the following pages. The royal acceptance of the patronage is dated 1543.
40. Silvio Zavala is probably the scholar who has done most for the visibility of Vasco de Quiroga. For this vision, see the three main works, the primer *La "Utopía" de Tomás Moro en la Nueva España y Otros Estudios* (México: Antigua Librer'a Robredo, de José Porrúa e Hijos, 1937), the *Recuerdo de Vasco de Quiroga* (México: Porrúa, 1965), and finally a recent repetition of the same ideas in *La Utopía Mexicana del Siglo XVI: Lo bello, lo verdadero y lo bueno* (Italy: Grupo Azabache, 1992).
41. See A. Pagden, "The humanism of Vasco de Quiroga's *Información en Derecho*," included in *The Uncertainties of Empire* (Brookfield, Vermont: Variorum, 1994): pp. 133-142.
42. See M. M. Lacas in "A Social Welfare Organizer in Sixteenth Century new Spain: Don Vasco de Quiroga, First Bishop of Michoacán," *TA* (Vol. XIV, July, 1957-April 1958): pp. 57-86.
43. See Dagmar Bechtloff in "La formación de una sociedad intercultural: las cofradías en el Michoacán colonial, " *HM* (Vol. XLIII, Octubre-Diciembre, 1993, Núm. 2): pp. 251-263.
44. The complete title being, "Reglas y *Ordenanzas* para el Gobierno de los Hospitales de Santa Fé de México y Michoacán, Dispuestas por su Fundador el Rmo. y Venerable Sr. Don Vasco de Quiroga, Primer Obispo de Michoacán," (Serrano Gassent, p. 265). These three fundamental documents, the *Rules and Regulations*, the *Testament*, and *Legal Matters*, my proposed translation for *Información en Derecho*, are included in the recent edition entitled *La Utopía en América*, edited by Paz Serrano Gassent (Madrid: Historia 16, Crónicas de América-num. 73, 1992). All quotes to these three documents refer to this edition unless otherwise indicated.
45. My edition has been, *Libro Anual 1974-Segunda Parte* (México: Instituto Superior de Estudios Eclesiásticos Eclesiásticos, 1975): pp. 183-200.

46. My edition has been the beautiful bilingual facsimile version, *The New Laws of the Indies for the Good Treatment and Preservation of the Indians, promulgated by the Emperor Charles V*, originally by the late Henry Stevens of Vermont and Fred W. Lucas, London, Priv. print at the Chiswick Press, 1893 (New York: AMS Press, 1971).

47. I have used the version included in the complete edition, *Cartas y Documentos*, edited by Mario Hernández Sánchez Barba (México: Porrúa, 1963).

48. Greenblatt comments on the "astonishingly short" utopian workday of six hours by the standards set in Tudor statutes, and I quote, "The Henrician Acte concernyng Artificers & Labourers" specifies labor daybreak to night from mid-September to mid-March; before 5:00 a.m. to between 7:00 and 8:00 p.m. from mid-March to mid-September (Hexter and Surtz in Greenblatt), ibidem, p. 40, and footnote 45 on p. 264. For the nightmare of working conditions in the United Kingdom three centuries later, see *The Marx Engels Reader* (New York: W.W. Norton, 1978): pp. 361-390.

49. My two main sources have been, *Cedulario de Puga* (Original Edition by Pedro Ocharte, 1563, reprinted by México, José María Sandoval, Impresor, 2 vols. 1878), and *Colección de Documentos para la Historia de la Formación Social de Hispanoamérica 1493-1810. Volumen 1* (1493-1592), by Richard Konetzke (Madrid: Consejo Superior de Investigaciones Científicas, 1953).

50. A quote such as the following, "There one is constrained to a felicity of geometric idylls, of adjusted ecstasies, of a thousand disgusting wonders necessarily offered by the spectacle of a perfect world, a fabricated world," misses the historicity of construction of utopianism. Cioran, ibidem, p. 82-83.

51. Pablo Beaumont speaks of the universal imposition of this normative uniformity in all hospitals as a necessity for survival (Crónica de Michoacán, III), pp. 148, 158-159 and 162.

52. This glorious line trying to circumscribe the utopian impulse is included in Fredric Jameson's important *The Seeds of Time* (New York: Columbia University Press, 1994): p. 91.

53. More's harsh ideal of panoptic visibility is also articulated in the life-long choice of a mate. Within the clause that stipulates the vision of the naked body of the bride-to-be so that the vigor and youth may be ascertained, the marriage-structuring of the social body admits no exceptions. Strictly restrained from promiscuous intercourse, clandestine premarital intercourse is severely punished and the household suffers public disgrace. Utopians are said to be "the only people in the world who practice monogamy." Divorce, although a laborious legal process, is nonetheless allowed with the Senate approval. Violators of the marriage bond are punished with the strictest form of social degradation or slavery (see Logan's edition, p. 189-193). In Tommaso Campanella (1568-1639), a determined disentangling of the couple arrangement mostly attending to the fecundity of the woman is at work in *The City of the Sun* (1623). Intricate copulation arrangements follow apocalyptic

numerological patterns, astronomical observation, etc. Like Quiroga, Campanella's vision of a different and ideal society is largely within the universal messianism of absolutist Monarchy. Despite much turncoat and contradiction, the Calabria-born Campanella did not hesitate to propose the universal ideal of the Spanish Monarchy. See *A Discourse Touching the Spanish Monarchy* (London: printed for Philemon Stephens, English translation of 1654). In this, see chapter nine, for the ideal copulation ritual of the King and Queen. See chapter fifteen "Of the Soldiery," for a copulation arrangement of national allegories. See also *La Monarchia del Messia* (Edizioni di storia e letteratura, 1995). These themes also emerge in Campanella's poetry. See the anthologic collection, *Poesie* (Guerini e Associati, n/d). See also Anthony Pagden in *Spanish Imperialism and the Political Imagination* (New Haven: Yale University Press, 1990).

54. In the *Cedulario de Puga*, the *Laws of Burgos*, as in Cortés's *ordenanzas*, specifically mention that the civilizational imposition of the couple arrangement was to be enforced. One may wonder about the state usufruct in such imposition.

55. These "female duties" ("oficios mujeriles") could be related to the native social organization of the *guatapera*, a "woman's community house [where] young girls were educated and trained there in the crafts essential for marriage. They were also instructed in the performance of various services for the female priests. The term *guatapera* came to be used for the many hospitals which were found in the region by don Vasco." Which may well lead us to suggest if only tentatively a relative symbiosis of native social forms within Quiroga's repressive culture. See, *Collision of Utopias: Vasco de Quiroga's Mission to the Purépecha-Chichimec of Michoacán, México, 1537-1565* by Bernardino Verástique (Harvard University: PhD Dissertation, 1990): p. 214ff.

56. We must no doubt see this construction of sameness, or synchronism, as an imposition inside the communitarian precincts yet also one view among others in competition. We may bring to memory Gruzinski's rich account of the colonial semiosis and slow deterioration of indigenous time cycles, ritualistic in a non-Christian way, yet receiving the impact of Christianity proper, the work cycles affected by colonial labor impositions, the calendar cycles for the Michoacán region with ritualized cycles for fasting and sexual abstinence, nocturnal and diurnal cycles, the changes pertaining to eating habits and clothing, the restriction of the social differentiation as pertains to cannibalism, the communal work cycles, even the ritualized confluence to conflict and war destructured by the official colonial periodicity of the collection of tribute, etc., in *The Conquest of Mexico* (Cambridge: Polity Press, 1993): pp. 88-97.

57. For greater detail into this, see Halpern, ibidem, p. 160.

58. There is also a big difference in dimension, scope and numbers. Ruiz de Montoya in his *Spiritual Conquest* (1639) will speak of 60,000 missionized peoples made prisoners by the intense *bandeirante* activity or the rapacity of

slave-holders. See the important document by Montoya, edited in English by The Institute of Jesuit Sources (St. Louis, 1993). Alberto Armani's comprehensive text for some global periodization, useful chronology and tentative numbers, *Ciudad de Dios y Ciudad del Sol: El "Estado" Jesuita de los Guaraníes (1609-1768,* México: Fondo de Cultura Económica, 1987).

59. See more of the needs of this inevitably bureaucratic world and the need for an archive, in "Las Tierras Comunales Indígenas de la Nueva España en el siglo XVI," by Delfina E. López Sarrelangue, in *Estudios de Historia Novohispana* (México 1966, Vol. 1): pp. 131-148. Any indigenous communitarianism must have passed no doubt through the diligent application to this legalistic paperwork.

60. For a determined repudiation of the "grotesque en rose" of the naiveté and the inanity in the conception of a different society, see the contemporary reading by Cioran in *History and Utopia* (New York: Seaver Books, 1987), particularly chapter four, "Mechanism of Utopia." The early modern desirability of social sameness and synchronicity finds in Cioran a fierce pronouncement on the unreadability of the utopian genre as constructed upon the fearfully and disgusting geometric adjustments of automatons devoid of any psychological instinct. A valid contemporary Hungarian parallel to O'Gorman's critical reading of the Western knowledge production of an outside Utopia, Cioran also proclaims the West "theoreticians of the duty it [the West] evades."

61. In the Utopian neutralization of market value, or value reversal, "[t]hey are amazed at the madness of any man who considers himself a nobler fellow because he wears clothing of specially fine wool. No matter how fine the thread, they say, a sheep wore it once, and still was nothing but a sheep;" "[a]s far as a garment's usefulness goes, why is fine woollen thread better than coarse?" and "[t]hey like linen cloth to be white and woold cloth to be clean; but they do not value fineness of texture" (*Thomas More's Utopia*, Edited by Logan, Adams and Miller, Cambridge: at the University Press, 1995, pp. 133, 155, and 167).

62. James Harrington's great dictum in *Oceana* (1656), has it that "[the] structuring of the commonwealth [based] upon the natural principle of the same which is justice," is paradoxically divorced from "the manners that are rooted in men [and which] bow the tenderness of a commonwealth coming up by twigs unto their bent." My edition, *The Commonwealth of Oceana and A System of Politics*, edited by J. G. A. Pocock (Cambridge: University Press, 1992), pp. 62 and 67.

63. In relation to these structural interpenetrations between colonial conditions of imposition (or forced labor) and incipient predations of money economy against the larger background of barter economy, see Branislava Susnik for rich explanations of the standard practice of cloth-payment and the official prohibition of payment in the form of wine, honey, chicha or coca. In the specificity of the remote Amazon context of today's Paraguay, Susnik convincingly describes the regulated length of the cloth-payment ("pago en

lienzo") and the standard abuses that took place, in *El Indio Colonial del Paraguay. Los trece Pueblos Guaranies de las Misiones (1767-1803)* (Asunción: Museo Etnográfico "Andrés Barbero," 2 Volumes, 1965): pp. 43-44, 150-152.

64. At the end of the *Testament* in 1226, St. Francis writes: "In virtue of obedience, I strictly forbid any of my friars, clerics or lay brothers, to interpret the Rule or these words, saying "This is what they mean." God inspired me to write the Rule and these words plainly and simply, and so you too must understand them plainly and simply, and live by them, doing good to the last" (*English Omnibus*, ibidem, p. 69).

65. Michel De Certeau has suggested, "the "literal" pretext for a law that legitimizes as "literal" the interpretation given by socially authorized professionals and intellectuals (*clercs* or *letrados*),"see *The Practice of Everyday Life* (Berkeley: University of California Press, 1984): pp. 170-174.

66. For a brief account of the four levels of interpretation, see the *Rule of St. Benedict* (The 1980 Liturgical Edition): pp. 473-476. One must resist the temptation that would take us too far away from our topic. Yet I would like to include the medieval saying: "Littera gesta docet, quid credas allegoria, moralis quid agas, quo tendas anagogia," in the illustration of the simultaneity of vision in the literal or the raw data or fact, the allegorical or grid of Christological intelligibility, the tropological or moral or anthropological meaning giving meaning to the doing, and the anagogical or the teleology, the whys and wherefores of the doing. For some contemporary possibilities of appropriation of this interpretive wealth, see Fredric Jameson in *The Political Unconscious. Narrative as a Socially Symbolic Act* (Ithaca: Cornell University Press, 1981): pp. 28-36.

67. Who can ever forget the splendid vistas into the timely, efficient and clean dining halls in More's islands? Enough food to satisfy anybody's hunger, earthenware dishes, glass cups, finely made but inexpensive, most special attention to the elders, intellectual readings by an appointed Utopian citizen, "no evening meal without music, no dessert course is ever scanted, they burn incense and scatter perfume, omitting nothing which will cheer up the diners." Not an isolated activity, utopian eating is then a radically centralized and communal activity, rather than beggars' banquet, truly love feast and agape (*Utopia*, Logan edition, pp. 139-143).

68. Enrique Dussel has given us wonderful pages for a philosophy of poverty in times of (colonial) cholera and some possibilities and expectations of the *pauper ante festum*, originally a Marxist expression. See his proposals for a Philosophy of Liberation at the table of the great European philosophers in *The Underside of Modernity: Apel, Ricoeur, Rorty, Taylor and the Philosophy of Liberation* (New Jersey: Humanities Press, 1996): pp. 88-93.

69. What follows is a good example of the scholarly fall into this temptation. In the inmediate context of the *indigenista* novel, Cornejo Polar has left us with delicate pages about the technique of allegorization of nature, which he

translates as "exacerbation of mimesis" or the transformation of "the likely and believable into the truthful" or the refusal to accept a cancellation of a(ny) past and the desire to trascend, if only textually, the history-as-usual or literal meaning of unresolved social tensions. See his latest *Escribir en el Aire. Ensayo sobre la Heterogeneidad Socio-Cultural en las Literaturas Andinas* (Lima: Editorial Horizonte, 1994): pp. 198, 205.

70. See these documents in *Documentos Inéditos Referentes al Ilustrísimo Señor Don Vasco de Quiroga Existentes en el Archivo General de Indias,* recopilados por Nicolás León (México: Porrúa, 1940): pp. 1-7.

71. *Crónica de Michoacán,* vol. III, ibidem, p. 127.

72. In *Documentos Inéditos del Siglo XVI para la Historia de México,* edited by Mariano Cuevas (México: Porrúa, 1975): pp. 76-77.

73. "His consecration took place at sometime between November 26, 1538 and January 14, 1539, as is indicated in the acts of the ecclesiastical cabildo of Mexico. On the earlier date he is referred to as bishop-elect; on the latter, as bishop. The general consensus of authors indicates that he was consecrated during December 1538, although the document of his consecration has not come to light," in Warren, p. 88.

74. See Warren, pp. 55-60.

75. Nicolas León, ibidem, 40-84.

76. Beaumont, *Crónica de Michoacán,* Tomo III, Chapters XVII and XIX, pp. 95-140 and Chapter XXIV, pp. 211-253. In the first lawsuit, and despite Quiroga's nomination as bishop in 1537, Beaumont comments that he managed to claim a previous usurpation of two previous years of his rights (p.127).

77. *Don Fray Juan de Zumárraga. Primer Obispo y Arzobispo de México* (México: Porrúa, 1947): pp. 175-188.

78. *Crónica de Michoacán,* vol. 3, pp. 266-286.

79. Tena Ramírez includes a summary of these 16 years of legal in-fighting between Quiroga and various others, ibidem, pp. 41-46. These data are all taken from Warren's biography, see this evidence on page 73, but also the panoramic legal battlefield in chapters five, "Difficulties of Santa Fe de Mexico," and chapter six, "Michoacan and the Founding of Santa Fe de la Laguna."

80. Tena Ramírez, ibidem, pp. 117-124.

81. Beaumont asserts the following in relation to the lawsuit, Quiroga vs. the influential *encomendero* Juan Infante: "No sólo el señor Quiroga (*en su viaje a la Corte, donde residió algunos años*) atendió a contener las pretensiones injustas del poderoso encomendero Juan Infante...sino que tambión quiso mirar por la conservación y bienestar del pueblo y hospital de Santa Fe de la Laguna, de que era patrono y fundador, como asimismo del de Santa Fe... *trayéndoles nuevos privilegios de vuelta de España, a más de los que antes había conseguido.* Luego que estos hospitales estuvieron acabados (que fue antes del año de 1535), *alcanzó su fundador un privilegio de su Majestad, de inmunidad de tributos a favor de los natruales de ellos...y en virtud de este*

privilegio dejaron de pagar el real tributo por tiempo inmemorial" (my emphasis). Lack of documentation is explained by Beaumont in relation to a fire which destroyed the Cathedral of Michoacán in 1688 (Beaumont, p. 286, also on p. 289). We may advance the connection between the bishopric status ("la mitra"), and the seemingly achieved objetives of exemption from tribute and municipal independence.

82. The original article which makes a close-reading comparison of the transatlantic connection between More and Quiroga is "La Utopía de Tomás Moro en la Nueva España y Otros Estudios," (México: Antigua Librería Robredo, de José Porrúa e Hijos, Biblioteca Histórica Mexicana de Obras Inéditas, num. 4, 1937). These findings were later reprinted, without a fundamental change in perspective or approach to Quiroga's experimentation in the more recent *Recuerdo de Vasco de Quiroga* (México: Editorial Porrúa, 1965) and *La Utopía Mexicana del Siglo XVI: Lo bello, lo verdadero y lo bueno* (Italy: Grupo Azabache, 1992).

83. I quote from Warren: "In the bull of [Quiroga's] nomination to the bishopric of Michoacán he was designated as a licenciate in sacred theology but, with a lawyer's scrupulosity for exactness in official documents, he asked the Holy See that this error be corrected, since his licenciate was in canon law. The correction was made in an apostolic brief, 'Exponis nobis,' of July 8, 1550," in *Vasco de Quiroga and His Pueblo-Hospitals of Santa Fe*, ibidem, p. 11.

84. Tena Ramírez includes the 1767 rewritings of Quiroga's original document here discussed. Of a much reduced and tasteless quality, these latest *ordenanzas* visibly illustrate the debilitation and final demise of Quiroga's enterprise, pp. 206-212.

85. Future endeavors will have to take us to *Archivo de Indias* (Seville), where literally thousands of pages of unpublished courtooom litigation regarding Vasco de Quiroga still await a patient, critical investigation. There is fortunately a detailed catalogue assembled by Armando M. Escobar Olmedo for this solitary navigation, *Catálogo de Documentos Michoacanos en Archivos Españoles* (Universidad Michoacana de San Nicolás de Hidalgo, 1990).

86. *Recuerdo de Vasco de Quiroga*, p. 7.

87. In Beaumont, "[el señor don Vasco] fundó en Pátzcuaro un colegio de niños españoles," and "un colegio donde los hijos de los españoles legítimos e mestizos, y algunos indios, por ser lenguas, para que puedan mejor aprovechar con ellos, deprenden gramática, e juntamente con ellos, los indios hablar nuestra lengua castellana, cosa muy util e necesaria," ibidem, p. 290 and 292.

88. It is also true, however, that the work that these populations had to do for the project of Vasco de Quiroga was a constant source of litigation and investigation by the authorities. There were constant claims on the abusive nature of the work demanded by Quiroga on his citizens, for example in the construction of the monumental Cathedral of St. Salvador. Quiroga was exonerated of these charges in relation to the secretive investigation, already mentioned, conducted

by the *oidor* Francisco Loaysa. See also the "quejas de los indios de tzintzuntzan contra el Señor Quiroga (1555)," "Quejas de los vecinos de Guayangareo contra el Señor Quiroga (1567)" and "Los vecinos de Guayangareo (1567)," Nicolás León, *Documentos Inéditos*, ibidem, pp. 35-85.

89. Except for Beaumont's exceedingly generous number of twenty hospitals associated to Vasco de Quiroga, Tena Ramírez is alone in the defense of three hospitals, instead of the standard two. We do not find Tena Ramírez's explanations convincing, see ibidem, pp. 22-24 and 131-160.

90. Warren's account has given us some information about it: "Financially the pueblos seem to have had considerable success, especially Santa Fé de Mexico. The 3,000-4,000 *pesos* which this pueblo was grossing annually at the time of Quiroga's death was undoubtedly the major reason why the City of Mexico kept casting greedy glances in its direction. We have very little information about the financial success of Santa Fé de la Laguna, although from the words of Bishop Medina, we can judge that it was paying its own way and fulfilling its obligations" (p. 118).

91. For the careful historical exegesis of the notion of "miserable," see Carlos Sempat Assadourian in "Fray Bartolomé de las Casas obispo: La naturaleza miserable de las naciones indianas y el derecho de la Iglesia. Un escrito de 1545," *HM* (Vol. XL, Enero-Marzo, 1991, Núm. 3): pp. 387-451.

92. However, this anonymity may be partially reconstructed thanks to Beaumont's narrative: 1) After Quiroga's death, Don Pedro de Yepes, treasurer of the church of Valladolid, Michoacán, presents cédula ratification of the municipal independence granted to the Cabildo de Michoacán in 1565 (p. 290); 2) In the lawsuit against the Bishop of New Galicia, don Pedro Gómez Maraver, Juan de Uribe, "in the name of the Bishop of Michoacán," asks for the execution of a state prerogative in 1552 (p. 250); 3) before Quiroga's s death and in relation to the big lawsuit between our Bishop of Michoacán and Zumarraga, the Bishop of Mexico City, Pedro de Yepes, and Alvaro Gutierrez, "canónigo" and "mayordomo" respectively of the Cathedral of Michoacán, "en nombre y con poder de don Vasco de Quiroga, primer obispo de la Catedral de Michoacán," present a petition against the still rebellious *chichimeca* community in the *hacienda* of Guaanajuato, which then belonged to Rodrigo Vázquez, to the judge Antonio de Godoy appointed to the "white chichimecas" (literally, "los chichimecas blancos," p. 131).

93. Verástique Bernardino, *Collision of Utopias*, ibidem, writes the following: "Pérez Gordillo emerges in this period as Quiroga's war captain in the feuds with the regular orders.... During Quiroga's long stay in Spain between the years of 1547 to 1554, Pérez Gordillo who received full orders of the priesthood from Don Vasco in the early 1540s, increasingly became Quiroga's powerbroker in Michoacán (pp. 171-172).

94. The important document for the immediate post-Quiroga years is "Noticias para la Historia del Antiguo Colegio de San Nicolás de Michoacán" in *Boletín del Archivo General de la Nación* (Num. 1, Tomo X, México 1939): pp. 24-

106. This document, written by an anonymous Jesuit during the XVII century, contains detailed socioeconomic evidence of the incipient wealth of the Jesuit patrimony, of which the Colegio de San Nicolás became one asset. The document is indeed also very eloquent about the early status of regional reverence regarding Vasco de Quiroga, the official complications of an almost state burial, and the regional conflict regarding the final settlement of the Cathedral, and of Quiroga's remains, between Valladolid and Pátzcuaro. The travelling of this illustrious dead finished very recently, Kripper-Martínez details the latest change in 1990 of Quiroga's remains to a mausoleum located in the modern Basílica de Nuestra Señora de la Salud, Pátzcuaro, and the official ceremonies surrounding the event, in "Discourse of Domination. Discourse of Hope: The Contradictory Vision of Don Vasco de Quiroga," (*Images of Conquest: Text and Context in Colonial Mexico*, diss. University of Wisconsin-Madison, 1993): pp. 130-232.

95. "La Compañía de Jesús y la Evangelización de América y Filipinas en los Archivos de la Orden," by Francisco de Borja Medina, S.J., pp. 31-61 (photocopied article, incomplete reference, n/d).

96. In the document "Noticias para la Historia del Antiguo Colegio de San Nicolás de Michoacán," it is also mentioned that the Jesuits who took over after Quiroga's decease enjoyed, by official dictum of Viceroy Manrique de Zúñiga, the benefit of indigenous personal service, in what appears to have been a standard colonial practice (pp. 93-94).

Chapter III

1. The equation, law as repression, is directly taken from Jesús Lalinde-Abadía, whose abundant scholarship on the historicity of legal scholarship and politics, historiography and Hispanism has been a constant source of inspiration for this work. His most encompassing single work is *Las Culturas Represivas de la Humanidad* (h. 1945) (Zaragoza: Universidad de Zaragoza, 1992). There is a very useful and synthetic essay, "Depuración Histórica del Concepto de Estado," included in the anthology *El Estado Español en su Dimensión Histórica* (Barcelona: PPU, 1984): pp. 17-58. Most of his numerous articles have been published by *Anuario de Historia del Derecho Español*.

2. I have in mind Ortega y Gasset's notion of "creencia" (belief). One is ("está") in the collectivity of the historical belief, which is humanly pliable and changing and also necessarily always interpenetrated by doubts. See the "Ideas y Creencias (1940)," included in *Obras Completas. Tomo V* (1933-1941) (Madrid: Revista de Occidente, 1947): pp. 375-405.

3. See Hernán Vidal's warnings in *Socio-Historia de la Literatura Colonial Hispanoamericana: Tres Lecturas Orgánicas* (Minneapolis: Institute for the Study of Ideologies and Literature, 1985, 1985): pp. 18-43.

4. I feel I need to intervene into the excessive visibility of Todorov's *Conquest of America: The Question of the Other* (New York: Harper & Row, 1982). I am

260   *Good Places and Non-Places in Colonial Mexico*

taking into account Jameson's critique of typologies, included in "Figural Relativism; or, The Poetics of Historiography," included in *The Ideologies of Theory. Essays 1971-1986. Volume 1: Situations of Theory* (Minneapolis: University of Minnesota Press, 1988, pp. 153-165 [160], and also briefly in *Marxism and Form* (Princeton: Princeton University Press, 1971): pp. 93-94. Although Jameson is not directly concerned with colonial Latin America, this will be the historical and social laboratory to some of these provocative remarks. See also the four scholarly or historiographic possibilities included in the essay "Marxism and Historicism," *The Ideologies of Theory. Essays 1971-1986. Volume 2: Syntax of History* (Minneapolis: University of Minnesota Press, 1988), pp. 148-177.

5.   For example, Jorge Klor de Alva. See the controversial essay (1st version), "Colonialism and Post Colonialism as (Latin) American Mirages," *Colonial Latin American Review* (Vol. 1., Nos. 1-2, 1992): pp. 3-23. See the latest version, "The Postcolonization of the (Latin) American Experience: A Reconsideration of "Colonialism," "Postcolonialism" and "Mestizaje," "included in the volume by Gyan Prakash, *After Colonialism: Imperial Histories and Postcolonial Displacements* (Princeton: Princeton University Press, 1995): pp. 241-275. We must take into account the work on Sahagún: *The Work of Bernardino de Sahagún: Pionner Ethnographer of Sixteenth Century Aztec Mexico* (New York: Univ. of Texas Press, 1988). To give depth to Klor de Alva, see the four essays published in the massive, four-volume work *De Palabra y Obra en el Nuevo Mundo*, edited by Miguel León-Portilla, Manuel Gutiérrez-Estévez, Gary H. Gossen and J.Jorge Klor de Alva (eds.), (Madrid: Siglo XXI, 1992). A nutshell of his controversial thesis (there is no colonization of the Americas), is repeated in one of these essays, "La Disputa sobre un Nuevo Occidente: Política Cultural e Identidades Múltiples en el Fin de Siglo," pp. 508-539 [pp. 516-517].

6.   Besides the dense, almost programatic essay previously quoted, "Colonialidad y Modernidad-Racionalidad," see also the complete *Modernidad, Identidad y Utopía en América Latina* (Quito: El Conejo, 1990). A more accessible selection of this text for an English audience, with some important variations in the translation, is included in *The Postmodernism Debate in Latin America*, A special issue of Boundary 2, edited by John Beverley and José Oviedo (Durham: Duke University Press, 1993).

7.   My references have been, Immanuel Wallerstein's *The Modern World System. Capitalist Agriculture and the Origins of the European World-Economy in the Sixteenth Century. Vol. 1* (New York: Academic Press, 1974); Giovanni Arrighi's *The Long Twentieth Century* (New York: Verso, 1994); and Enrique Dussel's *The Invention of the Americas: Eclipse of "the Other" and the Myth of Modernity* (New York: Continuum, 1995).

8.   Vidal speaks of the conquest as the making of the commercial private capital with relatively little direct involvement by the Crown, and also of the capitalism

of the *capitulaciones*. The colonial world will then be the historical concretization of the farce (the attack of reason and logic), whereby alienated social production by dominated American majorities is tragically out of step with their concrete demands and needs for education, health, shelter, nourishment, etc. The colonial world is thus this painfully real "outside" of the sole imaginary place of the collective satisfaction of need (or historical *fuera de lugar*), ibidem, pp. 21-42.

9. This is my synthetic definition taken from the double critique of A. G Frank's classic work by Ernesto Laclau and Carlos Sempat Assadourian, included in *Modos de Producción en América Latina* (Córdoba, Buenos Aires: Cuadernos de Pasado y Presente, num. 40, 1974): pp. 23-82. Laclau defines the capitalist mode of production as the birth of the free wage labor, and thus the making of labor/merchandise (or "relación asalariada," p. 39), which will coexist historically with other arrangements. Sempat Assadourian emphasizes the crucial consideration of the appropriation of the surplus and introduces the cautious warning about the felicitous formula of the center-periphery which may risk, if not handled tactfully, intellectual obfuscation and the emptying out of all concrete historical content (p. 50-1). We will soon include Steve Stern's suggestions.

10. I hope following pages will give a convincing rendering of what I consider to be Quiroga's reformist or contractual vision of the social polity if only incipient or protocapitalist. I have in mind, Marx's critique on "Wage Labor and Capital"and the *Grundisse* moments about wage labor (*The Marx-Engels Reader*. Edited by Robert C. Tucker (New York: Norton, 1978): pp. 203-217, 254-276. In the explorations of repressive or juridical culture and labor, I also make references to the "Chapter on Money," in *Grundisse: Introduction to the Critique of Political Economy* (London: Penguin Books, 1973): pp. 115-238.

11. This work wishes to join all those efforts against the banality of evil of the euphemism explicit in the "Encounter of Two Worlds" formula. We find O'Gorman's language much more convincing, "apoderamiento" against "encuentro," in the ontological-philosophical reduction of American reality inside the historically hegemonic belief-system of European modernity (O'Gorman explicitly mentions Ortega y Gasset). See this combative hermeneutic discrimination against León-Portilla, in the "Encuentro de Dos Mundos o lo Superfluo" by O'Gorman, CA (Año 1, Vol. 2, Marzo-Abril (2), 1987): pp. 192-213. One must take into account the lengthier development of these objections in *La Idea del Descubrimiento de América. Historia de esa Interpretación y Crítica de sus Fundamentos* (México: Centro de Estudios Filosóficos, 1951). For a panoramic view of who's who in Mexican historiography, see the volume edited by E. Florescano and R. Pérez-Monfort, *Historiadores de México en el Siglo XX* (México: Fondo de Cultura Económica, 1995).

12. "¿Proto-Industria Colonial?" by M. Miño Grijalva, *HM* (Vol. XXXVIII, Abril-Junio, 1989, Núm. 4): pp. 793-818, and "La Despoblación Indígena en Perú y Nueva España Durante el Siglo XVI y la Formación de la Economía Colonial," in *HM* (Vol. XXXVIII, Enero-Marzo, 1989, Núm. 3, 151): pp. 419-453. Grijalva speaks of proto-industrial enclaves in rural locations near commercial centers, and he is careful to highlight that proto-industrial situations do not necessarily lead to industrialism. There is a book length elaboration, *La Protoindustria Colonial Hispanoamericana* (México, Fondo de Cultura Económica, 1993). In sharp contrast, Vidal ascertains "the mechanism of appropriation of wealth...in the strict prohibition of artisan manufactures in the Americas" (ibidem, p. 23).

13. Sempat Assadourian speaks of the quite shameless application of an intensified colonial criterion of economic profitability as regards the American possessions by Philip II, see "La despoblación indígena en Perú y Nueva España durant el siglo XVI y la formación de la economía colonial," in *HM* (Vol. XXXVIII, Enero-Marzo 1989, Núm. 3, 151): pp. 419-453.

14. R. Adorno has convincingly developed in direct relation to the specific early modern colonial condition the notion of "paradigmatic loss" ("Paradigmas Perdidos: Guamán Poma examina la Sociedad Española Colonial, " *Revista Chungará*, num. 13, Nov. 1984, 67-91, Universidad de Tarapacá, Arica-Chile), and W. Mignolo, the notion of "colonial semiosis" in *The Darker Side of the Renaissance*, ibidem (pp. 7-9, 20, 29, 332-334). We wish to juxtapose to this primordial consideration of "sign," the messy or chaotic historical condition of labor in the periphery, and thus take into account Steve J. Stern's article "Feudalism, Capitalism and the World-System in the Pespective of Latin America and the Caribbean," *American Historical Review* (vol. 93-N. 4, oct. 1988): pp. 829-872. We will get back to Stern's suggestions, and his important disagreement with Wallerstein, once we describe Quiroga's concrete plans for the reformation of coloniality.

15. It is approximately the breaking point in Braudel's long sixteenth century (1450-1650). We have, always according to Arrighi, the mutation or the supreme agility of the decision-making centers of high finance in seizing the historical day of Spanish expansionism, the strengths of cosmopolitan networks of accumulation working with the strongest available network of power, the Habsburg/Pope alliance to save what could be saved of the disintegration of the medieval system of rule, which could not quite hold expansionism together, etc. (Arrighi, pp. 40-47, 109-158).

16. The highest increase of Genoese in Seville (1503-1530), between 1530-1539, the largest part of the peninsula comes under Spanish domination during this time frame (Wallerstein, ibidem pp. 173, 176).

17. Wallerstein, ibidem, p. 201.

18. Manuel Miño Grijalva, ibidem, has also spoken of the 1530-1570 period, Quiroga's chronology in New Spain, as a transitional period, the most dynamic and extensive of the proto-industrial manufacture. Sempat Assadourian, ibidem,

has also spoken beautifully of the money-novelty as catalyst for some pockets of proto-industrial or comercial exchange, but only in the first moment detached from a rigid cause-effect connectedness to demographic collapse, and always immersed in economic maximization of economic profit and a long-term *diezmo*-tax increase affecting several Mexican regions, among these Michoacán (pp. 431, 438).

19. *The Protestant Ethic and the Spirit of Capitalism*, translated by Talcott Parsons, with a foreword by R. H. Tawney (New York: Scribner, 1958).

20. See *Semiperipheral Development: The Politics of Southern Europe in the Twentieth Century*, edited by Giovanni Arrighi (London: Sage Publications, 1985).

21. See Fredric Jameson on Arrighi in "Culture and Finance Capital," *Critical Inquiry* (Autumn 1997, Vol. 24, Num. 1): pp. 246-265.

22. To illustrate this standard forgetfulness, see the work by Richard Tuck: a) the essay "The 'modern' [*sic*] theory of natural law," included in Anthony Pagden's volume *The Languages of Political Theory in Early Modern Europe* (Cambridge: Cambridge University Press, 1979), and b) his lengthier elaboration in *Natural Rights Theories: Their Origin and Development* (Cambridge: Cambridge University Press, 1979). The poet was right: "*Castilla miserable desprecia cuanto ignora.*"

23. The inevitable reference for this insinuation of the suspension of the hegemonic European periodizations for world history is again Enrique Dussel. These are perhaps the two most accessible recent translations of his work: *The Invention of the Americas: Eclipse of the "Other" and the Myth of Modernity* (New York: Continuum, 1995); and the *The Underside of Modernity: Apel, Ricoeur, Rorty, Taylor and the Philosophy of Liberation* (New Jersey: Humanities Press, 1996).

24. At the narrow disciplinary level of Renaissance or early modern studies, this questioning has already been taking place, see Stephen Greenblatt's *Redrawing the Boundaries* (New York: The Modern Language Association of America, 1992). Another more ambitious and penetrating intervention followed, Fredric Jameson's "On 'Cultural Studies'" (*Social Text* 34 (1993): 17-52.

25. *La Ciudad Letrada* (Hanover: Ediciones del Norte, 1984). For a recent evaluation of Rama's work, see *Angel Rama y los Estudios Latinoamericanos*, Mabel Moraña, Ed. (Pittsburgh: Serie Críticas, 1997).

26. Wallerstein, ibidem, p. 180.

27. Arrighi, ibidem, p. 156.

28. "In the end, the total loss of the Fuggers in unpaid debts of the Hapsburgo the middle of the seventeenth century" is certainly not put too high at 8 million Rhenish gulden" (p. 174), in Wallerstein, ibidem, pp. 173-181. The inevitable reference on this alliance is of course ón Carande's monumental work, *Carlos V y sus Banqueros. La Vida Económica en Castilla (1516-1556)* (Madrid: Sociedad de Estudios y Publicaciones, 2a edición, 1965).

29. The official whereabouts of the Emperor have been recorded by the "enemy" of Bernal Díaz del Castillo, López de Gómara. I have consulted the bilingual edition, *Annals of the Emperor Charles V*, carefully translated and edited by Roger Bigelow Merriman (Oxford: the Clarendon Press, 1912).

30. It is impossible here not to remember Ortega y Gasset's beautiful pages after Charles V's grand retirement, surrounded by clocks and the inventions of the Flemish Juanelo Turriano, "true magician," in "Ensimismamiento y Alteración" (1939), *Obras Completas*, ibidem, pp. 367-371.

31. The Crowns of Spain and Portugal were united for 1580-1640, datum included in J. I. Israel's *Race, Class and Politics in Colonial Mexico, 1610-1670* (Oxford: Oxford University Press, 1975): p. 67.

32. Arrighi, ibidem, p. 126.

33. Wallerstein, ibidem, pp. 183-5.

34. This is taken from the excellent critical edition of Las Casas's *De Regia Potestate o Derecho de Autodeterminación*, by Pérez-Prendes, et al. (Madrid: Consejo Superior de Investigaciones Científicas, 1969): pp. xxi-civii [lxxii].

35. It's been said, "In the process [of wider reduction of economic and political power that affected all of Castile in the seventeenth century, the winners were peripheral areas near the coast, the aristocracy and especially the office-holding families in command of Castile's cities...the losers were the center of the peninsula, the old mercantile cities of Castile and especially the monarchy," Richard Kagan's *Lawsuits and Litigants in Castile (1500-1700)* (Chapel Hill: The University of North Carolina Press, 1981): pp. 235.

36. Weber's insights are useful but anachronistic. The bureaucratic state is, if not created, intensified under modernity or capitalism, and this is already happening in the first half of the sixteenth century in relation to American bureaucracies, inside which Quiroga is to be situated. See Max Weber's *Essays in Sociology*, trans. and ed. H. H. Gerth and C. Wright Mills (London, 1967): pp. 159-266.

37. F. Tomás y Valiente has given us excellent accounts in *Gobierno e Instituciones en la España del Antiguo Regimen* (Madrid: Alianza Editorial, 1982); *La Venta de Oficios en Indias (1492-1606)* (Madrid: Instituto de Estudios Administrativos, 1972), and on the institutionalization of political absentism in *Los Validos en la Monarquía Española del Siglo XVII* (Madrid: Siglo XXI, 1990).

38. Lalinde-Abadía has written persuasively about some of these historical struggles. We may suggest for the authoritarian character of Spanish law-making and the struggles between nuclear and peripheral tendencies, "La Creación del Derecho entre los Españoles" (*AHDE*, Tomo XXXVI, 1966): pp. 301-378; for some names and faces in these struggles, "Notas sobre el Papel de las Fuerzas Políticas y Sociales en el Desarrollo de los Sistemas Iushistóricos Españoles," (*AHDE*, Tomo XLVIII, 1978): pp. 249-268; & for the historicist (or situationist?) emphasis against German legal historiography, "Historia del Derecho Frente a Filosofía del Derecho (Contrarréplica

extemporánea a Hans Kelsen)," (*AHDE*, Tomo LXV, 1995): pp. 1023-1035. Sempat Assadourian has spoken of the cunning ("sigilo") of Philip II and the magnificent ambiguity ("excelsa ambiguedad") of legal interpretation, bypassing all explicit contradictions, in a political pursuit of intensified rotatory compulsive labor and maximum economic benefits (ibidem, pp. 426-7, 433-5).

39. Raup Wagner, ibidem, pp. 121-194.

40. Antonio F. García-Abasolo's *Martín Enriquez y la Reforma de 1568 en Nueva España* (Sevilla: Diputación Provincial de Sevilla, 1983).

41. Miguel de León-Portilla, *La Flecha en el Blanco* (Mexico: Diana, 1995).

42. Raup Wagner attributes to Las Casas the main inspiration for the gestation of the New Laws, ibidem, pp. 108-120; the revocation of the Law of Inheritance included in these laws is dated Oct. 20, 1545 [p. 157]. R. Adorno's comments that "[they were] promulgated in 1542, never enforced in Mexico and rescinded three years later," included in "History, Law and the Eyewitness Protocols of Authority in Bernal Dóaz del Castillo's *Historia Verdadera de la Conquista de la Nueva España*," in *The Project of Prose in Early Modern Europe and the New World* (New York: Cambridge University Press, 1997): pp. 154-175 [169].

43. Data from Charles Gibson, *The Aztecs under Spanish Rule* (Stanford: Stanford University Press, 1964): pp. 62-63, 84-5.

44. See the excellent critical volume by Ernesto De la Torre Villar, *Las Congregaciones de los Pueblos de Indios. Fase Terminal: Aprobaciones y Rectificaciones* (México: Universidad nacional Autónoma de México, 1995).

45. It is indeed not easy to try to come to terms with the historical first-generation intensity of this impact. The work by Barbara E. Mundy may help, *The Mapping of New Spain: Indigenous Cartography and the Maps of the Relaciones Geográficas* (Chicago: The University of Chicago Press, 1996). Putting institutional demands side by side "indigenous" meaning-making practices may add some more intensity, see the classic anthology by Donald Robertson, *Mexican Manuscript Painting of the Early Colonial Period. The Metropolitan Schools* (Norman and London: University of Oklahoma Press, [1959], new edition of 1994).

46. Against Wallerstein's reductive tripartite division of labor, Stern proposes a more complicated, or "heterogeneous" labor pattern for colonial Latin America: "approximations of wage labor, complicated tenancy, share and debt-credit, forced labor rafts and slavery into a single productive process" (p. 870). See the tense exchange between Steve J. Stern and Immanuel Wallerstein apropos Stern's "Feudalism, Capitalism, and the World-System in the Perspective of Latin America and the Caribbean," *American Historical Review* (vol. 93, No. 4, oct. 1988): pp. 829-897.

47. This collaboration appears to have been particularly intense in the case of the Michoacán region and the Tarascan or Purépecha communities oppossing the Aztec domination and allies with the Spaniards since the very beginning of the

Spanish colonization. See the work by López-Sarrelangue, *La Nobleza Indígena de Pátzcuaro en la Epoca Virreinal* (México: Universidad Nacional Autónoma de México, Instituto de Investigaciones Históricas, 1965) for a detailed elaboration of the social and political privileges granted to the indigenous nobility engaged in bureaucratic work in the sixteenth century Michoacán area (mostly, chapters five and six, pp. 81-148). See also Díaz Rementería, *El Cacique en el Virreinato del Perú. Estudio Histórico-Jurídico* (Sevilla: Universidad de Sevilla, 1977).

48. An excellent reference to enforce a salutary estrangement regarding alphabetization and "books" in colonial situations, is of course the already quoted work by Walter Mignolo, *The Darker Side of the Renaissance*, but also his collaboration with Elizabeth Hill Boone, *Writing Without Words: Alternative Literacies in Mesoamerica and the Andes* (Durham: Duke University Press, 1994).

49. The classic case is Cortés's soldier, Bernal Díaz del Castillo (1495-1584). For the largely mono-lingual protocols of the repressive culture as pertain to the exercise of arms and letters, see Adorno in "The Discursive Encounter of Spain and America: the Authority of Eyewitness Testimony in the Writing of History," *The William and Mary Quarterly* (Vol. XLIX, No. 2, April 1992): pp. 210-228; and "Discourses on Colonialism: Bernal Díaz, Las Casas, and the Twentieth Century Reader," *MLN* (Vol. 103, No. 2, March 1988): pp. 239-258. The always slippery notion of "colonial writing" in the Spanish language is undoubtedly predominantly within the horizon of the politics of the notary public, see the excellent edition of *La Política de Escrituras de Nicolás de Yrolo Calar* (1605), Ma. del Pilar Martínez López-Cano, Editor (México: Universidad Nacional Autónoma de México, 1996).

50. Kagan has given us concrete and detailed accounts , inside this monumental and labyrinthine bureaucratic maze, of the most frequent social extraction and attitudes, the clothes, the wages (330,000 *maravedíes*), and some telling historical specificities of the *oidor*es in the period, in *Lawsuits and Litigants*, ibidem, pp. 103, 119, 135, 176, 182, 189, 192, 217.

51. An excellent account of this exchange and the scholarly edition of these two treatises by Matías de Paz and López de Palacios Rubios is provided by Silvio Zavala and Agustín Millares Carlo, *De las Islas del Mar Océano & Del Dominio de los Reyes de España sobre los Indios* (México: Fondo de Cultura Económica, 1954).

52. To contextualize political ideologies in the sixteenth century, the presence of J. A. Maravall is still inevitable. See, *Carlos V y el Pensamiento Político del Renacimiento* (Madrid: Instituto de Estudios Políticos, 1960), *La Oposición Política bajo los Austrias* (Barcelona: Ariel, 1972), *Utopía Y Reformismo en la España de los Austrias* (Madrid: Siglo XXI, 1982), and the magnificent panoramic work, *Estado Moderno y Mentalidad Social.Siglos XV al XVII* (Madrid: Revista de Occidente, 1972). It is still customary to put Vasco de

Quiroga close to Erasmism. The classic reference is of course, Marcel Bataillon, *Erasmo y España. Estudios sobre la Historia Espiritual del Siglo XVI* (México: Fondo de Cultura Económica, seg. ed. 1966), the last chapter deals with Erasmism in the Americas.

53. The scene between the illiterate barbarian teaching the political lesson of tolerance of difference to the Roman emperor is a commonplace on Quiroga's "moderate" political ideology (*Información en Derecho*, pp. 78-79). Américo Castro produced in his day a manageable compilation on Guevara, *El Villano del Danubio y Otros Fragmentos* (Princeton: Princeton University Press, 1945).

54. Bernal Díaz del Castillo is again our source, His monumental narrative *Historia Verdadera de la Conquista de la Nueva España* (Madrid: CSIC, 1991 [1632]), puts Quiroga at the negotiating table in the Valladolid Debates. The footsoldier says that Quiroga was "on our side" ("que era de nuestras parte, chapter CCXI, p. 887), this could well either that Quiroga was from the Americas, and thus he could exercise with all legitimacy the existential claim to truth, or that both men shared identical political goal, the defense of the *encomienda* system in perpetuity (p. 890), or both.

55. This delicate balance between the two main fiddlers of the Valladolid Debate, Ginés de Sepúlveda and Las Casas, was perceived in his day by the French Hispanist Marcel Bataillon before the appearance of the controversial treatise *De Debellandis Indis* and the scholarship of René de Acuña (which we will analyze in the following chapter). Bataillon's intuitions appear fundamentally correct still today. The reference is *Estudios Sobre Bartolomé de las Casas* (Barcelona: Ediciones Península, 1976): pp. 267-279.

56. There are two panoramic references, J. A. Fernández-Santamaría's *The State, War and Peace: Spanish Political Thought in the Renaissance, 1516-1559* (Cambridge: Cambridge University Press, 1977), and Anthony Pagden's *The Fall of Natural Man: The American Indian and the Origins of Comparative Ethnology* (Cambridge: Cambridge University Press, reprinted 1989). Fernández-Santamaría does not mention Quiroga at all. Pagden only mentions Quiroga once, in his endorsment of the commonplace of "decent independent lives for Indians in the Santa Fe communities"; conversion is also emphasized (p. 35). Pagden has called Quiroga a "humanist," in "The Humanism of Vasco de Quiroga's *Información en Derecho*," included in *The Uncertainties of Empire: Essays in Iberian and Ibero-American Intellectual History* (Collected Series: Series Variorum, 1994). I disagree with this qualification. Following Francisco Rico and Luis Gil Fernández, Juan Ginés de Sepúlveda, More, Erasmus and Nebrija are humanists, but Vitoria and Quiroga aren't.

57. Kagan, ibidem, pp. 35 & 93.

58. Serrano Gassent follows Marcel Bataillon's classic early essay quoted earlier in the supposition which bets on doctor Bernal Díaz de Luco. Quiroga's tone and the size and quality of the treatise clearly intended a decision-making superior, well versed in legal matters and acquainted with the early dilemmas

of coloniality. The other *oidores* were, besides Quiroga, Alonso Maldonado, Francisco Ceynos and Juan de Salmerón (p. 11).

59. According to Serrano Gassent, the *Segunda Audiencia* was carrying anti-slavery regulations, which found strong opposition in New Spain, to the point of state revocation. It is at this juncture that Quiroga writes *Información en Derecho*, "Quiroga wrote this [anti-slavery] treatise in defense of the indigenous liberty" (pp. 13-4, 28); it is also said that Quiroga is "less advanced than Vitoria in matters of slavery" (p. 26). I do not wish to affirm nor deny this; I rather want to think my way through this either-or and give a more concrete and persuasive historical definition to the articulation of freedom inside the more encompassing notion of early modern coloniality.

60. "At the Chancillería of Valladolid, the only tribunal for which this kind of information exists, unfinished lawsuits outnumbered those that obtained a final judgment by a ratio of approximately fifteen to one, a difference so large as to suggest that the parties involved in most disputes were willing to compromise and to bring a lawsuit to a halt" (Kagan, ibidem, p. 84).

61. The "información en derecho [was] the central task of an advocate...to research the law and substantiate the case. He has then to prepare a brief or *información en derecho* outlining the arguments central to his client's demands. A concise, well-prepared brief was a vital document and in many instances the key to success because presiding magistrates frequently based their own opinions upon the arguments an advocate had previously advanced. Briefs were so important that many litigants had their briefs printed and elaborately bound at considerable expense" (Kagan, ibidem, p. 61).

62. This abstract notion, freedom, is here meant in the Marxian sense of the social exchange in which each subject is capable of producing the annihilation, or the "object," of the need of other. This reciprocal satisfaction of need is what defines me and you as human, that is, the mutual reaching beyond his or her particular need. The acknowledgement of the common species-being is this transcendence of particularized or individualized need, or generosity. In Quiroga's colonial model, however, there are some latent contradictions. This reference, to which we will turn later, is found in *Grundisse. Foundations of the Critique of Political Economy (Rough Draft)* (London: Penguin Books, 1973): p. 273.

63. But isn't the appeal to taste a blatant petit-bourgeois tic we may have inherited, together with miopia, beauty spots, eating habits and thinning hair from our grandparents? The issue of taste takes me to the always delicate *escribidor* Julio Ramos. There is an important essay on the constitution of the juridical personality and the contradictory word of the slave qua slave, María Antonia Mandinga, in the Cuban context of XIX: "La ley es Otra: Literatura y Constitución de la Persona Jurídica" (*RCLL*, 1994, Núm. 40): pp. 305-335. There is a second version of this article with meaningful variations included in the volume, *Paradojas de la Letra* (Quito: Universidad Andina Simón Bolívar/ Sede Ecuador, Ediciones Excultura, 1996).

64. I have in mind the convincing work of Doris Sommer for the nineteenth century, *Foundational Fictions: the National Romances of Latin America* (Berkeley: University of California Press, 1991).

65. There is a beautiful video displaying some of the complexities of the *Codex Mendoza* for the generation to come. I am referring to *Tlacuilo* (1988), a film by Enrique Escalona, produced by the *Centro de Investigaciones y Estudios Superiores en Antropología Social* (CIESAS, Mexico).

66. Our edition has been the *Defensor Minor and De Translatio Imperii* by Marsiglio of Padua (1275-1342), edited by Cary J. Nederman (Cambridge: Cambridge University Press, 1993).

67. The towering intellectual figure of colonial law, Juan de Solórzano y Pereira (1575-1655), in his multi-volume *Política Indiana* (first printed in 1629), represents the first systematization of Spanish Indian Law. This will be almost one hundred years later than this official construction of legitimation. See the chapter XI in Vol. 1 of the classic edition prepared by Miguel Angel Ochoa Brun (Madrid: *Biblioteca de Autores Españoles*, Ediciones Atlas, 5 Vols. Num. 252-6, 1972).

68. For some biographic background, see the bit dated *Juan Ginés de Sepúlveda a Través de su "Epistolario" y Nuevos Documentos* by Angel Losada (Madrid: Instituto Francisco de Vitoria, 1949). See also the more recent pocketbook edition by Losada, *Epistolario de Juan Ginés de Sepúlveda (Selección)*, (Madrid: Ediciones de Cultura Hispánica, 1966).

69. See José Luis Abellán on Ginés de Sepúlveda for a classic pronouncement, *Historia Crítica del Pensamiento Español. Tomo II: La Edad de Oro* (Madrid: Espasa Calpe, 1986): pp.449-490.

70. I have used the bilingual *Tratado de las Justas Causas de la Guerra Contra los Indios* (México: Fondo de Cultura Económica, seg. ed. 1941). All quotes will refer to this edition.

71. For this early modern translation of this Aristotelian notion of "distributive justice" in the specific historical context of New Spain, see *Disceptación Sobre Justicia Distributiva y Sobre la Acepción de Personas a Ella Opuesta. Segunda Parte: En qué Cosas tiene Lugar la Acepción de Personas y la Injusta Distribución de Bienes* by Juan Zapata y Sandoval (Bishop of Chiapa 1613, Bishop of Guatemala 1630), (México: Universidad Nacional Autónoma de México, 1995).

72. I have used the following editions, *The Politics* (Penguin Books, 1992), and *Politics. Books 1 and 2*, translated with a commentary by Trevor J. Saunders (Oxford: Clarendon Press, 1995).

73. If state is an association, self-sufficiency is the traditional meaning attributed to perfection as regards the state. This is present in Aristotle, as well as Aquinas's modulation of Aristotle's gradation of the good: "there is perfect goodness when a thing is such that it is sufficient in itself to conduce to the end," in the *Treatise on Law*, included in *Basic Writings of Saint Thomas*

Aquinas (New York: Random House, 1944, [p. 807]). We will soon see how Vasco de Quiroga's *Información en Derecho* will be articulating locally the need for this self-sufficiency in relation to indigenized social sectors in the Americas.

74. See the concrete rendition of Ginés de Sepúlveda as the intellectual exposition of the first true modernity, in *The Invention of the Americas* (New York: Continuum, 1995): pp. 63-70.

75. Ginés de Sepúlveda almost perfectly exemplifies this ethnocentric vision, or civilizational prejudice, which will not hesitate to posit itself as the naturalized norm of protocapitalism: The one-way construction of the ontology of "humanity" coincides with the speaking position, which is clearly one vocal modality or visible position inside totality or "humanity," precisely for being a historical position of force and privilege. The others, inhabitants of another time, are said to follow behind this circular self-appointment as role model (or historical arrogance). This cognitive mechanism has been denounced as the denial of coevalness. See Johannes Fabian's *Time & the Other: How Anthropology Makes its Object* (New York; Columbia Press, 1983). To bring "those" people to the same "human" planet, the denial of the denial of coevalness must be put in hermeneutic practice. See Mignolo's programatic words in *The Darker Side*, ibidem, pp. 249-251, 254-58 & 329-30.

76. Lalinde-Abadía has spoken convincingly of the early modern period of normative expansionism and integration, also of official recopilation and Crown hegemony amid tensions between natural law and law of nations. The sixteenth century means the redefinition of notions of "foreigness" and the reinforcement of the authoritarian formulations of the rule of law in the Americas. See the breath-takingly panoramic work *Iniciaciòn Histórica al Derecho Español* (Barcelona: Ariel, 1970): pp. 178-210, 259-284, 298-302, 434-436.

77. See Philip II's emphasis on economic profitability for the American possessions in Sempat Assadourian's "La despoblación indígena en Perú y Nueva España..." ibidem, pp.

78. In his dialogue with the English historian Toynbee, Ortega y Gasset has indeed still beautiful pages on the distemper of the early modern enrichment with puts together the "I" and the "you" in combinatory games of similarity and differences. The Spanish philosopher speaks of the profound injury caused by the infinite diversity of the human being, i.e. the persistence of the difference in between the "you" and the "I." See *An Interpretation of Universal History* (New York: W.W. Norton, 1973): pp. 163-4.

79. See also Anthony Pagden's *The Fall of Natural Man: The American Indian and the Origins of Comparative Ethnology* (Cambridge: Cambridge University Press, 1982), and J. A. Fernández-Santamaría's *The State, War and Peace: Spanish Political Thought in the Renaissance 1516-1559* (Cambridge: Cambridge University Press, 1977), for different variations on Ginés de Sepúlveda.

80. The link between coercion and law surely exceeds our framework of the early modern Spanish Law. Lalinde-Abadía does not hesitate to speak of the essential link between authoritarianism and the repressive culture. See his synthetic discourse of reception to the *Real Academia de Buenas Letras de Barcelona, Poder, Represión e Historia* (Barcelona, 1988).

81. One could very well use the Hegelian equation of the master (Pozzo) and the slave (Lucky) as long as the historical specificity and concreteness of the situation of domination, subordination or destruction is not thrown out the window. Ginés de Sepúlveda prefigures the civilizing prejudice of the Hegel of the Lectures of History, where the Americas is nothing but pre-history. My edition has been *Lectures on the Philosophy of World History* (Cambridge: Cambridge University Press, 1975). This Hegel gives philosophical dimension to Weber's parochialism. What gets called civilization is more often than not the migratory cores of capital accummulation and high finance. Enrique Dussel's critique of Hegelian Eurocentrism is everpresent in *The Invention of the Americas*, ibidem, see particularly 19-26. In a personal communication, Dussel has emphasized to me that the charge of anti-Hegelianism in relation to his work is incorrect. In his own words, his project is neither pro-Hegalian nor anti-Hegelian, but is something else. For a further reading, see the recent "Beyond Eurocentrism: the World-System and the Limits of Modernity," in *The Cultures of Globalization* edited by Fredric Jameson and Masao Miyoshi (Durham: Duke University Press, 1998): pp. 3-31.

82. Not to go gentle into the good night of the subaltern category, see the essay by Irene Silverblatt, "Becoming Indian in the Central Andes of Seventeenth Century Peru," in *After Colonialism: Imperial Histories and Postcolonial Displacements* (Princeton: Princeton University Press, 1995); pp. 279-298. See also the synthetic version, "El Surgimiento de la Indianidad en los Andes del Perú Central: El Nativismo del Siglo XVII y los Muchos Significados de "Indio,"" included in De Palabra y Obra en el Nuevo Mundo. Vol 3. La Formación del Otro (México/España: Siglo XXI Editores, 1992): pp. 459-481.

83. Mignolo has spoken, inspired by Ortega y Gasset and Rodolfo Kusch, of the discursivity "out of place" ("decires fuera de lugar"), in relation to the colonial world. See this work inside the first Berkeley Colloquium on the problem of the subject in relation to colonial Latin America (Nov. 12-13, 1993), included in *Revista de Crítica Literaria Latinoamericana* (Año XXI, Núm. 41): pp. 9-31.

84. I am here drawing inspiration from the excelent edition on Bartolomé de Las Casas's *De Regia Potestate o Derecho de Autodeterminación*, by Luciano Pereña, J. M. Pérez-Prendes, Vidal Abril and Joaquín Azcarraga (Madrid: Consejo Superior de Investigaciones Científicas, 1969): pp. xxiv-xxv (Manuel Colmeiro's paragraph), & p. liv.

85. Exegeses of the economy in the colonial world were traditionally grappling with the dualism or less often with the blurring of dualism as to whether the

early modern economy in the Americas was feudalism or capitalism. See Ernesto Laclau's classic reference "Feudalism and Capitalism in Latin America, *New Left Review* (No. 67, May-June 1971): pp. 19-38. See also in this line, *Social Classes in Agrarian Societies* by Rodolfo Stavenhagen (New York: Anchor Books, 1975), and the panoramic anthology *Modos de Producción en América Latina: Assadourian, Cardoso, Ciafardini, Garavaglia, Laclau* (Córdoba: Cuadernos d e Pasado y Presente/40, 1974).

86. Besides the already mentioned reference to Steve Stern, "Feudalism, Capitalism, and the World System…" and his debate with Wallerstein, latest developments will take us in the direction of local specificity as pertains to labor arrangements in the colonial world. To see into this historical regionalization and colonial specificity, *El Sistema de la Economía Colonial* by Sempat Assadourian (Lima: Instituto de Estudios Peruanos, 1982), and the panoramic *La Participación Indígena en los Mercados Surandinos* edited by O. Harris, B. Larson and E. Tandeter (La Paz: Centro de Estudios de la Realidad Económica y Social, Ceres, 1987).

87. A historical definition is needed: "Mero y misto [*sic*] imperio es término jurídico; decláralo Ulpiano, en la ley imperium. ff. de iurisd. [*sic*] omnium iuidicum: Imperium aut merum, aut mixtum est; merum imperium est habere gladii potestatem animadvertendi in facinerosos homines, quod etiam potestas appellatur; mixtum imperium est, cui etiam iurisdictio inest, quod in danda bonorum possessione consistit. Lo demás se remite a los juristas [*sic*]," in *Tesoro de la Lengua Castellana o Española* (1611), by Sebastián de Covarrubias Horozco (Madrid: Turner, 1977): p. 801.

88. A second historical definition is needed: "Feudo: Es nombre godo, que entre los latinos se tiene por bárbaro. Significa un cierto género de reconocimiento, con el qual se dio alguno por el príncipe o señor la dignidad o estado o ciudad o villa o territorio, etc. para que assí el que ha recebido esta merced como sus sucessores y herederos en ella, reconozcan perpetuamente a quien les hizo la merced y la gracia. Verisímil [*sic*] es averse [*sic*] dicho feudo de fee y de dar, porque se da en fe y confianza de que han de tenerla con quien les haze la gracia, vel a foedere [*sic*], aunque se escribe sin diphtongo, feudum," included in *Tesoro*, ibidem, p. 590.

89. Some of the historical pain implicit in this dissolution or "destructuration" has been classically analyzed by Nathan Wachtel. See chapter seven, "The Indian and the Spanish Conquest" included in *The Cambridge History of Latin America. Volume l*, edited by Leslie Bethell (Cambridge University Press, 1984): pp. 207-248. For the *requerimiento*, see Lewis Hanke's *La Lucha por la Justicia en la Conquista de América* (Buenos Aires: Editorial Sudamericana, 1949): pp. 47-55.

90. The official letter of the *cédulas* leave initially no doubt that the Indians are, like the Spaniards, vassals to the Crown and cannot be made into slaves, quite unlike African populations, provided they comply with *requerimiento*

regulations appertaining to the "just war." Slavery remains perfectly intelligible to the legal system, though, and there are also of course numerous hesitations and contradictions. Yet the penalty for illegally enslaving the Indians is the death penalty. See *Cedulario de Puga* (Mexico: Pedro Ocharte, 2 Vols., 1879 [1563]): (1) 29-36.

91. See Rolena Adorno por political reforms in relation to the "indio ladino" in the Peruvian context, "El Indio Ladino en el Perú Colonial," included in *De Palabra y Obra en el Nuevo Mundo, Vol. 1. Imágenes Interétnicas*, ibidem, pp. 369-395; "Colonial Reform or Utopia? Guaman Poma's Empire of the Four Parts of the World," included in *Amerindian Images and the Legacy of Columbus*, René Jara and Nicholas Spadaccini, Editors (Minneapolis: University of Minnesota Press, 1992): pp. 346-374; and "The Genesis of Felipe Guaman Poma de Ayala's Nueva Coronica y Buen Gobierno," in *Colonial Latin American Review (Vol. 2, Nos. 1-2, 1993)*: pp. 53-91.

92. The beautiful language of this terrible quote reads thus: "Porque yo veo que Motezuma que fue el que presidía entre ellos cuando esta tierra se ganó, a quien acataban y tenían como a diso, tenía las condiciones del uno malo,...que él era adorado e tenido y reverenciado, no como hombre humano, de gente libre, sino casi como dios de gente captiva, opresa y servil, que son las condiciones del uno malo y tirano; e quería e trabajaba que sus súbditos ni pudiesen ni supiesen ni entendiesen, ni toviesen libertad de alzar los ojos a mirarle, ni traer buenas mantas ni calzado delante de él ni aun oler, según todos afirman, ciertas rosas, porque eran buenas y olorosas, ni de comer gallinas y cosas buenas semejantes. Y la pena de quien así no le acataba e obedecía, dicen era sacrificarle e matarle o cosa semejante, como agora también se manifiesta a quien ve la manera e subjección de los que eran sus súbditos, y su opresión servil y tiránica que aún les queda" (pp. 95-96).

93. See the excellent document for the mockery of colonial justice by a corrupt state official, the "Proceso, tormento y muerte del Cazonci, último Gran Señor de los Tarascos" por Nuño Guzmán, 1530," edited by Armando M. Escobar Olmedo (Morelia: Frente de Afirmación Hispanista, 1997). For the protocols of justice on the disciplining of Nuño de Guzmán, see the *Cedulario de Puga*, ibidem, (1) 154-166, 184-193, 244, 264-290, 380.

94. There are two important sources for the situation of early colonial Michoacán: one is the Humanist Francisco Cervantes de Salazar (1513-1575), translator of Luis Vives into Spanish, and author of *Crónica de La Nueva España* (México: Porrúa, 1985); the second one is by the antagonist of the foot soldier Bernal Díaz del Castillo, the secretary to Hernán Cortés and Crown chronicler, Francisco López de Gómara (1511-1559). See *La Conquista de México* (Madrid: Historia 16, 1986), for this description of early colonial Michoacan (pp. 316-320, 405-409 & 440-483). Charles Gibson, in *The Aztecs Under Spanish Rule*, ibidem, has written on how the Spanish conquest served to weaken the position of the strongest tribal units, and how these "suffered a

loss of identity," and how it reinforced on the other hand the positions of the intermediate peoples who managed to survive (pp. 25, 30). It is plausible to envisage the Michoacán region in this explanation in the latter position. For the figure of *Hidalgo*, see two celebratory accounts in *Aspectos de la Vida Pre-Insurgente de Hidalgo (Hacendado, Litigante y Administrador*, published by the Universidad Michoacana, and also *Hidalgo. Antes del Grito de Dolore*s by Carlos Herrejón Pereda (incomplete reference).

95. Kagan, quoting from Lockhart, has given us historical evidence of the institutional desire which indeed gets very close to More's dream: the banishment of the legal profession. The Spanish Crown agreed in 1529 to ban all lawyers from its new Peruvian colonial center! Surely the measure could not last for too long , *Lawsuits and Litigants*, ibidem, p. 19.

96. The multi-edited effort on *Bartolomé de las Casas. De Regia Potestate o Derecho de Autodeterminación* edited by Pereña, Perez-Prendes, Abril and Azcarraga, ibidem, is an excellent example of historicist scholarship on this historical extremity, namely the self-government for an early modern Americas.

97. See Gutiérrez's *En Busca de los Pobres de Jesucristo: El Pensamiento de Bartolomé de las Casas* (Lima: Instituto Bartolomé de las Casas/CEP, 1992). See also Dussel's critique of the myth of the modernity in relation to Las Casas in *The Invention of the Americas*, ibidem, pp. 64-72.

98. We have already mentioned Mundy's important work on the state mapping (or *Relaciones Geográficas*). There are also excellent examples of this modern desire to put peoples in places; for example, the *Ordenanzas* by Philip II for the foundation of villages in New Spain, included in *BAGN* (Tomo VI, Mayo-Junio 1935, Num. 3): pp. 321-360.

99. See Gustavo Gutiérrez, ibidem, on this political desire for the "best Indies," pp. 23-25.

100. Las Casas's fierce critique, i.e. the accusation implicit in the historical suspension of justice and reason ("Àcon qué derecho y en qué conciencia...?"), is scrupulously modern in this specific sense of the desire for the legalization of the totality of humanity (or *genus homo*), and the intimate marriage or dissolution of facts into regulations with no (human) reality left outside this horizon of regulation. Coloniality (Vidal's farce of human logic and need) is thus the superficial painting of the "fact" with the "law" ("pintar el hecho con el derecho," and the permanent fracture of the rule of law. Law is sameness ("ley es precepto común para bien común"). See Las Casas's dramatic account of the Burgos Meeting and the Montesinos's sermon in *Historia de las Indias. Vol. II*, edition by Agustín Millares Carlo and Lewis Hanke (México: Fondo de Cultura Económica, 1951): pp. 439-471.

101. The rich colonial notion of "asiento" is strongly suggestive of the lettered, official city of the pencilled record, but also of the place, sense, maturity, possibility and propriety of the settlement and the social contract among parties. See Martín Alonso's *Enciclopedia del Idioma* (1958, p. 528-9). See also the *Historical Dictionary of the Spanish Empire, 1402-1975*, (ibidem, p. 56).

Against popularized distortions, such as Spielberg's film *Amistad* (1994), it is important to remind ourselves of the generalized practice of the slave market. Arrighi's *The Long Twentieth Century*, ibidem, states, "In the course of the War of Spanish Succession, the Treaty of Methuen (1703) had granted England privileged access to the Portuguese domestic and colonial markets and to the rapidly expanding supplies of Brazilian gold, and the Treaty of Utrecht (1713) had granted [England] exclusive control over the slave trade with Spanish America" (p. 205). "[T]he earliest beginnings of the nineteenth century free trade movement can be traced to the Atlantic slave trade," already in British and Dutch hands (p. 244-5).

102. Some philological fastidiousness is needed about the notion of "protocol." We may recall Adorno's already classic essay on Bernal Díaz del Castillo, ibidem, giving historical specificity to González Echevarría's centrality of the law for Latin American literature. Yet, we must however highlight that the early modern "protocol" is however quite concrete and specific, i.e. the front-page summary of an attached legal treatise. See Martín Alonso's *Enciclopedia del Idioma* (1958, p. 3421), and also the *Covarrubias* (1611, p. 885). It is then clear that early modern "protocolo" is related to "asiento" (see previous footnote). Literary flights of fancy are not welcome for the most part in this colonial horizon where "libro" (or "book") is mostly "libro de registros" or "libro matrícula," or ledger and "reading" is quite far from a silent solitary pastime, almost exclusively the public performance of "tomar cuentas" or the official book-keeping for the historical record (*Cedulario de Puga*, ibidem, p. 234, and in the landmark *Leyes de Burgos* (1512-3), in the edition in *Libro Anual 1974-Segunda Parte* (México: Instituto Superior de Estudios Eclesiásticos, 1975): pp. 183-200 [195]).

103. I have been unable to verify this term which is likely a mispelled approximation to a related *nahuatl* term as perceived by the Spanish ears of our *oidor*. It appears to mean ethnic lord. The compact *Codex Mendoza* includes the series of homonyms (at least to a Spanish-accustomed ear): *tacatecle: tlacaele, tlacatecatl, tlacateclatl warrior, tlacatectli, tlacatecuhtl, tlacatl* (p. 266). Gibson's magisterial *The Aztecs Under Spanish Rule*, ibidem, includes two references to Quiroga. One of them speaks of Quiroga's admiration for native election rituals: this "foreign" sign in Quiroga's Spanish may well mean a slow incorporation of traditionally indigenous election mechanisms into the local administration of the "Indian cabildos" (p. 175).

104. These are the three direct references to Thomas More and his *Utopia* included in *Información en Derecho*: "Tomás Moro...fue grand griego y gran experto y de mucha auctoridad" (p. 229), "tengo para mí, por cierto, que sabido y entendido por el autor del muy buen estado de la república, de donde como de dechado se sacó el de [*sic*] parecer, varón ilustre y de genio más que humano, el arte y manera de las gentes simplic'simas deste Nuevo Mundo (p. 228)," and "avisos muchos que de él se pueden tomar en ello, harto sabio y sutil, y aun a mi ver no menos verdaderamente, si no me engaño, y por asaz elegante

estilo, a lo menos en el latín, donde yo a la letra lo saqué y traduje para este fin y efecto, y porque a todos fuese más familiar y no se les defendiese [?] algún rato, como hizo a mí algo con todo quitado [?], aunque no de la sustancia e intento de la sentencia para mejor aplicarlo a mi propósito; por el mismo Tomás Morus [*sic*], autor de aqueste muy buen estado de república...donde su intención parece que haya sido proponer, alegar, fundar y probar por razones las causas por que sentía por muy fácil, útil, probable y necesaria la tal república entre una gente tal que fuese de la cualidad de aquesta natural [de este] Nuevo Mundo , que en hecho de verdad es cuasi en todo y por todo como él allí [*Utopia*] sin haberlo visto lo pone, pinta y describe, en tanta manera que me hace muchas veces admirar" (pp. 245-6).

105. The historiographic masterpiece on the official rationality of the early stages of the Spanish Indian state of law is still Mario Gongora's *El Estado en el Derecho Indiano: La Epoca de Fundación (1492-1570)* (Santiago, Chile: Editorial Universitaria, 1951). This work would like to remain always a bit restless and dissatisfied about the notions of legality and the state. If the Chilean scholar is the best example of the historiography of the rule of law and its fractures, my analysis, owing a great deal to Góngora's serious scholarship, seeks to imagine historically plausible hermeneutic possibilities, if only future-oriented, around and beyond the official (hi)story of the rule of law.

106. Charles Gibson includes a panoramic view of existing tribes —his word choice—before the Spanish conquest. His work provides the gradual display of the Spanish incorporation of those tribes into the multi-layered political system (*The Aztecs Under Spanish Rule*, ibidem, particularly chapter two and the appendixes.

107. For the seeds of this potential, if only future-oriented, for self-government, see the "Treinta Proposiciones Muy Jurídicas," *Obras Completas. Vol 10: Tratados de 1552*, Ed. Ramón Hernández and Lorenzo Galmés (Madrid: Alianza Editorial/Quinto Centenario, 1992): pp. 200-214.

108. The excellent *Suma y Epíloga de toda la Descripción de Tlaxcala* (1588-9), edited by R. Acuña gives us a panoramic view of some of the most common Spanish historical categories for the local government in the colonial period. Some of these are still commonly used today. It is clear that the resulting colonial semiosis of these *Relaciones Geográficas* gives us the "main tone" of the official mapping, largely in the Spanish language, in tense coexistence with a myriad of indigenous languages. For example, the interrelational maze of Spanish hierarchies gives us from the smallest to the most important unit, the "corregimiento," "alcaldía mayor," "gobernación," "villa" and "ciudad," inside "provincias" or counties. Bureaucratic measures are arranged according to main populations (or "cabeceras"), which may or may not coincide with original indigenous settlements. This official nomenclature creates a three-level colonial palimpsest with religious jurisdictions. Quiroga's legacy attests to internal conflicts among these. We must also insert the "feudos" or "encomiendas" of settlers with negotiable jurisdictional arrangements for one

or two generations. Given the endless boundary-disputation and profoundly temporary arrangements, it is not strange to see in this *Relación* a special emphasis on boundary markers ("terminos" and "mojones"). Sergio Quezada's *Pueblos y Caciques Yucatecos (1550-1580)* (México: El Colegio de México, 1993), has given us an excellent account of this early colonial slippery gerrymandering. Against this colonial ocean, Quiroga had to negotiate the no-place, good-place location of his insular village-hospitals.

109. My edition for this comparison has been Eugenio Imaz's classic anthology, *Utopías del Renacimiento: Moro/Campanella/Bacon* (Mexico: Fondo de Cultura Económica, 1941 [1993]).

110. It is impossible not to notice the overabundance of almost silly or superfluous detail in More's *Utopia*. We may feel that More's proto-bourgeois plot-free narrative is nothing but details! It is precisely this reality effect created by the dwelling upon the concrete and the numeral, which keeps this *Utopia* going! What difference does it make to know that the Utopian technique for egg-breeding requires no hens?, or to have the old and new words for the same political office? What do we make of the emphasis on the adverb, that *Amauroto* is "almost" in the center of the island, and is of "almost" square shape? Should we be all too rigorous about the illusion of the precision implicit in the numeral (there is a 24-mile, or 1-day travel distance between the cities, and there are 54 cities with are absolutely identical in language, manners and customs, institutions and laws)? What difference would it make if future editions of *Utopia* include the typos of 56 cities, 34-mile 3-day distance, etc.? What about the 6 working hours for everybody and the 2 sets of clothing? We may recall Roland Barthes's *Writing Degree Zero* (New York: Hill and Wang, 1968), and "The Reality Effect," *French Literary Theory Today* (Cambridge: Cambridge University Press, 1982): pp. 11-17. Should we then extrapolate this illusionary precision-producing device to the entire political structure? And, since we have previously cut short the device of ironic meaning inside the repressive culture, how would we then deal with Quiroga's model? Quiroga's writings insistently represent the debilitation of the fictionalization: numbers do appear to matter a great deal as in the negotiation of boundaries with neighbouring *encomiendas*. More's nimble humanist cleverness is not historically interchangeable despite explicit borrowings with Quiroga's shoe-flavored canon-law severities.

111. Sempat-Assadourian's formulation, "coeficiente de explotación [del] trabajo estacional compulsivo," "La Despoblación Indígena en Perú y Nueva España...," ibidem, pp. 433, 447.

112. "The Chapter on Capital," in *Grundise: Introduction to the Critique of Political Economy*, ibidem, pp. 242-244.

113. "The Chapter on Capital," in *Grundise*, ibidem, pp. 246-249.

114. See the "naborías" or allocated Indians in the minefields in the excellent document, *Estratificación social, Esclavos y Naborías en el Puerto Rico*

Minero del Siglo XVI. La información de Francisco Manuel de Lando, Edited by Julio Damiani Cósimi (Puerto Rico: Universidad de Puerto rico, Río Piedras: Centro de Investigaciones Históricas, Departamento de Historia, Núm. 1, 1994).

115. See *Pre-Capitalist Modes of Production* by Barry Hindness and Paul Q. Hirst (London: Routledge and Kegan Paul, 1975), for an intricate defense of the slave mode of production, the coexistence of slave labor with peasant and artisan production, a strong emphasis upon the historicity of the institution away from humanistic mythology including provocations for Marxian historiography (mostly chapter three, pp. 109-177, and the conclusion, pp. 308-323).

116. See the excellent document, *Proyecto para la Abolición de la Esclavitud en Puerto Rico* (10 de Abril de 1867), presented to the *Junta de Información*, Madrid by Segundo Ruiz Belvis, José Julián Acosta and Francisco Mariano Quiñones (Puerto Rico, Ríos Piedras: Edil, 1978).

117. Again, the *Covarrubias* Dictionary (1616) is eloquent about this, "rescatar: recobrar por precio lo que el enemigo ha robado, de res, latine re, que vale iterum, y catar, que es mirar, que vale tanto como bolver a mirar uno en su presencia lo que se avía ausentado della." A panoramic view is provided by Silvio Zavala's major contribution, *Esclavos Indios en Nueva España* (México: El Colegio Nacional, 1967).

118. The most accessible edition of Vitoria's lectures ("relectiones") for an English audience is probably the edition by Anthony Pagden's *Political Writings* (Cambridge: Cambridge University Press, 1991).

119. For a convincing contextualization of Quiroga's historical surroundings, see the telling document by the Franciscan Zumárraga, first Archbishop of New Spain, "Segundo Parecer de Zumárraga sobre la Esclavitud (1536)," included by Carlos Herrejón Peredo in his *Textos Políticos en la Nueva España*, ibidem, pp. 174-183. The worldview for the legal repression of the historical intelligibility of slavery is very similar to Quiroga's attitude in *Información en Derecho*: "que el primer pie que en estas tierras se metiere sea el derecho…; es muy necesario…que su Majestad ponga otra muy diferente manera de gobernación en estas tierras (p. 183).

120. These are several references on Quiroga's puzzlement over what he (mis)understood to be the indigenous slavery: "muy diferente de la nuestra" (p. 128), "corrupto el vocablo" (p. 129), "ni saber qué cosa sea esclavo, ellos truecan sin pesadumbre" (p. 158), "no hay vocablo entre ellos para esclavitud" (p. 166), and "corrupto el vocablo" (p. 183).

121. These questions owe a great deal to the following essays, "Marxism and Historicism," by Fredric Jameson, *The Ideologies of Theory*, ibidem, and also the provocative "Representations of Subjectivity," in *Discours Social/Social Discourse: the Non-Cartesian Subjects, East and West* (Winter-Spring 1994): pp. 47-60. See also in the same volume Darko Suvin, "Polity or Disaster:

From Individualist Self Toward Personal Valences and Collective Subjects" (pp. 181-210).

122. The crisis of the legal logic does not mean that the legal machine will vanish tomorrow. Quite the contrary, the legal crisis could display the cutting teeth of historical longevity. (p. 257). The fact is, the very practice of the law becomes the patrimony of professional groups, and authoritarianism is no other thing but the historical sign of concentration of power in a social group (p. 257). If I understand Lalinde-Abadía correctly, the incongruence of the legal logic is the very essence of the legal logic ("Los defectos de incongruencia son "paralogismos jurídicos," p. 256), and the totality of vision must hence take into account internal or juridical paralogisms as well as historical or exogenous paralogisms. Hence, there is no way to go but towards the ideology of those professional groups, or in Ortega's words, the belief-system of those groups always already against others. The ideology of the natural law ("iusnaturalismo católico") is, according to Lalinde-Abadía, the ideology of the monarchy (p. 263-4). Isn't the crisis of the legal logic a mechanism to grow stronger? And how far is one willing to go down the para-logic road? These words on paralogism are included in "Notas sobre el Papel de las Fuerzas Políticas" (ibidem, pp. 256-257, 264-266).

123. These two notions "casuism" and "particularism" are included by Ismael Sánchez Bella in his panoramic *Historia del Derecho Indiano* (Madrid: Colección Mapfre 1492, 1992): p. 91. He gives thus historical concretization to the abstract formulation by G. Deleuze a propos the seriality of jurisprudence with no concrete subject of rights: "the function of singularity replaces that of universality (in a field in which there is no use for the universal), this can be seen even in law: the judicial notion of "case" or "jurisprudence" dismisses the universal to the benefit of emissions of singularities and functions of prolongation [or "seriality"?, FG]. A conception of law based upon jurisprudence does not need any "subject" of rights. Conversely, a philosophy without subject [theme?, plot?, FG] has a conception of law based on jurisprudence," this in included in the essay "A Philosophical Concept," included in the volume, *Who Comes After the Subject?*, edited by Jean-Luc Nancy, Peter Connor and Eduardo Cadava (New York: Routledge, 1991).

124. See "The Insurmountable Contradictions of Liberalism: Human Rights and the Rights of Peoples in the Geoculture of the Modern World-System," by Wallerstein, in V.Y. Mudimbe's *Nations, Identities, Cultures* (Durham: Duke University Press, 1997): pp. 181-198.

125. Other good examples of millenarianism in Quiroga's treatise are located in pp. 98-9, 192-3, 195, 202, 217-9, 221-2, 224-227.

126. The explicit millenarian figure of the crumbling statue and the fifth kingdom is to be found in the arresting pages of the *De las Islas del Mar Océano* (1515-1516?), by the distinguished Salamanca scholar, state representative and advisor in legal matters, President of the prestigious *Mesta* organization, etc. This

canonic millenarian jargon of authenticity is included in the excellent edition by Zavala and Millares Carlo, ibidem, pp. 18, 23-24, 72, 79-80 and 107.

127. I have in mind the famous *testimonio, Me llamo Rigoberta Menchú y Así me Nació La Conciencia* (Barcelona: Seix Barral, 4th edition, nov. 1993).

Chapter IV

1. The edition is by René Acuña, *De Debellandis Indis: Un tratado desconocido* (Mexico: Universidad Nacional Autónoma, 1988). The literal translation would be something like, "The War that Must be Waged Against the Indians." I agree with Acuña that the title is slightly misleading (p. 32), since it does not synthesize the essence of this treatise which is incomplete. All references relate to this edition unless otherwise indicated. I will be using the shorthand *Indis* to refer to this controversial legal document. All page numbers refer to this edition. All translations are mine unless indicated otherwise.

2. The masterpiece of the social exercise of the letters is *Panorama Social del Humanismo Español* (1500-1800), by Luis Gil Fernández (Madrid: Tecnos, 2nd. edition, [1981] 1997). For the specific colonial exercise exercise of the letters, see the excellent work by Tamar Herzog, *Mediación, Archivos y Ejercicio: Los escribanos en Quito (siglo XVII)* (Vittorio Klostermann Frankfurt am Main, 1996), and *La Administración como Fenómeno Social: La justicia Penal de la Ciudad de Quito (1650-1750)* (Madrid: Centro de Estudios Constitucionales, 1995).

3. *Vasco de Quiroga and his pueblo-hospitales* (Washington: Academy of American Franciscan History, 1963): p. 66.

4. There are numerous accounts of the Valladolid Debates. We would like to highlight two: *La Lucha por la Justicia en la Conquista de América* by Lewis Hanke (Buenos Aires: Editorial Sudamericana, 1949), and *En Busca de los Pobres de Jesucristo: El Pensamiento de Bartolomé de las Casas* by Gustavo Gutiérrez (Lima: Instituto Bartolomé de las Casas-Rimac, 1992). For the Las Casas's legal machinery, see the voluminous bilingual edition of the "Apologia," included in *Obras Completas/9*, edited by Angel Losada (Madrid: Alianza Editorial/V Centenario del Descubrimiento de América/ Consejería De Cultura, Junta de Andalucía, 1988).

5. These include: Bartolomé de Las Casas, Juan Ginés de Sepúlveda, the members of the *Real Consejo de Indias*, Luis Hurtado de Mendoza (Marqués de Mondéjar), *licenciados* Gracián de Briviesca, Gregorio López, Francisco Tello de Sandoval, Gutierre Velázquez, the *doctores* Hernán Pérez de la Fuente and Gonzalo Pérez de Rivadeneyra, and the religious members, Bernardino de Arévalo, Melchor Cano, Bartolomé Carranza de Miranda and Domingo de Soto (p. 20).

6. For some of these colonial complexities, see the panoramic volume *Writing Without Words: Alternative Literacies in Mesoamerica and the Andes*, edited by Elizabeth Hill Boone and Walter D. Mignolo (Durham: Duke University Press, 1994). For some reasons to circumvent Derrida in relation to the idea

of writing in colonial situations, see the afterword by Mignolo, particularly pp. 302-310.

7. The "writings" of the most important intellectual of the period, Francisco de Vitoria, were also left untouched by the print in his lifetime. What we today know about him is exclusively through the disciples attending his Salamanca lectures, which no doubt adds a tremendous sense of historical fragility and generational unpredictability to the whole early modern period and beyond. See, *Francisco de Vitoria. Political Writings*, edited by Anthony Pagden and Jeremy Lawrance (Cambridge University Press, 1991), and for a panoramic, preliminary view on the Salamanca School, see also by Padgen *The Uncertainties of Empire: Essays in Iberian and Ibero-American Intellectual History* (Brookfield, Vermont: Variorum, 1994).

8. "Vasco de Quiroga y Bartolomé de las Casas," included in the Spanish version *Estudios sobre Bartolomé de las Casas* (Barcelona: Ediciones Península, 1976): pp. 267-279.

9. See "Don Vasco de Quiroga y su tratado *De Debellandis Indis* (ll)," by Benno Biermann and "En torno al tratado De debellandis Indis de Vasco de Quiroga," by Silvio Zavala in *HM* (Vol. XVIII, Abril-Junio 1969, Núm. 4): pp. 615-626. See the *Memoria de la Mesa Redonda sobre Vasco de Quiroga* (Instituto Dr. José María Luis Mora, 1982). See also Zavala's latest pronouncement I have been able to collect, "Algo más sobre Vasco de Quiroga," *HM* (vol. XXXVIII, Enero-Marzo 1989, Núm. 3, 151): pp. 533-549.

10. The already classic edition is *Santo Tomás More y "La Utopía de Tomás Moro en la Nueva España"* by Justino Fernández and Edmundo O'Gorman (Mexico: Alcancia, 1934).

11. I have in mind specifically O'Gorman's *Fundamentos de la Historia en América* (México: Imprenta Universitaria, 1942) and *Crisis y Porvenir de la Ciencia Histórica* (México: Imprenta Universitaria, 1947), and Bataillon's *Dos concepciones de la Tarea Histórica* (México: Imprenta Universitaria, 1955). See also Mignolo's evaluation of this controversy in "La Historia de la Escritura y la Escritura de la Historia," included in *De la Crónica a la Nueva Narrativa Mexicana: Coloquio sobre Literatura Mexicana*, edited by Merlín H. Forster and Julio Ortega (Mexico: Editorial Oasis/Colección Alfonso Reyes, 1986): pp. 13-28.

12. See his chapter four, "Discouse of Domination, Discourse of Hope: The Contradictory Vision of Vasco de Quiroga," included in *Images of Conquest: Text and Context in Colonial Mexico* (University of Wisconsin-Madison, Dissertation 1993): pp. 130-232. I have had access to a paper presentation by Kripper-Martínez entitled "Paternalism and the Colonial Utopia of Vasco de Quiroga," (*The Society for Utopian Studies*, 22nd Meeting, Memphis, TN, Oct. 16-19, 1997).

13. Krippner-Martínez concludes his latest evaluation with the following sentence: "Vasco de Quiroga thought of himself as an ethical encomendero" ("Paternalism and the Colonial Utopia of Vasco de Quiroga," manuscript, ibidem, p. 15).

14. See, "Beyond Eurocentrism: The World-System and the Limits of Modernity" by Enrique Dussel and "Globalization, Civilization Processes and the Relocation of Languages and Cultures," by Walter D. Mignolo included in the recent volume *The Cultures of Globalization*, edited by Fredric Jameson and Masao Miyoshi (Durham: Duke University Press, 1998): pp. 3-31, 32-53.

15. Lewis Hanke and Agustín Millares Carlo have spoken of the alliance between high bourgeois society in New Spain, represented by Juan Velázquez de Salazar, *regidor* in the *Cabildo* of Mexico (1554) and Juan Ginés de Sepúlveda with gift of money and jewels to the Humanist scholar to give him courage in the future ("para animarle en el futuro"), *Cuerpo de Documentos del Siglo XVI Sobre los Derechos de España en las Indias y Filipinas* (México: Fondo de Cultura Económica, 1943): pp. xxiii-xxvii.

16. For the desirable historicization of the notion of Humanism, see Gil Fernández, ibidem. See also *El Sueño del Humanismo: De Petrarca a Erasmo* by Francisco Rico (Madrid: Alianza Universidad, 1997).

17. To see this humanitarian dehistoricization of the historical figure of Quiroga, see *Humanistas del Siglo XVI* by Gabriel Méndez-Plancarte (Mexico: Universidad Nacional Autónoma, 1946), the *Memoria de la Mesa Redonda sobre Vasco de Quiroga (Rafael Moreno, José Miguel Quintana & Silvio Zavala)* (México: Instituto Dr. José María Luis Mora, 1982?), and the recent *El Humanismo en el Nuevo Mundo: Ensayo Histórico y Perspectivas Contemporáneas* by Raúl Horta (México: Miguel Angel Porrúa Grupo Editorial, 1997), prologued by Silvio Zavala.

18. "The Humanism of Vasco de Quiroga's "Información en Derecho," "included in *The Uncertainties of Empire*, ibidem, pp. 133-142.

19. *Cuerpo de Documentos del Siglo XVI*, ibidem, pp. 3-9.

20. The *locus classicus* is Francisco deVitoria's Salamanca lectures *On the American Indians and On the Law of War* (1539), included in *Francisco de Vitoria: Political Writings* edited by Anthony Pagden and Jeremy Lawrance (Cambridge: Cambridge University Press, 1991): pp. 231-327. For some desirable contextualization, see *La Conquista Justificada* by Guillermo Vázquez-Franco (Montevideo: Tauro, 1968), and by Silvio Zavala, *Ensayos sobre la Colonización Española en América* (Buenos Aires: Emecé, 1944) and *The Political Philosophy of the Conquest of America* (Mexico, Editorial Cultura, T.G., 1953).

21. See the excellent edition of *De las Islas del Mar Océano por Juan López de Palacios Rubios & Del Dominio de los Reyes de España sobre los Indios por Fray Matías de Paz* by Silvio Zavala and Agustín Millares Carlo (México: Fondo de Cultura Económica, 1954).

22. See the excellent facsimile document, *Narración histórico-jurídica del derecho del Patronato Real: Títulos que se afianza y extensión dellos, que dirigie el zelo y amor a la augusta Magestad de España* (Perkins Library Reference (282.46. N234), Duke University, n.p., n.p., n.d.).

23. For the official historical definiton of the powers of the Church, see Vitoria's lectures, Pagden and Lawrance's *Francisco de Vitoria: Political Writings*, ibidem, pp. 45-151. For the knotty issues of boundaries, see "Derecho y Poder en el Pensamiento Jurídico Español del Siglo XVI. El Problema de los Límites del Poder" by Ramón Martínez Tapia in *Pensamiento* (Madrid: Vol. 54, Núm. 208, Enero-Abril 1998): pp. 45-83.

24. See *Real Patronato de Granada. El Arzobispo de Talavera, la Iglesia y el Estado Moderno (1486-1516). Estudios y Documentos*, by Jesús Suberbiola-Martínez (Granada: Caja General de Ahorros y Monte de Piedad de Granada, 1985).

25. *Vasco de Quiroga and his Pueblo-Hospitales of Santa Fé*, ibidem, pp. 12-17.

26. It was Ortega y Gasset who spoke of history as the vast system of incorporation and decadence or desintegration. Historicity or dynamism is hence the human forcefield with integrating or unifying and disintegrating or differentiating forces. In the specific history of the Iberian peninsula, Ortega y Gasset suggests the symbolic date of 1580 for the end of the process of ascension or accumulation and the beginning of a terribly long process of disintegration and dispersion well into this century. There is a painful grain of truth in this vision. See his *España Invertebrada* (Madrid: La Lectura, 1922).

27. See "Nebrija en México" by José Luis Martínez, *NRFH* (Tomo XLI, 1993, Núm. 1): pp. 1-17.

28. See specifically the final section "Vida y Costumbres del Humanista" in *De Las Disciplinas* (*De Disciplinis*, 1531) and the *Arte de Hablar* (*De Ratione Dicendi*, 1532) by Luis Vives, Early Modern international "public intellectual" to see some concrete historical specificities of the notion of "humanist;" included in *Obras Completas* (Madrid, Aguilar, 1948): pp. 670-687 & 689-806.

29. *Dos Diálogos escritos por Juan de Valdés* (n/d, n/p, 1850).

30. See Americo Castro's abbreviated edition, *El Villano del Danubio y Otros Fragmentos* (Princeton: Princeton University Press, 1945). We must explain however that this fragment is a *locus classicus* inside two colossal compositions in the romance language by the Franciscan Guevara (1480-1545) who, well inside the print culture, became influential member of the Inquisition and official chronicler of Charles V. These two monumental works must be necessarily framed inside the formal education of princes after Christian-Roman models (or *De Regimine Principum* tradition). For these two references which say politely that the emperor is naked (or early modern reformation), see *Obras Completas/1: Libro Aureo de Marco Aurelio* (Turner: Biblioteca Castro, 1994): pp. 122-133 & *Obras Completas /2: Relox de Príncipes*, ibidem, pp. 633-650.

31. It reinforces this point to remind ourselves that Quiroga held a degree in canon law and not theology, *Vasco de Quiroga and his Pueblo-Hospitals of Santa Fe*, ibidem, pp. 10-11.

32. In a largely illiterate culture on both sides of the Atlantic, the necessity for the literalness of the ceremonies of the repressive cultures is justified in so far as the shunning of idolatry and the foreshadowing of Christ. Ritualization and sacralization thus go hand in hand also in relation to the repressive culture in this Thomist construction of ontologies. See the rather detailed Question Cl "On the Ceremonial Precepts in Themselves" and beyond, in *Basic Writings of Saint Thomas Aquinas. Volume Two*, edited by Anton C. Pegis (New York: Random House, 1944): pp. 853-948.

33. For convincing pages on the early modern conceptualization of imperial domination, see mostly chapter two in Mario Góngora's *Studies in the Colonial History of Spanish America* (Cambridge: Cambridge University Press, 1975): pp. 33-66, 220-225.

34. See Pagden's "The Preservation of Order: The School of Salamanca and the 'Ius Naturae,'" in *The Uncertainties of Empire: Essays in Iberian and Ibero-American Intellectual History* (Aldershot: Variorum, 1994); pp. 147-166 [166].

35. We will draw inspiration from Mortimer J. Adler's "A Question about Law," included in *Essays in Thomism*, edited by Robert E. Brennan (New York: Sheed & Ward, 1942): pp. 205-236, and also Ramón Martínez-Tapia's "Derecho y Poder en el Pensamiento Jurídico Español del Siglo XVI: El Problema de los Límites del Poder," *Pensamiento* (Madrid: Vol. 54 (1998), Núm. 208): pp. 45-83.

36. Acuña includes the following definition from the *Reader's Digest* of the medieval period, Saint Isidoro's *Etymologiae* (VII century): "Derecho de Gentes equivale a la ocupación de las sedes, edificación, fortificación, guerras, cautividades, servidumbres, postliminios, tratados, paces, armisticios, juramento de respetar los legados, bodas prohibidas entre extraños. De ahí que reciba el nombre de Derecho de Gentes porque casi todas las gentes usan de él [*sic*]," (endnote 153, p. 213).

37. An exceedingly rich notion, title or *título* is according to its rich etymology: "origen o fundamento jurídico de derecho, demonstración auténtica del mismo por medio de un razonamiento, cada una de las partes principales en que se suelen dividir las leyes, reglamentos, etc." (Martín Alonso).

38. *The Bible: Authorized King James Version*, edited by Robert Carroll and Stephen Prickett (Oxford: Oxford University Press, 1997): p. 807.

39. The arguments in *Indis* are essentially, distressingly the same, almost one thousand years later, as Saint Augustine's, whom the author of *Indis* explicitly refers to, but with some confusions, as Acuña is quick to point out. Using Cold War American language, there are no "doves" here. For the official messianism and the war mechanism of cleansing of infidels in relation to the declining Roman Empire, see the fourth and fifth Books in *The City of God* (New York: The Modern Library, 1950): pp. 110-141 & 151-179.

40. See the important document *Open the Social Sciences. Report of the Gulbenkian Commission on the Rethinking of the Social Sciences* (Stanford:

Stanford University Press, 1996) for the historical rendition, from the eighteenth century until 1945, of the tension between these two models: the nomothetic model based upon general principles, measurability and comparability and the idiographic model based upon particularized historical or local knowledges. There is no explicit mention of the repressive culture here, yet I still find this vocabulary relevant to the exercise of the law, which cannot quite do without these two tendencies (literalist or textualist in the narrow sense on the one hand and historical and contextualist on the other). This report suggest the desirability of a third space, that is, the opening of the social sciences, noting however the difficulties, which are no doubt political (p. 76). Is it fair to equate the idiographic model to Mignolo's call for "pluritopic hermeutics" in the conflation of the (false) difference between "subject" and "object" of knowledge in a radically inter-subjective situation of knowledge production? I would dare say so. See the afterword to *The Darker Side of the Renaissance*, ibidem, pp. 315-334, particularly 328-332.

41. This *Proceso de Residencia* of Vasco de Quiroga is to be found in the collection of primary material gathered by the Mexican scholar Nicolás León (1859-1929), *Documentos Inéditos Referentes al Ilustrísimo Señor Don Vasco de Quiroga Existentes en el Archivo General de Indias* (México: Antigua Librería Robredo de José Porrúa e Hijos, Biblioteca Histórica Mexicana de Obras Inéditas/17, 1940): pp. 40-84. It is important to note that this is according to León's own words not the complete document of the general *Proceso de Residencia* involving all the four judges of the High Court. These forty-four pages are the ones León found most relevant in relation to Quiroga. I will abbreviate this document henceforth as simply *Residencia*. All page numbers refer to this edition.

42. For some additional information, see the *Historical Dictionary of the Spanish Empire, 1402-1975* (New York: Greenwood Press, 1975): p. 516.

43. In León's own words: "En las páginas 311 a 315 del proceso de residencia del oidor don Vasco de Quiroga" and the location given is "Estante 47, caj. 6, leg. 20/15, núm. 3," ibidem, p. 40.

44. We are using "protocol" in the generic contemporary sense. Yet we need to be careful with the strict Early Modern sense of the word, "initial summary of the attached document." León's 1940 edition includes two of these protocols which give will give force to the generic charge against Quiroga. These are: 1) document V or "Quejas de los Indios de Tzintzuntzan contra el Señor Quiroga (1555)," and 2) document VI or "Quejas de los Vecinos de Guayangareo contra el Señor Quiroga (1567); ibidem, pp. 35-6 .

45. For the always desirable historical qualification of these "foreigners," see the good introductory article by Stuart B. Schwartz "New world nobility: Social Aspirations and Mobility in the Conquest and Colonization of Spanish America," *Social Groups and Religious Ideas in the Sixteenth Century* edited by Miriam Usher Chrisman and Otto Grundler (Kalamazoo, Michigan: Western Michigan University/ The Medieval Institute, 1978): 23-37.

46. To the production of the historical heterogeneity as pertains to the abstract notion of readership, which is *not* historically central to this *Residencia* theater, see Maxime Chevalier's *Lectura y Lectores en la España de los Siglos XVI y XVII* (Madrid: Turner, 1976), on the culture of entertainment, Ricardo Senabre's *Literatura y Público* (Madrid: Paraninfo, 1987), on the formation of communities of readers and interpreters and (mis)communications with authors, and also the excellent work by Jesús A. Martínez Martín, *Lectura y Lectores en el Madrid del Siglo XIX* (Madrid: Consejo Superior de Investigaciones Científicas, 1991), on the print serialization and professionalization for mass consumption. We must not forget the classic reference for the print culture or the "book" culture in the early modern Americas, Irving A. Leonard's *Books of the Brave* (Berkeley: University of California Press, [1949]1992).

47. According to Armando Escobar-Olmedo, the file number 188, which is Quiroga's *Residencia*, includes 638 "sheets" in three separate "volumes" ("638 hojas en tres piezas"). Escobar-Olmedo's "protocol-like" summary of this document 188, which must be León's original, includes the following relevant information: 1) of the 27 charges, only one charge, the number 26, is against Quiroga, 2) Loayza's questions to the witnesses are only 30, 3) several witness names are introduced which are not included in León's document, 4) this original *Residencia* includes a list of tributes of several *pueblos-corregimientos* in the Michoacán region, which León omits, 4) there is no word about Loaysa's final sentence. Future endeavors will take me to try to acquire this complete file which I will then have to compare with León's 1940 version. The reference is, *Catálogo de Documentos Michoacanos en Archivos Españoles* (Morelia, Mich.: Universidad Michoacana de San Nicolás de Hidalgo, 1990): pp. 92-3.

48. We must remember again the useful notions of "sujeto dicente" and "decires fuera de lugar." See Mignolo on the historical problem of the "subject" in direct relation to the scholarly field of colonial Latin American studies, *Revista de Crítica Literaria Latinoamericana* (Año XXI, Núm. 41): pp. 9-31.

49. For the historical specificity of this notion, see "Fray Bartolomé de las Casas obispo: la naturaleza mierable de las naciones indianas y el derecho de la Iglesia. Un escrito de 1545," by Carlos Sempat Assadourian (*HM*, Vol. XL, Enero-Marzo 1991, Núm. 3): pp. 387-451.

50. I have in mind Ortega y Gasset's *vitalismo*, the ground of *vivir*, that is, *lo que hay*, the everyday travail, the carelessness and also its extravagant tree-like greenness. In the tremendous years of international war conflict and exile, Ortega's anti-idealist proposals are for a courageous joviality, the mockery of the seriousness of the philosophical discipline, the "superficial" condition of the new philosophy looking after the threatened naturalness of life, my life and yours, the "ground" which cannot be doubted and yet frustrates the exercise of the intelligence, in *¿Qué es Filosofía? (Obras Completas. Tomo VII (1948-1958)* (Madrid: Revista de Occidente, 2a edición/1964): pp. 275-438.

51. See Enrique Dussel on the reconfiguration of the philosophical ground: the destruction of contractualist and communicational societal models based upon the economic fact of poverty and hunger, for a majority of the population, especially chapter ten in *The Underside of Modernity: Apel, Ricoeur, Rorty, Taylor and the Philosophy of Liberation* (New Jersey: Humanities Press, 1996): pp. 213-239 and the essay "La Introducción de la "Transformación de la Filosofía" de K. O. Apel y la Filosofía de la Liberación (Reflexiones desde una perspectiva latinoamericana)" (n/d).

52. We have already mentioned in chapter three the assocation with the hospitals depicted by Luis Vives's *De Subventione Pauperum* (1525). We must also include the major work *De Concordia et Discordia in Humano Genere* (1529), firmly strictured according to the tradition of scholarly advise to kings or *De Regimine Principum*, addressed to Charles V, and the continuation in *De Pacificatione* (1529), addressed to the Archbishop of Seville Don Alfonso Enrique, for the political ethos which permeates Quiroga's political orthodoxy. I am not aware of any direct links between Vives and Quiroga, but I find it hard to believe that our historical figure had not been familiar with the Valencia-born international intellectual.

53. For the historical contextualization of Quiroga's beneficence inside monasticism, see Pedro Borges's "Vasco de Quiroga en el ambiente misionero de la Nueva España," *MH* (Año XXIII, Núm. 69): 297-340. Borges downplays and relativizes Quiroga's hospital-villages in relation to the most encompassing and long-lasting Franciscan dissemination. Borges's axiology is clear: *Oidor* Quiroga is intellectually and politically much more relevant as Bishop Quiroga (p. 297). Borges does not quite subsume Quiroga's utopiansim to beneficence and charity (p. 330).

54. The crucial reference for indigenous nobility in the colonial context of the Michoacan region is, *La Nobleza Indígena de Pátzcuaro en la Epoca Virreinal* by Delfina Esmeralda López Sarrelangue (Mexico: Instituto de Investigaciones Históricas/Universidad Nacional Autónoma de México, 1965). There is information about a Don Pedro Cuiniharángari, "El Gobernador," (p. 203) in charge of Quiroga's hospital (p. 209), which is perhaps related to the don Pedro "señor de Mechuacan" [*sic*] who according to Andrés Suárez (witness thirty-three) had three or four wives (*Residencia*, p. 80). There is also a Don Alonso Huitzinméngari, main *regidor* writing affectionately to Quiroga (p. 226). López-Sarrelangue includes listings of indigenous peoples in positions for local government and *cacicazgo* privileges well into the XVIII. It is thus historically not unlikely, so we are forced to speculate, the historical collaboration between Quiroga and selected members of the indigenous nobility.

55. Warren's biography, *Vasco de Quiroga and his Pueblo-Hospitals of Santa Fé*, ibidem, is the most reliable and thorough account of these historical tensions over land jurisdictions and ownership rights. If the ideal city is thematically quite close to More's utopia, and Warren follows Zavala on this (pp. 35-42),

this is clearly an almost dream-like oasis in the middle of incredible tensions affecting Quiroga directly. For some of these difficulties see especially chapters five and six. For the collaboration between Quiroga and the Tarascan-Chichimecs against the *encomendero* Infante occasionally on the verge of military confrontation, see the rather dramatic episode (pp. 95-101).

56. Ross Dealy has told us how to this day (1976) "Indians" light candles before church images in honor of the "Tata Vasco," and how popular veneration draws attention to the preservation of a spot where his foot allegedly sank into the mud, and to the various relics of Quiroga's remains. León is said to have measured his skull, and these findings are said to be included in his biography on Quiroga which I have not yet been able to situate. Canonization plans are also under way. For further information on this, see Dealy's *The Politics of an Erasmian Lawyer: Vasco de Quiroga* (Malibu: Undena Publications, 1976): pp. 1-2, 21. See also Krippner-Martínez's conclusion to the dissertation chapter "Discourse of domination, discourse of hope: the contradictory vision of Don Vasco de Quiroga"(University of Wisconsin-Madison, 1993), for the account of the 1990 transfer of Quiroga's remains to the mausoleum in the modern Basilica de Nuestra Señora de Salud, Pátzcuaro and the various celebrations around this event (pp. 203-207).

57. To come closer to the early modern horizon, we must account for the rather standard vilification of the mechanical arts. Quiroga's colonial utopianism is to be situated in this historical vicinity of manual labor ("los que viven de sus manos"), and marginality in the American periphery receiving the influx of all those who want to get out to get luckily better off ("mudar de lugar [para] mejorar de estado"). See "Trabajo y exclusión: El trabajador manual en el sistema social español de la primera modernidad" by J.A. Maravall, *Les problemes de l'exclusion en Espagne (XVI-XVII siecles): Idéologie et Discours*, Augustin Redondo, Ed. (Paris: Publications de la Sorbonne, 1983): pp. 135-159.

58. For some tentative differences among these four *oidor* members of the *Segunda Audiencia*, see Ross Dealy, ibidem, pp. 10-16.

Bibliography

Vasco de Quiroga, Primary Material: Colonial Sources (16th–17th Centuries) and Monographic Editions

Acuña, René, Ed. *Relaciones Geográficas del Siglo XVI: Michoacán.* México: Universidad Nacional Autónoma de México, 1987.

———.*Vasco de Quiroga. De Debellandis Indis. Un tratado desconocido.* México: Universidad Nacional Autónoma de México, 1988.

Aguayo, Spencer, Rafael. *Don Vasco de Quiroga: Taumaturgo de la Organización Social Seguido de un Apéndice Documental* (Mexico: Oasis, 1970).

Arriaga, Antonio. "Vasco de Quiroga Fundador de Pueblos," *EHN* (México, vol.1, 1966): pp. 149-155.

"Breve Descripción del Obispado de Michoacán (Finales del Siglo XVIII)," *BAGN* (Mexico, Tomo XI, Num. 1, 1940): pp. 125-145.

Banazak, Gregory A. *The Ecclesiology of Vasco de Quiroga.* Dissertation. Roma: Pontificia Universitatis Gregorianae, 1991.

Bechtloff, Dagmar. "La Formación de una sociedad intercultural: las cofradías en el Michoacán colonial," *HM* (Vol. XLIII, Octubre-Diciembre 1993, Núm. 2): pp. 251-263.

Borges, Pedro. "Vasco de Quiroga en el Ambiente Misionero de la Nueva España," *MH* (Año XXIII, Set.-Dic., Núm. 69): pp. 297-340.

Cabrero, Leoncio, Ed. *Relación de Michoacán. Anónimo.* Madrid: Historia 16, Col. Crónicas de América, núm. 52, 1989.

Callens, Paul L. *Tata Vasco. Un Gran Reformador del Siglo XVI.* México: Editorial Jus, 1959.

Castañeda-Delgado, Paulino, Ed. *Don Vasco de Quiroga y su "Información en Derecho."* Madrid: Ediciones Jóse Porrua Turanzas, 1974.

Cro, Stelio. "La Utopía Cristiano-Social en el Nuevo Mundo," *ALH* (26/l, 1997): pp. 87-129.

Cuevas, Mariano, Ed. *Documentos Inéditos del Siglo XVI para la Historia de Mexico.* Mexico: Editorial Porrúa, 2a edition, 1975.

Dealy, Ross. *The Politics of an Erasmian Lawyer, Vasco de Quiroga.* Malibu: Undena Publications, 1976.

Escobar-Olmedo, Armando M. *Catálogo de Documentos Michoacanos en Archivos Españoles*. Morelia, México: Universidad Michoacana de San Nicolás de Hidalgo, 1990.

Gómes Moreira, José Aparecido. *Conquista y Conciencia Cristiana. El Pensamiento indigenista y jurídico-teológico de Don Vasco de Quiroga (+1565)*. Quito: Ediciones Abyá-Yala, 1990.

González-Dávila, Gil. *Teatro Eclesiástico de la Primitiva Iglesia de la Nueva España en las Indias Occidentales*. Madrid: José Porrúa Turanzas, 1959.

Hermida-Lazcano, Pablo. "Topografía de una Utopía: De la Utopía de Tomás Moro a los Pueblos-Hospitales de Vasco de Quiroga," *RDI* (Mayo-Agosto 1995, Núm. 204, Vol. LV): pp. 357-203.

Herrejón Peredo, Carlos. "Fuentes Patrísticas, Jurídicas y Escolásticas del Pensamiento Quiroguiano," in *Textos Políticos en la Nueva España*, México: Universidad Nacional Autónoma de México, 1984.

Krippner-Martínez, James. *Images of Conquest: Text and Context in Colonial Mexico*. University of Wisconsin-Madison, Dissertation 1993.

Lacas, M. M. "A Social Welfare Organizer in Sixteenth Century New Spain: Don Vasco de Quiroga, First Bishop of Michoacán," *TA* (Vol. XIV, July 1957-April 1958): pp. 57-86.

Landa, Rubén. *Don Vasco de Quirhoga*. Barcelona: Ediciones Grijalbo, 1965.

Lejarza, Fidel de. "Don Vasco de Quiroga en las Crónicas Franciscanas," *MH* (Año XXIII, Mayo-Agosto, Núm. 68): pp. 129-244.

Lemoine Villicaña, Ernesto. "Documentos para la Historia de la Ciudad de Valladolid, hoy Morelia (1541-1624)," *BAGN* (Mexico, Tomo III, Núm. 1, 1962): pp. 5-97.

———. "Mandamientos del Virrey Conde de Monterrey para la Congregación de Pueblos de Indios en la Alcaldía Mayor de Valladolid (1601-1603)," *BAGN* (Mexico, Tomo I, Num. 1, 1960): pp. 5-55.

———. "La Relación de la Guacana, Michoacán, de Baltasar Dorantes Carranza, Año de 1605," *BAGN* (Mexico, Tomo III, Num. 4, 1962): pp. 669-702.

———. "Un Notable Escrito Póstumo del Obispo de Michoacán, Fray Antonio de San Miguel, sobre la situación social, económica y eclesiástica de la Nueva España, en 1804," *BAGN* (Mexico, Tomo V, Num. 1, 1964): pp. 5-66.

León, Nicolás, Ed. *Documentos Inéditos Referentes al Ilustrísimo Señor Don Vasco de Quiroga Existentes en el Archivo General de Indias*. Mexico: Antigua Librería Robredo, de José Porrúa e Hijos, Biblioteca Histórica Mexicana de Obras Inéditas, number 17, 1940.

Lietz, Paul S. *Don Vasco de Quiroga and the Second Audiencia of New Spain*. A Loyola University. Dissertation, 1940 [Brown University Library, Microfilm Version].

Martin, Cheryl E. "Modes of Production in Colonial Mexico: The Case of Morelos," *EHN* (Mexico, Instituto de Investigaciones Históricas, 1992): pp. 107-121.

———. *Rural Society in Colonial Morelos*. Albuquerque: University of New Mexico Press, 1985.

Martín-Hernández, Francisco. *Don Vasco de Quiroga (Protector de los Indios)*. Salamanca: Universidad Pontificia & Caja Salamanca y Soria, 1993.

Méndez-Arceo, Sergio. "Contribución a la Historia de Vasco de Quiroga," *Abside* (Enero, 1941, V-1): pp. 59-68.

————. "Contribución a la Historia de Vasco de Quiroga. Nuevas Aclaraciones y Documentos," *Abside* (Marzo, 1941, V-3): pp. 196-208.

Méndez-Plancarte, Gabriel. *Humanistas del Siglo XVI*. México: Ediciones de la Universidad Nacional Autónoma, 1946.

Merino, Manuel. "Don Vasco de Quiroga en los Cronistas Agustinos," *MH*(Año XXIII, Enero-Abril, Num. 67): pp. 89-112.

Miranda Godínez, Francisco. *El Real Colegio de San Nicolás de Pátzcuaro. Dissertatio ad Laureaum in Facultate Historiae Ecclesiasticae Pontificiae Universitatis Greforianae*. Zamora: Centro Intercultural, 1967.

Muriel, Josefina. *Hospitales de la Nueva España. Tomo I: Fundaciones del Siglo XVI*. Mexico: Universidad Nacional Autónoma de México/Cruz Roja Mexicana, Instituto de Investigaciones Históricas, Serie Historia Novohispana/12, [1956] 1990.

————.*Hospitales de la Nueva España. Tomo II: Fundaciones de los Siglos XVII y XVIII*. Mexico: Universidad Nacional Autónoma de México/Cruz Roja Mexicana, Instide Investigaciones Históricas, Serie Historia Novohispana/15, [1960] 1991.

O'Gorman, E., Ed."Noticias Para La Historia del Antiguo Colegio de San Nicolás de Michoacán, Anonymous [Jesuit, XVII], *BAGN* (1.Tomo X. México, 1939): pp. 24-106.

O'Gorman, Ed. and Fernández, Justino. *Santo Tomás More y "La Utopía de Tomás Moro en la Nueva España."* México: Alcancia, 1937.

Pagden, Anthony. "The Humanism of Vasco de Quiroga's Información en Derecho," in *The Uncertainties of Empire: Essays in Iberian and Ibero-American Intellectual History* (Collected Series. Series Variorum, 1994). (incomplete ref.)

Pérez San Vicente, Guadalupe. "La Introducción del Estudio del Derecho en el Colegio de San Nicolás de Valladolid," *EHN* (México 1967, vol 2, 1967): pp. 79-109.

Reglas y Ordenanzas Para el Gobierno de los Hospitales de Santa Fé de México, Michoacán Dispuestas por su Fundador el Rmo. Y Venerable Señor Don Vasco de Quiroga, Primer Obispo de Michoacán. Facsimile Edition, Mexico, 1940.

Serrano Gassent, Paz, Ed.*Vasco de Quiroga: La Utopía en América*. Madrid: Historia 16, 1992.

Trueba, Alfonso. *Don Vasco*. México: Editorial Jus, 1958.

Verástique, Bernardino. *Collision of utopias: Vasco de Quiroga's mission to the Purhépecha-Chichimec of Michoacán, México 1537-1565*. Harvard University, Dissertation, 1990.

Warren, Fintan B. "Documents. The Construction of Santa Fé de México," *TA* (Vol. XX., July, 1964, Num. 1): pp. 69-78.

————. *Vasco de Quiroga and his Pueblo-Hospitales of Santa Fe.* Washington: Academy of American Franciscan History, 1963.

————. "Vasco de Quiroga, fundador de hospitales y colegios," *MH* (Enero-Abril, Año XXlll, Núm. 67): pp. 25-46.

Zavala, Silvio. "Algo Más Sobre Vasco de Quiroga," *HA* (Vol. XXXVIII, Enero-Marzo 1989, Num. 3, 151): pp. 533-549.

————. "Letras de Utopía: Carta a Don Alfonso Reyes," *CA* (Año l, Vol. ll/2, Marzo-Abril 1942): pp. 46-158.

————. *La "Utopia" de Tomás Moro en la Nueva España y Otros Estudios.* México: Antigua Librería Robredo, de José Porrúa e Hijos, Biblioteca Histórica Mexicana de Obras Inéditas, number 4, 1937.

————. *Recuerdo de Vasco de Quiroga.* México: Editoria Porrúa, 1965.

————. *Sir Thomas More in New Spain: A Utopian Adventure of the Renaissance.* London: Hispanic & Luso-Brazilian Councils, 1956.

Zavala, Silvio et el. *Memoria de la Mesa Redonda sobre Vasco de Quiroga.* México: Instituto Dr. José María Luis Mora, 1982.

Zavala, Silvio, León-Portilla, Miguel and Tovar de Teresa, Guillermo. *La Utopía Mexicana del Siglo XVI: Lo bello, lo Verdadero y lo Bueno.* Mexico: GrupoAzabache, 1992.

The Region of Michoacán: Primary Sources (Pre-Hispanic and Colonial Sources) and Monographic Studies

Anawalt, Patricia R. and Berdan, Frances F., Eds. *The Essential Codex Mendoza.* Berkeley: University of California Press, 1997.

Beaumont, Pablo. *Crónica de Michoacán.* México: Talleres Gráficos de la Nación, 1932.

Beltrán, Ulises. *El Michoacán Antiguo. Estado y Sociedad Tarascos en la Epoca Prehispánica.* Zamora, Mich.: El Colegio de Michoacán/Gobierno del Estado de Michoacán, 1994.

Carreño, Alberto María. *Don Fray Juan de Zumárraga: Teólogo y Editor, Humanista e Inquisidor (documentos inéditos).* Mexico: Jus, 1950.

Carrillo-Cázares, Alberto. *Partidos y Padrones del Obispado de Michoacán, 1680-1685.* Michoacán: El Colegio de Michoacán/Gobierno del Estado de Michoacán, 1996.

Cline, S. L., Ed. *The Book of Tributes: Early Sixteenth-Century Nahuatl Censuses from Morelos.* Los Angeles: UCLA Latin American Center Publications & University of California, 1993.

Códice Osuna. Reproducción Facsimilar de la Obra del Mismo Título, Editada en Madrid, 1878. México: Instituto Indigenista Interamericano, 1947.

Cortés, Fernando. *Relación de Algunas Cosas de la Nueva España y de la Gran Ciudad de Temestitán México.* México: José Porrúa e Hijos, 1961.

Díaz del Castillo, Bernal. *Historia Verdadera de la Conquista de la Nueva España.* Madrid: Alianza Editorial, 1991.

Dietz, Gunther. *Teoría y Práctica del Indigenismo. El caso del fomento de la alfarer'a en Michoacán (México)*. Quito: Biblioteca Abya-Yala, 1995.

Escobar-Olmedo, Armando M. *"Proceso, Tormento y Muerte del Cazonzi, último Gran Señor de los Tarascos" por Nuño de Guzmán (1530)*. Morelia, Michoacán: Frene de Afirmación Hispanista, 1997.

Florescano, Enrique, Ed. *Historia General de Michoacán*. México: Gobierno de Michoacán, 1989.

García Izcalbaceta, Joaquín. *Don Fray Juan de Zumárraga: Primer Obispo y Arzobispo de Mexico*. Mexico: Editorial Porrúa, 4 vols. 1947.

———. *México en 1554 de Francisco Cervantes de Salazar*. México: Ediciones de la Universidad Nacional Autónoma, 1939.

Garibay K., Angel María, Ed. *Historia de las Indias de Nueva España e Islas de la Tierra Firme*. Escrita por Fray Diego Durán (XVI). Mexico: Porrúa, núms. 36-37, 1967.

Gonzalbo-Aizpuru, Pilar. *Historia de la Educación en la Epoca Colonial: El Mundo Indígena*. Mexico: El Colegio de México, 1990.

Herrejón-Peredo, Carlos. *El Colegio de San Miguel de Guayangareo*. Morelia, Michoacán: Universidad Michoacana de San Nicolás de Hidalgo, 1989.

Kobayashi, José María. *La Educación como Conquista*. México: El Colegio de México, 1974.

Las Casas, Bartolomé de. *Apología*. Madrid: Alianza Editorial/Obras Completas/ núm. 9, 1992.

———. *Apologética. Historia Sumaria I*. Madrid: Alianza Editorial/Obras Completas/num. 6, 1992.

———. *De Regia Potestate o Derecho de Autodeterminación*. Edición Crítica Bilingue por Luciano Pereña, J. M. Pérez-Prendes, Vidal Abril and Joaquín Azcarraga. Madrid: Consejo Superior de Investigaciones Científicas, 1969.

———. *Tratados de 1552*. Madrid: Alianza Editorial/Obras Completas/num. 10, 1992.

López-Sarrelangue, Delfina E. *La Nobleza Indígena de Pátzcuaro en la Epoca Virreinal*. México: Instituto de Investigaciones Históricas, Universidad Nacional Autónoma de México, 1965.

Osorio-Romero, Ignacio. *La Enseñanza del Latín a los Indios*. México: Universidad Autónoma de México, 1990.

Ramírez, José F. and Rayon, Ignacio L., Eds. *Proceso de Residencia contra Pedro de Alvarado*. Mexico: Valdés y Redondas, 1847.

Rubí, Alma Rosa, Ed. *El Lienzo de Carapán*. México: Instituto Nacional de Antropología e Historia/ Cuaderno de Trabajo/2, 1989.

Ruiz Medrano, Ethelia. *Gobierno y Sociedad en Nueva España: Segunda Audiencia y Antonio de Mendoza*. Zamora, Mich.: El Colegio de Michoacán, 1991.

The Tlaxcatlan Actas. A Compendium of the Records of the Cabildo of Tlaxcala (1545-1627). Edition by James Lockhart, Frances Berdan & Arthur J. O. Anderson. Salt Lake City: University of Utah Press, 1986.

Valadés, Fray Diego. *Retórica Cristiana*. México: Fondo de Cultura Económica, Biblioteca Americana, 1989.

Vázquez, Germán. *Varios. Relaciones de la Nueva España*. Madrid: Historia 16, 1990.

Warren, Benedict J. *The Conquest of Michoacán. The Spanish Domination of the Tarascan Kingdom in Western Mexico, 1521-1530*. Norman: The University of Oklahoma Press, 1985.

Colonial Mexico: Historical Background and Criticism

Aiton, Author Scott. *Antonio de Mendoza: First Viceroy of New Spain*. Durham: Duke University Press, 1927.

Anawalt, Patricia R., and Berdan, Frances F. *The Essential Codex Mendoza*. Berkeley: University of California Press, 1997.

Bacigalupo, Marvyn Helen. *A Changing Perspective: Attitudes Toward Creole Society in New Spain (1521-1610)*. London: Tamesis Books, 1981.

Baudet, Georges, Ed. *Fray Andrés de Olmos. Tratado de Hechicerías y Sortilegios*. México: Universidad Nacional Autónoma de México, 1990.

―――. *Utopia and History in Mexico. The First Chroniclers of Mexican Civilization*. Niwot, Colorado: University Press of Colorado, 1995.

Blanco-Sánchez, Antonio. *Aislados en su Lengua (1521-1995)*. Madrid: Anejos del Boletín de la Real Academia Española, Anejo LIV, 1997.

Borah, Woodrow. *Justice by Insurance: The General Indian Court of Colonial Mexico and the Legal Aides of the Half Real*. Berkeley: University of California Press, 1983.

Bribiesca-Sumano, Ma. Elena, et al. *Catálogo de Protocolos de la Notaría No. 1 de Toluca 1558-1785. Volumen IV*. Mexico: Universidad Autónoma del Estado de Mexico, 1994.

Connaughton, Brian F., ed. *Las Fuentes Eclesiásticas para la Historia Social de México*. México: Universidad Autónoma Metropolitana, 1996.

Cutter, Charles R. *The Protector de Indios in Colonial New Mexico 1659-1821*. Albuquerque: University of New Mexico Press, 1986.

Durand, José. *La transformación Social del Conquistador*. México: Porrúa, 1953.

Ferná□índez, Justino. *Santo Tomás More y La Utopia de More en la Nueva España*. Mexico: Alcancia, 1937.

Florescano, Enrique, Ed. *México en 500 Libros*. México: Nueva Imagen, 1980.

Florescano, Enrique and Gil-Sánchez, Isabel, Eds. *Descripcioens Económicas y Regionales de Nueva España. Provincias del Centro, Sudeste y Sur, 1766-1827*. Mexico: Instituto Nacional de Antropología e Historia, 1976.

Florescano, Enrique and Pérez-Montfort, R. Eds. *Historiadores de México en el Siglo XX*. México: Fondo de Cultura Económica, 1995.

Forst, Elsa C. *Este Nuevo Orbe*. México: Universidad Nacional Autónoma de México, 1996.

García-Abasolo, Antonio F. *Martín Enriquez y la Reforma de 1568 en Nueva España*. Sevilla: Excma. Diputación Provincial de Sevilla, 1983.

Gerhard, Peter. *A Guide to the Historical Geography of New Spain*. Cambridge: Cambridge University Press, 1972.

————. *Síntesis e Indice de los Mandamientos Virreinales 1548-1553*. México: Universidad Nacional Autónoma de México, 1992.

Gibson, Charles. *The Aztecs Under Spanish Rule. A History of the Indians of the Valley of Mexico, 1519-1810*. Stanford: Stanford University Press, 1964.

————. *Tlaxcala in the Sixteenth Century*. New Haven: Yale University Press, 1952.

Grijalva, Juan de. *Crónica de la Orden de N.P.S. Agustín en la Provincias de la Nueva España*. Mexico: Imprenta Victoria [1624], 1924.

Grijalva, Manuel Miño. "¿Proto-Industria Colonial?," *HM* (Vol. XXXVIII, Abril-Junio 1989, Núm. 4): pp. 793-818.

Gruzinski, Serge. *The Conquest of Mexico*. Cambridge: Polity Press, 1993.

————. *Painting the Conquest: The Mexican Indians and the European Renaissance*. Unesco: Flammarion, 1992.

Herzog, Tamar. "Sobre la Cultura Jurídica en la América Colonial (Siglos XVI-XVIII)," in *AHDE* (Tomo LXV. Madrid, 1995): pp. 903-911.

Horta, Raúl. *El Humanismo en el Nuevo Mundo. Ensayo Histórico y Perspectivas Contemporáneas*. Mexico: Miguel angel Porrúa, 1997.

Israel, J. I. *Race, Class and Politics in Colonial Mexico 1610-1670*. Oxford: Oxford University Press, 1975.

Kellogg, Susan. *Law and the Transformation of Aztec Culture, 1500-1700*. Norman: University of Oklahoma Press, 1995.

Klor de Alva, J. Jorge. "Colonialism and Post Colonialism as (Latin) American Mirages. *CLAR* (Vol. 1. Nos. 1-2, 1992): pp. 3-23.

————. *The Work of Bernardino de Sahagún: Pioneer Ethnographer of Sixteenth-Century Aztec Mexico*. New York:University of Texas Press, 1988.

Klor de Alva, J. Jorge, Ed. and Miguel León-Portilla, Manuel Gutiérrez-Estévez, Gary H. Gossen, *De Palabra y Obra en el Nuevo Mundo* (Madrid: Siglo XXI, 1992).

León-Portilla, Miguel. *Endangered Cultures*. Dallas: Southern Methodist University Press, 1990.

————. *La Flecha en el Blanco: Francisco Tenamaztle y Bartolomé de las Casas en lucha por los derechos de los indígenas 1541-1556*. Mexico: Editorial Diana, 1995.

Llaguno, José A. *La Personalidad Jurídica del Indio y el III Concilio Provincial Mexicano (1585)*. México: Editorial Porrúa, 1963.

Lockhart, James. *The Nahuas After the Conquest*. Stanford: Stanford University Press, 1992.

————. *We People Here. Nahuatl Accounts of the Conquest of Mexico*. Berkeley: University of California Press, 1993.

López-Cervantes, Gonzalo and García-García, Rosa. *Ensayo Bibliográfico del Período Colonial en México*. Mexico: Instituto Nacional de Antropología e Historia, 1989.

Mundy, Barbara E. *The Mapping of New Spain: Indigenous Cartography and the Map of the Relaciones Geográficas*. Chicago: The University of Chicago Press, 1996.

Offner, Jerome A. *Law and Politics in Aztec Texcoco*. Cambridge: Cambridge University Press, 1983.

O'Gorman, Edmundo. *Crisis y Porvenir de la Ciencia Histórica*. México: Imprenta Universitaria, 1947.

———. *Fundamentos de la Historia de América*. México: Imprenta Universitaria, 1942.

———. *La Idea del Descubrimiento de América*. Historia de esa Interpretación y Crítica de sus Fundamentos. México: Centro de Estudios Filosóficos, 1951.

———. *La Invención de América. El Universalismo de la Cultura de Occidente*. México: Fondo de Cultura Económica, 1958.

O'Gorman, Edmundo, Ed. *México en 1554 y Túmulo Imperial de Francisco Cervantes de Salazar*. México: Ed. Porrúa, 1972.

O'Gorman, Edmundo and Bataillon, Marcel. *Dos Concepciones de la Tarea Histórica con motivo de la Idea del Descubrimiento de America*. México: Imprenta Universitaria, 1955.

Paz, Octavio. *Sor Juana Inés de la Cruz o Las Trampas de la Fé*. Barcelona: Seix Barral, 1982.

Pérez-Bustamante, C. *Don Antonio de Mendoza: Primer Virrey de la Nueva España* (1535-1550). Santiago, Mexico: Tip. de "El Eco Franciscano," 1928.

Phelan, John Leddy. *The Millennial Kingdom of the Franciscans in the New World*. Berkeley: University of California Press, 1970.

Quiñones-Keber, Eloise, ed. *Codex Telleriano-Remensis: Ritual, Divination, and History in a Pictorial Aztec Manuscript*. Austin: University of Texas Press, 1995.

Ricard, Robert. *La Conquista Espiritual de México*. México: Editorial Jus/Polis, 1947.

Robertson, Donald. *Mexican Manuscript Painting of the Early Colonial Period. The Metropolitan Schools*. Norman and London: University of Oklahoma Press, 1994.

Román-Gutiérrez, José Francisco. *Sociedad y Evangelización en Nueva Galicia durante el Siglo XVI*. Córdoba, Mexico: Instituto Nacional de Antropología e Historia, 1993.

Rubio Mañé, José Ignacio. *El Virreinato*. 4 Volumes. México: Fondo de Cultura Económica, 1983.

Sánchez de Tagle, Esteban, Ed. *Ciudad de México. Epoca Colonial. Bibliografía*. México: Departamento del Distrito Federal/Dirección de Estudios Históricos (INAH), 1993.

Seed, Patricia. *Ceremonies of Possession in Europe's Conquest of the New World, 1492-1640*. Cambridge: Cambridge University Press, 1995.

————. *To Love, Honor and Obey in Colonial Mexico: Conflict over Marriage Choice, 1574-1821*. Stanford: Stanford University Press, 1988.

Spores, Ronald & Hassig, Ross. *Five Centuries of Law and Politics in Central Mexico*. Nashville: Vanderbilt University/ Publications in Anthropology/30, 1984.

Sterne, Steve. *The Secret History of Gender: Women, Men and Power in Late Colonial Mexico*. Chapel Hill: The University of North Carolina Press, 1995.

Taylor, William B. *Magistrates of the Sacred: Priests and Parishioners in Eighteenth-Century Mexico*. Stanford: Stanford University Press, 1996.

Thomas, Hugh. *The Conquest of Mexico*. London: Hutchinson, 1993.

de la Torre Villar, Ernesto. *Estudios de Historia Jurídica*. México: Universidad Nacional Autónoma de México, 1994.

Vance, John T. *The Background of Hispanic-American Law*. New York: Central Book Company, 1943.

Von Wobeser, Gisela. *San Carlos Borromeo. Endeudamiento de una Hacienda Colonial (1608-1729)*. México: Universidad Nacional Autónoma de México, 1980.

Zavala, Silvio A. *La Encomienda Indiana*. Mexico: Editorial Porrúa, 1992.

————. *Esclavos Indios en Nueva España*. Mexico: Edición de El Colegio Nacional, 1967.

————. *Estudios Indianos*. México: El Colegio Nacional, 1984.

————. *Instituciones Jurídicas en la Conquista de América*. Mexico: Porrúa, 1971.

————. *Por la Senda Hispana de la Libertad*. Mexico: Fondo de Cultura Económica/Mapfre, 1993.

————. *Recuerdo de Vasco de Quiroga*. México: Porrúa, 1965.

————. *Servicio Personal de los Indios en la Nueva España*. Mexico: El Colegio de Mexico/El Colegio Nacional, Vols. 1-3. 1984.

————. *Suplemento Documental y Bibliográfico a la Encomienda Indiana*. México: Universidad Nacional Autónoma de México, 1994.

————. *La "Utopia" de Tomás Moro en la Nueva España y Otros Estudios*. México: Antigua Librería Robredo, de José Porrúa e Hijos, Biblioteca Histórica Mexicana de Obras Inéditas/ 4, 1937.

————. *La Utopía Mexicana del Siglo XVI: Lo bello, lo verdadero y lo bueno*. Italy: Grupo Azabache, 1992.

Colonial Latin America: Primary Sources, Background and Criticism

Adorno, Rolena. *Felipe Guamán Poma de Ayala. Nueva Crónica y Buen Gobierno*. Madrid: Historia 16, 1987.

————. "The Genesis of Felipe Guaman Poma de Ayala's Nueva Corónica y Buen Gobierno." *CLAR* (Vol. 2, Nos. 1-2, 1993): pp. 53-92.

Armani, Alberto. *Ciudad de Dios y Ciudad del Sol: El "Estado" Jesuita de los Guaraníes (1609-1768)*. México: Fondo de Cultura Económica, 1987.

Arnoldsson, Sverker. *Los Momentos Históricos de América según la Historiografía Hispanoamericana del período colonial*. Madrid: Insula, 1956.

Arranz, Luis, Ed. *Cristobal Colón: Diario de a Bordo*. Madrid: Historia 16, 1985.

Arzans de Orsúa y Vela, Bartolomé. *Historia de la Villa Imperial de Potosí*. Lewis Hanke y Gunnar Mendoz, Eds. Providence: Brown University Press, 1965.

Bacigalupo, Marvyn Helen. *A Changing Perspective: Attitudes Towards Creole Society in New Spain (1521-1610)*. London: Tamesis Books Limited, 1981.

Bayón, Damián. *History of South American Colonial Art and Architecture*. Barcelona: Ediciones Polígrafa, 1989.

Beverley, John. *Against Literature*. Minneapolis: Minnesota Press, 1993.

————. *Del Lazarillo al Sandinismo: Estudios de la Función Ideológica de la Literatura Española e Hispanoamericana*. Minneapolis: The Prisma Institute, 1987.

————. *Literature and Politics in the Central American Revolutions*. Austin: University of Texas Press, 1990.

Bonilla, Heraclio, Ed. *Los Conquistados: 1492 y la población indígena de las Américas*. Colombia: Tercer Mundo Editores, 1992.

Burga, Manuel. *De la Encomienda a la Hacienda Capitalista: El valle del Jequetepeque del siglo XVI al XX*. Lima: IEP Ediciones, 1976.

————. *Nacimiento de una Utopía: Muerte y Resurrección de los Incas*. México: Instituto de Apoyo Agrario, 1988.

Burkholder, Mark A. *Colonial Latin America*. New York: Oxford University Press, 1994.

Carbonell de Masy, Rafael. *Estrategias de Desarrollo Rural en los Pueblos Guaraníes* (1609-1767). Barcelona: Antoni Bosch Editor, 1992.

Cevallos-Candau, Francisco J., Ed. *Coded Encounters: Writing, Gender, and Ethnicity in Colonial Latin America*. Amherst: University of Massachusetts Press, 1994.

Chanady, Amaryll. *Latin American Identity and Constructions of Difference*. Minneapolis: University of Minnesota Press, 1994.

Chang-Rodríguez, Raquel. *La apropiación del signo. Tres cronistas indígenas del Perú*. Tempe: Arizona State University, 1988.

Chichizola Debernardi, José. *El Manierismo en Lima*. Perú: Pontificia Universidad Católica del Perú, 1983.

Cook, Noble David., Ed. *Tasa de la Visita General de Francisco de Toledo*. Lima: Universidad Nacional Mayor de San Marcos, 1975.

Cossio del Pomar, F. *Peruvian Colonial Art: The Cuzco School of Painting*. New York: Wittenborn and Company, 1964.

————. *Historia Crítica de la Pintura en el Cuzco*. Cuzco: Universidad del Cuzco, H.G. Rozas, 1922.

Cro, Stelio. *The American Foundations of the Hispanic Utopia. Volume 1: The Literary Utopia* and *Volume 2: The Empirical Utopia.* Tallahassee, Florida: The DeSoto Press, 1994.

————. "Las reducciones jesuíticas en la encrucijada de dos utopías," Las Utopías en el Mundo Hispánico/ Les Utopies dans le Monde Hispanique. Madrid: Universidad Complutense/Casa de Velázquez, 1990.

Dean, Carolyn S. "Ethnic Conflict and Corpus Christi in Colonial Cuzco," *CLAR* (Vol. 2, Nos. 1-2 1993): pp. 93-120.

De la Puente Brunke, José. *Encomiendas y Encomenderos en el Perú. Estudio Social y Político de una Institución Colonial.* Sevilla: Diputación Provincial, 1992.

De la Torre Villar, Ernesto. *Las Congregaciones de los Pueblos de Indios.* México: Universidad Nacional Autónoma de México, 1995.

Delgado-Gómez, Angel, Ed. *Spanish Historical Writing about the New World (1493-1700).* Providence, Rhode Island: Published by the John Carter Brown Library in Recognition of the Quincentenary Year, 1992.

Díaz-Rementería, Carlos J. *El Cacique en el Virreinato del Perú: Estudio Jurídico-Histórico.* Sevilla: Universidad de Sevilla, 1977.

Dunn, Oliver, Ed. *The Diario of Christopher Columbus's First Voyage to America 1492-1493.* Norman and London: University of Oklahoma Press, 1989.

Dussel, Enrique. *Desintegración de la Cristiandad Colonial y Liberación.* Salamanca: Ediciones Sígueme, 1978.

————. *1492, El Encubrimiento del Otro: Hacia el Origen del "Mito de la Modernidad."* Santafé de Bogotá: Anthropos, 1992.

————. *El Episcopado Hispanoamericano. Institución Misionera en Defensa del Indio, 1504-1620.* Cuernavaca, México: Centro Intercultural de Documentación (CIDOC), Sondeos Nos. 32, 35, 37; vols. 1, 4, 6, 1969-1970.

————. *El Episcopado Hispanoamericano. Institución Misionera en Defensa del Indio, 1504-1620.* Apéndices Documentales. Cuernavaca, México: Centro Intercultural de Documentación (CIDOC), No. 71, vs. 8-9, 1970.

————. *Hipótesis para una Historia de la Iglesia en América Latina.* Barcelona: Estela-IEPAL, 1967.

————. *The Invention of the Americas.* New York: Continuum, 1995.

————. *Liberación Latinoamericana y Emmanuel Levinas.* Buenos Aires: Editorial Bonum, 1975.

————. *Teología de la Liberación. Un Panorama de su Desarrollo.* Mexico: Potrerillos Editores, 1995.

————. *The Underside of Modernity: Apel, Ricoeur, Rorty, Taylor and the Philosophy of Liberation.* New Jersey: Humanities Press, 1996.

Flores Galindo, Alberto. *Buscando un Inca: Identidad y Utopía en los Andes.* La Habana: Casa de las Américas, 1986.

————. *Tupac Amaru II-1780.* Antología. Lima: Ediciones Retablo de Papel, 1976.

Forgues, Roland. Mariátegui: *La Utopía Realizable.* Lima: Amauta, 1995.

300   *Good Places and Non-Places in Colonial Mexico*

Fraser, Valerie. *The Architecture of Conquest: Building in the Viceroyalty of Peru, 1535-1635.* Cambridge: Cambridge University Press, 1990.

Gibson, Charles and Peckham, Howard, Eds. *Attitudes of Colonial Powers Toward the American Indian.* Salt Lake City: University of Utah Press, 1969.

Giménez Fernández, Manuel. *Bartolomé de las Casas. Volumen Primero. Delegado de Cisneros para la Reformación de los Indios (1516-1517).* Sevilla: Escuela de Estudios Hispano-Americanos, 1953.

————. *Bartolomé de las Casas. Volumen Segundo. Capellán de S.M. Carlos I. Poblador de Cumaná (1517-1523).* Sevilla: Escuela de Estudios Hispano-Americanos, 1960.

Góngora, Mario. *Encomenderos y Estancieros. Estudios Acerca de la Constitución Social Aristocrática de Chile después de la Conquista 1580-1660.* Santiago de Chile: Universidad de Chile, 1970.

————. *El Estado en el Derecho Indiano.* Epoca de Fundación (1492-1570). Chile: Instituto de Investigaciones Histórico-Culturales, 1951.

————. *Origen de los "Inquilinos" de Chile Central.* Santiago de Chile: Editorial Universitariña, 1960.

————. *Studies in the Colonial History of Spanish America.* Cambridge: Cambridge University Press, 1975.

González Echevarría, Roberto. *Myth and Archive: A Theory of Latin American Narrative.* Cambridge: Cambridge University Press, 1990.

Gugelberger, Georg M., Ed. *The Real Thing: Testimonial Discourse and Latin America.* Durham: Duke University Press, 1996.

Gutiérrez, Gustavo. *Dios o el Oro en las Indias.* Lima: Instituto Bartolomé de las Casas, CEP, 1989.

————. *En Busca de los Pobres de Jesucristo. El Pensamiento de Bartolomé de las Casas* (Lima: Instituto Bartolomé de las Casas/CEP, 1992).

————. *Entre las Calandrias. Un Ensayo sobre José María Arguedas.* Lima: Instituto Bartolomé de las Casas, CEP, 1990.

————. *La Verdad los hará libres.* Confrontaciones. Lima: Instituto Bartolomé de las Casas, CEP, 1986.

————. *Teología de la Liberación.* Perspectivas. Salamanca: Sígueme, 1973.

————. *A Theology of Liberation. History, Politics and Salvation.* New York: Orbis Books, 1973.

Gutiérrez, Ramón. *Evolución Urbanística y Arquitectónica del Paraguay (1537-1911).* Argentina: Departamento de Historia de la Arquitectura. Universidad Nacional del Nordeste, 1978.

Hanke, Lewis. *The First Social Experiments in America. A Study in the Development of Spanish Indian Policy in the Sixteenth Century.* Cambridge: Harvard University Press, 1935.

————. *La lucha por la Justicia en la Conquista de América.* Buenos Aires: Editorial Sudamericana, 1949.

Hanke, Lewis and Millares-Carlo, Agustín. *Cuerpo de Documentos del Siglo XVI:*

Sobre los derechos de España en las Indias y las Filipinas. Mexico: Fondo de Cultura Economica, 1943.

Hanke, Lewis, Ed. *Do the Americas have a Common History? A Critique of the Bolton Theory.* New York: Alfred A. Knopf, 1965.

Hanke, Lewis and Rausch, Jane M., Eds. *People and Issues in Latin American History. The Colonial Experience.* New York and Princeton: Markus Wiener Publishing, 1993.

Hernández, Pablo. *Organización Social de las Doctrinas Guaraníes de la Compañía de Jesús.* 2 Volumes. Barcelona: Gustavo Gili, 1913.

Herzog, Tamar. *La Administración como un Fenómeno Social: la Justicia Penal de la Ciudad de Quito (1650-1750).* Madrid: Centro de Estudios Constitucionales, 1995.

———. *Mediación, Archivos y Ejercicio: Los escribanos de Quito (siglo XVI).* Frankfurt: Vittorio Klostermann, 1996.

———. *Los Ministros de la Audiencia de Quito (1650-1750).* Colombia: Ediciones Libri Mundi/Enrique Grosse-Luemern, 1995.

Hilton, Sylvia L., Ed. *La Florida del Inca.* Madrid: Historia 16, 1986.

Kristal, Efraín. *The Andes Viewed from the City: Literary and Political Discourse in Peru 1848-1930.* New York: Peter Lang, 1987.

Larsen, Neil. *Reading North by South: On Latin American Literature, Culture and Politics.* Minneapolis: University of Minnesota Press, 1995.

Larson, Brooke. *Cochabamba, 1550-1900: Colonialism and Agrarian Transformation in Bolivia.* Duke and London: Duke University Press, 1998.

Lavallé, Bernard. *Las Promesas Ambiguas: Criollismo Colonial en los Andes.* Lima: Instituto Riva-Aguero de la Pontificia Universidad Católica del Perú, 1993.

León-Caparó, Raúl. *Racionalidad Andina en el Uso del Espacio.* Lima: Pontificia Universidad Católica del Perú. Fondo Editorial, 1994.

Levene, Ricardo. *Introducción a la Historia del Derecho Indiano.* Buenos Aires: Librería Jurídica Lavalle, 1924.

Lienhard, Martín. *Testimonios, Cartas y Manifiestos Indígenas (De la conquista hasta comienzos del siglo XX).* Caracas: Ayacucho, 1992.

———. *La voz y su huella: Escritura y conflicto étnico-social en América Latina 1492-1988.* México: Ediciones del Norte, 1991

López-Baralt, Mercedes. *Guaman Poma. Autor y Artista.* Lima: Pontificia Universidad Católica del Perú, 1993.

———Ed. *Iconografía Política del Nuevo Mundo.* Ríos Piedras, Puerto Rico: Editorial de la Universidad de Puerto Rico, 1990.

Maeder, Ernesto J. A. *Misiones del Paraguay: Conflicto y Disolución de la Sociedad Guaraní.* Madrid: Editorial Mapfre, 1992.

MacCormack, Sabine. "Pachacuti: Miracles, Punishments, and Last Judgment: Visonary Past and Prophetic Future in Early Colonial Peru," *AHR* (Vol. 93, No. 4, October 1988): pp. 960-1006.

Malagón-Barceló. "The Role of the Letrado in the Colonization of America," *TA* (Vol. XVIII, July 1961, Num. 1): pp. 1-17.

Mannheim, Bruce. *The Language of the Inka since the European Invasion.* Austin: University of Texas Press, 1991.

Mariátegui, José Carlos. *Antología de José Carlos Mariátegui.* México: B. Costa-Amic, Editor, 1966.

————. *El Alma Matinal y Otras Estaciones del Hombre de Hoy.* Lima: Empresa Editora Amauta, 1950.

————*Siete Ensayos de Interpretación de la Realidad Peruana.* México: Ediciones Era, 1979.

Markman, Sidney D. *Arquitecture and Urbanization of Colonial Central America.* 2 Volumes. Tempe: Arizona State University, 1995.

————. *Arquitecture and Urbanization of Colonial Chiapas, Mexico.* Philadelphia: The American Philosophical Society, 1974.

————. *Colonial Architecture of Antigua Guatemala.* Philadelphia: The American Philosophical Society, 1966.

Martínez López-Cano, María P., Coordinadora. *La Política de Escrituras de Nicolás de Yrolo Calar.* México: Universidad Nacional Autónoma de México, 1996.

Mazzotti, José A. "Betanzos: De la 'Epica' Incaica a la Escritura Coral. Aportes para una Tipología del Sujeto Colonial en la Historiografía Andina," in *RLL* (Año XX, Num. 40, 2do. semestre de 1994): pp. 239-258.

————. *Coros Meñstizos del Inca Garcilaso.* Resonancias Andinas. Perú; Bolsa de Valores de Lima Otorongo Producciones, Fondo de Cultura Económica, 1996.

Mignolo, Walter. *The Darker Side of the Renaissance: Literacy, Territoriality and Colonization.* Ann Arbor: University of Michigan, 1995.

————. "El Metatexto Historiográfico y la Historiografía Indiana," *MLN* (Vol. 96/No. 2, March 1981): pp. 358-402.

————. "El mandato y la ofrenda: La Descripción de la ciudad y provincia de Tlaxcala, de Diego Muñoz Camargo, y las Relaciones de Indias," *NRFH* (Tomo XXXV, 1987, Núm. 2): pp. 451-484.

Mignolo, Walter and Hill Boone, Elizabeth, Eds. *Writing Without Words: Alternative Literacies in Mesoamerica & the Andes.* Durham: Duke University Press, 1994.

Milhou, Alain. *Colón y su Mentalidad Mesiánica en el Ambiente Franciscanista Español.* Valladolid: Casa-Museo de Colón y Seminario Americanista de la Universidad de Valladolid, 1983.

Milla Batres, Carlos, Ed. *Compendio Histórico del Perú. 2/3 Tomos.* Lima: Editorial Milla Batres, 1993.

Millones, Luis, Ed. *La Tradición Andina en Tiempos Modernos.* Osaka: National Museum of Ethnology, 1996.

Miño-Grijalva, Manuel. *La Protoindustria colonial hispanoamericana.* México: El Colegio de México/Fidei. Historia de las Américas, 1993.

Miró Quesada, Aurelio, Ed. *Inca Garcilaso de la Vega: Comentarios Reales de los Incas.* Caracas: Ayacucho, nums. 5/6, 1985.

Moraña, Mabel, Ed. *Angel Rama y los Estudios Latinoamericano*s. Pittsburgh: Instituto Internacional de Literatura Iberoamericana, 1997.

Morner, Magnus, Ed. *The Expulsion of the Jesuits from Latin America*. New York: Alfred A. Knopf, 1965.

———. *Local Communities and Actors in Latin America's Past*. Stockhlom: Institute of Latin American Studies, 1994.

———. *Perfil de la Sociedad Rural del Cuzco a fines de la Colonia*. Lima: Universidad del Pacífico/Instituto de Estudios Latinoamericanos, Stockholm, 1978.

———. *The Political and Economic Activities of the Jesuits in the La Plata Region. The Hapsburg Era*. Stockholm: Library and Institute of Ibero-American Studies, 1953.

———. *Region and State in Latin America's Past*. Baltimore: The Johns Hopkins University Press, 1993.

———. *El Sector Agrario en América Latina. Estructura Económica y Cambio Social*. Stockholm: Institute of Latin American Studies, 1979.

Ots-Capdequí, J. M. *El Estado Español en las Indias*. Mexico: Fondo de Cultura Económica, n/d.

Pastor-Bodmer, Beatriz. *Discursos Narrativos de la Conquista: Mitificación Y Emergencia*. Hanover: Ediciones del Norte, Segunda Edición, 1988.

———. *El Jardín y el Peregrino. Ensayos sobre el Pensamiento Utópico Latinoamericano 1492-1695*. Amsterdam, Atlanta: Rodopi, 1996.

Pease, Franklin, Ed. *Felipe Guaman Poma de Ayala: Nueva Coronica y Buen Gobierno*. Caracas: Ayacucho, nums. 75/76, 1980.

Peralta-Ruiz, Víctor. *En pos del tributo: Burocracia estatal, elite regional y comunidades indígenas en el Cusco rural (1826-1854)*. Cusco: Centro de Estudios Regionales Andinos "Bartolomé de las Casas," 1991.

Rabasa, José, Ed. *Dispositio/n. American Journal of Cultural Histories and Theories*. Ann Arbor: The University of Michigan, Vol. XIX, No. 46, 1994 [1996].

———. *Inventing America: Spanish Historiography and the Formation of Eurocentrism*. London: University of Oklahoma Press and Norman Publishing Division, 1993.

Ramos, Demetrio, Ed. *Las Capitulaciones de Descubrimiento y Rescate*. Valladoli: Casa-Museo de Colón y Seminario Americanista de la Universidad, 1981.

Rodríguez G. de Ceballos, Alfonso. "El Urbanismo de las Misiones Jesuiticas de America Meridional: Génesis, Tipología y Significado. Relaciones Artísticas entre España y América." Madrid: Consejo Superior de Investigaciones Científicas, 1990): pp. 151-171.

Schwartz, Stuart B. *Slaves, Peasants, and Rebels*. Urbana: University of Illinois Press, 1992.

Sempat-Assadourian, Carlos. "La Despoblación Indígena en Perú y Nueva España Durante el Siglo XVI y la Formación de la Economía Colonial," *HM* (Vol. XXXVIII, Enero-Marzo 1989, Núm. 3, 151): pp. 419-453.

———. *El Sistema de la Economía Colonial: Mercado Interno, Regiones y Espacio Económico*. Lima: Instituto de Estudios Peruanos, 1982.

————. et. al. *Modos de Producción en América Latina*. Córdoba: Cuadernos de Pasado y Presente/40, sec, ed. 1974.

Sepúlveda, César. *Derecho Internacional Público*. México: Porrúa, 1964.

Spadaccini, Nicholas, Ed. *Amerindian Images and The Legacy of Columbus*. Minneapolis: University of Minnesota Press, 1992.

————. *1492/1992: Re/Discovering Colonial Writing*. Minneapolis: The Prisma Institute, 1989.

Sierra, María Teresa. "Indian Rights and Customary Law in Mexico: A Study of the Nahuas in the Sierra de Puebla," in *LSR* (Vol. 29, Num. 2,1995): pp. 227-254.

Silverblatt, Irene. *Moon, Sun, and Witches: Gender Ideologies and Class in Inca and Colonial Peru*. Princeton: Princeton University Press, 1987.

Stavenhagen, Rodolfo. *Social Classes in Agrarian Societies*. New York: Anchor Books/ Doubleday, 1975.

Stern, Steve. "Feudalism, Capitalism and the World-System in the Perspective of Latin America and the Caribbean," *AHR* (Vol. 93, No. 4, October 1988): pp. 829-872.

————. *Peru's Indian Peoples and the Challenge of Spanish Conquest. Huamanga to 1640*. Madison: The University of Wisconsin Press, 1982.

————. "Reply: 'Ever More Solitary.'" *AHR* (Vol. 93, No. 4, October 1988): pp. 886-897.

Suskin, Branislava. *El Indio Colonial del Paraguay*. 2 Volumes. Asunción, Paraguay: Museo Etnográfico "Andrés Barbero," 1965.

Tandeter, Enrique, Harris, Olivia and Larson, Brooke, Eds. *La Participación Indígena en los Mercados Surandinos*. La Paz: Centro de Estudios de la Realidad Económica y Social (CERES), 1987.

Todorov, Tzvetan. *The Conquest of America. The Question of the Other*. New York: Harper & Row, 1982.

Varela, Consuelo. *Cristóbal Colón.Textos y Docummentos Completos*. Madrid: Alianza, 1989.

Vidal, Hernán. *Poética de la Población Marginal: Fundamentos Materialistas para una Historiografía Estética*. Minneapolis: Institute for the Study of Ideologies and Literature, 1987.

————. *Sentido y Práctica de la Crítica Literaria Sociohistórica: Panfleto para la Proposición de una Arqueología Acotada*. Minneapolis: Institute for the Study of Ideologies and Literature, 1984.

————. *Socio-Historia de la Literatura Colonial Hispanoamericana: Tres Lecturas Orgánicas*. Minneapolis: Institute for the Study of Ideologies and Literature, 1985.

Wachtel, Nathan. *Sociedad e Ideología: Ensayos de Historia y Antropología Andinas*. Lima: Instituto de Estudios Peruanos, IEP, 1973.

Wagner, Henry R. *The Life and Writings of Bartolomé de las Casas*. Albuquerque: The University of New Mexico Press, 1967.

Watson, Alan. *Slave Law in the Americas*. Athens: University of Georgia Press, 1989.

Williamson, Edwin. *The Penguin History of Latin America*. London: Penguin Books, 1992.

Weber, David J., Ed. *Where Cultures Meet: Frontiers in Latin American History*. Wilmington: A Scholarly Resources Inc., 1994.

Wright, Ronald. *Continentes Robados*. Madrid: Anaya, 1994.

Golden Age, Iberian Peninsula: Primary Sources (Sixteenth and Seventeenth Centuries)

Aldea-Vaquero, Quintín, Ed. *Diego Saavedra Faajardo. Empresas Políticas*. 2 Vols. Madrid: Editoria Nacional, 1976.

Beverley, John, Ed. *Soledades*. Madrid: Cátedra, 1979.

Blanco, Emilio, Ed. *Relox de Príncipes. Confres* (Conferencia de Ministros Provinciales de España), ABL Editor, 1994.

Ginés de Sepúlveda, Juan. *Historia del Nuevo Mundo*. Madrid: Alianza, 1987.

———. *Sobre las Justas Causas de la Guerra contra los Indios*. Pánuco, Mex.: Fondo de Cultura Económica, 1941.

Guevara, Antonio de. *Menosprecio de Corte y Alabanza de Aldea*. Madrid: Ediciones de "la Lectura," 1928.

———. *El Villano del Danubio y Otros fragmentos*. Princeton: Princeton University Press, 1945.

Isidoro de Sevilla, San. *Etimologías*. Oroz Reta, J. and Marcos Casquero, M.A., Eds. Madrid: Biblioteca de Autores Cristianos (BAC), 2 vols. 1983.

de León Pinelo, Antonio. *El Paraíso en el Nuevo Mundo*. Edited by R. Porras Barrenechea. Lima: Auspiciado por el Comité del IV Centenario del Descubrimiento del Amazonas, 2 Volumes, 1943.

Lisón Tolosana, Carmelo. *La Imagen del Rey: Monarquía, Realeza y Poder Ritual en la Casa de los Austrias*. Madrid: Espasa Calpe, 1991.

MacLachlan, Colin M. *Spain's Empire in the New World: The Role of Ideas in Institutional and Social Change*. Berkeley: University of California Press, 1988.

Pagden, Anthony, Ed. *Francisco Vitoria. Political Writings*. Cambridge: University Press, 1991.

Paz, Julian. *Catálogo de Manuscritos de América Existentes en la Biblioteca Nacional*. Madrid: Ministerio de Cultura, 1992.

Ramos, Demetrio. *El Mito de El Dorado*. Madrid: Colegio Universitario de Ediciones Istmo, 1988.

Saint-Lú, André, Ed. *Bartolomé de las Casas. Historia de las Indias*. Caracas: Ayacucho, nums. 108-110, 1956.

Solórzano y Pereira, Juan de. *Política Indiana*. Madrid: Ediciones Atlas, 1972.

Vives, Juan Luis. *Obras Completas*. Madrid: Aguilar, 1948.

Golden Age, Iberian Peninsula: Historical Background and Criticism

Abellán, José Luis. *Filosofía Española en América (1936-1966)*. Madrid: Ediciones Guadarrama con Seminarios y Ediciones, 1967.

———. *Historia Crítica del Pensamiento Español*. Tomo 1: Metodología e Introducción Histórica. Madrid: Espasa-Calpe, 1988.

———. *Historia Crítica del Pensamiento Español. Tomo II: La Edad de Oro*. Madrid: Espasa-Calpe, 1986.

Avalla-Arce, Juan Bautista. *Dintorno de una Epoca Dorada*. Madrid: José Porrúa Turanzas Ediciones, 1978.

Barrientos-García, José. *El Tratado "De Iustitia et Jure (1590)" de Pedro de Aragon*. Salamanca: Ediciones Universidad de Salamanca, 1978.

Bataillon, Marcel. *Estudios sobre Bartolomé de las Casas*. Barcelona: Ediciones Península, 1976.

———. *Erasmo Y España: Estudios sobre la Historia Espiritual del Siglo XVI*. Mexico: Fondo de Cultura Económica, seg. ed. 1966.

Batllori, Miguel. *Humanismo y Renacimiento. Estudios Hispano-Europeos*. Barcelona, 1987.

———. "Discurso de Contestación," *Los Factores de la Idea de Progreso en el Renacimiento Español* by J. A. Maravall-Casesnoves. Madrid: Real Academia de la Historia, 1963.

Brea, José Luis. *Nuevas Estrategias Alegóricas*. Madrid: Tecnos, 1991.

Brown Scott, James. *Francúisco de Vitoria and His Law of Nations*. Oxford: The Clarendon Press, 1934.

Brufau-Prats, Jaime. *La Escuela de Salamanca ante el Descubrimiento del Nuevo Mundo*. Salamanca: San Esteban, 1989.

———. *El Pensamiento Político de Domingo de Soto y su Concepción de Poder*. Salamanca: Universidad de Salamanca, 1960.

Carande, Ramón. *Carlos V y sus Banqueros. La vida económica en Castilla (1516-1556)*. Madrid: Sociedad de Estudios y Publicaciones, 1965.

Castillo, Miguel A. *Renacimiento y Manierismo en España*. Madrid: Historia 16, 1989.

Checa, Fernando et al. *Arquitectura del Renacimiento en España, 1488-1599*. Madrid: Cátedra, Manuales de Arte, 1989.

———. *Felipe II: Mecenas de las Artes*. Madrid: Nerea, 1993.

Chevalier, Maxime. *Lectura y Lectores en la España de los Siglos XVI y XVII*. Madrid: Turner, 1976.

Collins, Roger. "Literacy and the Laity in Early Medieval Spain," *The Uses of Literacy in Early Mediaeval Europe*. Edited by R. McKitterick. Cambridge: Cambirdge University Press, n/d.

Di Camillo, Ottavio. *El Humanismo Castellano del Siglo XV*. Valencia: J. Domenech, 1976.

————. "Interpretations of the Renaissance in Spanish Historical Thought." *RQ* (Vol. XLVIII. Núm. 2., 1995): pp. 352-365.

————. "Interpretations of the Renaissance in Spanish Historical Thought: The Last Thirty Years," *RQ* (Vol. XLIX. Núm. 2., 1996): pp. 360-383.

Fernández Herrero, Beatriz. *La Utopía de América: Teorías, Leyes, Experimentos.* Barcelona: Anthropos, 1992.

Fernández-Santamaría, J. A. *The State, War and Peace: Spanish Political Thought in the Renaissance 1516-1559.* Cambridge: Cambridge University Press, 1977.

Escudero-López, José Antonio. "La historiografía general del Derecho Inglés," *AHDE* (Madrid, Tomo XXXV, 1965): pp. 217-356.

Estudios sobre Política Indigenista Española en América. Simposio Conmemorativo del V Centenario del Padre Las Casas. Terceras Jornadas Americanistas de la Universidad de Valladolid, 1975.

Fernández-Rodríguez, Pedro. *Los Dominicos en la Primera Evangelización de México.* Salamanca: San Esteban, 1994.

Fernández-Santamaría, José A. *Razón de Estado y Política en el Pensamientodel Barroco (1595-1640).* Madrid: Grafoffset sl, Centro de Estudios Constitucionales, 1986.

de la Flor, Fernando R. *Emblemas: Lecturas de la Imagen Simbólica.* Madrid: Alianza Editorial, 1995.

García de la Concha, Víctor., Ed. *Nebrija y la Introducción del Renacimiento en España.* Salamanca: Universidad de Salamanca, 1983.

García-de-Enterría, Eduardo. *La Lengua de los Derechos. La formación del Derecho Público europeo tras la Revolución Francesa.* Madrid: Alianza, 1995.

García-Gallo, Alfonso. "La Ciencia Jurídica en la Formación del Derecho Hispanoamericano en los Siglos XVI al XVIII," *AHDE* (Madrid, Tomo XLIV, 1974): pp. 157-200.

Gil-Fernández, Luis. *Panorama Social del Humanismo Español (1500-1800).* Madrid: Tecnos, [1981] 1997.

Guy, Alain. *Ortega y Gasset: Crítico de Aristóteles.* Madrid: Espasa-Calpe, 1968.

Hamilton, Bernice. *Political Thought in Sixteenth Century Spain.* Oxford: Clarendon Press, 1963.

Hernández, Ramón. *Derechos Humanos en Francisco de Vitoria.* Salamanca: San Esteban, 1984.

Kagan, Richard L. *Lawsuits and Litigants in Castile (1500-1700).* Chapel Hill: The University of North Carolina Press, 1981.

————. *Students and Society in Early Modern Spain.* Baltimore and London: The Johns Hopkins University Press, 1974.

Lalinde-Abadía, Jesús. "Apuntes sobre las "Ideologías en el Derecho Histórico Español," *AHDE* (Madrid, Tomo XLV, 1975): pp. 123-157.

————. "La Creación del Derecho entre los Españoles," *AHDE* (Madrid, Tomo XXXVI, 1966): pp. 301-378.

————. "La Cultura Represiva [Apostillas al libro *Las Culturas Represivas de la*

Humanidad (hasta 1945)], *AHDE* (Madrid, Tomo LXIII-LXIV, 1993-1994): pp. 1135-1191.

———. "Depuración Histórica del Concepto de Estado," in *El Estado Español en su Dimensión Histórica*. Barcelona: Promoción Publicaciones Universitarias, 1984.

———. "Los Gastos del Proceso en el Derecho Histórico Español," *AHDE* (Madrid, Tomo XXXIV, 1964): pp. 249-416.

———. "El Hispanismo Norteamericano en la Historia de las Instituciones de Indias," *AHDE* (Madrid, Tomo LVI, 1986): pp. 953-76.

———. "Historia del Derecho frente a Filosofía del Derecho," *AHDE* (Madrid, Tomo LXV, 1995): pp. 1023-1035.

———. "La Iushistoriografía Española y Europea en el Umbral del Siglo XX," *AHDE* (Madrid, Tomo LVI, 1986): pp. 977-994.

———. *Iniciación Histórica al Derecho Español*. Barcelona: Ariel, 1970.

———. "Notas Sobre el Papel de las Fuerzas Políticas y Sociales en el Desarrollo de los Sistemas Iushistóricos Españoles," *AHDE* (Madrid, Tomo XLVIII, 1978): pp. 249-268.

———. "Sánchez-Albornoz, Medievalista Institucional," *AHDE* (Madrid, Tomo LXIII-LXIV, 1993-1994): pp. 1098-1122.

López Estrada, Francisco. "Un centenario humanístico: Tomás Moro (1478-1978), *Seis Lecciones sobre la España de los Siglos de Oro. Homenaje a Marcel Bataillon*. Sevilla: Universidad de Sevilla-Université de Bordeaux, 1981.

Maravall, José Antonio. *Antiguos y Modernos: La idea de Progreso en el Desarrollo Inicial de Una Sociedad*. Madrid: Sociedad de Estudios y Publicaciones, 1966.

———. *Carlos V y el Pensamiento Político del Renacimiento*. Madrid: Instituto de Estudios Políticos, 1960.

———. *El Concepto de España en la Edad Media*. Madrid: Instituto de Estudios Políticos, 1954.

———. *Culture of the Baroque: Analysis of a Historical Structure*. Minneapolis: University of Minnesota Press, 1986.

———. *Estado Moderno y Mentalidad Social*. Madrid: Ediciones de la Revista de Occidente, 1972.

———. *Estudios de Historia del Pensamiento Español*. Madrid: Ediciones de Cultura Hispánica, 1967.

———. *Los Factores de la Idea de Progreso en el Renacimiento Español*. Madrid: Real Academia de la Historia, 1963.

———. *La Literatura Picaresca desde la Historia Social (Siglos XVI y XVII)*. Madrid: Taurus, 1987.

———. *La Oposición Política bajo los Austrias*. Barcelona: Ariel, 1972.

———. *Utopia and Counterutopia in the "Quixote."* Detroit: Wayne State University Press, 1991.

———. *Utopía y Reformismo en la España de los Austrias*. Madrid: Siglo XXI Editores, 1982.

Márquez-Villanueva, Francisco. "Letrados, Consejeros y Justicias (Artículo-Reseña)," *HR* (Vol. 53, Spring 1985, Number 2): pp. 201-227.

Martínez-Cardos, José. *Las Indias y las Cortes de Castilla durante los siglos XVI y XVII.* Madrid: Consejo Superior de Investigaciones Científicas, 1956.

Martínez-Gijón, José. "La comenda en el Derecho Español. l. La comenda-depósito," *AHDE* (Madrid: Vol. XXXIV, 1964): pp. 31-140.

Martínez-Martín, Jesús A. *Lectura y Lectores en el Madrid del Siglo XIX.* Madrid: Consejo Superior de Investigaciones Científicas, 1991.

Milhou, Alain. *Colón y su Mentalidad Mesiánica en el Ambiente Franciscanista Español.* Valladolid: Casa-Museo de Colón y Seminario Americanista de la Universidad de Valladolid, 1983.

Millares-Carlo, Agustín, Ed. *De las Islas del Mar Océano* por Juan López de Palacios Rubios [1498] and *Del Dominio de los Reyes de España sobre los Indios* por Fray Matías de Paz [1512?]. Mexico: Fondo de Cultura Económica, 1954.

Muro-Orejón, Antonio, Ed. *Cedulario Americano del Siglo XVIII. Colección de Disposiciones Legales Indianas desde 1680 a 1800 en los Cedularios del Archivo General de Indias III. Cédulas de Luis I (1724), Cédulas de Felipe V 1724-46).* Sevilla: Escuela de Estudios Hispano-Americanos de Sevilla y la Cátedra de Historia del Derecho Indiano de la Universidad de Sevilla, 1977.

Navarro-García, Luis. *Las Reformas Borbónicas en América. El Plan de Intendencias y su Aplicación.* Sevilla: Universidad de Sevilla, 1995.

Ortega y Gasset, José. *An Interpretation of Universal History.* Translated by Mildred Adams. New York: Norton & Company, 1973.

———. *Origen y Epílogo de la Filosofía.* Madrid: Revista de Occidente, 1967.

———. *Sobre la Razón Histórica.* Madrid: Revista de Occidente, Alianza Editorial, 1980.

Pagden, Anthony. "Dispossessing the barbarian: the language of Spanish Thomism and the debate over the property rights of the American Indians," in *The Languages of Political Theory in Early-Modern Europe.* Anthony Pagden, Ed. Cambridge: Cambridge University Press, 1987: pp. 79-98.

———. "Identity Formation in Spanish America," in *Colonial Identity in the Atlantic World, 1500-1800.* Edited by Nicholas Canny and Anthony Pagden. Princeton: Princeton University Press, 1987.

———. *The Fall of Natural Man: The American Indian and the Origins of Comparative Ethnology.* Cambridge: Cambridge University Press, 1982.

———. *Lords of All the World: Ideologies of Empire in Spain, Britain and France.* New Haven: Yale University Press, 1995.

———. *Spanish Imperialism and the Political Imagination.* New Haven: Yale University Press, 1990.

———. *The Uncertainties of Empire. Essays in Iberian and Ibero-American Intellectual History.* Brookfield: Variourum, 1994.

Parry, J. H. *The Spanish Seaborne Empire.* London: Hutchinson, 1966.

———. *The Spanish Theory of Empire in the Sixteenth Century.* Cambridge: Cambridge University Press, 1940.

Scott, Samuel P., Ed. *Las Siete Partidas*. Chicago: The Comparative Law Bureau of The American Bar Association, 1931.

Peiró-Martín, I. and Pasamar-Alzuria, G. *La Escuela Superior de Diplomática (Los Archiveros en la Historiografía Española Contemporánea)*. Madrid: Asociación Española de Archiveros, Bibliotecarios, Museólogos y Documentalistas, 1996.

Perry, Mary E. *Gender and Disorder in Early Modern Seville*. Princeton: Princeton University Press, 1990.

Piñero-Ramírez, Pedro M. and Reyes-Cano, Rogelio, Eds. *Seis Lecciones sobre la España de los Siglos de Oro (Literatura e Historia)*. Sevilla: Universidad de Sevilla/Université de Bordeaux III, 1981.

Rico, Francisco. *El Sueño del Humanismo: De Petrarca a Erasmo*. Madrid: Alianza Universidad, 1993.

———. *El Pequeño Mundo del Hombre*. Madrid: Alianza, 1988.

Romera-Navarro, M., Ed. *El Criticón*. 3 Vols. Philadelphia: University of Pennsylvania Press, Published in Cooperation with the MLA, 1940.

Sánchez Bella, Ismael et al. *Historia del Derecho Indiano*. Madrid: Colección Mapfre 1492, 1992.

Sánchez-Albornoz, Claudio. *Estudios Sobre las Instituciones Medievales Españolas*. Mexico: Instituto de Investigaciones Históricas, 1965.

———. *Viejos y Nuevos Estudios Sobre las Instituciones Medievales Eapañolas*. Madrid: Espasa Calpe, Vols. I & II, 1976.

Serrano, Antonio. "La Rata en el Laberinto o La Historia como Observatorio Jurídico," *AHDE* (Madrid, Tomo LXII, 1992): pp. 675-713.

Thompson, I. A. A. *Crown and Cortes: Government, Institutions and Representation in Early-Modern Castile*. Aldershot, Hampshire: Variorum, 1993.

Tomás y Valiente, Francisco. *A Orillas del Estado*. Madrid: Taurus, 1996.

———. *Gobierno e Instituciones en la España del Antiguo Régimen*. Madrid: Alianza Universidad, 1982.

———. *La Venta de Oficios en Indias (1492-1606)*. Madrid: Instituto de Estudios Administrativos, 1972.

Ynduráin, Domingo. *Humanismo y Renacimiento en España*. Madrid: Cátedra, 1994.

Other Historical Contexts, Theories of Utopianism, Legal Scholarship

Adams, Robert M., Ed. *Utopia*. New York: Norton, 1992.

Adorno, Theodor. *The Jargon of Authenticity*. Evanston: Northwestern University Press, 1973.

———. *Negative Dialectics*. New York: Continuum, 1994.

———. *Prisms*. Cambridge: The MIT Press, 1995.

Aguero, Oscar & Cerutti-Guldberg, Horacio, Eds. *Utopía y Nuestra América*. Quito: Abya-Yala, 1996.

Alexander, Peter, Ed. *Utopias*. London: Duckworth, 1984.

Althusser, Louis and Balibar, Etienne. *Reading Capital*. London: NLB, 1970.

Anderson, Perry. *Imagined Communities*. New York: Verso, 1991.

————. *Lineages of the Absolutist State*. London: Verso, 1987.

Aram Veeser, H., Ed. *The New Historicism*. New York: Routledge, 1989.

Arrighi, Giovanni. *The Long Twentieth Century*. London: Verso, 1994.

Ashcroft, Bill, Ed. *The Post-Colonial Studies Reader*. New York: Routledge, 1995.

Auerbach, Erich. "Figura." *Scenes from the Drama of European Literature*. Minneapolis: University of Minnesota Press, Theory and History of Literature, 1984: pp. 11-76.

Basadre, Jorge. *En la Biblioteca Nacional. Ante el Problema de las Elites*. Lima: Talleres Gráficos P.L. Villanueva, 1968.

————. *Historia del Derecho Peruano*. Lima: Editorial Antena, 1937.

————. *Los Fundamentos de la Historia del Derecho*. Lima: Librería Internacional del Perú, 1956.

Bhabha, Homi K. *The Location of Culture*. New York: Routledge, 1994.

Barthes, Roland. *Writing Degree Zero*. New York: Hill and Wang, 1953.

Benjamin, Walter.*The Origin of German Tragic Drama*. New York: Verso, 1984.

————. *Reflections. Essays, Aphorisms, Autobiographical Writings*. New York: Schocken Books, 1978.

Berger, Harry, Jr. *Second World and Green World: Studies in Renaissance Fiction Making*. Berkeley, Los Angeles: University of California Press, 1988.

Biagioli, Mario. *Galileo, Courtier. The Practice of Science in the Culture of Absolutism*. Chicago: The University of Chicago Press, 1993.

Blake, Peter. *No Place like Utopia: Modern Architecture and the Company We keep*. New York: Alfred A. Knopf, 1993.

Blaut, J. M. *The Colonizer's Model of the World: Geographical Diffusionism and Eurocentric History*. New York: The Guilford Press, 1993.

Bloch, Ernst. *The Principle of Hope*. Cambridge: MIT Press, 1986.

Bolton, Herbert E. *New Spain and the Anglo-American West. Historical Historical Contributions Presented to Herbert Eugene Bolton. 2 Volumes*. Los Angeles: Privately Printed, 1932.

Braudel, Fernand. *The Mediterranean and the Mediterranean World in the Age of Philip II*. New York: Harper & Row Publishers, 1973.

Bousquet, Jacques. *La Peinture Manieriste*. Neuchatel: Ides et Calendes, 1964.

Brundage, James A. *Medieval Canon Law*. London: Longman, 1995.

Campanella,Tommaso. *La Monarchia del Messia*. Roma: Edizioni di Storia e Letteratura, 1995.

————. *Poesie*. Milano: Guerini e Associati, 1992.

Campos, Paul F. et al. *Against the Law*. Durham: Duke University Press, 1996.

Castañeda, Jorge G. *Utopía Desarmada*. México: Joaquín Mortiz-Planeta, 1993.

Chambers, R. W. *Thomas More*. New York: Harcourt Brace, 1935.

Cole, Peter, Ed. *Language in the Andes*. Newark: Latin American Studies, 1994.

312 *Good Places and Non-Places in Colonial Mexico*

Colie, Rosalie L. *Light and Enlightenment. A Study of the Cambridge Platonists and The Dutch Arminians*. Cambridge: Cambridge University Press, 1957.

———. *Paradoxia Epidemica. The Renaissance Tradition of Paradox*. Hamden, Conn.: Archon Books, 1976.

———. *The Resources of a Kind: Genre-Theory in the Renaissance*. Berkeley: University of California Press, 1973.

Corcuera de Mancera, Sonia. *Voces y Silencios en la Historia. Siglos XIX y XX*. México: Fondo de Cultura Económica, 1997.

Davies, Thomas M. *Indian Integration in Peru: A Half Century of Experience 1900-1948*. Lincoln: University of Nebraska Press, 1974.

Davis, J. C. *Utopia and the Ideal Society. A Study of English Utopian Writing (1516-1700)*. Cambridge: Cambridge University Press, 1981.

DeGrazia, Margreta, et al., Ed. *Subject and Object in Renaissance Culture*. Cambridge: Cambridge University Press, 1996.

DeMan, Paul. "The Epistemology of Metaphor." *Critical Enquiry* (Autumn 1978, Volume 5. Number 1): pp. 13-30.

———. *The Resistance to Theory*. Minneapolis: University of Minnesota Press, 1986.

Denvir, John, Ed. *Legal Reelism: Movies as Legal Texts*. Urbana and Chicago: University of Illinois Press, 1996.

Díaz Martínez, Antonio. *Ayacucho: Hambre y Esperanza*. Lima: Mosca Azul Editores, 2a ed., 1985.

Eco, Umberto. *Apocalípticos e Integrados*. Barcelona: Editorial Lumen, 1985.

———. *Apocalypse Postponed*. Bloomington: British Film Institute, 1994.

———. *Travels in Hyperreality*. Essays. San Diego: Harcourt Brace Jovanovich, Publishers, 1986.

Eco, Umberto and Marmo, Costantino. *On the Medieval Theory of Signs*. Amsterdam, Philadelphia: John Benjamins Publishing Company, 1989.

Eisenstein, Elizabeth L. *The Printing Revolution in Early Modern Europe*. New York: Cambridge University Press, 1983.

Eliav-Ferldon, Miriam. "Secret societies, utopias, and peace plans: the case of Francesco Pucci." *JMRS* (14, 1984:2): pp. 139-158.

———. *Realistic Utopias: The Ideal Imaginary Societies of the Renaissance 1516-1630*. Oxford: Clarendon Press, 1982.

Fabian, Johannes. *Time and the Other: How Anthropology Makes its Object*. New York: Columbia University Press, 1983.

Falkowski, James E. *Indian Law/Race Law: A Five-Hundred-Year History*. New York: Praeger, 1992.

Finnis, John. *Natural Law*. New York: New York University Press, 1991.

Fish, Stanley. *Self-Consuming Artifacts: The Experience of Seventeenth-Century Literature*. Berkeley: University of California Press, 1972.

Fortunati, Vita, Ed. *Utopías*. Buenos Aires: Editorial Corregidor, 1994.

Galanter, Marc. "Why the "Haves" Come out Ahead: Speculations on the Limits of Legal Change," in *LSR* (Vol.9, Num.1/Fall 1974): pp. 95-160.

García Calvo, Agustín. *Contra el Tiempo*. Zamora: Lucina, 1993.
———. *De la Construcción*. Madrid: Lucina, 1983.
García Canclini, Néstor. *Hybrid Cultures: Strategies for Entering and Leaving Modernity*. Minneapolis: University of Minnesota Press, 1995.
García Márquez, Gabriel. *Elogio de la Utopía. Una entrevista de Nahuel Maciel*. Argentina: Ediciones El Cronista, 1992.
Geertz, Clifford. *After the Fact*. Cambridge: Harvard University Press, 1995.
González Casanova, Pablo. *Un Utopista Mexicano*. México: Secretaría de Educación Pública, 1986.
Greenblatt, Stephen. *Marvelous Possessions: The Wonder of the New World*. Chicago: The University of Chicago Press, 1991.
———. *Redrawing the Boundaries*. New York: The Modern Language Association of America, 1992.
Gurkind, E. A. "The Renaissance. The Geometric Spider." *International History of City Development. Volume IV. Urban Development in Southern Europe: Italy and Greece*. (Incomplete reference; chapter 4): pp. 106-135.
Gutiérrez, Miguel. *Poderes Secretos*. Lima: Jaime Campodonico Editor, 1995.
Halpern, Richard. *The Poetics of Primitive Accumulation. English Renaissance Culture and the Genealogy of Capital*. Ithaca: Cornell University Press, 1991.
Haraszti-Takacs, Marianne. *The Masters of Mannerism*. Budapest: Corvina Press, 1968.
Harrison, Regina. *Signs, Songs and Memory in the Andes. Translating Quechua Language and Culture*. Austin: University of Texas Press, 1989.
Hart, H. L. A. *The Concept of Law*. Oxford: Clarendon Press, [1961] 1997.
Harvey, David. *The Condition of Postmodernity*. Cambridge: Blackwell, 1990.
Huntington, Samuel P. *The Clash of Civilizations and the Remaking of the World Order*. New York: Simon & Schuster, 1996.
Headley, John M. *Tommaso Campanella and the Transformation of the World*. Princeton, New Jersey: Princeton University Press, 1997.
Henríquez Ureña, Pedro. *La Utopía de América*. Caracas: Ayacucho, 1989.
Hexter, J.H. *The Vision of Politics on the Eve of the Reformation: More, Machiavelli, and Seyssel*. New York: Basic Books, 1973.
Hindness, Barry & Hirst, Paul Q. *Pre-capitalista Modes of Production*. London: Routledge & Kegan Paul, 1975.
Holm, John. *Pidgins and Creoles*. Cambridge: Cambridge University Press, 1989.
Hulme, Peter. *Colonial Encounters: Europe and the Native Caribbean, 1492-1797*. New York: Methuen, n/d.
Ibáñez, Alfonso. *Para Repensar Nuestras Utopías*. Lima: Sur Tarea, 1993.
Imaz, Eugenio. *Utopías del Renacimiento: Moro, Campanella, Bacon*. Mexico: Fondo de Cultura Económica, 1993.
Irigaray, Luce. *I Love to You. Sketch of a Possible Felicity in History*. New York and London: Routledge, 1996.
Jameson, Fredric. *Marxism and Form: Twentieth-Century Dialectical Theories of Literature*. Princeton, New Jersey: Princeton University Press, 1971.

————. *The Ideologies of Theory. Essays (1971-1986). Two Volumes*. Minneapolis: University of Minnesota Press, sec. print. 1989.

————. "Reading without Interpretation: Postmodernism and the Video-Text," in *The Linguistics of Writing: Arguments between Language and Literature*. Edited by Nigel Fabb, Derek Attridge, Alan Durant and Colin MacCabe (New York: Methuen, 1987): pp. 199-223.

————. "Representations of Subjectivity," in *Discours Social/Social Discourse: The Non-Cartesian Subjects, East and West/Les Sujets Non-Cartésiens, Orient/ Occident* (Montreal: Volume 6: 1-2): pp. 47-60.

————. *The Political Unconscious: Narrative as a Socially Symbolic Act*. Ithaca, New York: Cornell University Press, 1981.

————. *The Seeds of Time*. New York: Columbia University Press, 1994.

————. *Signatures of the Visible*. New York: Routledge, 1992.

Jameson, Fredric and Miyoshi, Masao, Eds. *The Cultures of Globalization*. Durham: Duke University Press, 1998.

Jardine, Lisa. Erasmus, *Man of Letters. The Construction of Charisma in Print*. Princeton: Princeton University Press, 1993.

Julien, Catherine J. Ed. *Toledo y los Lupacas: Las Tasas de 1574 y 1579*. Bonn: Holos/ Bas 23, Bonner Amerikanistische Studien/Estudios Americanistas de Bonn, 1993.

Kamps, Ivo, Ed. *Materialist Shakespeare: A History*. New York: Verso, 1995.

————. *Shakespeare and Gender: A History*. New York: Verso, 1995.

Kantorowicz, Ernst H. *Los dos Cuerpos del Rey: Un Estudio de Teología Política Medieval*. Madrid: Alianza, 1985.

Kateb, George. *Utopia and Its Enemies*. New York: Schocken Books, 1972.

Kaufman, Terrence. *Language Contact, Creolization and Genetic Linguistics*. Berkeley: University of California Press, 1988.

Kelley, Donald R. *Renaissance Humanism*. Boston: Twayne Publishers, 1991.

Kenyon, Timothy. *Utopian Communism and Political Thought in Early Modern England*. London: Pinter Publishers, 1989.

Kinney, Arthur F. *Humanist Poetics: Thought, Rhetoric, and Fiction in Sixteenth-Century England*. Amherst: The University of Massachusetts Press, 1986.

Kuklick, Henrika. *The Savage Within: The Social History of British Anthropology, 1885-1945*. Cambridge: Cambridge University Press (n/d).

Kumar, Krishan, Ed. *News from Nowhere*. Cambridge: Cambridge University Press, 1995.

————. *Utopias and the Millennium*. London: Reaktion Books, 1993.

Lasky, Melvin J. *Utopia and Revolution*. Chicago and London: The University of Chicago Press, 1976.

Lazarus-Black, Mindie. *Legitimate Acts and Illegal Encounters: Law and Society in Antigua and Barbuda*. Washington: Smithsonian Institution Press, 1994.

Lefebvre, Henri. *The Production of Space*. Oxford: Blackwell, 1991.

Levitas, Ruth. *The Concept of Utopia*. New York: Philip Allan, 1990.

Locke, John. *An Essay Concerning Human Understanding.* Peter H. Nidditch, Ed. Oxford: Clarendon Press, 1975.

Loftis, John. *Renaissance Drama in England and Spain: Topical Allusion and History Plays.* Princeton: Princeton University Press, 1987.

Logan, George M. et altri, Ed. *Thomas More's Utopia.* Cambridge: Cambridge University Press, 1995.

Lubar, Steven, e al. Ed. *History from Things. Essays on Material Culture.* Washington and London: Smithsonian Institution Press, 1993.

Mannheim, Karl. *Essays on the Sociology of Knowledge.* New York: Oxford University Press, 1952.

————. *Ideology and Utopia. An Introduction to the Sociology of Knowledge.* New York: Harcourt Brace & Company, 1936.

Manuel, Frank E. *Utopias and Utopian Thought.* Cambridge: The Riverside Press, 1966.

————. *Utopian Thought in the Western World.* Cambridge: The Belknap Press of Harvard University Press, 1979.

Marcuse, Hebert. *One-Dimensional Man. Studies in the Ideology of Advanced Industrial Society.* Boston: Beacon P   ress, 1968.

————. "Repressive Tolerance," in *A Critique of Pure Tolerance.* Boston: Beacon Press, 1965.

Margolin, Victor. *The Struggle for Utopia: Rodchenko, Lissitzky, Moholy-Nagy 1917-1946.* Chicago: The University of Chicago Press, 1997.

Marin, Louis. *The Semiotics of the Passion Narrative.* Topics and Figures. Pittsburgh: The Pickwick Press, 1980.

————. *Utopics: Spatial Play.* New Jersey: Humanities Press, 1984.

McInerny, Ralph, Ed. *St. Thomas Aquinas. Treatise on Law.* Washington: Regnery Publishing, 1996.

Mintz, Sidney W. *Sweetness and Power: The Place of Sugar in Modern History.* New York: Elisabeth Sifton Books/Viking (n/d).

Morgan, Arthur E. *Nowhere was Somewhere.* Chapel Hill: The University of North Carolina Press, 1946.

Nancy, Jean-Luc, Connor, Peter and Cadava, Eduardo, Eds. *Who Comes After the Subject?* New York: Routledge, 1991.

Nederneveen Pieterse, Jan, Ed. *The Decolonization of Imagination. Culture, Knowledge and Power.* London: Zed Books Ltd, 1995.

Negley, Glenn. *Utopian Literature. A Bibliography with a Supplementary Listing of Works Influential in Utopian Thought.* Lawrence: The Regents Press of Kansas, 1977.

Ortega y Gasset, José. *España Invertebrada.* Madrid: La Lectura, 1922.

Osborne, Peter, Ed. *A Critical Sense: Interviews with Intellectuals.* London: Routledge, 1996.

Ossío-Acuña, Juan. *Las Paradojas del Perú Oficial: Indigenismo, Democraciay Crisis Estructural.* Lima: Pontificia Universidad Católica del Perú, 1994.b

Pashukanis, Eugeny B. *Law and Marxism. A General Theory.* London: Ink Links, 1978.

Pfaelzer, Jean. *The Utopian Novel in America 1886-1896. The Politics of Form.* Pittsburgh: University of Pittsburgh Press, 1984.

Pietz, W. *Fetishim as Cultural Discourse.* Ithaca and London: Cornell University Press, 1993.

Pocock, J. G. A., Ed. James Harrington. *The Commonwealth of Oceana and A System of Politics.* Cambridge: Cambridge University Press, 1992.

Posner, Richard A. *Overcoming Law.* Cambridge: Harvard University Press, 1995.

Post, Robert, Ed. *Law and the Order of Culture.* Berkeley: University of California Press, 1991.

Pratt, Mary Louise. *Imperial Eyes: Travel Writing and Transculturation.* London: Routledge, 1992.

————. "Linguistic Utopias," in *The Linguistics of Writing: Arguments between Language and Literature,* edited by Nigel Fabb et al., (New York: Methuen Inc., 1987): pp. 48-66.

Quijano, Aníbal. *Dominación y Cultura: Lo cholo y el conflicto cultural en el Perú.* Perú: Mosca Azul Editores, 1980.

Rabil, Albert, Jr., Ed. *Renaissance Humanism. Foundations, Forms and Legacy. Volume 1: Humanism in Italy.* Philadelphia: University of Pennsylvania Press, 1988.

————. *Renaissance Humanism. Foundations, Forms and Legacy. Volume 2: Humanism Beyond Italy.* Philadelphia: University of Pennsylvania Press, 1988.

————. *Renaissance Humanism. Foundations, Forms and Legacy. Volume 3: Humanism and the Disciplines.* Philadelphia: University of Pennsylvania Press, 1988.

Rafael, Vicente L. *Contracting Colonialism: Translation and Christian Conversion in Tagalog Society Under Spanish Rule.* Durham: Duke University Press, 1993.

Rama, Angel. *La Ciudad Letrada.* Hanover: Ediciones del Norte, 1984.

Rama, Carlos M. *Historia de las Relaciones Culturales entre España y la América Latina. Siglo XIX.* Mexico: Fondo de Cultura Económica, 1982.

Ramos, Julio. *Desencuentros de la Modernidad en América Latina. Literatura y Política en el Siglo XIX.* México: Fondo de Cultura Económica, 1989.

————. *Paradojas de la Letra.* Caracas: Ediciones eXcultura, 1996.

Rappaport, Joanne. *The Politics of Memory: Native Historical Interpretation in the Colombian Andes.* Cambridge: Cambridge University Press, 1990.

Reyes, Alfonso. *Ultima Tule. Tentativas y Orientaciones. No hay tal lugar...* Mexico: Fondo de Cultura Económica, Obras Completas de Alfonso Reyes, 1960.

Rincón, Carlos. *La no simultaneidad de lo simultáneo: Postmodernidad, globalización y culturas en América Latina.* Colombia: Editorial Universidad Nacional, 1995.

Roig, Arturo Andrés. *La Utopía en el Ecuador.* Quito: Editora Nacional, 1987.

Romero, Raúl R., Ed. *Música, Danzas y Máscaras en los Andes.* Lima, Perú: Instituto Riva-Aguero, 1988.

Rose, Mark. *Authors and Owners: The Invention of Copyright.* Cambridge: Harvard University Press, 1993.

Rubert de Ventós, Xavier. *Las Metopias: Metodologías y Utopías de Nuestro Tiempo.* Barcelona: Montesinos, 1984.

Saccaro del Buffa, Giuseppa. *Utopia per Gli Anni Ottanta.* Roma: Gangemi, 1986.

Said, Edward W. *Culture and Imperialism.* New York: Alfred A. Knopf, 1994.

Saldívar, José David. *Dialectics of Our America.* Durham: Duke University Press, 1991.

Samuel, Raphael. *Theatres of Memory. Volume 1. Past and Present in Contemporary Culture.* London: Verso, 1994.

Sánchez, Rosaura. *Telling Identities: The Californio Testimonios.* Minneapolis: University of Minnesota Press, 1995.

Saunders, Trevor J. *Aristotle Politics. Books I and II.* Oxford: Clarendon Press, 1995.

Schoemburgk, Robert H., Ed. Francis Drake. *The Discover of the Empire of Guiana.* London: The Hakluyt Society, 1848.

Schwartz, Stuart B., Ed. *Implicit Understandings: Observing, Reporting, and the Reflecting on the Encounters Between Europeans and Other Peoples in the Early Modern Era.* Cambridge: Cambridge University Press, 1994.

Siebers, Tobin. *Heterotopia: Postmodern Utopia and the Body Politic.* Ann Arbor: The University of Michigan Press, 1994.

Sinfield, Alan. *Faultlines: Cultural Materialism and the Politics of Dissident Reading.* Berkeley and Los Angeles, California: University of California Press, 1992.

de Sousa Santos, Boaventura. "Three Metaphors for a New Conception of Law: The Frontier, the Baroque and the South," in *LSR* (Vol. 29, No. 4, 1995): pp. 569-584.

Spurr, David. *The Rhetoric of Empire: Colonial Discourse in Journalism, Travel Writing and Imperial Administration.* Durham: Duke University Press, 1994.

Stobbart, Lorainne. *Utopia: Fact or Fiction? The Evidence from the Americas.* The United Kingdom: Alan Sutton Publishing Inc., 1992.

Suvin, Darko. "Polity or Disaster: From Individualist Self Toward Personal Valences and Collective Subjects," *Discours Social/Social Discourse: The Non-Cartesian Subjects, East and West/Les Sujets Non-Cartésiens, Orient/Occident* (Montreal: Volume 6: 1-2): pp. 181-210.

Tafuri, Manfredo. *Architecture and Utopia: Design and Capitalist Development.* Cambridge: The MIT Press, ninth printing, 1994.

Thompson, E. P. *The Poverty of Theory & Other Essays.* New York: Monthly Review Press, 1978.

Trousson, Raymond. *Historia de la Literatura Utópica.* Barcelona: Ediciones Península, 1995.

Tuck, Richard. *Natural Rights Theories: Their Origin and Development.* Cambridge: Cambridge University Press, 1979.

————. *Philosophy and Government, 1572-1651.* Cambridge: Cambridge University Press, 1993.
Tucker, Robert C., Ed. *The Marx-Engels Reader.* New York: W.W. Norton & Company, 1978.
Tuve, Rosemond. *Allegorical Imagery: Some Medieval Books and Their Posterity.* Princeton, New Jersey: Princeton University Press, 1966.
Vázquez-Montalbán, Manuel. *El Escriba Sentado.* Barcelona: Grijalbo-Mondadori, 1997.
Wallerstein, Immanuel. *After Liberalism.* New York: The New Press, 1995.
————. "Comments on Stern's Critical Terms," *AHR* (Vol. 93, No. 4, October 1988): pp. 873-885.
————. *Geopolitics and Geoculture: Essays on the Changing World-System.* Cambridge: Cambridge University Press, 1994.
————. *Historical Capitalism.* London: Verso, 1974.
————. *The Modern World-System. Capitalist Agriculture and the Origins of the European World-Economy in the Sixteenth Century.* New York: Academic Press, 1974.
————. *The Modern World-System. Mercantilism and the Consolidation of the European World-Economy 1600-1750.* New York: Academic Press, 1980.
————. *Utopistics or Historical Choices of the Twenty-First Century.* New York: The New Press, 1998.
Wegner, Phillip E. *Horizons of Future Worlds, Borders of Present States. Utopian Narratives, History and the Nation.* Durham: Duke University Diss., 1993.